HISTORICAL ESSAYS AND LECTURES

CLASSIC EUROPEAN HISTORIANS

A SERIES EDITED BY LEONARD KRIEGER

François Guizot

HISTORICAL ESSAYS
AND
LECTURES

Edited and with an Introduction

by Stanley Mellon

THE UNIVERSITY OF CHICAGO PRESS
CHICAGO & LONDON

THE UNIVERSITY OF CHICAGO PRESS, CHICAGO 60637
THE UNIVERSITY OF CHICAGO PRESS, LTD., LONDON

© 1972 by The University of Chicago
All rights reserved. Published 1972
Printed in the United States of America

International Standard Book Number: 0–226–31049–3
Library of Congress Catalog Card Number: 72–76486

When Guizot contrasts European Civilization to all others with the observation that in Europe no principle, idea, group, or class has ever triumphed in an absolute form and that to this is due its progressive character and constant growth, we cannot but take heed. He knows what he is talking about; the expression of his thought is negative and therefore inadequate, but the words are charged with insight. As one knows the diver by the smell of the ocean still clinging to him, so do we recognize in Guizot a man who has plunged into the depths of European history. Indeed, it seems incredible that at the beginning of the nineteenth century, a time of rhetoric and confusion, there should have been written such a book as The History of European Civilization. *Even a man of today can learn from it how liberty and plurality are reciprocal and between them constitute the permanent heart of Europe.*

José Ortega y Gasset

Contents

Series Editor's Preface

OF THE twin purposes to which the series of Classic European Historians is dedicated—the revival of great historical works and the recall of the great historiographers who have shaped our point of view—certainly this volume of selections from François Guizot would seem to weigh heavily on the historiographical side of the scale. The imbalance is accountable not so much to the negative consideration that all of Guizot's histories are now deemed dated and none accorded classic status—for it can be argued that there is a sense in which they have not been superseded and remain valuable as history—but rather to the positive factor of the especially prominent place which Guizot holds in western historiography. His prominence in this regard stems from two functions—his combination of a political career with the profession of historian and his explicit exposition of the historiographical principles behind his actual practice of history. In both he remains a distinctive representative—distinctive because he represents purely and transparently what is obscure and hybrid in others of his set—of two general types in our historiography: the politician-historian who has epitomized the pervasive problem of the relations between past knowledge and present action; and the first-generation historicist of early nineteenth-century provenance who believed both in the infinite variety of history and in unifying laws governing it and who thus spawned the ambiguous definitions of historicism from which we still suffer. It was, indeed, Guizot's anomalous role as a unique exemplar of these important types that explains the incongruity of a practising historian who has remained more important than has the history that he practised.

When we think of politician-historians, two species usually come to mind. First, there are the famous political leaders who wrote history—the likes of Caesar, Augustus, Frederick the Great, Jaurès, Churchill, and de Gaulle. Second, there are the historians, whether amateur or professional, who were also political officials or representatives—the likes of Machiavelli, Guicciardini, Leibniz, Macaulay, Mommsen, Miliukov, Nicolson, and Heuss. Both types are imperfect as loci for the study of the interaction between history and politics, the first because their history was either derivative or avocational, the second either because their historical and political careers were too interlaced for separate identification or because their public positions were too irresponsible for their politics to exercise an independent force. But with Guizot we have the only case that comes to mind of a professional historian who became a political leader. Guizot wrote the bulk of his history while he was politically active but before he became the dominant figure in France's bourgeois monarchy, and Professor Mellon deftly traces the effect of his mediatory political attitudes upon his choice and treatment of historical subject, thus showing how Guizot's politically conditioned history could itself become relevant to his politics. Guizot, then, became the supreme authority in France with his political views already fixed in a definite historical mold, and it is the subsequent career of this historicized de facto sovereign that gives us a rare insight into the relationship of history and decision-making. The result in Guizot's case was hardly glorious, but since the subsequent careers of professional historians in politics have not greatly improved upon his record, Guizot remains a most instructive example.

In his sensitive introduction to Guizot, Professor Mellon reconstructs the man as a representative of the age that produced him. If we look to Guizot's position in European historiography, we should regard him analogously as a representative rather than pioneer among the historians of the early nineteenth-century. For his most definite value as a historian undoubtedly lies in the frank expositions and crystalline applications of the historicist tenets he shared with his less theoretically articulate nineteenth-century colleagues who founded the modern discipline of history. Like them he not only accepted but appreciated the manifold and fractious heterogeneity of human affairs which required discriminating research into every particular, and like them he not only required the formulation of unifying themes in history as a condition for its understanding but also claimed to see these unities in history as facts of human relations. But unlike the bulk of his contemporaries, he was so consistent in his equal acknowledgment of both diversity and unity in history and so transparent in the historiographical devices he used to reconcile them that he affords a unique insight into the fruitful consequences of the historicist ambiguity. Precisely because Guizot is as sententious as he is and precisely because the structure of his historical writing is as coarse grained as it is, his work is a revelation of the rationale behind some of the most characteristic features of nineteenth-century historiography. A summary of these features in Guizot from the point of view of his rationale for them may serve as a guide both to what is representative in him and to the explanation of the nineteenth-century historical mechanics he represents.

First, the "big" subjects which were the pride of nineteenth-century historians and have been the envy of their twentieth-century successors can be seen to have been just so many deliberate intersections of unified and multiplex history. In Guizot's model, indeed, they are explicitly universal histories in empirically manageable form—the only form in which the scientifically minded nineteenth-century would accept universal history. Consequently, we find Guizot continually justifying his historical subjects by explicitly deriving them from a fundamental process of human history as the historiographically practicable focus of the process, which is historiographically impracticable in itself. Thus his subjects were institutions, countries, and periods, each considered as the knowable historical realization of a historically unknowable general principle. He ensconced the principle of freedom in the history of representative institutions, the principle of civilization in the history of France, and the principle of progress in the synoptic history of revolutions. When he wanted to write the history of civilization on a European basis, he divided it into an external history of social action and an internal history of individual thought and morality, and he insisted he could only write on one—the external. When he wrote long-range history, he stipulated his concentration on that historical dimension whose effects were transmitted continuously from age to age. Behind these Guizotian devices for a historical incarnation of universal human principles that would respect the infinite variety of human life was his belief that lawful unity and circumstantial plurality met in the great dualities of history: representation and absolutism, people and government, and humanity and society were pairings which could be known historically and which testified to the progress of the great unities—freedom, state, and civilization. Such were the assumptions, explicit in Guizot and implicit in his contemporaries, of the great historical canvases of the nineteenth-century.

A second feature of his period's historiography that is illuminated in Guizot is the confusing relationship between rational analysis and history. Like his contemporaries Guizot rejected the imposition of a priori systems, whether of faith or reason, upon history and claimed that the knowledge of history could only be derived from what is found in it. And yet from the welter of facts which he acknowledged to be the chaotic raw materials of history, he, like his contemporaries, emerged with awe-inspiring patterns of symmetrical and rationally coherent human relations. The very format of Guizot's historical writings, obvious in Professor Mellon's revealing choice of selections, furnishes the key to the thorny problem of the real and the rational in nineteenth-century historiography. Guizot began each of his important works with a general theoretical disquisition on the subject whose history he was about to present, because, as he frankly stated, the history would be incomprehensible without such a preliminary analysis. For Guizot himself this habitual sequence of analysis and history shows how he translated his political doctrine of the golden mean into the terms of his history, but it also shows something more basic for the historiography of the nineteenth-century. Through the very mechanics of his writing Guizot here exhibits the unquestioning, if usually unstated, belief of nineteenth-century historians in the rational structure existing within history itself, created by men of the past in the organizations, traditions, and ideas which they have extended over large human spaces and have continued through long flows of human time in the effort to weave threads of logic into their multifarious existence. Because this immanent logic has been inevitably intermingled with the particular circumstances and individual actions which it is designed both to order and respect, and because these logical facts can be recognized by the discursive mode in which past men have actually cast them, rational exposition of general themes is required to identify them in the historical process. Guizot's theoretical prologomena, cast as introductory definitions of general historical terms corresponding to the general facts in history itself, are irrefutable witnesses of the assumptions about human rationality which synthesized scientific and philosophical history in the nineteenth-century.

But it is the third of Guizot's representative features that is perhaps the most revealing of all, for in his historical writing we see the gears which meshed the nineteenth-century historians' anomalous attitudes toward the role of the past and the present in history. On the one hand they exalted the ideal of the historian's impartiality, with the corollary stipulating his detachment of the past from the interests of the present and his understanding of past events and eras in their own terms; but on the other hand they also assumed an actual relevance of the past to the present, and this assumption not only legitimated their unabashed criticism of past sources with present standards of truth but also helped to produce the great works of committed, or partial, history which marked the actual achievement of the nineteenth-century. As Professor Mellon demonstrates, Guizot defined impartiality toward the past precisely in terms of its necessary connection to the present; he did this by identifying the historian's immersion in the past with his biased sympathy for one of its parties, and by identifying the progressive illuminations of the past through successive presents with the expansion of partial into impartial historical judgment. Not only did Guizot make this connection between past and present explicit, but he also made explicit the conditions that were necessary for this connection: first, the past in question—the historical past—must be the dimension of the past which, transmitted by successive ages, has in fact been connected with the present, thus ensuring a continuity of historical views; and secondly, that there is cumulative progress in historical knowledge, wherein new perspectives are not simply added to the old ones but actually transcend and comprehend them. Since Guizot also insisted—particularly in his revolutionary histories—upon the historian's sympathetic re-creation of the individual flavor of this past, and since he objected to his contemporaries' imposition of current partisan views upon the past, he was clearly not asserting either relevance or detachment as such but rather a right rather than a wrong way of connecting the past and the present. Guizot's argument thus shows that for nineteenth-century historians neither the insulation of the past from the present nor the connections as such of the past and the present were what distinguished the valid historical approach. What did distinguish it was vague in most historians, but again it becomes explicit in Guizot: ostensibly, it is history as distinguished from partial history, in the most general sense of the confrontation connoted by these terms—that is, judgment by standards of the whole rather than by interests of the part. Actually, however, Guizot reveals a root of the distinction which reaches far deeper than these familiar terms of discrimination among historians. When, in his lectures on the *History of Civilization in Europe,* he invoked the "inevitable alliance of philosophy and history" to derive historical truth from the "nature of the true development of society and man," he betrayed the underlying faith of nineteenth-century men in absolute principles of human truth which served to measure the truth of past and present alike and which associated past history and present historian as mutual correctives in its service. The merit of nineteenth-century historians lay in their efforts to expand the orbit of absolute truth to include past and contemporary humanity alike; but then, as Guizot pointed out, they could associate past and present in no other way, and they could acknowledge meaningful history according to no other standard. How refreshing to meet an honest historian at last!

Hence Guizot's contribution to historiography was his inimitable exposition of the principles he shared with contemporaries who wrote more memorable history on less definite principles. But there is something more. To read Guizot is to experience an unanticipated satisfaction that goes beyond the appreciation of so symmetrical a congruence between the method and the content of his history. Precisely because he is so consistent in the application of the balance between unity and multiformity in his historiographical principles, the past that he evokes is both coherent and alive. His general themes—whether European civilization or the French nation or the representative system—are embodied in real institutions and events. His singular subjects—whether George Washington or Madame de Rumford's salon—become the vehicles of universal themes or cultural continuities. On all levels there is clearly at work a mind that has interpreted the history of our culture as the arena in which the fundamental problems of the culture have been posed and provisionally resolved. To readers who knew Guizot only as the middle-of-the-road politician who became a narrow-minded conservative, the scope and the flow of the history which he wrote must come as a surprise and a delight.

Leonard Krieger

Editor's Introduction

I

THE *Petit Larousse*—that best and most succinct guide to all things French—says of François Guizot:

> Statesman and French historian, born at Nîmes, minister under Louis Philippe, he was the rival of Thiers, and the defender of conservative ideas as well as a policy that was too timid in relation to England. His faults had not a little to do with the revolution of 1848. Historian of great merit, he wrote *History of the English Revolution, History of Civilization in Europe and in France*, etc. (1787-1874).

No ordinary person could be held even partly responsible for something so complex and vast as the Revolution of 1848. Guizot's name has survived in French history as the author of an unfortunate phrase, *"Enrichissez-vous,"* and the object of the cry from the streets of Paris in 1848, *"à bas Guizot."*

When a man is remembered in history, the first and most often invoked reason is that he belonged to the future, that he was the ancestor of some perfectly acceptable modern point of view or the originator of some idea or movement which has triumphed in our own time. There is considerable ancestor worship in historical thinking; we tend to honor those who first invented, discovered, founded—those who were the prophets belonging to the party of the future. François Guizot can make no such claim for our attention. If one looks for the modern disciples and interpreters of Guizot—the Guizotins—he will find that they simply do not exist. Guizot was a remarkably poor prophet;

everything that he feared and resisted came to pass; all those things he believed could not endure, triumphed.

History is not only concerned with the successful, however; it is also concerned with those who failed and sank into obscurity. Often their very neglect affords a different approach for the historian, who can ask us to remember the forgotten one because he was in some way a typical or representative man of his time. This approach can be a great challenge for the historian because it sometimes demands that he grapple with third-rate ideas, books that did not make the best-seller lists, heresies that were wiped out, revolutions that failed. For the man, movement, or idea—no matter how obscure or unsuccessful—might illustrate something much larger and more important. It is conceivable that François Guizot could be studied in this way. He could be taken as spokesman for a small, influential political sect of liberals, the original Doctrinaires. He could be regarded as an archetype of the nineteenth-century liberal, professor and intellectual, a symbol of the July Monarchy, a representative leader of the French middle class. The truth is, however, that Guizot was not a satisfactory specimen for any of these. He was too complicated, too unique, too individual to be used as a simple symbol of an important failure; in fact, the closer one gets to Guizot the more difficult he is to categorize. We discover, for example, that most nineteenth-century intellectuals despised him, that Louis Philippe did not like him, and that the middle class did not regard him as one of their own.

If Guizot fails as a voice of the future or symbol of the past, the historian still has a good reason to justify his being remembered: his importance in his own time. Obvious though this may be, it presents one of the great problems in any kind of historical investigation. To understand an age, one must first have a map of the age drawn to scale. One must know it the way a contemporary would have known it. Yet this seemingly simple reconstruction is often what is hardest to achieve. To the amazement of their modern audiences, historians are repeatedly offering the discovery that those figures best known to us were often obscure in their own time, or were regarded as minor figures or crackpots. On the other hand, we are repeatedly being offered as examples of bad judgment and vulgar taste those considered to be heroes in their own time. Leaving aside the question of the propriety of one age's judging another at all, it is clear that just as reputations do not survive the transfer from one culture to another, so they do not weather well with time. Those reputations that do not survive present the historian with the immediate problem of discovering what an earlier age regarded as important. We have our own failures of vision to overcome. Our own perspective is inevitably distorted because we are so accustomed to seeing an age with certain eyes that we often fail to grasp what is placed directly before us.

For instance, the most important thing about Paris in the 1840s seems at first to have been the presence of three obscure Germans—Heinrich Heine, Richard Wagner, and Karl Marx. Yet, if we perform a Cartesian operation and clear the mind of the extraordinary contributions of these three Germans, and if we confront their age as they knew it, what will we then discover? Their Paris was the Paris of François Guizot. Both Heine and Marx would not have doubted this. Heine, who while in Paris supported himself by writing dispatches for the *Augsburger Allgemeine Zeitung*, wrote:

> Guizot is a man of resistance but not of reaction. . . . His real business is the practical maintenance of the regime of the bourgeoisie which is as grimly threatened by the marauding stranglers of the past as it is by the plunder-seeking avant-garde of the future. Monsieur Guizot has laid out a hard task for himself and more's the pity—nobody thanks him for it. And truly most ungrateful of all to him are those good citizens whom his strong hand protects and guards, but to whom he never gives the hand in confidence and with whose petty passions he never makes a common cause. They love him not at all, for neither does he laugh with them at Voltarian witticisms, nor is he "industrial"; neither does he dance with them around the May pole of *la Gloire!* He bears his head very high and a melancholy pride shows itself in every trait and seems to say "I could do something better perhaps than waste my life in a weary daily struggle for this blackguard pack." That is in fact the man who does not woo very passionately for popularity, and has even assumed the principle

that a good minister must be unpopular. He has never cared to please the multitude, not even in those days of the Restoration when he was honored most gloriously as a learned tribune of the people. When he delivered in the Sorbonne his memorable lectures, and the approbation of the assembled youth went to extremes, he subdued the flattering tumult with the firm words, "Gentlemen, order must prevail even in enthusiasm." Love of order is a predominant trait in the character of Guizot, and even on this account his ministry worked most advantageously in the confusion of the present. On account of this love of order he has often been accused of pedantry, and I confess that the stiff seriousness of his personal appearance is softened by a certain associated, learned, pedagogical mien which recalls our German homeland, especially Göttingen. . . . There is in fact something German in his nature, but German of the best kind; he is thoroughly erudite, honorable, generally humane, and universal. We Germans, who would have been proud of him were he one of us, should at least do him justice where his personal worth and dignity is in question. . . . He lately paid to one of my fellow countrymen the naive compliment, "A German would never regard me as a reactionary."

(Heine, *Lutitia*)

The other young German began his pamphlet of the year 1848 by invoking the chief conservative powers of Europe, and he put it this way:

A spectre is haunting Europe—the spectre of Communism. All the powers of old Europe have entered into a holy alliance to exorcise this spectre; Pope and Czar, Metternich and Guizot, French radicals and German police spies.

Both for Marx and for Heine—as well as for Metternich, Wellington, and Tsar Nicholas—Guizot was a major figure in the political life of the nineteenth century.

Contemporaries could differ over Guizot's stature in politics, but there was little disagreement that he was the outstanding historian of the nineteenth century. This judgment would be set aside today as the extravagant partiality of the conscientious biographer who has been living too long with his subject, though it would only be echoing the verdict of such disinterested observers as John Stuart Mill and Lord Acton, and such hostile ones as Sainte-Beuve, who called Guizot "the greatest of our professors." Guizot should be remembered if only because in an age of great historians his ideas were at the center of historical debate. How easily in time even this has been forgotten. Jules Michelet and his famous doctrine of "resurrection" are remembered. Yet when Michelet first coined that word in a popular work of 1846, he did so to establish the distinction between his work and that of the leading historians of his day. "Thierry saw there a narrative and Monsieur Guizot an analysis: I have named it resurrection and that name will remain."

In each of these figures cited—Heine, Marx, Michelet—we could note a strong personal connection which affected each of their references to Guizot. Heine was drawing a small pension from the French Foreign Office thanks to Guizot; Marx was forced to leave Paris on Guizot's order; and Michelet had been given jobs, promotions, and the opportunity to write his great history of France because of Guizot's intervention. The fact, however, that all their acknowledgments of Guizot's importance could stem from these personal experiences does not in any way diminish Guizot's significance. Indeed, it leads us to the real reason why the student of the nineteenth century should know François Guizot: because not merely Heine or Marx, but everyone who lived at the time, knew him. Whether admired, hated, talked or written about, he was known. Obscure young philosophers like Auguste Comte were flattered to discuss things with him. Other young men, like Alexis de Tocqueville and Guiseppe Mazzini, were his students. Guizot seemed to have touched the life of every major figure of the first half of the nineteenth century. He was warmly esteemed by Goethe and Hegel, hated by Chateaubriand, and distrusted by Metternich. He lived for eighty-seven years and was able to influence powerfully a whole younger generation of Frenchmen—including men like Ernest Renan and Hippolyte Taine.

II

The chief merit of a historian, according to Nisard, "is to differ from the histories which have preceded him, be it by real discoveries, be it by facts reestablished or completed, be it by errors refuted." François Guizot did all of these things.

It was by chance that Guizot became a professor of history

in 1812; Napoleon, who appointed him to that position, could just as easily have appointed him professor of philosophy or literature instead. Yet once he was appointed, it was no accident that Guizot committed himself wholeheartedly. As Nietzsche understood so well, history was the natural vocation for men of the nineteenth century, who had lived through a revolution, who had watched empires rise and fall, who had seen a king's head in a basket, and who could reflect upon the marriage between a parvenu named Napoleon Bonaparte and a Hapsburg princess. What was different in Guizot's case was that he went on to become one of the great historians of his century.

History was a discovery made by many young men of the generation after 1789; conservatives like Scott and Chateaubriand discovered it first, but the liberal generation was not far behind. This search for roots—common enough after twenty-five years of revolution—had a special poignancy for Guizot, who found that history fulfilled a particular and personal need. Where did he belong? In Nîmes? Or Geneva? Or in an imperial Paris that was trying to be a new Rome? Napoleon's Paris was no Jerusalem for Guizot; he felt estranged from the France that he saw all about him. A Protestant, a provincial, soaked in German culture and English literature, Guizot was eighteen years old when he arrived in Paris, a foreign city to him. He could not have been thrilled by the sight of the Tricolor being carried to the four corners of Europe. He could neither believe in nor identify with a France that had dreamed of world conquest for the rights of man yet had delivered itself at the same time into the hands of Napoleon.

History was for François Guizot a personal way out of this dilemma. If he could not find roots in either of the two Frances, he could go back beyond the recent revolution and civil war and find another France, eternal, historic, a home at last. It was while he was developing his course for 1820–22 that Guizot found his roots and announced his discovery of that historic France. More European than French in training and instinct, Guizot was now able to proclaim to his French students that France had been and was still the very center of European civilization. Earlier in the

Empire, none could have doubted this, though, to many, France had become an enemy of the Europe she had conquered. Guizot could now assure his audience that in studying France they were studying Europe. His own research into French history had dispelled his reservations and taught him that France possessed a great European past, teeming with examples and illustrations of the struggle for human liberty. There was now more to France than Napoleon or Louis XVIII.

What Guizot had sought in all his studies was a reconciliation that could serve as a prelude to a practical political reconciliation in the nation. For Guizot the political problem of nineteenth-century France could be posed simply: how could France, which had become two nations in the course of twenty-five years of revolution, become whole and one again? Guizot expected no miraculous solution. It would be slow and laborious work; charters and compromises might help, but the real work of reconciliation would be something taking place in the minds of the next generation. This new generation must first be taught that the France of the Old Regime was not an enemy. The task of the French historian was to "introduce" one France to another and foster an acquaintance which would reveal that there was really only one France—the historic, eternal one. Such an introduction would establish that the France of the Revolution need not be ashamed of the Old Regime and that the Revolution had been wrong to despise the French past. This was the liberal Guizot's awesome conception of what history could do for nineteenth-century France, a view he shared with the other liberal historians of the period. He could offer no greater praise of Barante than to say, "he has always presented the spirit of the old France to the new France."

This belief in history was a major amendment which many nineteenth-century liberals made to the reformist philosophies of the eighteenth century. It was an important correction, for, according to liberal nineteenth-century critics from Guizot to Matthew Arnold, the denial of history was the fundamental fault of that century of philosophy. To put the matter in the way favored by the Doctrinaires: the eighteenth century had destroyed; the nineteenth century's task was one of reconstruction. The new spirit was one of moderation and reconciliation with one's historic adversaries. This new tone, mild and historical, which was represented by Guizot and the Doctrinaires, drew the attacks of the next generation of historians deeply committed to the Revolution. Edgar Quinet, describing the Doctrinaire historical spirit, said, "It raised, it rehabilitated, it praised, it patronized its adversaries."

The adoption of history by liberals like Guizot was one of the turning points in the development of liberalism; it was more than just a break with the eighteenth century. It was natural to expect the conservatives to construct their defenses around a return to a lost past, a golden age of French history, to construct a historical system totally rejected by the eighteenth century. It was quite another matter to find that liberals, by an unexpected and a surprising work of human will, had become restorers and ancestor worshipers too. To unreconstructed eighteenth-century "liberals" like Quinet, this spectacle of "liberal restorers" was ludicrous.

> With what conscience, with what seriousness was the task of restoring the past divided up among the men of the future. . . .
> All seemed to work on a preconceived plan. . . . Nothing could upset for a moment this concert of all the friends of unity for raising and resurrecting what they hated most.

Quinet's anger at the Doctrinaires led him to an important insight. The liberal discovery of history was in effect a resurrection of something which liberals had previously fought. It would have been more consistent of the nineteenth-century liberal, truer to his revolutionary traditions, if he had continued to despise the French past. If we follow Quinet, the real liberal historian of the nineteenth century would be a man for whom European history began with 1789.

Guizot, however, tried to do for Europeans in the nineteenth century what those early anthropologists had done for their world in the seventeenth and eighteenth centuries. The philosophe, disgusted with a Europe which still seemed tied to its medieval past, had turned to the primitive and had discovered there excitement, joy, and a virtue not present in Europe. What the nineteenth-century historians did was to recapture for the European liberal imagination the richness and wonder of its own past. The liberal historian, studying the Dark Ages, discovered in Europe's own primitive past, in those Gauls and Franks, all the strange, wondrous customs, the simple yet exotic traits possessed by Diderot's Polynesians and Voltaire's Indians. Guizot discovered that his European ancestors were very much like J. Fenimore Cooper's savages, and just as interesting.

Writing after a century of great partisan debate about European history, Guizot saw a way out. One did not have to accept French history either as a glorious, unbroken, thousand-year reign of kings, or as an uninterrupted story of liberty. The truth was much subtler and much greater. For Guizot, the truth lay in the diverse forms the struggle for liberty had taken and in the way those seeking liberty had been influenced by their struggle. To understand history as the story of liberty, the liberal historian must first understand such hostile elements as monarchy, church, and aristocracy; he must study them not as the prosecuting attorney, but sympathetically, to see how, in their very resistance to liberty, they worked, often unconsciously, toward the creation of modern society.

In the first part of the nineteenth century, Europe found itself psychologically in the state of a new nation. Europe had a past, but that past had been consciously rejected by the French Revolution, whose major purpose had been to sever any connection with history and to uproot the physical reminders of that past. Many Europeans, sympathetic to the Revolution, had willingly accepted this denial of history and preferred to conceive of themselves psychologically as Americans, a people born anew without the burden of a history. The French Revolution offered many substitutes for that scorned and rejected French past. It promised for the living the radical reconstruction of society, and for future generations the building of a new Europe.

The thwarting of the hopes spawned by the French Revolution, however, left European liberals in a deep quandary. They had been taught to disbelieve in that old Europe which had been overthrown; the Revolution had had extraordinary success in breaking links with the past. Yet the Revolution itself had ultimately failed, and countless Europeans simply felt disconnected. This was the challenge to the new liberal history; Guizot's solution was to convince Europeans that they did possess a past and that this past could be admired. Guizot understood why it had been necessary for a revolution to uproot the past and to deny it any value. But the great advantage of this second generation of revolutionaries was their ability to understand that the eighteenth century had been too sweeping in its denunciation, too one-sided in its rejection.

This discovery of the past was no simple matter. It raised all of the questions and exposed all of the difficulties concerning the relation of past to present. What position should the historian of the nineteenth century occupy? Should he immerse himself in the past or remain the cool, detached, modern observer? Should he passionately identify himself with some liberal part of that past or attempt to embrace it all? In the opening lecture of the first course of history he ever gave, Guizot raised the question that was to concern him throughout his life. He deliberately stated the case in its extreme form by making the polemical suggestion that the historian should not really be interested in the "past," in merely re-creating the excitement of a bygone moment. There were really two pasts, only one of which was of real concern to the historian.

> It may be said, to a certain extent, that there are two pasts, the one entirely extinct and without real interest, because its influence has not extended beyond its actual duration; the other enduring forever by the empire it has exercised over succeeding ages.

Two years previously, in 1810, Guizot was reviewing Kotzebue's *History of Prussia*. As the young Guizot analyzed it, Kotzebue's mistake was that he had immersed himself completely in the past and had become so partisan that he had, in fact, produced a history which could have been written by one of the historical actors themselves. For Guizot, this meant that the historian, by "losing himself" in the past, had forfeited all of those advantages that distance and time afforded. Above all, by joining history, Kotzebue had forfeited the possibility of judging fairly. "Because it is generally recognized today that liberty is a good thing, he [Kotzebue] thunders against the popes and against the feudal regime . . . without thinking that today the time for thundering is past, and the time for judgment has come." But judgment precisely required not occupying some position in the past, not enlisting in one party or cause, but assuming the true position of the judge, the man who listens to all sides of the story, who sympathetically enters into the testimony of all litigants. Quite early in his life Guizot suspected that history was for many a superior form of grave-robbing; he suspected those who studied the past merely to punish those who were already dead. "What does it serve to declaim against the dead, whom we no more resemble?"

Kotzebue, for example, had delighted in reviving the Teutonic knights and arraigning them for their historic crimes. Yet, because he had judged solely from the point of view of the victims of those crimes, he had failed in his responsibility as a historian to appreciate the achievements of the Teutonic knights—to comprehend the permanent and often useful historic results that flowed from such particular "crimes" as forced conversions. Guizot had written this review while Jules Michelet was still a child, but he had already pointed to the fatal weakness of that whole future school of history which believed that the historian's role was to become a partisan in past conflicts. In opposition to this view of history, Guizot proposed postponing judgment to some future time. Without denying the possibility of moral judgment ("I am far from thinking that such considerations can prevent the condemnation of the guilty knights"), Guizot called for another kind of judgment, a disinterested one. The Teutonic knights, the historian had to recognize, were the agents for the spread of Christianity to the East. For Guizot, the historical question was, Were the Prussian barbarians better off before the coming of Christianity? Kotzebue plainly thought that the conversion to Christianity had been a disaster for the Slavs, and Guizot criticized him for this shortsighted judgment. Kotzebue, concerned with narrating the crimes and painting the horrors, had quite forgotten his primary duty as historian: "The philosopher must precede the painter."

For Guizot Kotzebue had become an enemy of the Teutonic knights and had identified himself with those Prussians being Christianized and Teutonized. This sympathetic passion, which was the guiding spirit of Kotzebue's history, was in Guizot's opinion the ultimate historical sin.

Guizot could not find words in French sufficient to characterize the deadly effects of such a partisan approach, so he turned to German. In reviewing Bérenger's book on criminal justice in France, Guizot found the author to be typical of those writers created by the French Revolution—generous and sympathetic to one world, hostile and unfeeling to the other. In groping for the word to characterize this attitude Guizot selected *Einseitigkeit*, which, he explained, was not exactly the French word *partialité*, and which he defined as "the fault of only seeing one side of things." In this word, which few Frenchmen could even pronounce, lies one great key to understanding Guizot's historical outlook.

Post-revolutionary Europe found itself occupied by a new race of people, all suffering from the symptoms of this new "disease." They were all victims of *Einseitigkeit*—the inability to see the other side, a total commitment, a belief in blacks and whites (or, as they said at the time, a belief in whites and blues), a party of "virtue" fighting "vice," the newest form of Manicheanism. This cast of mind was for Guizot the real enemy in politics and in history, for it committed Europe politically to an endless renewal of civil war. In the study of history it blinded one to the simplest understanding. Whatever was the opposite of *Einseitigkeit* would be the secret weapon of the Doctrinaires, their great psychological tool. What would distinguish them from both the party of revolution and the party of reaction was their ability to see all sides of the question, to appreciate virtue everywhere they found it, to see some possible good in the darkest part of the European forest. *Einseitigkeit* was the enemy that Guizot would combat all his life in the politics of legitimists and republicans. In his histories he would build his system on this ability to see all sides and around all corners. As historian, Guizot was committed to studying all parties and—unlike Kotzebue—in some way appreciating and understanding them.

Where did Guizot's doctrine come from? Politically, it was the response of a new generation seeking a way out of the passions of a revolutionary age. Psychologically, it was a doctrine that suited a man trying to come to terms with two Frances, neither of which he could totally accept or reject. Philosophically, it stemmed from what we would call a Hegelian conception of the universe. For if all things exist for their own purposes in the historical universe, if each element constantly produces its opposite, and if there is good in bad and bad in good, then the historian cannot approach any subject from any simple point of view. Whatever is, possesses some kind of justification, some place in the historical scheme. Nothing is purely accidental or ephemeral; everything can, with some effort, be understood.

This determination to be fair to both sides, to dispense justice and mercy everywhere, would carry François Guizot into many strange positions and into the defense of some of the most curious and despised figures of the nineteenth century. For Guizot there were no monsters, no men beneath the possibility of understanding; the more they were universally despised, the more drawn he was to make the attempt at historical understanding. Indeed, he was always at his greatest when called upon to make some special effort to judge one with whom he was fundamentally unsympathetic. This involvement with the other side always seemed to touch some deep, hidden reserve of feeling in Guizot. Of Chateaubriand's mistress, Madame Récamier, he would write, "I have not lived under her charm," and this first step into another's existence would seem to bring forth a firm and warm appreciation. When impelled at first to criticize, Guizot, by reflex, would draw back and redress the scale, seek out and record some redeeming feature even in the most abandoned of human creatures. Guizot elevated this instinct into a conscious system of historical magnanimity. Never collapsing into a sterile relativism, he did not dodge the necessity of judgment; but once having pronounced it, Guizot immediately sought to extend sympathy to the defeated, to the losers in history. He lived and wrote by Pascal's dictum: "If I find man lowered I shall raise him."

Guizot not only lived by this *pensée*, he consistently applied it in judging all other historians. For him the greatest virtue, the sure mark of a historical intelligence, was this ability to sympathize after rendering judgment. In 1828 Guizot translated Hallam's *Constitutional History of England*, a work he obviously admired. In an introduction he singled out Hallam's balanced judgment for particular praise. Yet there was one exception he felt compelled to note, one instance when Hallam's equanimity seemed to have deserted him, and that was in the treatment of Strafford. Guizot agreed with Hallam that Strafford had been wrong and was justly condemned to the gallows. "But it is not everything that a condemnation be just; one must still be just to the condemned." Guizot conceded that the men of the seventeenth century were correct in punishing Strafford, but the historian of the nineteenth century had the additional obligation to render justice humanely. "The justice of the gallows is not the justice of history." This was the decisive distinction between the partisan living in the seventeenth century and the historian writing in the present. If Guizot had been a member of that seventeenth-century parliamentary jury, he would have condemned Strafford. But the later historian need not be of the seventeenth century; his job was understanding. The historian must study the man and get behind the crime, for there was a man Strafford separate from his crime. "There were crimes in his conduct which laws could not touch; there were qualities in his character untouched by his crimes." The headsman having performed his task in the year 1641, it was not the historian's task to resurrect the past, to repeat the work, or to drag Strafford through his trial and execution yet another time. Precisely because the seventeenth century had been so unanimous and severe in its condemnation, the nineteenth century must temper this judgment with mercy.

Hegel's idea of "the cunning of history" was understandably

appealing to a nineteenth-century historian. If one accepted the notion, one admitted that neither Kotzebue's Teutonic knights nor their victims could possibly have understood their own true significance. Guizot believed that ultimately the past, although existing by its own right, could only be illuminated by light from the present. Further, some ages were peculiarly suited to unraveling the secrets of others. He believed that the French Revolution had so rearranged history, that it had given to past centuries a significance they had never had before. Thanks to the Revolution, it was now possible to go back and recast the entire history of Europe in a new light. This is one reason why Guizot did not write a history of the French Revolution, although he did something at least as important. He wrote a history of European civilization as revealed by the French Revolution. Guizot thought of the French Revolution as a kind of eighteenth-century earthquake which had so shaken Europe as to reveal its geological structure underneath, making it possible to study for the first time other strata of that civilization, strata which had lain unobserved in calmer times. For example, it had taken the French Revolution to reveal the fact that the French aristocrat was hated in the countryside. Now, thanks to this observation, one could return to the Middle Ages, study the origins of this phenomenon, and reconstruct from the documents *why* the aristocrat was hated. Knowledge thus drawn from the psychology of recent revolution could aid the historian. The revolution had left gaping wounds which had exposed in the European past the true relations between classes and institutions—a hidden history obscured by time and defeat.

The belief by nineteenth-century historians that they were the first truly to understand the past was common and natural. They did not think that they had invented history or that previous ages did not know history, but rather that it was not possible for one who had lived before the French Revolution really to understand certain episodes of that history. These nineteenth-century historians believed that because they had seen such things, participated in such events, witnessed such horrors, their vision had been expanded and their nerves sensitized. They therefore had a far richer and more sophisticated grasp of European history than their less involved ancestors.

This attitude, however, could easily produce a "Whig history" in which the European experience would be arranged merely to justify the French Revolution. It was the greatness of Guizot (and one reason for his present neglect) that he rose above this temptation. There were at the time many liberals in Europe as well as in France who wanted to enlist history in a kind of cultural "cold war" against the European Restoration. Guizot for a time lent himself to this enterprise, but what saved him was another side of his nature and experience. He possessed the instincts of a man who, in the post-revolutionary era, was determined to find reconciliation. He rejected the *Einseitigkeit* of other pro-Revolution historians and their heirs. He would spend his time studying all sides, including those institutions that had been overthrown. He would study the defeated races and lost causes. He would give them time, attention, and historical understanding. He would study the monarchy, the church, the aristocracy, and decide what made them oppressors and oppressed in turn.

The opening lecture of 1820 was Guizot's strongest statement of a particular liberal reading of the French past. It should be understood as a piece of special pleading before a very special kind of audience. It was not a general defense of the past, but an argument designed to convince an audience which Guizot correctly judged to be antihistorical. Few professors of history had ever labored under such difficulties. Guizot believed that the way of convincing the young liberal generation that history was a possible and honorable discipline was by proving to them that history, if properly understood, would be their possession.

From the time of Burke and Chateaubriand, liberals had grown accustomed to "conceding" history to the conservatives. One attacked revolution by an appeal to history, to the greatness of an unbroken English tradition, or to the glories of the French past. Those who had taken part in the French Revolution seemed undisturbed by this invocation of history. They proudly accepted the call in 1789 to "begin history over again" (to use Barrère's phrase). The primary task of the French Revolution had been the destruction of institutions which had been accumulating for thirteen centuries; it had been, as Burke charged, a revolt against history. As a man of 1789, Guizot paid tribute to that feeling, acknowledging that it was in the nature of a revolution to do this. All revolutions were to some degree rejections of history. Presumably, if one were in love with one's past, one would not become a revolutionary, and Guizot noted the tendency to burn documents in both the English and French Revolutions.

But this rejection of history, though understandable, had, in Guizot's opinion, been a mistake of the eighteenth century. The men of the French Revolution, whether they recognized them or not, did have ancestors; the desire for liberty was not something newly sprung from the brain of the Assembly of 1789. If one turned to the past, one could find examples of courage, energy, and political wisdom which could have served as inspiration for men making a revolution. Guizot realized that revolutions could also make use of traditions. Liberals of his own day could root themselves in the past just as easily as the conservatives, for in French history there was a specific, usable liberal past.

Guizot recognized, of course, that it was very difficult for the men of 1789 to grasp the idea of a liberal tradition of revolt preceding theirs. Here Guizot's doctrine of the present conditioning one's understanding of the past was of particular importance. While it was not seen in 1789, this tradition of revolt did exist, and it became easier to grasp in 1820. It was indeed the French Revolution itself which made this new vision possible. Seen through the prism of the Revolution, France's long buried liberal past could now be disclosed. Now Guizot could conduct his audience into these dark corners, and guide them through a history of representative institutions. This would have seemed impossible in the eighteenth century; but a France which had lived through 1789, through estates, assemblies, conventions, and which had seen the nation win liberty, lose it, and recapture it again was prepared to take this journey.

Of equal importance was Guizot's discovery of the middle class as the chief carrier of this liberal tradition. Guizot and the Doctrinaires launched a large scale, ill-fated effort to persuade the nineteenth-century middle class that it was descended from a race of heroes. For Doctrinaires like Royer-Collard and Rémusat, as for Broglie and Barante, the right of the middle class to rule modern society was a new and exciting idea, part of the doctrine to be taught. But for Guizot it was more than an idea; it touched his deepest feelings, since it made sense of his own life. More than any of the others, François Guizot was a bourgeois. Neither he nor his family could have made any claims to be anything else. Like Rousseau, that earlier Genevan in Paris, Guizot had in his first association with Parisian society developed a strong sense of class consciousness—a cool contempt for that great world above him and a pride in his own class. Although there were to be many changes in the life of François Guizot (he would eventually address kings and queens with familiarity and have a Russian princess for a mistress), one belief was to remain unaltered: his deep and constant faith in the virtue and the historic role of the middle class from which he sprang. Accepting the Doctrinaire belief in the middle class because it corresponded to his own deepest experience, Guizot then proceeded to transform it into a principle, and it became one of the great themes of all of his work, at the center of both his history and his politics.

In choosing to defend the middle class at the outset of the nineteenth century, Guizot and the Doctrinaires could not know that they had chosen to go against the currents of the age. They knew they would have to meet a conservative counterattack, but they could not yet anticipate the attack from the socialists. The conservatives and the socialists shared one important insight: both denounced the narrowness of middle-class rule, its selfish character, and the parochialism of its triumph in 1789. Both attacked the bourgeoisie at its most sensitive point, its theory of representation.

This theory was, in fact, a talisman for the nineteenth-century middle class. At the heart of their claim to rule was the belief that they did "represent" what was best in European civilization, that they had been for ten centuries the economically productive class, that their men—writers, artists, philosophers—had been the mind of Europe and its glory even while aristocrats and kings ruled. And now in the nineteenth century, possessing money and intellect, they had arrived at the proper moment to assume the political direction of society as well. Guizot was well aware of his class's history of struggle, of its coming to power through force, through the violent overthrow of the old regime.

> For more than thirteen centuries France has contained two peoples, conquerors and conquered. For more than thirteen centuries the conquered people battled to throw off the yoke of the conquerors. Our history is the history of the struggle. In our time, a decisive battle has been waged. It is called Revolution.

It follows that far from having to wipe out the memories of an unfortunate past, French nineteenth-century liberals could turn to history with confidence and excitement. Liberals now had, in fact, a deeper, richer pedigree than just the Assembly of 1789. Those who believed in that Revolution could now go back to the darkest part of the Dark Ages, and find there their ancestors.

Yet the French liberals did not need to go so far back. They could also turn to the example of seventeenth-century England. As the one nation that had succeeded in making its liberal revolution permanent, seventeenth-century England held the practical secret that Doctrinaires like Guizot sought: how to end a revolution successfully and absorb it into the fabric of the nation. In the preface to his history of the English Revolution, Guizot stressed the similarities between the seventeenth- and the eighteenth-century revolutions.

Both the French and English revolutions, according to Guizot, "neither said, did, nor wished anything that had not been said, wished, or done hundreds of times before." This was Guizot's argument against Burke's catastrophic theory of revolution, which had become a commonplace of conservative attack during the Restoration. Guizot felt that this kind of conservative criticism dealt unfairly with both the English and the French revolutions, for not only were both these revolutions deeply rooted in the national past of each country, but they also marked decisive stages in the general progress of European civilization. "The principles, designs, efforts, which are exclusively attributed to the English and French revolutions not only preceded them by several centuries, but are precisely those to which society in Europe owes all its progress."

Guizot believed, however, that the English themselves had ceased to "live" in their seventeenth century; they no longer felt the true force of the image of Revolution, and therefore missed its true meaning. However, someone who had just lived through another, more recent revolution, would, Guizot felt, be in a better position to see the true significance of that earlier revolution. To illustrate his point, Guizot contrasted the erudite English works on Cromwell with the biography by Villemain, one of his own Doctrinaire colleagues. Villemain's Cromwell possessed a force lacking in the English versions because Villemain

> looked at and judged the English Revolution from the midst of that of France; he found in the men and events beneath his own eyes the key to understanding those he had to paint; he drew life from his own times.

This was precisely the advantage that Guizot felt he too possessed. He thought that, as a man of the French Revolution, he could understand this English Revolution because it was, after all, part of the same tradition. Thus, though lacking the erudition of the English commentators, Guizot would be able to invoke these dead scenes with all the force of the Romantics. Frenchmen of the Restoration could sit down and tell sad tales of the deaths of kings in a way that Englishmen had forgotten, and when Guizot wrote of Charles I at the block, he was mindful of the fate of Louis XVI as well.

Guizot, however, was writing a history of a people who were regarded by most of his countrymen as the hated national enemy. He had to take great care to justify his history, appealing to that same liberal audience of the Restoration which had welcomed Thiers' history of the French Revolution and Thierry's liberal version of the French past. He had urged his young students in 1820 to consider a new possibility in French history. That battle won, he now asked the French reading audience of the Restoration to accept the history of England as part of their heritage, particularly when that history encompassed the revolutions of the seventeenth century.

One would expect so polemical an introduction to be followed by a typical Whig or liberal history, or by a paen to the English Revolution and an indictment of the evils of absolute monarchy. Indeed, after reading Guizot on England, Sismondi noted in his journal, "It makes me feel more than any other work I have ever read the necessity and the justice of the Revolution." Yet, Guizot's history of England was more than just another liberal tract. He had performed the most difficult of historical tasks: to give an account that was philosophically sympathetic to the revolution but personally sympathetic to the defeated party. Despite its obvious intention, the work is impressive for its astonishing balance and neutrality. The reader could never forget that this English Revolution was ultimately a good thing (Guizot never lost sight of its historical necessity), but in the course of the story his feelings are drawn to the defeated and the rejected, to Laud, to Strafford, and, above all, to Charles I.

Guizot's natural sympathies for these underdogs created the real tension of his work. In his portrait of Strafford, for example, we are given a man clearly guilty of great crimes, though innocent of the particular ones with which he was charged—a man who, in his death, achieved a kind of nobility. Guizot chose as the natural climax of his history the trial and execution of Charles I. Reviled in his own time, Charles needed the greatest sympathy; he needed to be portrayed as a human being who made mistakes and suffered for them; he needed to be rescued from the *Einseitigkeit* of later generations. In the midst of the French Restoration, with all the official piety and mourning surrounding the execution of Louis XVI, there was no more delicate subject that Guizot could have chosen, for no French reader could respond to such a scene dispassionately.

Thus, the nineteenth-century historian who had lived through the Revolution, who had experienced all forms and varieties of liberty and dictatorship, who had seen the rise and fall of kings and classes, could make better sense out of the past than those who had lived before 1789. Thus, men of the nineteenth century were in a better position to understand the English Revolution than men of the seventeenth century; thus, Guizot was in a better position to write a history of early Europe around the theme of representative institutions; thus, Augustin Thierry could write a history of the Third Estate; thus, a historian of 1830 could sense the importance of the urban Roman middle class far better than Edward Gibbon. Guizot insisted that a nineteenth-century historian in a liberal era could understand and convey the excitement of earlier revolutions far better than historians in a reactionary period who, though closer in time, were hostile to the spirit of the event. He described to Barante his own excitement as he plunged into the history of seventeenth-century England and as his knowledge of the men grew: "I know the age of each, his face, his *entouré*, his tastes. I speak, they reply to me. With the parings of history I could make novels."

III

Both in his own time and throughout the nineteenth century, Guizot's speculations and his approach to history were subject to friendly doubts and sharp criticism. As with any system, however, Guizot's historical philosophy can best be understood when presented against the prevailing ideas of his own time. His history was designed to rescue the European past from the prevailing distortions of the Left and the Right. It was an attempt to find a historical *juste milieu* between the total rejection of history by the Revolution and the worship of a particular part of the past by the conservatives. It was an attempt to use history as a kind of political mediating force. Guizot was reconstructing a French past that liberals could accept. He gave France a history that would not divide her—a history of struggles and conflict, to be sure, but one in which there were no villains, and in which every part of the French past could be seen sympathetically. In Guizot's version there emerged from a dialectical struggle of monarchy, church, aristocracy, and middle class a

France recognizable and admirable. Nineteenth-century France could be understood as the just summation of all of French history as well as of the European past. It was a history which could explain and justify the French Revolution while at the same time serving as a firm basis for a new national unity. Guizot's sharpest challenge as the leading French historian of the nineteenth century came from Jules Michelet, who offers an instructive contrast because his reputation has survived and because he has continued to be read and to influence historians in the twentieth century. In a preface of 1869 Michelet grudgingly acknowledged his debt to Guizot, in a summary which at once said too little and revealed too much.

At my first steps he was benevolent to me, little guessing my future audacities. He opened the archives to me, he gave me a small position, then later increased it. He promised me the honor of being his *suppléant* at the Sorbonne. In 1833 when I emerged he did not retract his promise, but he could not conceal how often he would be opposed to me. I took his place for one year in 1834. It was under his last ministry, 1847, that my course at the College de France was suspended.

From this bare and inaccurate recital one could scarcely guess the richness of the relation and how much Michelet really owed to Guizot. It was Guizot who advised Michelet to take the job as tutor for the Duchesse de Berry; it was Guizot who gave Michelet his job at the Archives (no small thing, since it placed Michelet in a position to become the great historian of France); it was Guizot who backed Michelet for a post at the Collège de France after 1830 and, when that fell through, did the next best thing and made Michelet his *suppléant* at the Sorbonne, not for one year but for two; it was Guizot who helped arrange an easy transfer so that Michelet could emerge after 1830 as tutor to an Orleanist princess; it was Guizot, first as Minister of the Interior and later as Minister of Education, who cleared the way for Michelet's career, as for so many others. Michelet's most sympathetic biographer, Gabriel Monod, acknowledged all of this, even if Michelet would not. Michelet himself, when younger, could not totally falsify the record. After July 1830 he wrote enthusiastically to Quinet, urging him to hurry and come to Paris, where careers were now open to talents. "Our friends are in power. Guizot is at the Interior, and at Education Villemain, Vatimesnil, or Cousin. Hurry then."

In those first years of the July Monarchy, Michelet in fact basked in the special favor of Minister Guizot. If later his disagreements with Guizot and their open break made him forget, an earlier record acknowledges his gratitude. In his opening lecture of 1834, after paying tribute to the great names that had been part of the Sorbonne, Michelet spoke of more recent examples that had honored that tradition. Of Guizot he said:

> France would never forget with what brilliance history, philosophy, and literature had been recently taught in this chair. When will the day come when I can see my illustrious master and friend return to his chair, when we can hear for the second time those simple, strong, clear, and fertile words, words which extracted science from all passions of the moment, from all partiality, from all falsehood of fact or of style and elevated history to the dignity of law?

At this early stage in his career, Michelet was even willing to recognize the role that Guizot had played in his own success. Writing to Guizot in 1835, suggesting which of his two jobs he wanted to continue in, Michelet remarked, "I wish to speak to you on a subject in which you have always interested yourself, myself and my position." Despite the honor of being Guizot's *suppléant,* he indicated that he preferred to teach at the Ecole Normale, where he would continue to have a very special relation with Guizot. "You have wished to send your son to that school. I am to complete his historical training. It will be to recognize what I owe you."

This early relation between Guizot and Michelet is remarkable since, as historians, they differed so profoundly. Guizot was worried about the impact of Michelet's lectures at the Ecole Normale and later his influence on the younger generation, including his own son, who did become Michelet's student. While in England Guizot even wrote to his daughter urging her not to read Michelet. Despite these deep differences in manner and outlook, Guizot recognized Michelet's quality and did everything to further his career.

Why then was Guizot an early supporter of Michelet? Like so many others, he misunderstood or did not clearly perceive the direction of Michelet's work. It was an easy mistake to make. Michelet began his history of France, as had Guizot, with the Middle Ages. In his first volume Michelet celebrated the role of the Church as part of a hymn to the greatness of the French past. Though vastly different in tone and style, this position, nevertheless, coincided with the Doctrinaire rediscovery of medieval France. In 1833–34 Michelet seemed, if anything, to belong to the conservative-romantic, even religious, school. At the very least, he was far removed from the Voltairians, and his work was welcomed as such. Liberals like Armand Carrel of the *National* thought of him this way, and he was warmly praised by the Catholic romantic mystical school, even though some, like Montalembert, were sensible enough to sense the differences. Indeed, it was a persistent weakness of the Doctrinaires to imagine that anyone genuinely interested in the French past was on their side; they thought at first that a resurrection of the French past such as Michelet's could only lead to the reconciliation of the two Frances and therefore redound to the advantage of the policy of the July Monarchy. However, Michelet taught the Doctrinaires that history could also serve other purposes: he carried this rediscovery of the past to the extreme of national pride and patriotic identification.

Michelet's approach was not without its advantages. Nettement described the effect of reading one of Michelet's "resurrections" as that of watching the excavation of an ancient city. For the first time the reader could see the city and could easily imagine it as moving and alive. Yet for all this vivid color and life—things which Guizot's history lacked—Michelet's archeological technique forfeited the advantages of time and distance. Nettement argued that the advantages of such a technique were great when dealing with a period very remote from the present, where the most important task was to bring to life something which had been dead and buried for so long. Thus Michelet was most effective when "resurrecting" Roman history or the medieval past. But as Michelet came closer to modern times, the difficulties of this kind of passionate excavating became more apparent. In practice, these resurrections meant the identification by the historian with one particular part of that past. Michelet had realized that one could not re-create a period *toute entière*, that one could not get inside an age by presenting all sides of every conflict. To adopt all parties would have the effect of canceling out the vividness of the resurrection and would doom one to Doctrinaire history. Since Michelet was committed to writing a complete history of France, the problem was to select those men or institutions which in his mind clearly embodied France in different epochs. In the early history of France this presented no particular problem. One could accept a Gothic church or Joan or Arc as the embodiment of the nation. There may indeed have been those who opposed Joan of Arc and may even have opposed the building of Gothic cathedrals, but they could easily be dismissed as anti-French. But how would Michelet treat those great conflicts, those civil wars in French history, those periods when France was not a single nation? Guizot had no such difficulty. He could admire the French monarchy, the church, even the aristocracy at different periods. Guizot could demonstrate how each in its turn had contributed to the formation of modern France. Since Michelet scorned this kind of historical equanimity, he had to decide which of these forces in each century represented the true France.

For Michelet then, the French Revolution posed a problem. He could not pretend that there was a single France any longer but had to choose between the Old Regime and the French Revolution. Michelet decided that it was the French Revolution which embodied France in the eighteenth century, as Gothic cathedrals had in the twelfth. He plunged pell-mell into the Revolution and carried its defense to new lengths. His reader becomes part of that mob marching on Versailles and shares all of the passions, prejudices, stupidities of those revolutionary days. The pamphlets of the time are raised to the level of historical judgments. One believes all those stories about Marie Antoinette and the king. The result is an extraordinary evocation of the actual days of revolution, but the line between the historian and the chronicler is blurred, and all pretense of historical objectivity and balanced judgment is gone. With Michelet we have lost the commodity so precious to Guizot—that Doctrinaire secret of understanding what one does not like. With Michelet we have *Einseitigkeit* raised to an ideology.

Guizot and Michelet may have lived in the same nineteenth century, but they belonged to different intellectual worlds. One was pledged to the world of the disinterested liberal intelligence, the other to the world of the democratic, revolutionary apocalypse. Guizot believed that his generation was peculiarly qualified to understand the past because of its experiences with the revolution. For Michelet, the peculiar virtue of the nineteenth century was that it contained the past—that the present was the literal and fully alive summation of all that had gone before, that history "is in us." The best way to understand the past, therefore, was to interrogate the present as though it were the past. Thus, Michelet believed that he was himself an excellent source for French history because as an individual he recapitulated that history. "We know what we have not learned. We have the memory of what we have not seen. We feel the heavy weight of the emotions of those we do not know."

Michelet's development as a historian was directly opposite to that of Guizot. He began his career with a general interest in the history of civilization and became more and more a historian of France. The more he studied France, the more the rest of Europe receded into a series of external enemies. In the later histories England emerged as the great national enemy, and French history was treated as the efforts of Frenchmen through the centuries to sever that fatal connection with England. For Michelet France was born out of a hundred years of war with England, a war which had never really ended. He saw his teaching as creating Frenchmen, his history as serving the nation-state. His lectures were sermons, his histories patriotic hymns to the greatness of France. Nisard, an early sympathizer with Michelet, saw the distinction between Guizot and Michelet clearly: "Guizot is dominated by the march of civilization; Michelet by the unity of France."

It is true that when we move from Guizot to Michelet we are in a world that is richer and more vivid; but it is also one that is more parochial. For Guizot the theme of European history was the development of representative institutions through the agency of the middle class. (To a later generation of historians this too would seem parochial.) Such institutions, classes, and liberal ideas all had the advantage of being present everywhere in Europe. Guizot always made it clear that in studying France one studied in microcosm these larger European phenonmena. He had chosen the history of France only because that country was at the center of European civilization. It was his hope that the study of French history would free the younger generation from the narrow passion of the Revolution and have a liberating and liberalizing effect on the nineteenth century.

. . . .

Since this volume is designed to introduce Guizot the historian to the twentieth-century audience, and since it is appearing in a series devoted to great historians, the editor has confined his selections to Guizot's historical writing. This is to leave out a great deal of Guizot: his literary works, political pamphlets, and his own memoirs, speeches, and letters. There was a Guizot who wrote on Renaissance painters and Corneille and who late in life engaged in religious polemics and philosophical dissertations. Guizot, in addition to being a historian, was a great editor, journalist, and translator—and all this, too, will be absent from this volume. Yet even when one confines oneself to Guizot as historian, there is an enormous range to choose from, and one can only sample that range.

The opening discourse of 1812 is included because it was Guizot's first historical lecture. The introduction to his translation of Shakespeare (1821) and his essay on Washington (1839) are included to suggest the variety of his interests. His first great work to be published was a *History of England* (begun in 1825), and the preface to that has also been included. The essay on Madame de Rumford is included as an example of Guizot's writing on a contemporary topic. It was Guizot's personal encounter with Madame de Rumford that became the point of departure for his examination and judgment of the eighteenth century. The bulk of this volume is drawn from the two courses on the general history of Europe, which Guizot gave at the Sorbonne in the years 1820–22 and 1828–30. He continued to write histories to the very end of his life (including the so-called *History for My Grandchildren*, often translated as the *History of France*), but it is on these two sets of lectures that François Guizot's fame as a historian still rests.

These translations may strike the modern reader as archaic and perhaps even stilted. They do, however, have the advantage of being nineteenth-century English versions of nineteenth-century French classics. Furthermore, these are the very translations which made Guizot's essays and lectures standard reading in English and American universities and which helped make his name a household word in the nineteenth-century Anglo-Saxon world. Occasionally, when archaisms interfered with or obscured Guizot's meaning, I have been compelled in the interest of clarity to take the liberty of retranslating certain words and phrases. For example, Guizot's nineteenth-century translators rendered *bourgeois* as "burgher" and *commune* as "commons." In cases such as these, where the French has happily entered our historical language, it was possible to restore the original. There was one critical case (in Lecture VII of *History of the Origin of Representative Government in Europe*) where Guizot used the French phrase *la lutte des classes*. The nineteenth-century English translator, knowing nothing of Karl Marx (who, indeed, was only ten years old at the time), translated this as "the contest of classes." For a closer rendering of Guizot's sense, I have changed this to "the class struggle," that Marxian phrase which is perfectly familiar to the modern reader, for even in 1821 Guizot was writing of the very phenomenon which Marx would later help to make famous in his own words.

STANLEY MELLON

xlv

HISTORICAL ESSAYS AND LECTURES

1

Discourse Delivered by M. Guizot on the Opening of His First Course of Lectures on Modern History, December 11th, 1812

A STATESMAN equally celebrated for his character and misfortunes, Sir Walter Raleigh, had published the first part of a *History of the World;* while confined in the Tower, he employed himself in finishing the second. A quarrel arose in one of the courts of the prison; he looked on attentively at the contest, which became sanguinary, and left the window with his imagination strongly impressed by the scene that had passed under his eyes. On the morrow a friend came to visit him, and related what had occurred. But great was his surprise when this friend, who had been present at and even engaged in the occurrence of the preceding day, proved to him that this event, in its result as well as in its particulars, was precisely the contrary of what he had believed he saw. Raleigh, when left alone, took up his manuscript and threw it in the fire; convinced that, as he had been so completely deceived with respect to the details of an incident he had actually witnessed, he could know nothing whatever of those he had just described with his pen.

Are we better informed or more fortunate than Sir Walter

Reprinted from *Memoirs to Illustrate the History of My Time,* translated by J. W. Cole (London: Richard Bentley, 1858), from *Memoires pour Servir a l'Histoire de mon Temps.*

3

Raleigh? The most confident historian would hesitate to answer this question directly in the affirmative. History relates a long series of events, and depicts a vast number of characters; and let us recollect, gentlemen, the difficulty of thoroughly understanding a single character or a solitary event. Montaigne, after having passed his life in self-study, was continually making new discoveries on his own nature; he has filled a long work with them, and ends by saying, "Man is a subject so diversified, so uncertain and vain, that it is difficult to pronounce any fixed and uniform opinion on him." He is, in fact, an obscure compound of an infinity of ideas and sentiments, which change and modify themselves reciprocally, and of which it is as difficult to disentangle the sources as to foresee the results. An uncertain product of a multiplicity of circumstances, sometimes impenetrable, always complicated, often unknown to the person influenced by them, and not even suspected by those who surround him, man scarcely learns how to know himself, and is never more than guessed at by others. The simplest mind, if it attempted to examine and describe itself, would impart to us a thousand secrets, of which we have not the most remote suspicion. And how many different men are comprised in an event! how many whose characters have influenced that event, and have modified its nature, progress, and effects! Bring together circumstances in perfect accordance; suppose situations exactly similar: let a single actor change, and all is changed. He is urged by fresh motives, and desires new objects. Take the same actors, and alter but one of those circumstances independent of human will, which are called chance or destiny; and all is changed again. It is from this infinity of details, where everything is obscure, and nothing isolated, that history is composed; and man, proud of what he knows, because he forgets to think of how much he is ignorant, believes that he has acquired a full knowledge of history when he has read what some few have told him, who had no better means of understanding the times in which they lived, than we possess of justly estimating our own.

What then are we to seek and find in the darkness of the past, which thickens as it recedes from us? If Cæsar, Sallust, or Tacitus have only been able to transmit doubtful and imperfect notions, can we rely on what they relate? And if we are not to trust them, how are we to supply ourselves with information? Shall we be capable of disembarrassing our minds of those ideas and manners, and of that new existence, which a new order of things has produced, to adopt momentarily in our thoughts other manners and ideas, and a different character of being? Must we learn to become Greeks, Romans, or Barbarians, in order to understand these Romans, Barbarians, or Greeks, before we venture to judge them? And even if we could attain this difficult abnegation of an actual and imperious reality, should we become then as well acquainted with the history of the times of which they tell us, as were Cæsar, Sallust, or Tacitus? After being thus transported to the midst of the world they describe, we should find gaps in their delineations, of which we have at present no conception, and of which they were not always sensible themselves. That multiplicity of facts, which, grouped together and viewed from a distance, appear to fill time and space, would present to us, if we found ourselves placed on the ground they occupy, as voids which we should find it impossible to fill up, and which the historians leave there designedly, because he who relates or describes what he sees, to others who see equally with himself, never feels called upon to recapitulate all that he knows.

Let us therefore refrain from supposing that history can present to us, in reality, an exact picture of the past; the world is too extensive, the night of time too obscure, and man too weak for such a portrait to be ever a complete reflection.

But can it be true that such important knowledge is entirely interdicted to us?—that in what we can acquire, all is a subject of doubt and error? Does the mind only enlighten itself to increase its wavering? Does it develop all its strength, merely to end in a confession of ignorance?—a painful and disheartening idea, which many men of superior intellect have encountered in their course, but by which they ought never to have been impeded!

Man seldom asks himself what he really requires to know, in his ardent pursuit of knowledge; he need only cast a glance upon his studies, to discover two divisions, the difference between

5

which is striking, although we may be unable to assign the boundaries that separate them. Everywhere we perceive a certain innocent but futile labour, which attaches itself to questions and inquiries equally inaccessible and without results—which has no other object than to satisfy the restless curiosity of minds, the first want of which is occupation; and everywhere, also, we observe useful, productive, and interesting inquiry, nót only advantageous to those who indulge in it, but beneficial to human nature at large. What time and talent have men wasted in metaphysical lucubrations! They have sought to penetrate the internal nature of things, of the mind, and of matter; they have taken purely vague combinations of words for substantial realities; but these very researches, or others which have arisen out of them, have enlightened us upon the order of our faculties, the laws by which they are governed, and the progress of their development; we have acquired from thence a history, a statistic of the human mind; and if no one has been able to tell us what it is, we have at least learned how it acts, and how we ought to act to strengthen its justice and extend its range.

Was not the study of astronomy for a long time directed to the dreams of astrology? Gassendi himself began to investigate it with that view; and when science cured him of the prejudices of superstition, he repented that he so openly declared his conversion, because, he said, many persons formerly studied astronomy to become astrologers, and he now perceived that they ceased to learn astronomy, since he had condemned astrology. Who then can prove to us that, without the restlessness of anticipation which had led men to seek the future in the stars, the science, by which today our ships are directed, would ever have reached its present perfection?

It is thus that we shall ever find, in the labours of man, one half fruitless, by the side of another moiety profitable; we shall then no longer condemn the curiosity which leads to knowledge; we shall acknowledge that, if the human mind often wanders in its path, if it has not always selected the most direct road, it has finally arrived, by the necessity of its nature, at the discovery of important truths; but, with progressive enlightenment, we shall endeavour not to lose time, to go straight to the end by concentrating our strength on fruitful inquiries and profitable results; and we shall soon convince ourselves that what man cannot do is valueless, and that he can achieve all that is necessary. The application of this idea to history will soon remove the difficulty which its uncertainty raised at the outset. For example, it is of little consequence to us to know the exact personal appearance or the precise day of the birth of Constantine; to ascertain what particular motives or individual feelings may have influenced his determination or conduct on any given occasion; to be acquainted with all the details of his wars and victories in the struggles with Maxentius or Licinius: these minor points concern the monarch alone; and the monarch exists no longer. The anxiety some scholars display in hunting them out is merely a consequence of the interest which attaches to great names and important reminiscences. But the results of the conversion of Constantine, his administrative system, the political and religious principles which he established in his empire—these are the matters which it imports the present generation to investigate; for they do not expire with a particular age, they form the destiny and glory of nations, they confer or take away the use of the most noble faculties of man; they either plunge them silently into a state of misery alternately submissive and rebellious, or establish for them the foundation of a lasting happiness.

It may be said, to a certain extent, that there are two pasts, the one entirely extinct and without real interest, because its influence has not extended beyond its actual duration; the other enduring for ever by the empire it has exercised over succeeding ages, and by that alone preserved to our knowledge, since what remains of it is there to enlighten us upon what has perished. History presents us, at every epoch, with some predominant ideas, some great events which have decided the fortune and character of a long series of generations. These ideas and events have left monuments which still remain, or which long remained, on the face of the world; an extended trace, in perpetuating the memory and effect of their existence, has multiplied the materials suitable for our guidance in the researches of which they are the object; reason itself can here supply us with its positive data to conduct us through the uncertain labyrinth of facts. In a past event there may have been some particular circumstance at present unknown, which would completely alter the idea we have formed of it. Thus, we shall never discover the reason which delayed Hannibal at Capua, and saved Rome; but in an effect which has endured for a long time, we easily ascertain the nature of its cause. The despotic authority which the Roman Senate exercised for ages over the people, explains to us the ideas of liberty within which the Senators restricted themselves when they expelled their kings. Let us then follow the path in which we can have reason for our guide; let us apply the principles, with which she furnishes us, to the examples borrowed from history. Man, in the ignorance and weakness to which the narrow limits of his life and faculties condemn him, has received reason to supply knowledge, as industry is given to him in place of strength.

Such, gentlemen, is the point of view under which we shall endeavour to contemplate history. We shall seek, in the annals of nations, a knowledge of the human race; we shall try to discover what, in every age and state of civilization, have been the prevailing ideas and principles in general adoption, which have produced the happiness or misery of the generations subjected to their power, and have influenced the destiny of those which succeeded them. The subject is one of the most abundant in considerations of this nature. History presents to us periods of development, during which man, emerging from a state of barbarism and ignorance, arrives gradually at a condition of science and advancement, which may decline, but can never perish, for knowledge is an inheritance that always finds heirs. The civilization of the Egyptians and Phœnicians prepared that of the Greeks; while that of the Romans was not lost to the barbarians who established themselves upon the ruins of the Empire. No preceding age has ever enjoyed the advantage we possess, of studying this slow but real progression: while looking back on the past, we can recognize the route which the human race has followed in Europe for more than two thousand years. Modern history alone, from its vast scope, from the variety and extent of its duration, offers us the grandest and most complete picture which we could possibly possess of the civilization of a certain portion of the globe. A rapid glance will suffice to indicate the character and interest of the subject.

Rome had conquered what her pride delighted to call the world. Western Asia, from the frontiers of Persia, the North of Africa, Greece, Macedonia, Thrace, all the countries situated on the right bank of the Danube, from its source to its mouth, Italy, Gaul, Great Britain, and Spain, acknowledged her authority. That authority extended over more than a thousand leagues in breadth, from the Wall of Antoninus and the southern boundaries of Dacia, to Mount Atlas—and beyond fifteen hundred leagues in length, from the Euphrates to the Western Ocean. But if the immense extent of these conquests at first surprises the imagination, the astonishment diminishes when we consider how easy they were of accomplishment, and how uncertain of duration. In Asia, Rome had only to contend with effeminate races; in Europe, with ignorant savages, whose governments, without union, regularity, or vigour, were unable to contend with the strong constitution of the Roman aristocracy. Let us pause a moment to reflect on this. Rome found it more difficult to defend herself against Hannibal than to subjugate the world; and as soon as the world was subdued, Rome began to lose, by degrees, all that she had won by conquest. How could she maintain her power? The comparative state of civilization between the victors and the vanquished had prevented union or consolidation into one substantial and homogeneous whole; there was no extended and regular administration, no general and safe communication; the provinces were only connected with Rome by the tribute they paid; Rome was unknown in the provinces, except by the tribute she exacted. Everywhere, in Asia Minor, in Africa, in Spain, in Britain, in the North of Gallia, small colonies defended and maintained their independence; all the power of the Emperors was inadequate to compel the submission of the Isaurians. The whole formed a chaos of nations half vanquished and semibarbarous, without interest or existence in the State of which they were considered a portion, and which Rome denominated the Empire.

No sooner was this Empire conquered, than it began to dissolve, and that haughty city which looked upon every region as subdued where she could, by maintaining an army, appoint a proconsul, and levy imposts, soon saw herself compelled to abandon, almost voluntarily, the possessions she was unable to retain. In the year of Christ 270, Aurelian retired from Dacia, and tacitly abandoned that territory to the Goths; in 412, Honorius recognized the independence of Great Britain and Armorica; in 428, he wished the inhabitants of Gallia Narbonensis to govern themselves. On all sides we see the Romans abandoning, without being driven out, countries whose obedience, according to the expression of Montesquieu, *weighed upon them,* and which, never having been incorporated with the Empire, were sure to separate from it on the first shock.

The shock came from a quarter which the Romans, notwithstanding their pride, had never considered one of their provinces. Even more barbarous than the Gauls, the Britons, and the Spaniards, the Germans had never been conquered, because their innumerable tribes, without fixed residences or country, ever ready to advance or retreat, sometimes threw themselves, with their wives and flocks, upon the possessions of Rome, and at others retired before her armies, leaving nothing for conquest but a country without inhabitants, which they reoccupied as soon as the weakness or distance of the conquerors afforded them the opportunity. It is to this wandering life of a hunting nation, to this facility of flight and return, rather than to superior bravery, that the Germans were indebted for the preservation of their independence. The Gauls and Spaniards had also defended themselves courageously; but the one, surrounded by the ocean, knew not where to fly from enemies they could not expel; and the other, in a state of more advanced civilization, attacked by the Romans, to whom the Narbonnese province afforded, in the very heart of Gaul itself, an impregnable base, and repulsed by the Germans from the land into which they might have escaped, were also compelled to submit. Drusus and Germanicus had long before penetrated into Germany; they withdrew, because the

Germans always retreating before them, they would, by remaining, have only occupied territory without subjects.

When, from causes not connected with the Roman Empire, the Tartar tribes who wandered through the deserts of Sarmatia and Scythia, from the northern frontiers of China, marched upon Germany, the Germans, pressed by these new invaders, threw themselves upon the Roman provinces, to conquer possessions where they might establish themselves in perpetuity. Rome then fought in defence; the struggle was protracted; the skill and courage of some of the Emperors for a long time opposed a powerful barrier; but the Barbarians were the ultimate conquerors, because it was imperative on them to win the victory, and their swarms of warriors were inexhaustible. The Visigoths, the Alani, and the Suevi established themselves in the South of Gaul and Spain; the Vandals passed over into Africa; the Huns occupied the banks of the Danube; the Ostrogoths founded their kingdom in Italy; the Franks in the North of Gaul: Rome ceased to call herself the mistress of Europe; Constantinople does not apply to our present subject.

Those nations of the East and the North who transported themselves in a mass into the countries where they were destined to found States, the more durable because they conquered not to extend but to establish themselves, were barbarians, such as the Romans themselves had long remained. Force was their law, savage independence their delight; they were free because none of them had ever thought or believed that men as strong as themselves would submit to their domination; they were brave because courage with them was a necessity; they loved war because war brings occupation without labour; they desired lands because these new possessions supplied them with a thousand novel sources of enjoyment, which they could indulge in while giving themselves up to idleness. They had chiefs because men leagued together always have leaders, and because the bravest, ever held in high consideration, soon become the most powerful, and bequeath to their descendants a portion of their own personal influence. These chiefs became kings; the old subjects of Rome,

11

who at first had only been called upon to receive, to lodge, and feed their new masters, were soon compelled to surrender to them a portion of their estates; and as the labourer, as well as the plant, attaches himself to the soil that nourishes him, the lands and the labourers became the property of these turbulent and lazy owners. Thus feudalism was established—not suddenly, not by an express convention between the chief and his followers, not by an immediate and regular division of the conquered country amongst the conquerors, but by degrees, after long years of uncertainty, by the simple force of circumstances, as must always happen when conquest is followed by transplantation and continued possession.

We should be wrong in supposing that the barbarians were destitute of all moral convictions. Man, in that early epoch of civilization, does not reflect upon what we call duties; but he knows and respects, amongst his fellow beings, certain rights, some traces of which are discoverable even under the empire of the most absolute force. A simple code of justice, often violated, and cruelly avenged, regulates the simple intercourse of associated savages. The Germans, unacquainted with any other laws or ties, found themselves suddenly transported into the midst of an order of things founded on different ideas, and demanding different restrictions. This gave them no trouble; their passage was too rapid to enable them to ascertain and supply what was deficient in their legislature and policy. Bestowing little thought on their new subjects, they continued to follow the same principles and customs which recently, in the forests of Germany, had regulated their conduct and decided their quarrels. Thus the conquered people were, at first, more forgotten than vanquished, more despised than oppressed; they constituted the mass of the nation, and this mass found itself controlled without being reduced to servitude, because they were not thought of, and because the conquerors never suspected that they could possess rights which they feared to defend. From thence sprang, in the sequel, that long disorder at the commencement of the Middle Ages, during which everything was isolated, fortuitous, and partial; hence also proceeded the absolute separation between the nobles and the people, and those abuses of the feudal system which only became portions of a system when long possession had caused to be looked upon as a right, what at first was only the produce of conquest and chance.

The clergy alone, to whom the conversion of the victors afforded the means of acquiring a power so much the greater that its force and extent could only be judged by the opinion it directed, maintained their privileges, and secured their independence. The religion which the Germans embraced became the only channel through which they derived new ideas, the sole point of contact between them and the inhabitants of their adopted country. The clergy, at first, thought only of their own interest; in this mode of communication, all the immediate advantages of the invasion of the barbarians were reaped by them for themselves. The liberal and beneficent influences of Christianity expanded slowly; that of religious animosity and theological dispute was the first to make itself felt. It was only in the class occupied by those dissensions, and excited by those rancorous feelings, that energetic men were yet to be found in the Roman Empire; religious sentiments and duties had revived, in hearts penetrated with their importance, a degree of zeal long extinguished. St. Athanasius and St. Ambrose had alone resisted Constantine and Theodosius; their successors were the sole opponents who withstood the barbarians. This gave rise to the long empire of spiritual power, sustained with devotion and perseverance, and so weakly or fruitlessly assailed. We may say now, without fear, that the noblest characters, the men most distinguished by their ability or courage, throughout this period of misfortune and calamity, belonged to the ecclesiastical order; and no other epoch of history supplies, in such a remarkable manner, the confirmation of this truth, so honourable to human nature, and perhaps the most instructive of all others—that the most exalted virtues still spring up and develope themselves in the bosom of the most pernicious errors.

To these general features, intended to depict the ideas, manners, and conditions of men during the Middle Ages, it would be easy to add others, not less characteristic, and infinitely more minute. We should find poetry and literature, those beautiful and delightful emanations of the mind, the seeds of which have never been choked by all the follies and miseries of humanity, take birth in the very heart of barbarism, and charm the barbarians themselves by a new species of enjoyment. We should find the source and true character of that poetical, warlike, and religious enthusiasm which created chivalry and the crusades. We should probably discover, in the wandering lives of the knights and crusaders, the reflected influence of the roving habits of the German hunters, of that propensity move on, and that superabundance of population, which ever exist where social order is not sufficiently well regulated for man to feel satisfied with his condition and locality; and before laborious industry has taught him to compel the earth to supply him with certain and abundant subsistence. Perhaps, also, that principle of honour which inviolably attached the German barbarians to a leader of their own choice, that individual liberty of which it was the fruit, and which gives man such an elevated idea of his own individual importance; that empire of the imagination which obtains such control over all young nations, and induces them to attempt the first steps beyond physical wants and purely material incitements, might furnish us with the causes of the elevation, enthusiasm, and devotion which, sometimes detaching the nobles of the Middle Ages from their habitual rudeness, inspired them with the noble sentiments and virtues that even in the present day command our admiration. We should then feel little surprised at seeing barbarity and heroism united, so much energy combined with so much weakness, and the natural coarseness of man in a savage state blended with the most sublime aspirations of moral refinement.

It was reserved for the latter half of the fifteenth century to witness the birth of events destined to introduce new manners and a fresh order of politics into Europe, and to lead the world towards the direction it follows at present. Italy, we may say, discovered the civilization of the Greeks; the letters, arts, and ideas of that brilliant antiquity inspired universal enthusiasm. The long quarrels of the Italian Republics, after having forced men to display their utmost energy, made them also feel the necessity of a period of repose ennobled and charmed by the occupations of the mind. The study of classic literature supplied the means; they were seized with ardour.

Popes, cardinals, princes, nobles, and men of genius gave themselves up to learned researches; they wrote to each other, they travelled to communicate their mutual labours, to discover, to read, and to copy ancient manuscripts. The discovery of printing came to render these communications easy and prompt; to make this commerce of the mind extended and prolific. No other event has so powerfully influenced human civilization. Books became a tribune from which the world was addressed. That world was soon doubled. The compass opened safe roads across the monotonous immensity of the seas. America was discovered; and the sight of new manners, the agitation of new interests which were no longer the trifling concerns of one town or castle with another, but the great transactions of mighty powers, changed entirely the ideas of individuals and the political intercourse of States.

The invention of gunpowder had already altered their military relations; the issue of battles no longer depended on the isolated bravery of warriors, but on the power and skill of leaders. It has not yet been sufficiently investigated to what extent this discovery has secured monarchical authority, and given rise to the balance of power.

Finally, the Reformation struck a deadly blow against spiritual supremacy, the consequences of which are attributable to the bold examination of the theological questions and political shocks which led to the separation of religious sects, rather than to the new dogmas adopted by the Reformers as the foundation of their belief.

Figure to yourselves, gentlemen, the effect which these united causes were calculated to produce in the midst of the fermentation by which the human species was at that time excited, in the progress of the superabundant energy and activity which characterized the Middle Ages. From that time, this activity, so long unregulated, began to organize itself and advance towards a defined object; this energy submitted to laws; isolation disappeared;

the human race formed itself into one great body; public opinion assumed influence; and if an age of civil wars, of religious dissensions, presents the lengthened echo of that powerful shock which towards the end of the fifteenth century staggered Europe, under so many different forms, it is not the less to the ideas and discoveries which produced that blow that we are indebted for the two centuries of splendour, order, and peace during which civilization has reached the point where we find it in the present day.

This is not the place to follow the march of human nature during these two centuries. That history is so extensive, and composed of so many relations, alternately vast and minute, but always important; of so many events closely connected, brought about by causes so mixed together, and causes in their turn productive of such numerous effects, of so many different labours, that it is impossible to recapitulate them within a limited compass. Never have so many powerful and neighbouring States exercised upon each other such constant and complicated influence; never has their interior structure presented so many ramifications to study; never has the human mind advanced at once upon so many different roads; never have so many events, actors, and ideas been engaged in such an extended space, or produced such interesting and instructive results. Perhaps on some future occasion we may enter into this maze, and look for the clue to guide us through it. Called upon, at present, to study the first ages of modern history, we shall seek for their cradle in the forests of Germany, the country of our ancestors; after having drawn a picture of their manners, as complete as the number of facts which have reached our knowledge, the actual state of our information, and my efforts to reach that level will permit, we shall then glance at the condition of the Roman Empire at the moment when the barbarians invaded it to try to establish themselves; after that we shall investigate the long struggles which ensued between them and Rome, from their irruption into the West and South of Europe, down to the foundation of the principal modern monarchies. This foundation will thus become for us a resting point, from whence we shall depart again to follow the

16

course of the history of Europe, which is in fact our own; for if unity, the fruit of the Roman dominion, disappeared with it, there are always, nevertheless, between the different nations which rose upon its ruins, relations so multiplied, so continued, and so important, that from them, in the whole of modern history taken together, an actual unity results which we shall be compelled to acknowledge. This task is enormous; and when we contemplate its full extent, it is impossible not to recoil before the difficulty. Judge then, gentlemen, ought I not tremble at such an undertaking; but your indulgence and zeal will make up for the weakness of my resources: I shall be more than repaid if I am able to assist you in advancing even a few steps on the road which leads to truth!

2

History of the Origin of
Representative Government in Europe

REPRESENTATIVE INSTITUTIONS IN ENGLAND, FRANCE, AND SPAIN, FROM THE FIFTH TO THE ELEVENTH CENTURY

Lecture 1

SUCH is the immensity of human affairs, that, so far from exhibiting superannuation and decay with the progress of time, they seem to gain new youth, and to gird themselves afresh at frequent intervals, in order to appear under aspects hitherto unknown. Not only does each age receive a vocation to devote itself especially to a particular region of inquiry; but the same studies are to each age as a mine but little explored, or as an unknown territory where objects for discovery present themselves at every step. In the study of history this truth is especially apparent. The facts about which history concerns itself neither gain nor lose anything by being handed down from age to age; whatever we have seen in these facts, and whatever we can see, has been contained in them ever since they were originally accomplished; but they never allow themselves to be fully apprehended, nor permit all

Selections from *History of the Origin of Representative Government in Europe,* translated by Andrew R. Scoble (London: Henry G. Bohn, 1861), from *Histoire des Origines du Gouvernement Représentatif en Europe.*

their meaning to be thoroughly investigated; they have, so to speak, innumerable secrets, which slowly utter themselves after man has become prepared to recognise them. And as everything in man and around him changes, as the point of view from which he considers the facts of history, and the state of mind which he brings to the survey, continually vary, we may speak of the past as changing with the present; unperceived facts reveal themselves in ancient facts; other ideas, other feelings, are called up by the same names and the same narratives; and man thus learns that in the infinitude of space opened to his knowledge, everything remains constantly fresh and inexhaustible, in regard to his ever-active and ever-limited intelligence.

This combined view of the greatness of events and the feebleness of the human mind, never appears so startlingly distinct as upon the occurrence of those extraordinary crises, which, so to speak, entirely delocalize man, and transport him to a different sphere. Such revolutions, it is true, do not unfold themselves in an abrupt and sudden manner. They are conceived and nurtured in the womb of society long before they emerge to the light of day. But the moment arrives beyond which their full accomplishment cannot be delayed, and they then take possession of all that exists in society, transform it, and place everything in an entirely new position; so that if, after such a shock, man looks back upon the history of the past, he can scarcely recognise it. That which he sees, he had never seen before; what he saw once, no longer exists as he saw it; facts rise up before him with unknown faces, and speak to him in a strange language. He sets himself to the examination of them under the guidance of other principles of observation and appreciation. Whether he considers their causes, their nature, or their consequences, unknown prospects open before him on all sides. The actual spectacle remains the same, but it is viewed by another spectator occupying a different place; to his eyes all is changed.

What marvel is it, gentlemen, if, in this new state of things and of himself, man adopts, as the special objects of his study, questions and facts which connect themselves more immediately with the revolution which has just been accomplished—if he directs his gaze precisely towards that quarter where the change has been most profound? The grand crises in the life of humanity are not all of the same nature; although they, sooner or later, influence the whole mass of society, they act upon it and approach it, in some respects, from different sides. Sometimes it is by religious ideas, sometimes by political ideas, sometimes by a simple discovery, or a mechanical invention, that the world is ruled and changed. The apparent metamorphosis which the past then undergoes is effected chiefly in that which corresponds to the essential character of the revolution that is actually going forward in the present. Let us imagine, if we can, the light in which the traditions and religious recollections of Paganism must have appeared to the Christians of the first centuries, and then we shall understand the new aspects under which old facts present themselves in those times of renovation, which Providence has invested with a peculiar importance and significance.

Such is, gentlemen, up to a certain point, the position in which we ourselves are placed with regard to that subject which is to come before us in the present course of lectures. It is from the midst of the new political order which has commenced in Europe in our own days that we are about to consider, I do not say naturally, but necessarily, the history of the political institutions of Europe from the foundation of modern states. To descend from this point of view is not in our power. Against our will, and without our knowledge, the ideas which have occupied the present will follow us wherever we go in the study of the past. Vainly should we attempt to escape from the lights which they cast thereupon; those lights will only diffuse themselves around on all sides with more confusion and less utility. We will then frankly accept a position which, in my opinion, is favourable, and certainly inevitable. We attempt to-day, and with good reason, to reconnect what we now are with what we formerly were; we feel the necessity of bringing our habits into association with intelligent feeling, to connect our institutions with our recollections, and, in fine, to gather together the links in that chain of time, which never allows itself to be entirely broken, however violent may be the assaults made upon it. In accordance with the same principles, and guided by the same spirit, we shall not refuse the aid which can be derived from modern ideas and institutions, in order to guide our apprehension and judgment while studying ancient institutions, since we neither can, nor would wish to be separated from our proper selves, any more than we would attempt or desire to isolate ourselves from our forefathers.

This study, gentlemen, has been much neglected in our days; and when attempts have been made to revive it, it has been approached with such a strong preoccupation of mind, or with such a determined purpose, that the fruits of our labour have been damaged at the outset. Opinions which are partial and adopted before facts have been fairly examined, not only have the effect of vitiating the rectitude of judgment, but they moreover introduce a deplorable frivolity into researches which we may call material. As soon as the prejudiced mind has collected a few documents and proofs in support of its cherished notion, it is contented, and concludes its inquiry. On the one hand, it beholds in facts that which is not really contained in them; on the other hand, when it believes that the amount of information it already possesses will suffice, it does not seek further knowledge. Now, such has been the force of circumstances and passions among us, that they have disturbed even erudition itself. It has become a party weapon, an instrument of attack or defence; and facts themselves, inflexible and immutable facts, have been by turns invited or repulsed, perverted or mutilated, according to the interest or sentiment in favour of which they were summoned to appear.

In accordance with this prevailing circumstance of our times, two opposite tendencies are observable in those opinions and writings which have passed a verdict on the ancient political institutions of Europe. On the one hand, we see minds so overpowered by the splendour of the new day which has dawned upon mankind, that they see in the generations which preceded, only darkness, disorder, and oppression—objects either for their indignation or their contempt. Proud disdain of the past has taken possession of these minds—a disdain which exalts itself into a system. This system has presented all the characteristics of settled impiety. Laws, sentiments, ideas, customs, everything pertaining to our forefathers, it has treated with coldness or scorn. It would seem as if reason, regard for justice, love of liberty, all that makes society dignified and secure, were a discovery of today, made by the generation which has last appeared. In thus renouncing its ancestors, this generation forgets that it will soon join them in the tomb, and that in its turn it will leave its inheritance to its children.

This pride, gentlemen, is not less contrary to the truth of things than fatal to the society which entertains it. Providence does not so unequally deal with the generations of men, as to impoverish some in order that the rest may be lavishly endowed at their expense. It is doubtless true, that virtue and glory are not shared in a uniform degree by different ages; but there is no age which does not possess some legitimate claim upon the respect of its descendants. There is not one which has not borne its part in the grand struggle between good and evil, truth and error, liberty and oppression. And not only has each age maintained this laborious struggle on its own account, but whatever advantage it has been able to gain, it has transmitted to its successors. The superior vantage ground on which we were born, is a gift to us from our forefathers, who died upon the territory they themselves had won by conquest. It is then a blind and culpable ingratitude which affects to despise the days which are gone. We reap the fruits of their labours and sacrifices: is it too much for us to hallow the memory of those labours, and to render a just recompense for those sacrifices?

If those men who affect, or who actually feel, this irreverent disdain or indifference for ancient times, were better acquainted with these times and their history, they would find themselves constrained to entertain a different opinion. When, in fact, we investigate the cause of this unnatural state of mind, only one explanation can be found. At the moment of grand social reforms, during epochs full of ambition and hope, when important changes are on all sides demanded and necessary, the authority of the past is the one obstacle which opposes itself to all tendency to innovation. The present time seems devoted to errors and abuses, and the wisdom of centuries is appealed to by one party in order to resist the future to which the aspirations of the other party are directed. Accordingly, a kind of blind hatred of the past takes possession of a great number of men. They regard it as making common cause with the enemies of present amelioration, and the weapons employed by these latter confirm this idea in their mind. Gentlemen, the notion is full of falsehood and misapprehension. It is not true that injustice and abuses alone can shelter themselves under the authority of antiquity, that they only are capable of appealing to precedent and experience. Truth, justice, and rectitude, are also graced by venerable titles; and at no period has man allowed them to be proscribed. Take in succession all the moral needs, all the legitimate interests of our society, arrange them in systematic order, and then traverse the history of our country; you will find them constantly asserted and defended— all epochs will afford you innumerable proofs of struggles endured, of victories won, of concessions obtained in this holy cause. It has been carried on with different issues, but in no time or place has it been abandoned. There is not a truth or a right which cannot bring forward, from any period of history, monuments to consecrate, and facts to vindicate it. Justice has not retired from the world, even when it finds there least support: it has constantly sought and embraced, both with governments and in the midst of peoples, all opportunities for extending its dominion. It has struggled, protested, waited; and when it has had only glory to bestow upon those who have fought for it, it has bestowed that glory with a liberal hand.

Let us then, gentlemen, reassure ourselves with reference to the study of the past. It contains nothing which ought to alarm the friends of all that is good and true. It is into their hands, on the contrary, and in subservience to interests which are dear to them, that it will ever deposit the authority of antiquity and the lessons of experience.

This unjust contempt for ancient institutions, however, this wild attempt to dissever the present from its connexion with former ages and to begin society afresh, thus delivering it up to all the dangers of a position in which it is deprived of its roots and cast upon the protection of a wisdom which is yet in its infancy, is not an error of which we have been the first to give an example. In one of those ephemeral parliaments which attempted to maintain its existence under the yoke of Cromwell, it was seriously proposed to deliver up to the flames all the archives in the Tower of London, and thus to annihilate the monuments of the existence of England in former ages. These infatuated men wished to abolish the past, flattering themselves that they would then obtain an absolute control over the future. Their design was rejected, and their hope foiled; and very soon England, regaining, with new liberties, respect for all its recollections of the past, entered upon that career of development and prosperity which it has continued up to our times.

Side by side with this infatuation which has induced men, otherwise enlightened, to neglect the study of the ancient institutions of Europe, or only to regard their history with a hasty and supercilious glance, we have seen another infatuation arise, perhaps still more unreasonable and arrogant. Here, as elsewhere, impiety has been the herald of superstition. The past, so despised, so neglected by the one party, has become to the other an object of idolatrous veneration. The former desire that society, mutilating its own being, should disown its former life; the latter would have it return to its cradle, in order to remain there immovable and powerless. And as those lords of the future would in their own wild fancy create out of it, so far as regards government and social order, the most brilliant Utopias, so these, on the other hand, find their Utopia in their dreams of the past. The work might appear more difficult; the field open to the imagination may seem less open, and facts might be expected sometimes to press inconveniently against the conclusions sought. But what will not a preoccupied mind overcome? Plato and Harrington, giving to their thoughts the widest range, had constructed their ideal of a republic; and we, with still more confidence, have constructed our ideal of feudalism, of absolute power, and even of barbarism. Fully organized societies, adorned with freedom and morality, have been conceived and fashioned at leisure, in order thence to be transported into past ages. After having attempted to resolve, according to principles opposed to modern tendencies, the great problem of the harmony between liberty and power, between order and progress, we have required that ancient facts should receive these theories and adapt themselves to them. And since, in the vast number of facts, some are to be found which lend themselves with docility and readiness to the purposes which they are required to serve, the discoverers of this pretended antiquity have not lacked either quotations or proofs which might seem to give it an ascertained and definite existence in the past. Thus, France, after having spent more than five centuries in its struggles to escape from the feudal system, has all at once discovered that it was wrong in liberating itself from this system, for that in this state it possessed true happiness and freedom; and history, which believed itself to be chargeable with so many evils, iniquities, and convulsions, is surprised to learn that it only hands down to us recollections of two or three golden ages.

There is no necessity for me, gentlemen, to offer any very serious opposition to this fantastic and superstitious adoration of the past. It would hardly have merited even a passing allusion, were it not connected with systems and tendencies in which all society is interested. It is one of the collateral circumstances of the grand struggle which has never ceased to agitate the world. The interests and ideas which have successfully taken possession of society have always wished to render it stationary in the position which has given it over to their rule; and when it has escaped from them, it has ever, in so doing, had to withstand those seductive images and influences which these interests have called to their aid. There is no fear that the world will allow itself to be thus ensnared—progress is the law of its nature; hope, and not regret, is the spring of its movement—the future alone possesses an attractive virtue. Peoples who have emerged from slavery have always endeavoured by laws to prevent enfranchised man from again falling into servitude. Providence has not been less careful with regard to humanity; and the chains which have not sufficed to confine it, are still less able to resume the grasp which they have lost. But the efforts of a retrograde system have often perverted the study of ancient times. The Emperor Julian saw in the popular fables of Greece a philosophy capable of satisfying those moral necessities which Christianity had come to satisfy, and he demanded that men should see and honour in the history of decayed paganism that which only existed in his dreams. The same demands have been made with as little reason on behalf of the ancient political institutions of Europe. Justice, and justice alone, is due to that which no longer exists, as well as to that which still remains. Respect for the past means neither approbation nor silence for that which is false, culpable, or dangerous. The past deserves no gratitude or consideration from us, except on account of the truth which it has known, and the good which it has aimed at or accomplished. Time has not been endowed with the unhallowed office of consecrating evil or error; on the contrary, it unmasks and consumes them. To spare them because they are ancient, is not to respect the past, but it is to outrage truth, which is older than the world itself.

If I am not mistaken, gentlemen, we are at this time in an especially favourable position for avoiding both of the general errors which I have just described. Perhaps few persons think so; but impartiality, which is the duty of all times, is, in my opinion, the mission of ours—not that cold and unprofitable impartiality which is the offspring of indifference, but that energetic and fruitful impartiality which is inspired by the vision and admiration of truth. That equal and universal justice, which is now the deepest want of society, is also the ruling idea which is ever foremost in position and influence, wherever the spirit of man is found. Blind prejudices, insincere declamation, are no longer any more acceptable in the world of literature, than are iniquity and violence in the world of politics. They may still have some power to agitate society, but they are not permitted either to satisfy or to govern it. The particular state of our own country strengthens this disposition, or, if you please, this general tendency, of the European mind. We have not lived in that state of repose in which objects appear continually under almost the same aspects, in which the present is so changeless and regular as to present to man's view an horizon that seldom varies, in which old and powerful conventionalisms govern thought as well as life, in which opinions are well nigh habits, and soon become prejudices; we have been cast not only into new tracks, but these are continually interrupted and diversified. All theories, all practices, are displayed in union or in rivalry before our eyes. Facts of all kinds have appeared to us under a multitude of aspects. Human nature has been urged impetuously onwards, and laid bare, so to speak, in all the elements of which it is constituted. Affairs and men have all passed from system to system, from combination to combination; and the observer, while himself continually changing his point of view, has been the witness of a spectacle which changed as often as he. Such times, gentlemen, offer but little tranquillity, and prepare tremendous difficulties for those which shall follow them. But they certainly give to minds capable of sustaining their pressure an independent disposition and an extended survey, which do not belong to more serene and fortunate periods. The large number, and the unsettled character of the facts which appear before us, widen the range of our ideas; the diversity of trials which all things undergo within so short an interval, teach us to judge them with impartiality; human nature reveals itself in its simplicity, as well as in its wealth. Experience hastens to fulfil its course, and, in some sort, hoards its treasures; in the short space of one life, man sees, experiences, and attempts that which might have sufficed to fill several centuries. This advantage is sufficiently costly, gentlemen, to act at least as an inducement to our reaping it. It does not become us to entertain narrow views and obstinate prejudices; to petrify the form of our judgments by foregone conclusions; in fine, to ignore that diffusion of truth, which has been attested by so many vicissitudes, and which imposes on us the duty of seeking it everywhere, and rendering it homage wherever we meet it, if we would have its sanction to our thoughts, and its aid to our utterance.

In this spirit, gentlemen, we shall attempt to consider the ancient political institutions of Europe, and to sketch their history. While for this purpose we appropriate such lights as our age can furnish, we shall endeavour to carry with us none of the passions which divide it. We shall not approach past times under the guidance of such impressions belonging to the present, as those whose influence we have just deplored; we shall not address to them those questions which, by their very nature, dictate the answers which they shall receive. I have too much regard for those who listen to me, and for the truth after which I, in common with them, am seeking, to suppose that history can in any sense consent to suppress that which it has asserted, or to utter what is not affirmed by the voice of truth. We must interrogate it freely, and then leave it to full independence.

This study, gentlemen, requires a centre to which it may stand in relation—we must find for so large a number of facts, a bond which may unite and harmonize them. This bond exists in the facts themselves—nothing can be less doubtful. Unity and consecutiveness are not lacking in the moral world, as they are not in the physical. The moral world has, like the system of celestial bodies, its laws and activity; only the secret according to which it acts is more profound, and the human mind has more difficulty in discovering it. We have entered upon this inquiry so late, that events already accomplished may serve us as guides. We have no need to ask of some philosophical hypothesis, itself perhaps uncertain and incomplete, what, in the order of political development, has been the tendency of European civilization. A system which evidently, from a general view of the subject, adheres continually to the same principles, starts from the same necessities, and tends to the same results, manifests or proclaims its presence throughout the whole of Europe. Almost everywhere the representative form of government is demanded, allowed, or established. This fact is, assuredly, neither an accident, nor the symptom of a transient madness. It has certainly its roots in the past political career of the nations, as it has its motives in their present condition. And if, warned by this, we turn our attention to the past, we shall everywhere meet with attempts, more or less successful, either made with a conscious regard to this system so as to produce it naturally, or striving to attain it by the subjugation of contrary forces. England, France, Spain, Portugal, Germany and Sweden, supply us with numerous illustrations of this. If we look to one quarter we shall see these attempts after they have lasted for some time, and assumed an historical consistency; in another, they have hardly commenced before they issue in failure; in a third, they end in a kind of federation of the governments themselves. Their forms are as diverse as their fortunes. England alone continues these struggles without intermission, and enters at last into full enjoyment of their realization. But everywhere they take their place in history, and influence the destinies of nations. And when at last, no longer finding even the shadow of a representative government on the Continent of Europe, and beholding it only in the parliament of Great Britain, a man of genius inquires into its origin, he says that "this noble system was first found in the woods of Germany," from whence the ancestors of the whole of Europe have all equally proceeded.

In this opinion, as will be afterwards seen, I do not agree with Montesquieu; but it is evident, both from ancient facts and from those which we ourselves have witnessed, that the representative form of government has, so to speak, constantly hovered over Europe, ever since the founding of modern states. Its reappearance at so many times and in so many places, is not to be accounted for by the charm of any theory, or the power of any conspiracy. In the endeavour after it, men have often ignored its principles and mistaken its nature, but it has existed in European society as the basis of all its deepest wants and most enduring tendencies; sovereigns have invoked its aid in their hours of difficulty, and nations have ever returned to it during those intervals of prosperity and repose in which the march of civilization has been accelerated. Its most undeveloped efforts have left behind them indelible mementos. Indeed, ever since the birth of modern societies, their condition has been such, that in their institution, in their aspirations, and in the course of their history, the representative form of government, while hardly realized as such by the mind, has constantly loomed more or less distinctly in the distance, as the port at which they must at length arrive, in spite of the storms which scatter them, and the obstacles which confront and oppose their entrance.

We do not then, gentlemen, make an arbitrary choice, but one perfectly natural and necessary, when we make the representative form of government the central idea and aim of our history of the political institutions of Europe. To regard them from this point of view will not only give to our study of them the highest interest, but will enable us rightly to enter into the facts themselves, and truly to appreciate them. We shall then make this form of government the principal object of our consideration. We shall seek it wherever it has been thought to be discernible, wherever it has attempted to gain for itself a footing, wherever it has fully established itself. We shall inquire if it has in reality existed at times and in places where we have been accustomed to look for its germs. Whenever we find any indications of it, however crude and imperfect they may be, we shall inquire how it has been produced, what has been the extent of its power, and what influences have stifled it and arrested its progress. Arriving at last at the country where it has never ceased to consolidate and extend itself, from the thirteenth century to our own times, we shall remain there in order to follow it in its march, to unravel its vicissitudes, to watch the development of the principles and institutions with which it is associated, penetrating into their nature and observing their action—to study, in a word, the history of the representative system in that country where it really possesses a history which identifies itself with that of the people and their government.

Before undertaking this laborious task, it will be necessary for me, gentlemen, to exhibit before you, in a few words, the chief phases of the political condition of Europe, and the series of the principal systems of institutions through which it has passed. This anticipatory classification—which is but a general survey of facts which will afterwards reappear before you and bring their own evidence with them—is necessary, not only in order to clear the way before us in our study, but also to indicate the particular institutions and times which the point of view we have chosen for ourselves especially calls us to consider.

The history of the political institutions of Europe divides itself into four general epochs, during which society has been governed according to modes and forms essentially distinct.

The tribes of Germany, in establishing themselves on the Roman soil, carried thither with them their liberty, but none of those institutions by which its exercise is regulated and its permanence guaranteed. Individuals were free—a free society, however, was not constituted. I will say further, that a society was not then existent. It was only after the conquest, and in consequence of their territorial establishment, that a society really began to be formed either among the conquerors and the conquered, or among the victors themselves. The work was long and difficult. The positions in which they were placed were complicated and precarious, their forces scattered and irregular, the human mind little capable of extensive combinations and foresight. Different systems of institutions, or rather different tendencies, appeared and contended with each other. Individuals, for whom liberty then meant only personal independence and isolation, struggled to preserve it. Those who were strong succeeded in obtaining it, and became powerful; those who were weak lost it and fell under the yoke of the powerful. The kings, at first only the chiefs of warrior bands, and then the first of the great territorial proprietors, attempted to confirm and extend their power; but simultaneously with them an aristocracy was formed, by the local success of scattered forces and the concentration of properties, which did not allow royalty to establish itself with any vigour or to exert any wide-spread influence. The ancient liberty of the forest, the earliest attempts at monarchical system, the nascent elements of the feudal régime—such were the powers which were then struggling for preeminence in society. No general political order could establish itself in the midst of this conflict. It lasted till the eleventh century. Then the feudal system had become predominant. The primitive independence and wild equality of individuals had either become merged into a condition of servitude, or had submitted to the hierarchical subordination of feudalism. All central power, whether of kings or of ancient national assemblies, had well nigh disappeared; liberty existed coordinately with power; the sovereignty was scattered. This is the first epoch.[1]

1. On this see Guizot's *History of Civilization in France,* lectures 7 and 8.

The second epoch is that of the feudal system. Three essential characteristics belong to it: first, the reduction of the mass of the

31

people to slavery or a condition bordering thereon; second, the hierarchical and federative organization of the feudal aristocracy, extending in its application both to persons and lands; third, the almost entire dissolution of the sovereignty, which then devolved on every feudal proprietor capable of exercising and defending it; from whence resulted the feebleness of the royal power and the destruction of monarchical unity, which disappeared almost as completely as national unity. This system prevailed until the thirteenth century.

Then commenced a new epoch. The feudal lord, already possessed of royal power, aspired after royal dignity. A portion of the inhabitants of the territory, having regained somewhat of the power they had lost, longed to become free. The feudal aristocracy was attacked on the one hand by the enfranchisement of the townsmen and tenants, on the other hand by the extension of the royal power. Sovereignty tended to concentration, liberty to diffusion; national unity began to shape itself at the same time as monarchical unity appeared. This was at once indicated and promoted by attempts after a representative form of government, which were made and renewed during nearly three centuries, wherever the feudal system fell into decay, or the monarchical system prevailed. But soon sovereigns also began almost everywhere to distrust it in their turn. They could not behold with indifference that sovereignty, which after having been long diffused had been regained and concentrated by their efforts, now again divided at its very centre. Besides, the people were deficient alike in such strength and knowledge as would enable them to continue, on the one hand, against the feudal system, a struggle which had not yet ceased, and to sustain, on the other hand, a new struggle against the central power. It was evident that the times were not fully matured; that society, which had not thoroughly emerged from that condition of servitude which had been the successor of social chaos, was neither so firmly consolidated nor so mentally disciplined as to be able to secure at once order by the equitable administration of power, and liberty by the safeguards of large and influential public institutions. The efforts after representative government became more occasional and feeble, and at length disappeared. One country alone guarded and defended it, and advanced from one struggle to another, till it succeeded. In other places, the purely monarchical system prevailed. This result was accomplished in the sixteenth century.

The fourth epoch has lasted from that time to our own days. It is chiefly marked in England by the progress of the representative system; on the Continent, by the development of the purely monarchical system, with which are associated local privileges, judicial institutions which exercise a powerful influence on political order, and some remnants of those assemblies which, in epochs anterior to the present, appeared under a more general form, but which now confine themselves to certain provinces, and are almost exclusively occupied with administrative functions. Under this system, though political liberty is no longer met with, barbarism and feudalism finally disappear before absolute power; interior order, the reconciliation of different classes, civil justice, public resources and information, make rapid progress; nations become enlightened and prosperous, and their prosperity, material as well as moral, excites in them juster apprehensions of, and more earnest longings for, that representative system which they had sought in times when they possessed neither the knowledge nor the power requisite for its exercise and preservation.

This short epitome of facts has already indicated to you, gentlemen, the epochs towards which our studies will be principally directed. The objects of our search are the political institutions of various peoples. The representative system is that around which our researches will centre. Wherever, then, we do not meet with those general institutions, under the empire of which people unite themselves, and which demand the manifestation of general society in its government—wherever we perceive no trace of the representative system, and no direct effort to produce it—there we shall not linger. All forms and conditions of society present rich and curious subjects for observation; but in this inexhaustible series of facts we must choose only those which have a strict relation to one another, and a direct interest for us. The second and the fourth epochs therefore, that is to say, feudalism and absolute power, will occupy us but little. We shall only speak of them so far as a consideration of them is necessary to connect and explain the periods which will more directly claim our attention. I propose to study with you the first and the third epochs, and the fourth, so far as it relates to England. The first epoch, which shows us the German people establishing themselves on Roman soil—the struggle of their primitive institutions, or rather of their customs and habits, against the natural results of their new position—in fine, the throes attending the earliest formation of modern nations—has especial claims on our notice. I believe that, so far as regards political institutions, this time possessed nothing which deserves the name; but all the elements were there, in existence and commotion, as in the chaos which precedes creation. It is for us to watch this process, under which governments and peoples came into being. It is for us to ascertain whether, as has been asserted, public liberty and the representative system were actually there, whence some symptoms announced that they might one day emerge. When, in the third epoch, we see the feudal system being dissolved—when we watch the first movements towards a representative government appear at the same time with the efforts of a central power which aims at becoming general and organized—we shall recognize here, without difficulty, a subject which immediately belongs to us. We shall seek to learn what societies were then aroused, and by what means they have sought for trustworthy institutions, which might guarantee the continuance at once of order and of liberty. And when we have seen their hopes deceived by the calamities of the times, when we have detected in the vices of the social state, far more than in the influence of any disorderly or perverse desires, the causes of the ill-success of these magnanimous attempts, we shall be brought by our subject into the very midst of that people, then treated more leniently by fortune, which has paid dearly for free institutions, but which has guarded them to the last when they perished everywhere else, and which, while preserving and developing them for itself, has offered to other nations, if not a model, yet certainly an example.

Origin of Representative Government in Europe

It would be a small matter for us, gentlemen, thus to limit the field of our inquiries so far as epochs are concerned, if we did not also assign some boundaries in respect to place. The inquiry would be too large and protracted were we to follow the course of political institutions throughout the whole of Europe, according to the plan I have just indicated. Moreover, the diversity of events and conditions has been so great in Europe, that, notwithstanding certain general characteristics and certain philosophical results which the facts everywhere present, they very often resist all the attempts we may make to bring them under any uniform guiding principle. In vain do we strive to collect them together under the same horizon, or to force them into the same channel; ever do they release themselves from our grasp in order to assume elsewhere the place assigned to them by truth. We should therefore be compelled either to limit ourselves to generalities yielding but little instruction to those who have not sounded all their depths, or else continually to interrupt the course of our inquiry, in order to rove from one people to another with an attention which would be continually distracted and soon wearied. It will be more profitable for us to take a narrower range. England, France, and Spain, will supply us with abundant materials for our undertaking. In these countries we shall study political institutions under the different phases and in the various epochs which I have just exhibited before you. There we shall find that these epochs are more clearly defined, and that the chief facts which characterize them appear under more complete and simple forms. In France and Spain, moreover, the general attempts after a representative government, made in the thirteenth, fourteenth, and fifteenth centuries, assumed a more definite shape. We are therefore dissuaded by a variety of considerations from carrying our steps beyond these limits. Our researches will thereby gain both in interest and in solidity.

This interest, gentlemen, I must say at the outset, is not that merely which attaches itself to human affairs, which are ever attractive to man, however trivial may be the attention which he bestows upon them. The study of the ancient political institutions of Europe demands serious and assiduous effort. I am here to share this with you, not to undertake it for you. I shall be frequently obliged to enter into details, which may appear dry at first, but which are important because of the results to which they lead. I shall not content myself with merely presenting before you these results as a general expression of facts; I shall feel called upon to put you in possession of the facts themselves. The truths which they contain must be seen by yourselves to proceed naturally from them, and must not be allowed a final lodgment in your minds except as they are fortified by such evidence as can establish them. Gentlemen, it is to be borne in mind that truth, wheresoever we may seek it, is not easy of access. We must dig deep for it, as for precious metals, before we find it; we must not shrink from the difficulties, nor from the long duration of the enterprise. It only surrenders itself to resolute and patient endeavour. And not only on behalf of our peculiar study do I urge upon you that you should never allow yourselves to be baffled by the fatigue attendant upon some portions of the work—a more elevated motive, a more comprehensive claim, gives you this advice. Thrasea, when dying, said to his son-in-law, Helvidius Priscus, "Observe, young man: thou art living in times when it is well that the spirit should become fortified by such a scene as this; and learn how a brave man can die." Thankful should we be to Heaven that such lessons as these are not now required by us, and that the future does not demand such hard discipline in order that we may be prepared to meet it. But the free institutions which we are called upon to receive and maintain—these demand of us, from our earliest youth, those habits of laborious and patient application which will constitute our fittest preparation. They require that we should, among our first lessons, learn not to shrink either from the pain, or from the length and arduousness of duty. If our destiny is to be sublime, our studies must be severe. Liberty is not a treasure which can be acquired or defended by those who set a disproportionate value on personal ease and gratification; and if ever man attains it after having toiled for it under the influence merely of luxurious or impatient feelings, it denies to him those honours and advantages which he expected to gain from its possession. It was the error of the preceding age that, while it aimed at urging the minds of men into a wider and more active career, it yet fostered the impression that all was then to become easy, that study would be transformed into amusement, and that obstacles were removed from the first steps of a life that was to issue in something great and impressive. The effeminate weakness of such sentiments were relics of the feebleness of times when liberty did not exist. We who live in the present day, know that freedom requires from the man who would enjoy it a sterner exercise of his powers. We know that it allows neither indolence of soul nor fickleness of mind, and that those generations which devote their youth to laborious study can alone secure liberty for their manhood. You will find, gentlemen, as you watch the development of the political institutions of Europe, that the experience of all ages confirms this of our own. You will not find that those grand designs that have been formed for the promotion of truth, justice, and progress, have ever emanated from the abode of sloth, of frivolity, and antipathy to all that demands labour and patience. As you trace back such enterprises to their source, you will always find there, serious aspect and grave determination, existing, so to speak, in their early life. Only by men formed in this mould have public laws and liberties been defended. They have, according as the wants of their age impelled them, resisted disorder or oppression. In the gravity of their own life and thoughts they have found a true measure of their own dignity, and, in their own, of the dignity of humanity. And, gentlemen, do not doubt, in following their example, of achieving also their success. You will soon become convinced that, in spite of the tests to which it has been exposed, our age is not among the most unrestrained that have existed. You will see that patriotism, a respect for law and order, a reverence for all that is just and sacred, have often been purchased at a far heavier price, and have called for severer self-denial. You will find that there is as much feebleness as ingratitude in the disposition that is intimidated and discouraged by the sight of obstacles which still present themselves, when obstacles of a far more formidable character have not wearied the resolution of noble men of former times.

And thus, while early exercising your minds in all those habits which will prepare man for the duties of an exalted destiny, you will meet with nothing that will not continually deepen your attachment to your age and to your country.

So far as I myself am concerned, may I be allowed, gentlemen, in entering with you today upon the study of the ancient political institutions of Europe, to congratulate myself on being able to approach the subject with the liberty that is suitable to it. It was in works of a similar character that I commenced my intellectual life. But at that time the public exposition of such facts and of the ideas related to them, was hardly permitted. Power had arrived at that condition in which it fears equally any representation of the oppression of peoples, and of their efforts to obtain liberty; as if it must necessarily meet in these two series of historical reminiscences at once the condemnation of its past acts, and the prediction of its future perils. We are no longer in this deplorable position; the institutions which France has received from its sovereign have liberated at once the present and the past. Such is the moral strength possessed by a legitimate and constitutional monarchy, that it trembles neither at the recitals of history nor the criticisms of reason. It is based upon truth, and truth is consequently neither hostile nor dangerous to it. Wherever all the wants of society are recognised, and all its rights give each other mutual sanction and support, facts present only lessons of utility, and no longer hint at unwelcome allusions. The volume of history can now be spread out before us; and wherever we find the coincidence of legitimacy and constitutional order, we shall behold the prosperity both of governments and of peoples—the dignity of power ennobled and sustained by the dignity of obedience. In all positions, and however great may be the interval which separates them, we shall see man rendering honour to man; we shall see authority and liberty mutually regarding one another with that consideration and respect which can alone unite them in lasting connexion and guarantee their continued harmony. Let us congratulate ourselves, gentlemen, that we are living at a time in which this tutelary alliance has become a necessity—in which force without justice could only be an ephemeral power. The times to which we shall direct our attention experienced a harder lot;·they more than once beheld despotism root itself deeply in its position, and at the same time saw injustice assert its claim to a lasting rule. We, gentlemen, who have seen so many and diversified forms of oppression—we have seen them all fall into decay. Neither their most furious violence, nor their most imposing lustre, have sufficed to preserve them from the corruption that is inherent in their nature; and we have at length entered upon an order of things which admits neither the oppression of force which usurps power, nor that of anarchy which destroys it. Let us, gentlemen, reap all the advantages connected with such an order: let us show our respect for the distinguished author of this Charter by approving ourselves worthy of receiving, and capable of employing, the noble institutions which he has founded. Our gratitude can offer no purer homage.

Lecture 6

I propose to examine the political institutions of modern Europe in their early infancy, and to seek what they have in common with the representative system of government. My object will be to learn whether this form of government had then attained to any degree of development, or even existed only in germ; at what times, and in what places it first appeared, where and under what circumstances it prospered or failed. I have just examined the primitive institutions of the Anglo-Saxons. Before leaving our consideration of England, it might be well for me to compare these institutions with the essential type of representative government, in order to see how they agree and in what they differ. But this type is not yet in our possession. In order to find it I shall revert to the essential principle of representative government, to the original ideas out of which it springs; and I shall compare this idea with the fundamental idea that underlies Anglo-Saxon institutions.

The human mind is naturally led to judge of the nature of things, and to classify them according to their exterior forms; accordingly, governments have almost invariably been arranged according to distinctions which do not at all belong to their inherent character. Wherever none of those positive institutions have been immediately recognized which according to our present notions, represent and guarantee political liberty, it has been thought that no liberty could exist, and that power must be absolute. But in human affairs, various elements are mingled: nothing exists in a simple and pure state. As some traces of absolute power are to be found at the basis of free governments, so also some liberty has existed under governments to all appearance founded on absolutism. No form of society is completely devoid of reason and justice—for were all reason and justice to be withdrawn, society would perish. We may sometimes see governments of apparently the most opposite character produce the same effects. During the seventeenth and eighteenth centuries, representative government raised England to the highest elevation of moral and material prosperity; and France, during that same period, increased in splendour, wealth, and enlightenment, under an absolute monarchy. I do not intend by this to insinuate the impression that forms of government are unimportant, and that all produce results of equal quality and value; I merely wish to hint that we should not appreciate them by only a few of their results, or by their exterior indications. In order fully to appreciate a government, we must penetrate into its essential and constituent principles. We shall then perceive that many governments which differ considerably in their forms, are referable to the same principles; and that others which appear to resemble one another in their forms, are in fundamental respects different. Wherever elections and assemblies have presented themselves to view, it has been thought that the elements of a representative system were to be found. Montesquieu, looking at representative government in England, endeavoured to trace it back to the old Germanic institutions. "This noble system," he says, "originated in the woods." Appearances deceived Montesquieu; he merely took into consideration the exterior characteristics of representative government, not its true principles and its true tendencies. That is a superficial and false method which classifies governments according to their exterior characteristics;

making monarchy, government by one individual; aristocracy, government by several; democracy, government by the people, the sovereignty of all. This classification, which is based only upon one particular fact, and upon a certain material shape which power assumes, does not go to the heart of those questions, or rather of that question, by the solution of which the nature and tendency of governments is determined. This question is, "What is the source of the sovereign power, and what is its limit? Whence does it come, and where does it stop?" In the answer to this question is involved the real principle of government; for it is this principle whose influence, direct or indirect, latent or obvious, gives to societies their tendency and their fate.

Where are we to look for this principle? Is it a mere conventional arrangement by man? Is its existence anterior to that of society?

The two facts—society and government—mutually imply one another; society without government is no more possible than government without society. The very idea of society necessarily implies that of rule, of universal law, that is to say, of government.

What then is the first social law? I hasten to pronounce it: it is justice, reason, a rule of which every man has the germ within his own breast. If man only yields to a superior force, he does not truly submit to the law; there is no society and no government. If in his dealings with his fellows, man obeys not only force, but also a law, then society and good government exist. In the abnegation of force, and obedience to law, consists the fundamental principle of society and government. In the absence of these two conditions, neither society nor government can be properly said to exist.

This necessary coexistence of society and government shows the absurdity of the hypothesis of the social contract. Rousseau presents us with the picture of men already united together into a society, but without rule, and exerting themselves to create one; as if society did not itself presuppose the existence of a rule to which it was indebted for its existence. If there is no rule, there is no society; there are only individuals united and kept together

41

by force. This hypothesis then, of a primitive contract, as the only legitimate source of social law, rests upon an assumption that is necessarily false and impossible.

The opposite hypothesis, which places the origin of society in the family and in the right of the father over his children, is less objectionable, but it is incomplete. There is, certainly, a form of society among parents and their rising offspring; but it is a society in some sort unilateral, and of which one of the parties has not any true consciousness. Society, whether in the family or out of the family, is only complete when all its members, those who command as well as those who obey, recognise, more or less vaguely, a certain superior rule, which is neither the arbitrary caprice of will, nor the effect of force alone. The idea of society, therefore, implies necessarily another idea, that of government; and the idea of government contains in it two others, the idea of a collection of individuals, and that of a rule which is applicable to them—a rule which constitutes the right of the government itself; a rule which the individuals who submit to it have not themselves created, and to which they are morally bound to submit. No government ever totally disregarded this supreme rule, none ever proclaimed force or caprice as the only law of society. In seeking the principle of government, we have found the principle of social right to be the primary source of all legitimate sovereignty. In this law of laws, in this rule of all government, resides the principle of government.

Two important questions now present themselves. How is the law formed, and how is it applied? In this lies the distinctive character of the various forms of government; in this they differ.

Even until modern times, the belief has prevailed that the primitive and absolute right of law-making, that is, the right of sovereignty, resides in some portion of society, whether this right be vested in a single man, in several, or in all—an opinion which has been constantly contradicted by facts, and which cannot bear the test of reason. The right of determining and enforcing a rule, is the right to absolute power; that force which possesses this right inherently, possesses absolute power, that is to say, the right of tyranny. Take the three great forms of government, monarchy, aristocracy, and democracy, and see if a case can be found in which the right of sovereignty was held by one, by several or by all, in which tyranny did not necessarily arise. Facts have been logically correct—they have inferred from the principle its necessary consequence.

Such, however, is the force of truth, that this error could not reign alone and absolutely. At the very time when men appeared to believe, and did theoretically believe, that the primitive and absolute power of giving law belonged to some one, whether monarch, senate, or people, at the same time they struggled against that principle. At all times men have endeavoured to limit the power which they regarded as perfectly legitimate. Never has a force, although invested with the right of sovereignty, been allowed to develop that right to its full extent. The janissaries in Turkey sometimes served, sometimes abrogated, the absolute power of the Sultan. In democracies, where the right of sovereignty is invested in popular assemblies, efforts have been continually made to oppose conditions, obstacles, and limits to that sovereignty. Always, in all governments which are absolute in principle, some kind of protest has been made against the principle. Whence comes this universal protest? We might, looking merely at the surface of things, be tempted to say that it is only a struggle of powers. This has existed without doubt, but another and a grander element has existed along with it; there is an instinctive sense of justice and reason dwelling in every human spirit. Tyranny has been opposed, whether it were the tyranny of individuals or of multitudes, not only by a consciousness of power, but by a sentiment of right. It is this consciousneess of justice and right, that is to say, of a rule independent of human will—a consciousness often obscure but always powerful— which, sooner or later, rouses and assists men to resist all tyranny, whatever may be its name and form. The voice of humanity, then, has proclaimed that the right of sovereignty vested in men, whether in one, in many, or in all, is the iniquitous lie.

If, then, the right of sovereignty cannot be vested in any one man, or collection of men, where does it reside, and what is the principle on which it rests?

In his interior life—in his dealings with himself, if I may be allowed the expression, as well as in his exterior life, and in his dealings with his fellows—the man who feels himself free and capable of action, has ever a glimpse of a natural law by which his action is regulated. He recognises a something which is not his own will, and which must regulate his will. He feels himself bound by reason or morality to do certain things; he sees, or he feels that there are certain things which he ought or ought not to do. This something is the law which is superior to man, and made for him—the divine law. The true law of man is not the work of man; he receives, but does not create it; even when he submits to it, it is not his own—it is beyond and above him.

Man does not always submit; in the exercise of his free will and imperfect nature, he does not invariably obey this law. He is influenced by other principles of action than this, and although he perceives that the motives which impel him are vicious, nevertheless he often yields to them. But whether he obey or not, the supreme law for man is always existent—in his wildest dreams he recognises it, as placed above him.

We see, then, the individual always in presence of a law—one which he did not create, but which asserts its claim over him, and never abandons him. If he enters into society with his fellows, or finds himself thus associated, what other rule than this will he possess? Should human society involve an abdication of human nature? No; man in society must and does remain essentially the same as in his individual capacity; and as society is nothing but a collection of individuals, the supreme law of society must be the same as that which exercises a rightful control over individuals themselves.

Here, then, have we discovered the true law of society—the law of government—it is the same law as that which binds individuals. And as, for an individual, the true law is often obscure, and as the individual, even when he knows it thoroughly, does not always follow it implicitly; in the same manner with regard to government, whatever it may be, its true law—which must ever reach it through the medium of the human mind, which is ever biassed by passion and limited by frailty—is neither at all times apprehended nor always obeyed. It is then impossible to attribute to one man or to several the possession of an inherent right to sovereignty, since this would be to suppose that their ideas and inclinations were in all cases correspondent to the dictates of justice and of reason—a supposition which the radical imperfection of our nature will not allow us for a moment to admit.

It is, however, owing to the same imperfection that men have accepted, or rather created for themselves, idols and tyrants. A law ready made for them has appeared more convenient than that laborious and unremitting search after reason and justice which they felt themselves obliged to undertake by the imperious voice of that conscience which they could not entirely silence. Nevertheless, men have never been able entirely to deceive their conscience, or to stifle its utterances. Conscience defeats all the arrangements of human ignorance or indifference, and forces men to fight for themselves despite their own unwillingness. Never, in fact, have men fully accepted the sovereignty, the right of which they have admitted; and the impossibility of their thus consenting to it, plainly indicates the superhuman principle which sovereignty involves. In this principle we must seek for the true distinction between governments.

The classification which I am about to present is not, then, one that is merely arbitrary and factitious; it does not concern the exterior forms, but the essential nature of governments. I distinguish two kinds. First, there are those which attribute sovereignty as a right belonging exclusively to individuals, whether one, many, or all those composing a society; and these are, in principle, the founders of despotism, although facts always protest more or less strongly against the principle; and absolute obedience on the one hand, and absolute power on the other, never exist in full vigour. The second class of governments is founded on the truth that sovereignty belongs as a right to no individual whatever, since the perfect and continued apprehension, the fixed and inviolable application of justice and of reason, do not belong to our imperfect nature.

Representative government rests upon this truth. I do not say that it has been founded upon the full reflective acknowledgment of the principle in the form in which I have stated it. Governments do not, any more than great poems, form themselves on an a priori model, and in accordance with defined precepts. What I affirm is, that representative government does not attribute sovereignty as inherently residing in any person, that all its powers are directed to the discovery and faithful fulfilment of that rule which ought ever to govern their action, and that the right of sovereignty is only recognised on the condition that it should be continually justified.

Pascal has said, "Plurality which does not reduce itself to unity, is confusion. Unity which is not the result of plurality, is tyranny." This is the happiest expression and the most exact definition of representative government. The plurality is society; and the unity is truth, the whole of the laws of justice and reason which ought to govern society. If society remains in the condition of plurality, if isolated wills do not combine under the guidance of common rules, if they do not all equally recognise justice and reason, if they do not reduce themselves to unity, there is no society, there is only confusion. And the unity which does not arise from plurality, which has been violently imposed upon it by one or many, whatever may be their number, in virtue of a prerogative which they appropriate as their exclusive possession, is a false and arbitrary unit; it is tyranny. The aim of representative government is to oppose a barrier at once to tyranny and to confusion, and to bring plurality to unity by presenting itself for its recognition and acceptance.

Let us now see, in the central fact of this method of government, by what means it arrives at its end, and under what forms its principle is developed.

Representative government, wherever it has existed or does exist, is composed of different elements of power, equal among themselves, although one of them, the monarchical or the democratic, ordinarily retains certain peculiar rights. The number and form of these powers are not necessarily determinate or equal; in France, at the present time, there are three, the royal power, the House of Peers, and the Chamber of Deputies. These three powers emanate from different sources, and result from different social necessities. Neither of them, isolated from the rest, possesses a right of sovereignty: it is required of them that they seek the legitimate rule in common, and they are supposed to possess it only when they have found it in a united deliberation, before or after action. Society owes submission to this rule, thus discovered; but as these powers are not all fixed and immutable, so the sovereignty of right does not reside constantly among them. The elective principle, which is by its very nature changeful, can alter its idea and purpose, and exercise upon the other powers an influence that is periodically variable. If the different powers do not agree, they reduce themselves immediately to inaction. The sovereignty which exists in its own right then seems to hesitate to show itself, and government remains in suspense. In order to extricate it from this state, the right has been reserved to royalty of creating peers, and of dissolving the Chamber of Deputies. The powers then proceed afresh to seek for the true law, a work in which they ought not to rest until they have found it. Thus, no power is judged to possess fully the legitimate rule, which is rightfully the principle of sovereignty. The electors themselves are not its absolute interpreters, any more than are the peers, the deputies, or the king. The electors do not say at the outset to their deputies, "Such is our will: let that be the law." They enjoin upon them nothing precise; they simply confer upon them the mission of examining and deciding according to their reason. They must necessarily trust in the enlightenment of those whom they elect; election is a trial imposed on those who aspire to political power, and a sovereign but limited right exercised by those who confer political power upon such of the claimants as they may select.

From the political powers thus attributed to certain classes, let us now pass to the political rights which are vaguely distributed in the nation. These rights are among the essential conditions of representative government. The publicity of the debates in the deliberative assemblies imposes upon these powers the necessity of commending themselves to that sense of reason and justice which belongs to all, in order that every citizen may be convinced that their inquiries have been made with fidelity and intelligence, and that, knowing wherein they are deficient, he may himself have the opportunity, if he has the capacity, to indicate the remedy. Liberty opens up a career for this inquiry. In this way, every citizen may aid in the discovery of the true law. Thus does a representative government impel the whole body of society— those who exercise power, and those who possess rights—to enter upon a common search after reason and justice; it invites the multitude to reduce itself to unity, and it brings forth unity from the midst of plurality. The public powers—royalty, the deliberative houses, the electors—are bound and incessantly made to return to this work, by the essential nature of their relations, and by the laws of their action. Private citizens even can cooperate, by virtue of the publicity of the debates, and the liberty of the press.

I might pursue this idea, and show that all the institutions which are regarded as inherent in representative government, even those which have not been regarded as assisting in the search for those general rules which ought to preside in the conduct of government, are derived from the same principle, and tend to the same result. The publicity of judicial proceedings, and those who compose the jury, for example, supply a guarantee for the legitimate application of the law to particular cases. But our present concern is especially to determine the principle of those essential combinations by which a representative government is constituted; they all proceed evidently from this fact, that no individual is fully acquainted with and invariably consents to that reason, truth and justice, which can alone confer the right of sovereignty, and which ought to be the rule of sovereignty as actually exercised. They compel all powers to seek for this rule, and give to all citizens the right of assisting in this search, by taking cognizance of the mode in which the powers proceed to it, and in declaring themselves what they conceive to be the dictates of justice and of truth. In other words, to sum up what I have said, representative government rests in reality upon the following series of ideas. All power which exists as a fact, must, in order to become a right, act according to reason, justice, and truth, the sole sources of right. No man, and no body of men, can know and perform fully all that is required by reason, justice, and truth; but they have the faculty to discover it, and can be brought more and more to conform to it in their conduct. All the combinations of the poiltical machine then ought to tend, on the one hand, to extract whatever of reason, justice, or truth, exists in society, in order to apply it to the practical requirements of government; and, on the other hand, to promote the progress of society in reason, justice, and truth, and constantly to embody this progress of society in the actual structure of the government.

Lecture 7

I have, in my previous lecture, shown the error of those superficial classifications which only distinguish governments according to their exterior characteristics; I have recognised and separated with precision the two opposite principles, which are, both of them, the basis of all government; I have identified representative government with one of these principles; I have proved that it could not be deduced from the other; I wish now to compare the principle of representative government with the contrary principle, and to show the opposite condition of governments which refer to it as their starting point. I will begin by an examination of that form of government which is usually termed *aristocratic*.

There is a close connexion between the progressive changes that may be observed in language and those that belong to society. The word *aristocracy* originally signified the empire of the strong; Ἄρης, ἀρείων, ἄριστος, were, at first, terms applied to those who were physically the most powerful; then they were used to designate the most influential, the richest, and finally the best, those possessing the most ability or virtue. This is the history of the gradual acceptance of the word in the language from which it is borrowed; the same terms which were first applied to force, the superiority of force, came at length to designate moral and intellectual superiority—virtue.

Nothing can better characterise than this the progress of society, which begins with the predominance of force, and tends to pass under the empire of moral and intellectual superiority. The desire and tendency of society are in fact towards being governed by the best, by those who most thoroughly know and most heartily respond to the teachings of truth and justice; in this sense, all good governments, and preeminently the representative form of good government, have for their object to draw forth from the bosom of society that veritable and legitimate aristocracy, by which it has a right to be governed, and which has a right to govern it.

But such has not been the historical signification of the word *aristocracy*. If we take the word according as facts have interpreted it, we shall find its meaning to be, a government in which the sovereign power is placed at the disposal of a particular class of citizens, who are hereditarily invested with it, their only qualification being a certain descent, in a manner more or less exclusive, and sometimes almost completely exclusive.

I do not inquire whence this system of government has derived its origin; how, in the infancy of society, it has sprung almost invariably from the moral superiority of its first founders; how force, which was originally due to moral superiority, was afterwards perpetuated by itself, and became a usurper; these questions, which possess the highest interest, would carry me away from my main point. I am seeking for the fundamental principle of aristocratic government, and I believe it can be summed up in the following terms; the right of sovereignty, attributed in a manner if not entirely exclusive, yet especially and chiefly to a certain class of citizens, whose only claim is that of descent in a certain line.

This principle is no other than that of the sovereignty of the people confined to a small number of individuals—to a minority. In both cases, the right to sovereignty is derived, not from any presumed capacity to fulfill certain conditions, nor from intellectual and moral superiority proved in any particular manner, but from the solitary fact of birth, without any condition. In the aristocratic system, an individual is born to a position of sovereignty merely because he has been born into a privileged class; according to the democratic system, an individual is born to a position of sovereignty by the circumstance that he is born into humanity. The participation in sovereignty is in each case the result of a purely material fact, independent of the worth of him who possesses it, and of the judgment of those over whom it is to be exercised. It follows evidently from this, that aristocratic governments are to be classed among those which rest on the idea that the right of sovereignty exists, full and entire, somewhere on the earth—an idea directly contrary, as we have seen, to the principle of representative government.

If we look at the consequences of this idea—such consequences as have actually manifested themselves in the history of governments of this kind—we shall see that they are not less contrary to the consequences, historical as well as natural, of a representative government.

In order to maintain the right of sovereignty in the class to which it is exclusively attributed, it must necessarily establish a great inequality in fact, as well as in opinion, between this class and the rest of the citizens. Hence arise all those institutions and laws which characterise aristocratic governments, and which have for their object to concentrate, into the hands of the sole possessors of the sovereignty, all wealth and enlightenment, and all the various instruments of power. It is necessary that the sovereign class should not descend, and that others should not be elevated; otherwise actual power ceasing to approximate to rightful power, the legitimacy of the latter would soon be questioned, and, after a short time, its continuance endangered.

In the system of those governments which attribute to no individual upon earth a right of sovereignty, and which impose on the existing government the necessity of seeking continually for truth, reason, and justice, as the rule and source of rightful power, all classes of society are perpetually invited and urged to elevate and perfect themselves. Legitimate forms of supremacy are produced, and assume their position; illegitimate forms are unmasked and deposed. Factitious and violent inequalities are resisted and exhibited in their true colours; social forces are, so to speak, brought into competition, and the forces which struggle to possess them are moral.

A second consequence of the principle of aristocratic governments is their avoidance of publicity. When each one of those who participate in the rightful sovereignty possesses it by the mere accident of birth, and exercises it on his own individual responsibility, he need not recognise any one as claiming a right to call him to account. No one has any right to inquire into the use which he makes of his power, for he acts in virtue of a right which no one can contest because no one can deprive him of it. It is a right which needs not to justify itself, since it is connected with a fact that is palpable and permanent.

In the other system, on the contrary, publicity follows necessarily from the principle of government; for since the right to power is derived from superiority in the knowledge and practice of reason, truth, and justice, which no one is supposed to possess fully and at all times, it is imperative that this right should justify itself both before it is assumed and all the time that it is exercised.

It would be easy thus, proceeding continually within view of real facts, to compare the different consequences of the principle of purely aristocratic governments with those resulting from the principle of representative government, and to show that they are always opposed to one another. We should thereby demonstrate most completely the opposition of the principles themselves, and bring their true nature into clearer light; but I have already said enough on this point. And if any one asserts that I have too rigorously insisted upon inferences to be drawn from the principle of aristocratic governments, that the consequences which I have depicted do never fulfil themselves in so complete a manner, that, for example, the qualification of birth has never held exclusive possession of a right to sovereignty, that never has publicity been entirely quenched—I freely concede all this. At no time, in no place, has evil been allowed to gain exclusive possession of society and government; struggle between principles of good and evil is the permanent condition of the world. False ideas may achieve a more or less extended, a more or less durable success—they can never extirpate their godlike assailants. Truth is patient—it does not easily surrender its hold on society—it never abandons its purpose—it even exercises some sway over that region where error reigns most despotically. Providence never permits bad governments to become so bad as is logically demanded by the principle upon which they rest. So we have seen institutions of justice and liberty existing and even gaining a powerful existence, in the midst of societies ruled by the principle of hereditary right; these institutions have battled against the principle, and have modified it. When the worse principle has prevailed, then have society and government fallen into impotence and decay—this is the history of the Venetian republic. Elsewhere, the struggle has been attended with happier results: the good principle has possessed sufficient force to be able to introduce into the government elements which have made it vital, which have protected society against the effects of the evil principle, which have even in some sort saved the evil itself, rendering it tolerable by the good with which it is associated. This is the history of England, that striking example of the mixture and struggle of good and evil principles. But their mixture, however intimate it may be, does not prove that they are confounded in their interior character. Good never springs from evil; and representative government has not sprung in England, any more than elsewhere, from the exclusive principle of aristocratic governments; it has sprung from an entirely different principle; and so far from the distinction which I established at the commencement being compromised by the facts to which I have alluded, it is on the other hand triumphantly confirmed by them.

I have just proved, by a comparison between the principle of the aristocratic and that of the democratic form of government, that they are essentially different; I intend now to show that there is as fundamental a difference between the principle of representative government, and that of democratic government.

No one has ever understood the sovereignty of the people to mean, that after having consulted all opinions and all wills, the opinion and will of the greatest number constitutes the law, but that the minority would be free to disobey that which had been decided in opposition to its opinion and will. And yet this would be the necessary consequence of the pretended right attributed to each individual of being governed only by such laws as have received his individual assent. The absurdity of this consequence has not always induced its adherents to abandon the principle, but it has always obliged them to violate it. The sovereignty of the people is contradicted at the outset, by its being resolved into the empire of the majority over the minority. It is almost ridiculous to say that the minority may retire from the majority; this would be to keep society continually on the brink of dissolution. On every question the majority and the minority would disagree, and if all the successive minorities should retire, society would very soon exist no longer. The sovereignty of the people then must necessarily be reduced to the sovereignty of the majority only. When thus reduced, what does it amount to?

Its principle is, that the majority possesses right by the mere circumstance of its being the majority. But two very different ideas are included in the one expression—the majority; the idea of an opinion which is accredited, and that of a force which is preponderant. So far as force is concerned, the majority possesses no right different from that possessed by force itself, which cannot be, upon this ground alone, the legitimate sovereignty. As to the expression of opinion, is the majority infallible—does it always apprehend and respect the claims of reason and justice, which alone constitute true law, and confer legitimate sovereignty? Experience testifies to the contrary. The majority, by mere fact of its being a majority, that is to say, by the mere force of numbers, does not then possess legitimate sovereignty, either by virtue of power, which never does confer it, nor by virtue of infallibility, which it does not possess.

The principle of the sovereignty of the people starts from the supposition that each man possesses as his birthright, not merely an equal right of being governed, but an equal right of governing others. Like aristocratic governments, it connects the right to govern, not with capacity, but with birth. Aristocratic government is the sovereignty of the people in the minority; the sovereignty of the people is aristocratic despotism and privilege in the hands of the majority. In both cases, the principle is the same; a principle contrary, in the first place, to the fact of the inequality established by nature, between the powers and capacities of different individuals; secondly, to the fact of the inequality in capacity, occasioned by difference of position, a difference which exists everywhere, and which has its source in the natural inequality of men; thirdly, to the experience of the world, which has always seen the timid following the brave, the incompetent obeying the competent—in one word, those who are naturally inferior recognising and submitting themselves to their natural superiors. The principle of the sovereignty of the people, that is to say, the equal right of all individuals to exercise sovereignty, or merely the right of all individuals to concur in the exercise of sovereignty, is then radically false; for, under the pretext of maintaining legitimate equality, it violently introduces equality where none exists, and pays no regard to legitimate inequality. The consequences of this principle are the despotism of number, the domination of inferiorities over superiorities, that is, a tyranny of all others the most violent and unjust.

At the same time, it is of all others the most transient, for the principle is impossible of application. After its force has spent itself in excesses, number necessarily submits to capacity, the inferior retire to make room for the superior—these enter again into possession of their right, and society is reestablished.

Such cannot be the principle of representative government. No one disputes that the true law of government is that of reason, truth, and justice, which no one possesses but which certain men are more capable than others of seeking and discovering. Faithful to this aim, representative government rests upon the disposition of actual power in proportion to the capacity to act according to reason and justice, from whence power derives its right. It is the principle which, by the admission of all, and by virtue of its simple appeal to the common sense of the community, is applicable to ordinary life, and to the interest of individuals themselves. It is the principle which confers the sovereignty over persons, families, property, only to the individual who is presumed to be capable of using it reasonably, and which withdraws it from him who is seen to be positively incapable. Representative government applies to general interests, and to the government of society, the same principle which the good sense of the human race has led it to apply to individual interests and to the control of each man's private life. It distributes sovereignty according to the capacity required for it, that is to say, it only places actual power, or any portion of actual power, where it has discovered the presence of rightful power, presumed to exist by certain symptoms, or tested by certain proofs. It is remembered, that power though legitimate is not to be conceded fully and completely to any one, and not only is it not attributed to the mere fact of birth, but it cannot be allowed to remain by itself in irresponsible isolation, which is the second characteristic of representative government, by which, not less than by the preceding, it is distinguished from the sovereignty of the people.

It has been often said, that representative government is the government of the majority, and there is some truth in the assertion; but it must not be thought that this government of the majority is the same as that involved in the sovereignty of the people. The principle of the sovereignty of the people applies to all individuals, merely because they exist without demanding of them anything more. Thus, it takes the majority of these individuals, and says, Here is reason, here is law. Representative government proceeds in another way: it considers what is the kind of action to which individuals are called; it examines the amount of capacity requisite for this action; it then summons those individuals who are supposed to possess this capacity—all such, and such only. Then it seeks for a majority among those who are capable.

It is in this way, in fact, that men have everywhere proceeded, even when they have been supposed to act according to the idea of the sovereignty of the people. Never have they been entirely faithful to it; they have always demanded for political actions certain conditions, that is to say, indications of a certain capacity. They have been mistaken, more or less, and have excluded the capable, or invited the inefficient, and the error is a serious one. But they have followed the principle which measures right by capacity, even when they have professed the principle that right is derived from the simple fact of possessing a human nature.

Representative government, then, is not purely and simply the government of the numerical majority, it is government by the majority of those who are qualified to govern; sometimes assuming the existence of the qualification beforehand, sometimes requiring that it should be proved and exemplified. The peerage, the right to elect and to be elected, the royal power itself, are attached to a capacity presumed to exist, not only after certain conditions have been complied with, but by reason of the position occupied by those men in whom the capacity is presumed, in their relations to other powers, and in the limits of the functions assigned to them. No one is recognised as possessing an inherent right to an office or a function. Nor is this all; representative government does not content itself with demanding capacity before it confers power; as soon as the capacity is presumed or proved, it is placed in a position where it is open to a kind of legal suspicion, and where it must necessarily continue to legitimatize itself, in order to retain its power. According to the principle of the sovereignty of the people, absolute right resides with the majority; true sovereignty exists wherever this force is manifested; from this follows necessarily the oppression of the minority, and such has, in fact, generally been the result. The representative form of government, never forgetting that reason and justice, and consequently a right to sovereignty, do not reside fully and constantly in any part of the earth, presumes that they are to be found in the majority, but does not attribute them to it as their certain and abiding qualities. At the very moment when it presumes that the majority is right, it does not forget that it may be wrong, and its concern is to give full opportunity to the minority of proving that it is in fact right, and of becoming in its turn the majority. Electoral precautions, the debates in the deliberative assemblies, the publication of these debates, the liberty of the press, the responsibility of ministers, all these arrangements have for their object to insure that a majority shall be declared only after it has well authenticated itself, to compel it ever to legitimatize itself, for its own preservation, and to place the minority in such a position as that it may contest the power and right of the majority.

Thus, the considerations we have suggested show that a representative form of government regards the individuals whom it brings into activity, and the majority which it seeks, from quite another point of view than that involved in the sovereignty of the people. The latter admits that the right of sovereignty resides somewhere upon the earth; the former denies it: this finds the right in question in a purely numerical majority; that seeks it in the majority of those qualified to pronounce on the subject: the one attributes it fully and entirely to number; the other is satisfied with the presumption that it is there, admits at the same time that it may possibly not be there, and invites the minority to substantiate its claims, securing, meanwhile, every facility for its so doing. The sovereignty of the people sees legitimate power in the multitude; representative government sees it only in unity, that is to say, in the reason to which the multitude ought to reduce itself. The sovereignty of the people makes power to come from below; representative government recognizes the fact that all power comes from above, and at the same time obliges all who assume to be invested with it to substantiate the legitimacy of their pretensions before men who are capable of appreciating them. The one tends to lower those who are superior, the other to evaluate those who are inferior, by bringing them into communication with those who are naturally above them. The sovereignty of the people is full at once of pride and of envy; representative government renders homage to the dignity of our nature, without ignoring its frailty, and recognizes its frailty without outrage to its dignity. The principle of the sovereignty of the people is contrary to all the facts which reveal themselves in the actual origin of power, and in the progress of societies; representative government does not blink any one of these facts. Lastly, the sovereignty of the people is no sooner proclaimed, than it is compelled to abdicate its power, and to confess the impracticability of its aims; representative government moves naturally and steadily onward, and develops itself by its very existence.

So far, then, from deriving its existence from the principle of the sovereignty of the people, representative government disowns this principle, and rests upon an entirely different idea, and one which is attended with entirely different consequences. It matters little that this form of government has been often claimed in the name of the sovereignty of the people, and that its principal epochs of development have occurred at times when that idea predominated; the reasons for this fact are easily discovered. The sovereignty of the people is a great force which sometimes interferes to break up an inequality which has become excessive, or a power which has become absolute, when society can no longer accommodate itself to them; as despotism sometimes interferes, in the name of order, violently to restore a society on the brink of dissolution. It is only a weapon of attack and destruction, never an instrument for the foundation of liberty. It is not a principle of government, it is a terrible but transient dictatorship, exercised by the multitude—a dictatorship that ceases, and that ought to cease as soon as the multitude has accomplished its work of destruction.

Briefly, to conclude: as the object of these lectures is to trace the course of representative government in modern Europe wherever it has found any footing, I have looked for the primal type of this government in order to compare it with the government of the Anglo-Saxon monarchy, which we have already examined, and with the other primitive governments which we shall meet with in Europe. In order to distinguish precisely the character of a representative government, I have been obliged to go back to the source of all government. I think I have shown that we must classify all governments according to two different principles. The one class, allied to justice and reason, recognises these alone as their guides; and as it is not in the power of human feebleness, in this world, to follow infallibly these sacred leaders, these governments do not concede to any one the possession of an absolute right to sovereignty, and they call upon the entire body of society to aid in the discovery of the law of justice and reason, which can alone confer it. The other class, on the contrary, admitting a right inherent in man to make a law for himself, thus degrade the rightful sovereignty; which, as it belongs only to justice and reason, ought never to come under the absolute control of man, who is ever too ready to usurp sovereignty, in order to exercise it for the promotion of his private interests, or for the gratification of his passions. I have shown that a representative government alone renders homage to true principles, and that all other governments, democratic as well as aristocratic, ought to be arranged according to an entirely different scheme of classification. I have now to enter upon the examination of the exterior forms of representative government, and to compare its principle with the historical principle of the Anglo-Saxon monarchy, as it is exhibited before us in its institutions.

Lecture 8

The forms of a government are immediately related to its principle: the principle determines the forms, the forms reveal the principle. It does not therefore follow that the forms correspond exactly to the principle, nor that the principle can only realize itself under a peculiar form. As the principle itself is never alone nor omnipotent in its influence upon the facts, forms are necessarily diverse and mingled. In proportion as the action of any principle extends itself, the form which is truly correspondent to it is developed; but, in the course of this work, the principle embodies itself in the different forms which correspond to the condition of those facts which, in their aggregate, constitute society, and determine the position which it occupies in the scale of civilization.

The same principle can then be contained, and act under different forms. If the forms are the best that can be supplied for the principle, considering the existing state of society, and if, although they do not fully correspond to its nature, they insure the constant and regular progress of its action, there is no blame that can be charged upon them; each epoch, each state of society only allows of a certain development of the principle upon which its government rests. What is the measure of development possible to each epoch, and what is the form which corresponds to it in the present, which will secure for the future a more extended development, and which will bring with it new forms? This is the whole extent of the question—I mean, the question concerning the present, the only one with which political activity has to deal.

Nevertheless there are certain forms of government which are the general conditions of the presence and action of particular principles. Wherever the principle exists, it necessarily produces these forms; where they are wanting the principle does not exist or will soon cease to exist; its action and progress imperatively demand them: so far as they gain consistency at any place, the principle which they suppose is latently present and tends to become predominant.

What are the essential forms of the principle of representative government? By what external indications may we recognize the presence of this principle in a government? What conditions are required in order that it may act and develop itself?

We may, if I mistake not, reduce to three the conditions necessary, and the forms essential, to the representative system; all three are perhaps not equally necessary; their simultaneous existence is not perhaps indispensable in order to indicate the existence and secure the development of the principle from which they are derived. We may, however, justly consider them as fundamental. These forms are: first, the division of powers; second, election; third, publicity.

We have seen that no really existing power can be a rightful power, except in so far as it acts according to reason and truth, the only legitimate rule of action, the only source of right.

No existing power can fully know and constantly regard the guidance of reason and truth according to which it is bound to regulate its action. No actual power then is, or can be, in itself, a power by inherent right. In other words, as no existing power can be found that is infallible, there is none that may retain its existence on the tenure of absolute right.

Such is, however, the condition of human things that they need, as a last appeal, the intervention of a power which may declare the law to be the rule of government, and which shall impose it and cause it to be respected. In all the relations which the social state admits and to which it gives birth, from domestic order to political order, the presence of a power which may give and maintain the rule of action, is a necessary condition of the very existence of society.

We see then the dilemma in which society is placed. No actual power can vindicate a claim to become an absolute power; hence the necessity, in order to meet particular emergencies, of a power that is definite, that is to say, *actually* absolute.

The problem of government is—how to give society a guarantee that the power, which is in operation absolute, to which all social relations must necessarily be referred, shall be but the image, the expression, the organ of that power which is rightfully absolute and alone legitimate, and which is never to be found localized in this world? This is also, as we have seen, the problem which the representative system formally proposes to itself, since all its arrangements assume the existence of this problem and are framed with a purpose to resolve it.

To make actual power, as far as possible, identical with rightful power, by imposing upon it the abiding necessity of seeking for reason, truth, and justice—the sources of right; by investing it with practical power only when it has proved, that is to say, given a presumption of, its success in this search; and by compelling it ever to renew and confirm this presumption under penalty of losing power if it is unable to do so, this is the course of the representative system—this is the end at which it aims and according to which it directs, in their relations and their movement, all the resources which it brings into action.

In order to attain this end, it is indispensable that the existing power should not be simple, that is to say, that it should not be suffered to confine itself to one single instrument. As no force can possess in itself fully the right to authority, if there is one which possesses an absolute power, not only will it abuse this power, but it will very soon claim it as an inherent right. Alone it will become despotic, and in order to sustain its despotism it will call itself legitimately sovereign; and perhaps will end by believing and establishing the fiction. Such is the corrupting effect of despotism, that it destroys sooner or later, both in those who exercise it and in those who submit to it, even the feeling of its illegitimacy. Whoever is solitary in his sovereignty has only one step in order to become accredited as infallible. Alexander was right in wishing that he should be recognized as a god; he deduced a consequence that strictly followed from the fulness of the power which he possessed: and they also are right, who, attributing sovereignty to the multitude, take for their maxim, *Vox populi, vox Dei.* Everywhere where sovereignty rests with a single power, whatever may be the nature of that power, there is a danger that sovereignty will immediately be claimed as a right.

A division of the actual sovereignty is then a natural consequence of the principle, that a right to sovereignty does not belong to any person. It is necessary that there should be several powers, equal in extent and supplementary to each other in the exercise of actual sovereignty, in order that no one of them may be led to arrogate to itself the sovereignty of inherent right. The feeling of their reciprocal interdependence can alone prevent them from regarding themselves as entirely irresponsible.

Further: it is only in this way that the ruling power can be constrained to perpetuate its search for reason, truth, and justice; that is, for the rule which should govern its action, in order that it may become legitimate. The words of Pascal apply not only to the formation of power, they extend also to its exercise. Here are beings, individual or collective, who are called upon to perform the functions of sovereignty in common, each one under the supervision of his fellows. Do they possess among them, or by the fact of their existence, the right to power? No: they must seek it, they must on every opportunity manifest the truth which they proclaim as law. Isolated and distinct, they are only a multitude; when, after having deliberated and laboured, they find a ground of agreement in a common idea, from whence can proceed one will, then alone will the true unity, which resides in reason, be evolved; then there will be a presumption that the ruling power knows accurately and is well disposed to that legitimate rule which alone confers rightful power. If this work were not enforced, if this laborious and common search for the true law were not the necessary result of the reciprocal independence of the several powers, the end of government would not be attained. All the relations of the four great political powers which constitute, with us, the government (that is, the king, the two houses of parliament, and the electors) are intended to compel them to act in harmony, that is to say, to reduce themselves to unity.

The introduction of an elective, that is, a moveable element, into government, is as necessary as a division of forces to prevent the sovereignty from degenerating into the hands of those who exercise it into a full and permanent sovereignty of inherent right. It is therefore the necessary result of a representative government, and one of its principal characteristics. Accordingly we see that actual governments which have aimed at becoming absolute, have always endeavoured to destroy the elective principle. Venice gave a memorable illustration of this tendency, when, in 1319, it conferred an hereditary right on the grand council.[1] In the first age of governments, at the same time that we see power come from above, that is to say, acquire for itself by its superiority, of whatever kind that may be, either ability, riches, or courage, we see it also obliged to make its title recognised by those who can judge it. Election is the mode of this recognition—it is to be found in the infancy of all governments; but it is generally abolished after a time. It is when it reappears with sufficient energy to influence powerfully the administration of society, that a representative government is rising into being.

Theoretically, publicity is perhaps the most essential characteristic of a representative government. We have seen that it has for its object to call upon all individuals who possess rights, as well as those who exercise powers, to seek reason and justice, the source and rule of legitimate sovereignty. In publicity consists the bond between a society and its government. Looking, however, at facts, we find that of the elements essential to a representative government this is the last which is introduced and gains a firm footing. Its history is analogous to that of the elective principle. The *Champs de Mars* and *Mai* were held in the open air: many persons were present at them who took no part in the deliberation. The assembly of the Lombards at Pavia took place

1. This event is clearly and minutely related by Daru, in his *Histoire de Venise,* vol. 1, pp. 449–64.

circumstante immensa multitudine. It is probable that the same publicity attended also the *Wittenagemot* of the Saxons. When absolute or aristocratic government prevails, publicity disappears. When representative government begins to be formed by election, publicity does not at first enter into its constitution. In England, the House of Commons was for a long time a secret assembly; the first step towards publicity was to cause its acts, addresses and resolutions, to be printed. This step was taken by the Long Parliament under Charles I. Under Charles II its proceedings again became secret; some individuals demanded, but in vain, the publication of the acts passed by the House—the demand was resisted as dangerous. It was not till the eighteenth century that visitors were allowed to be present at the sittings of the English Parliament: this is not now granted as a right, and the demand of a single member who appeals to the ancient law, is sufficient to clear the gallery. Publicity has not then been invariably attached to a representative government; but it flows naturally from its principles—it is accordingly won almost necessarily, and may now be regarded as one of its most essential features. This result is owing to the press, which has rendered publicity easy without resorting to tumultuous meetings.

We have found the fundamental principle and the exterior and essential characteristics of a representative government; we have learnt what it is that constitutes it and distinguishes it from other governments: we may now pass to its history. We shall take care to admit its existence only where we recognise the presence or the approach of its true principles; and we shall be convinced that its progress has ever been identical with the development of these principles.

Lecture 23

At the commencement of the fifth century the subjects of the Empire were divided into three classes, forming three very distinct social conditions: (1) the privileged classes; (2) the curiales; (3) the common people. I speak only of free men.

The privileged class included: (1) the members of the Senate, and all those who were entitled to bear the name of *clarissimi;*

(2) the officers of the palace; (3) the clergy; (4) the cohortal militia, a sort of *gendarmerie* employed in the maintenance of the internal order of the State, and the execution of the laws; (5) the soldiers in general, whether included in the legions, or in the troops attached to the palace, or in the corps of barbarian auxiliaries. The class of curiales included all the citizens inhabiting towns, whether natives or settlers therein, who possessed a certain landed income, and did not belong, by any title, to the privileged class. The common people were the mass of the inhabitants of the towns, whose almost absolute want of property excluded them from a place among the curiales.

The privileged members of the first class were numerous, of various rank, and unequally distributed among the five orders of which it was composed; but that which was, in fact, the most important and most sought after of their privileges, that which alone was more valuable than all the rest, was common to the five orders which constituted this class—I mean, exemption from municipal functions and offices.

When we come to treat of the curiales, you will learn what was the extent of these duties; but you must first understand clearly who were exempt from them. (1) The whole army, from the lowest *cohortalis* to the *magister equitum peditumve*. (2) The entire body of the clergy, from the simple clerk to the archbishop. (3) It is an easy matter to define the two foregoing classes; but it is not so clear who were the members of the class of senators and *clarissimi*. The number of the senators was unlimited; the emperor appointed and dismissed them at his will, and could even raise the sons of freedmen to this rank. All those who had filled the principal magisterial offices in the Empire, or who had merely received from the prince the honorary title belonging to those magistratures, were called *clarissimi*, and had the right, when occasion required, of sitting in the Senate. Thus the class of *clarissimi* included all the functionaries of any importance: and they were all appointed and might be dismissed by the emperor.

The body of privileged individuals, then, was composed: (1) of the army; (2) of the clergy; (3) of all the public functionaries, whether employed at the Court and in the palace, or in the provinces. Thus despotism and privilege had made a close alliance; and, in this alliance, privilege, which depended almost absolutely on despotism, possessed neither liberty nor dignity, except perhaps in the body of the clergy.

This privilege, and especially exemption from curial functions, was not purely personal, but also hereditary. It was so, in the case of military men, on condition that the children also should embrace the profession of arms; and in the case of civilians, it was continued to those children who were born since their fathers had belonged to the class of *clarissimi*, or had occupied posts in the palace. Among the classes exempt from curial functions was the cohortal militia, a subaltern service to which those who entered it were hereditarily bound, and from which there was no means of passing into a superior class.

The class of curiales included all the inhabitants of the towns, whether natives thereof, *municipes*, or settlers therein, *incolœ*, who possessed a landed property of more than twenty-five acres, *jugera*, and did not belong to any privileged class. Members of the curial class became so either by origin, or by appointment. Every child of a curial was a curial also, and liable to all the charges attached to that quality. Every inhabitant who, by trade or otherwise, acquired a landed property of more than twenty-five acres, might be summoned to enter the *curia*, and could not refuse to do so. No curial could, by a voluntary act, pass into another condition. They were forbidden from dwelling in the country, entering the army, or engaging in employments which would have liberated them from municipal functions, until they had passed through every curial gradation, from that of a simple member of a *curia* to the highest civic magistracies. Then alone they might become military men, public functionaries, and senators. The children born to them before their elevation remained curiales. They were not allowed to enter the clergy except by granting the enjoyment of their property to any one who agreed to be a curial in their place, or by making a present of their possessions to the *curia* itself. As the curiales were incessantly striving to escape from their bondage, a multitude of laws were passed directing the prosecution of those who had escaped from their original condition, and succeeded in effecting their entrance furtively into the army, the clergy, public offices, or the Senate; and ordaining their restoration to the *curia* from which they had fled.

The following were the functions and charges of the curials thus confined, voluntarily or perforce, in the *curia*. (1) The administration of the affairs of the *municipium*, with its expenditure and revenues, either by deliberating thereon in the *curia*, or by discharging the magisterial offices of the town. In this double position, the curials were responsible not only for their individual management, but also for the necessities of the town, for which they were bound to provide out of their own resources, in case the municipal revenues were insufficient. (2) The collection of the public taxes, also under the responsibility of their private property in case of defaulters. Lands which were subject to the land tax and had been abandoned by their possessors, were allotted to the curia, which was bound to pay the tax thereon until it had found some one willing to take them off its hands. If it could find no one, the tax on the abandoned land was divided amongst the other estates. (3) No curial could sell the property from which he derived his qualification, without the permission of the governor of the province. (4) The heirs of curiales, when not members of the *curia*, and widows or daughters of curiales, who married men belonging to other classes, were bound to give a fourth part of their goods to the *curia*. (5) The curiales who had no children could not dispose, by will, of more than a fourth of their property: the other three-fourths went, by right, to the *curia*. (6) They were not allowed to absent themselves from their *municipium*, even for a limited time, without permission from the judge of the province. (7) When they had withdrawn from their *curia*, and could not be brought back, their property was confiscated to the benefit of their *curia*. (8) The tax known by the name of *aurum coronarium*, and which consisted in a sum to be paid to the prince, on the occasion of certain events, was levied on the curiales alone.

The only advantages granted to the curiales in compensation

for these burdens were: (1) Exemption from torture, except in very serious cases. (2) Exemption from certain afflictive and dishonouring punishments which were reserved for the populace; such as being condemned to work in the mines, to be burned alive, and so forth. (3) Decurions who had fallen into indigence were supported at the expense of the *municipium*. These were the only advantages possessed by the curiales over the common people, who, on the other hand, enjoyed the benefit that every career was open to them, and that, by entering the army, or engaging in public employments, they might raise themselves at once into the privileged class.

The condition of the curiales, then, both as citizens and in relation to the State, was onerous and devoid of liberty. Municipal administration was a burdensome service, to which the curiales were doomed, and not a right with which they were invested. Let us now see what was the condition of the curiales, not in relation to the State, and to the other classes of citizens, but in the *curia* and amongst themselves. Here still existed the forms, and even the principles, of liberty. All the curiales were members of the *curia*, and sat therein. The ability to bear the burdens of the office entailed that of exercising its rights, and taking part in its affairs; the names of all the curiales of each *municipium* were inscribed, in an order which was determined according to their dignity, age, and other circumstances, in a book called the *album curiæ*. When there was occasion to deliberate upon any matter, they were all convoked together by the superior magistrate of the town, the *duumvir, ædilis,* or *prætor,* and they all gave their opinions and their votes; everything was decided by the majority of votes: and no deliberation of the *curia* was valid unless two-thirds of the curiales were present.

The attributes of the *curia* as a body were: (1) the examination and decision of certain affairs; (2) the appointment of magistrates and municipal officers. Nowhere can I find an enumeration of the affairs which fell under the cognizance of the *curia* as a body. Everything, however, indicates that most of those municipal interests which required more than the simple execution of the laws or of orders already given, were discussed in the *curia*. The proper and independent authority of the municipal magistrates appears to have been very limited. For example, there is reason to believe that no expense could be incurred without the authorization of the *curia*. It fixed the time and place for holding fairs; it alone granted recompenses; and so forth.

There were even occasions on which the authorization of the *curia* was not sufficient, and when it was necessary to have the sanction of all the inhabitants, whether curiales or not; for example, for the sale of any property belonging to the commune, or for the despatch of deputies to wait on the emperor in reference to any grievance or request. On the other hand, it is evident that, by the general progress of despotism, the imperial power continued daily to interfere more and more in the affairs of the *municipia*, and to limit the independence of the *curiæ*. Thus they might not erect new buildings without the permission of the governor of the province; the reparation of the walls around the towns was subject to the same formality; and it was also necessary for the emancipation of slaves, and for all acts which tended to diminish the patrimony of the city. By degrees, also, even those affairs the final decision of which had previously belonged to the *curiæ* fell, by way of objection or appeal, under the authority of the emperor and his delegates in the provinces. This occurred in consequence of the absolute concentration of judicial and fiscal power in the hands of the imperial functionaries. The *curia* and curiales were then reduced to be nothing more than the lowest agents of the sovereign authority. There was left to them hardly anything beyond the right of consultation and the right of complaint.

With regard to the appointment to municipal magistracies, it remained for a long time, in reality, in the hands of the *curia*, without any necessity for its confirmation by the governor of the province, except in exceptional cases of towns which it was specially intended to ill-use or punish. But even this right soon became illusory by reason of the power given to provincial governors to annul the appointment on the demand of the person elected. When municipal functions had become merely burdensome, all the curials elected to discharge these offices, who had any influence with the governor, were able, under some pretext or another, to get their election annulled, and thus to escape from the load.

There were two kinds of municipal offices: the first, called *magistratus*, which conferred certain honours and a certain jurisdiction; the second, called *munera*, simple employments without jurisdiction and without any particular dignity. The *curia* appointed to both kinds of offices; only the magistrates proposed the men whom they thought competent to fulfil the *munera;* but even these were not really appointed until they had obtained the suffrages of the *curia.*

The *magistratus* were: (1) *Duumvir;* this was the most usual name of the chief municipal magistrate. He was also called, in certain localities, *quatuorvir, dictator, ædilis, prætor.* His tenure of office was for a year; it corresponded pretty nearly with that of our mayors; the *duumvir* presided over the *curia,* and directed the general administration of the affairs of the city. He had a jurisdiction confined to matters of small importance; he also exercised a police authority which gave him the right of inflicting certain punishments upon slaves, and of provisionally arresting freemen. (2) *Ædilis;* this was a magistrate generally inferior to the *duumvir;* he had the inspection of public edifices, of the streets, of corn, and of weights and measures. These two magistrates, the *duumvir* and *ædilis,* were expected to give public festivals and games. (3) *Curator reipublicæ;* this officer, like the ædile, exercised a certain oversight over public edifices; but his principal business was the administration of the finances; he farmed out the lands of the *municipium,* received the accounts of the public works, lent and borrowed money in the name of the city, and so forth.

The *munera* were: (1) *Susceptor,* the collector of taxes, under the responsibility of the curials who appointed him. (2) *Irenarchæ,* commissaries of police, whose duty it was to seek out and prosecute offences, in the first instance. (3) *Curatores,* officers charged with various particular municipal services; *curator frumenti, curator calendarii,* the lender out on good sureties of the money of the city, at his own risk and peril. (4) *Scribæ*, subaltern clerks in the two offices. To this class belonged the *tabelliones*, who performed almost the same functions as our notaries. In later times, when the decay of the municipal system became evident, when the ruin of the curiales and the impotence of all the municipal magistrates to protect the inhabitants of the cities against the vexations of the imperial administration, became evident to despotism itself; and when despotism, suffering at length the punishment of its own deeds, felt society abandoning it on every side, it attempted, by the creation of a new magistracy, to procure for the *municipia* some security and some independence. A *defensor* was given to every city: his original mission was to defend the people, especially the poor, against the oppression and injustice of the imperial officers and their agents. He soon surpassed all the other municipal magistrates in importance and influence. Justianian gave the defenders the right to exercise, in reference to each city, the functions of the governor of the province during the absence of that officer; he also granted them jurisdiction in all cases which did not involve a larger sum than 300 *aurei*. They had even a certain amount of authority in criminal matters, and two apparitors were attached to their person; and in order to give some guarantees of their power and independence, two means were employed; on the one hand, they had the right of passing over the various degrees in the public administration, and of carrying their complaints at once before the prætorian prefect; this was done with the intention of elevating their dignity by freeing them from the jurisdiction of the provincial authorities. On the other hand, they were elected, not by the *curia* merely, but by the general body of the inhabitants of the *municipium*, including the bishop and all the clergy; and as the clergy then alone possessed any energy and influence, this new institution, and consequently all that still remained of the municipal system, fell into its hands almost universally. This was insufficient to restore the vigour of the *municipia*, under the dominion of the empire; but it was enough to procure for the clergy great legal influence in the towns after the settlement of the Barbarians. The most important result of the institution of defenders was to place the bishops at the head of the municipal system, which otherwise would have dissolved of itself, through the ruin of its citizens and the nullity of its institutions.

Such are the facts: they demonstrate the phenomenon which I indicated at the outset, namely, the destruction of the middle class in the empire; it was destroyed materially by the ruin and dispersion of the curiales, and morally by the denial of all influence to the respectable population in the affairs of the State, and eventually in those of the city. Hence it arose that, in the fifth century, there was so much uncultivated land and so many towns almost deserted, or inhabited only by a famished and spiritless population. The system which I have just explained contributed, much more powerfully than the devastations of the Barbarians, to produce this result.

In order rightly to apprehend the true character and consequenses of these facts, we must reduce them to general ideas, and deduce therefrom all that they contain in regard to one of the greatest problems of social order. Let us first examine them on the relations of the municipal system with political order, of the city with the State. In this respect, the general fact which results from those which I have stated, is the absolute separation of political rights and interests from municipal rights and interests; a separation equally fatal to the political rights and interests, and to the municipal rights and interests of citizens. So long as the principal citizens possessed, at the centre of the State, real rights and an actual influence, the municipal system was not wanting in guarantees of security, and continued to develop itself. As soon as the principal citizens lost their influence at head quarters these guarantees disappeared, and the decay of the municipal system was not long in manifesting itself.

Let us now compare the course of things in the Roman world, with what has occurred in the modern states. In the Roman world, centralization was prompt and uninterrupted. In proportion as she conquered the world, Rome absorbed and retained within her walls the entire political existence of both victors and vanquished. There was nothing in common between the rights and liberties of the citizen, and the rights and liberties of the inhabitant; political life and municipal life were not confounded one in the other, and were not exhibited in the same localities. In regard to politics, the Roman people had, in truth, only one head; when that was stricken, political life ceased to exist; local liberties then found themselves unconnected by any bond, and without any common guarantee for their general protection.

Among modern nations, no such centralization has ever existed. On the contrary, it has been in the towns, and by the operation of municipal liberties, that the mass of the inhabitants, the middle class, has been formed, and has acquired importance in the State. But when once in possession of this point of support, this class soon felt itself to be in straits, and without security. The force of circumstances made it understand that, so long as it was not raised to the centre of the State, and constitutionally established there; so long as it did not possess, in political matters, rights which should prove the development and pledge of those which it exercised in municipal affairs—these last would be insufficient to protect it in all its interests, and even to protect themselves. Here is the origin of all the efforts which, from the thirteenth century onwards, either by Estates General or Parliaments, or by more indirect means, were made for the purpose of raising the burghers to political life, and associating with the rights and liberties of the inhabitant, the rights and liberties of the citizen. After three centuries of endeavour, these efforts were unsuccessful. The municipal system was unable to give birth to a political system which should correspond with it and become its guarantee. The centralization of power was effected without any centralization of rights. Thenceforward the municipal system proved weak and incapable of defending itself; it had been formed in spite of feudal domination; it was unable to exist in presence of a central authority, and in the midst of administrative monarchy. The towns gradually lost, obscurely and almost unresistingly, their ancient liberties. No one is ignorant that, at the moment when the French revolution broke out, the municipal system in France was nothing more than a vain shadow, without consistency or energy.

Thus although, in the Roman world and amongst ourselves,

matters have progressed in inverse proportion, although Rome began by the centralization of public liberties, and modern States by municipal freedom, in both cases facts alike reveal to us the double truth that the two orders of liberties and rights are indispensable to one another, that they cannot be separated without mutual injury, and that the ruin of one necessarily entails the ruin of that which at first survives.

A second result of no less importance is revealed to us by the same facts. The separation of the municipal from the political system led, in the Roman empire, to the legal classification of society and to the introduction of privilege. In modern States, an analogous classification and the presence of aristocratic privileges prevented the municipal system from raising itself to political influence, and from producing the rights of the citizen from the local rights of the inhabitant. Where, then, municipal and political life are strangers to one another, where they are not united in the same system and bound together in such a manner as reciprocally to guarantee each other's security, we may be certain that society either is or soon will be divided into distinct and unchangeable classes, and that privilege either already exists or is about to make its appearance. If the bourgeois have no share in the central power, if the citizens who exercise or share in the central power do not at the same time participate in the rights and interest of the bourgeoise, if political and municipal existence proceed thus collaterally, instead of being, as it were, included in each other, it is impossible for privilege not to gain a footing, even beneath the iron hand of despotism and in the midst of servitude.

If from all this we desire to deduce a still more general consequence, and to express it in a purely philosophical form, we shall acknowledge that, in order that right may certainly exist in any place, it must exist everywhere, that its presence at the centre is vain unless it be present also in localities; that, without political liberty, there can be no solid municipal liberties, and vice versa. If, however, we consider the facts already stated in reference to the municipal system taken in itself and in its internal constitution; if in these facts we look for principles—we shall meet with the most singular amalgamation of the principles of liberty with those of despotism; an amalgamation, perhaps, unexampled, and certainly inexplicable to those who have not well understood the course of circumstances, both in the formation and in the decline of the Roman world.

The presence of principles of liberty is evident. They were these. (1) Every inhabitant possessing a fortune which guaranteed his independence and intelligence, was a curial; and, as such, called upon to take part in the administration of the affairs of the city. Thus, the right was attached to presumed capacity, without any privilege of birth, or any limit as to number; and this right was not a simple right of election, but the right of full deliberation, of immediate participation in affairs, as far as they related to what occurred in the interior of a town, and to interests which might be understood and discussed by all those who were capable of raising themselves above the cares of individual existence. The *curia* was not a restricted and select council, it was an assembly of all the inhabitants who possessed the conditions of curial capacity. (2) An assembly cannot administrate—magistrates are necessary. These were all elected by the *curia*, for a very short time; and they answered for their administration by their private fortune. (3) In circumstances of importance, such as changing the condition of a city, or electing a magistrate invested with vague and more arbitrary authority, the *curia* itself was not sufficient; the whole body of the inhabitants was called in to take part in these solemn acts.

Who, on beholding such rights, would not think that he saw a small republic, in which municipal and political life were merged in one another, and in which the most democratic rule prevailed? Who would think that a municipality thus regulated formed a part of a great empire, and depended, by narrow and necessary bonds, on a remote and sovereign central power? Who would not, on the contrary, expect to meet with all the outbreaks of liberty, all the agitations and cabals, and frequently all the disorder and violence which, at all periods, characterize small societies thus shut up and governed within their own walls?

Nothing of the kind was the case, and all these principles of liberty were lifeless. Other principles existed which were fatal to them. (1) Such were the effects and exactions of the central despotism that the quality of curial ceased to be a right recognized as belonging to all who were capable of exercising it, and became a burden imposed upon all who were able to bear it. On the one hand, the government discharged itself from the care of providing for those public services which did not affect its own interests, and so cast the obligation on this class of citizens; and, on the other hand, it employed them to collect the taxes destined for its use, and made them responsible for the payment thereof. It ruined the curiales in order to pay its own functionaries and soldiers; and it granted to its own functionaries and soldiers all the advantages of privilege, in order to obtain their assistance forcibly to prevent the curiales from escaping from their impending ruin. Complete nullities as citizens, the curiales lived only to be fleeced. (2) All the elective magistrates were, in fact, merely the gratuitous agents of despotism, for whose benefit they robbed their fellow citizens, until they should be able, in some way or another, to free themselves from this unpleasant obligation. (3) Their election even was valueless, for the imperial delegate in the province could annul it, and they had the greatest personal interest in obtaining this favour from him; in this way also, they were at his mercy. (4) Lastly, their authority was not real, for it had no sanction. No effective jurisdiction was allowed them; they could do nothing that might not be annulled. Nay, more: as despotism daily perceived more clearly their impotence or ill will, it daily encroached further upon the domain of their attributes, either by its own personal action, or by its direct delegates. The business of the *curia* vanished successively with its powers; and a day was not far distant when the municipal system would be abolished at a single stroke in the rapidly decaying empire, "because," the legislator would say, "all these laws wander, in some sort, vaguely and objectless about the legal territory."

Thus, the municipal power, having become completely estranged from political and civil power, ceased to be a power itself. Thus, the principles and forms of liberty, isolated remains of the independent existence of that multitude of towns which were successfully added to the Roman empire, were impotent to defend themselves against the coalition of despotism and privilege. Thus, here also, we may learn what so many examples teach us; namely, that all the appearances of liberty, all the external acts which seem to attest its presence, may exist where liberty is not, and that it does not really exist unless those who possess it exercise a real power—a power, the exercise of which is connected with that of all powers. In the social state, liberty is participation in power; this participation is its true, or rather its only, guarantee. Where liberties are not rights, and where rights are not powers, neither rights nor liberties exist.

We must not, therefore, be surprised either at that complete disappearance of the nation which characterized the fall of the Roman empire, or at the influence which the clergy soon obtained in the new order of things. Both phenomena are explained by the state of society at that period, and particularly by that state of the municipal system which I have just described. The bishop had become, in every town, the natural chief of the inhabitants, the true mayor. His election, and the part which the citizens took in it, became the important business of the city. It is to the clergy that we owe the partial preservation, in the towns, of the Roman laws and customs, which were incorporated at a later period into the legislation of the State. Between the old municipal system of the Romans, and the civil-municipal system of the communes of the Middle Ages, the ecclesiastical municipal system occurred as a transition. This transition state lasted for several centuries. This important fact was nowhere so clearly and strongly developed as in the monarchy of the Visigoths in Spain.

PART II

ESSAYS OF REPRESENTATIVE GOVERNMENT IN
ENGLAND, FROM THE CONQUEST TILL THE
REIGN OF THE TUDORS

Lecture 1

I think it necessary to remind you, gentlemen, of the plan which I adopted last year with regard to our study of the political institutions of Europe. The essential object of that plan was to give some unity and compactness to this vast history. And this is not an arbitrary and self-chosen object. In the development of our continent, all its peoples and all its governments are connected together; in spite of all struggles and separations, there is really some unity and compactness in European civilization. This unity, which has been revealing itself from day to day, is now evident; never have geographical limits possessed less sway than in our times; never has such a community of ideas, feelings, aspirations, and efforts united, in spite of territorial demarcations, so great a mass of men. That which is now revealed has been labouring for more than twelve centuries to manifest itself; this external and apparent community has not always existed; but such has always been, at bottom, the unity of European civilization, that it is impossible thoroughly to understand the history of any of the great modern peoples without considering the history of Europe as a whole, and contemplating the course pursued by humanity in general. It is a vast drama in which every people has its part to perform, and with the general events of which we must be acquainted in order to understand the particular scenes connected therewith.

I have divided the history of the political institutions of Europe into four great epochs, which are distinguished from each other by essentially different characteristics. The first is the barbarian epoch; a time of conflict and confusion, in which no society could be established, no institution be founded and become regularly prevalent in any part of Europe; this epoch extends from the fifth to the tenth century. The second is the feudal epoch, and extends from the tenth to the fourteenth century. The third is the epoch of efforts towards constitutional monarchy; feudalism declines, the populations become free, and royalty employs them to extend and augment its power; this epoch embraces the period from the fourteenth to the sixteenth century. In the fourth period, on the Continent, all efforts towards a representative system have failed or almost entirely disappeared: pure monarchy prevails. England alone decidedly obtains a constitutional government. This epoch lasts from the sixteenth century to the French Revolution.

These epochs were not determined by an arbitrary choice—

their division results from the general facts which characterize them. They will not all form the subject of this course of lectures. I wish to study the political institutions of Europe with you, and representative government is the centre towards which all our studies tend. Where I perceive no trace of the representative system, and no direct effort to produce it, I turn aside, and transfer my attention to some other quarter. Nor shall I merely limit our studies in reference to epochs only; I shall limit them also in respect to places. Last year, in my lectures on the first epoch, I did not follow the progress of political institutions in the whole of Europe, but confined my observations to France, Spain, and England. We have now to study the third epoch; but the Estates General of France and the Cortes of Spain were only unfruitful attempts at representative government. I shall therefore postpone our study of them, and devote this year's course to the attentive examination of the origin of representative government in England, the only country in which it received uninterrupted and successful development. This study is particularly necessary to us at the present day, and we are ourselves well disposed to enter upon it with an earnest desire to reap advantage from it.

According to their political state, and in the degree of their civilization, do the peoples consider history under various aspects, and look to it for various kinds of interest. In the early ages of society, whilst all is new and attractive to the youthful imagination of man, he demands poetical interest; the memories of the past form the groundwork of brilliant and simple narratives, fitted to charm an eager and easily satisfied curiosity. If, in such a community, where social existence is in full vigour, and the human mind is in a state of excitement, Herodotus reads to the Greeks assembled at Olympia his patriotic narratives, and the discoveries of his voyages, the Greeks delight in them as in songs of Homer. If civilization is but little advanced—if men live more isolated—if "country," in the concrete, at least, exists but slightly for them—we find simple chronicles intermingled with fables and legends, but always marked with that *naïf* and poetical character which, in such a condition of existence, the human mind requires in all things. Such are the European chronicles from the tenth to the fifteenth century. If, at a later period, civilization becomes developed in a country without the coeval establishment of liberty, without an energetic and extensive political existence, when the period of enlightenment, of wealth, and of leisure, does arrive, men look for philosophical interest in history; it no longer belongs to the field of poetry; it loses its simplicity; it no longer wears its former real and living physiognomy; individual characters take up less space, and no longer appear under living forms; the mention of names becomes more rare; the narrative of events, and the description of men, are more its pretext than its subject; all becomes generalized; readers demand a summary of the development of civilization, a sort of theory of the peoples and of events; history becomes a series of dissertations on the progress of the human race, and the historian seems only to call up the skeleton of the past, in order to hang upon it general ideas and philosophic reflections. This occurred in the last century; the English historians of that period, Robertson, Gibbon, and Hume, have represented history under that aspect; and most of the German writers still follow the same system. The philosophy of history predominates; history, properly so called, is not to be found in them.

But if advanced civilization and a great development of the human intellect coincide, in a nation, with an animated and keen political existence; if the struggle for liberty, by exciting the mind, provoke energy of character; if the activity of public life be added to the general claims of thought, history appears in another light; it becomes, so to speak, practical. No longer is it required to charm easily excited imaginations by its narratives, nor to satisfy by its meditations active intellects debarred from exercising themselves upon aught but generalities. But men expect from it experience analogous to the wants they feel, to the life they live: they desire to understand the real nature and hidden springs of institutions; to enter into the movements of parties, to follow them in their combinations, to study the secret of the influence of the masses, and of the action of individuals; men and things must appear to them, no longer merely as an interest or diversion, but as a revelation of how rights, liberties, and power are to be acquired, exercised, and defended; how to combine opinions, interests, passions, the necessities of circumstances, all the elements of active political life. That is what history becomes for free nations; it is from that point of view that Thucydides wrote the history of the Peloponnesian war, Lord Clarendon and Bishop Burnet that of the English Revolution.

Generally, and by the very nature of things, it is in regular order, and at distant intervals, that history assumes one or other of these various kinds of interest in the eyes of the people. A taste for simple narratives, a liking for philosophic generalizations, and a craving for political instruction, almost always belong to very different times and degrees of civilization.

By a rare concurrence of circumstances, all these tastes and acquirements seem to unite at the present day; and history is now susceptible amongst us of all these kinds of interest. If it narrate to us with truth and simplicity the first attempts at social life, the manners of infant nations; that singular state of society in which ideas are few in number but keen, and wants are energetic although unvaried, in which all the pretensions of barbarian force struggle against all the habits of wild liberty, it will find us capable of understanding such a recital, and somewhat disposed to be charmed therewith. Fifty years ago, a faithful picture of this age in the life of peoples would have appeared only coarse and revolting; its interesting and poetical character would have been neither relished nor understood; conventions were then turned into habits, and factitious manners held sway over the whole of society; Homer himself, in an age so destitute of simplicity and naturalness, was admired on hearsay only; and if no one dared to call in question his title to glory, he was pitied for having been obliged to shed the lustre of his genius upon an epoch of barbarism and ignorance. Prodigious events have since renewed the state of society, broken up old forms, conventional habits, and factitious manners; simple ideas and natural feelings have resumed their empire; a kind of rejuvenation has taken place in the minds of men, and they have become capable of understanding at every degree of civilization, and of taking pleasure in the simple and poetic narratives of infant society. In our days it has been felt that barbarian times also deserved, in some respects, to be called heroic times; in our days, mankind has discovered the faculty, as well as the necessity, of obtaining a true knowledge of the institutions, ideas, and manners of peoples, on their entrance into social life. Thus this section of history has regained an interest which it had ceased to possess; it is no longer regarded as the patrimony of the erudite; it has been seized upon by novelists themselves, and the public have taken delight in following their footsteps.

At the same time, the need for broad philosophical views of the course of human affairs and the progress of society, has gained strength instead of becoming extinguished; we have not ceased to look to facts for something more than mere narratives; we still expect them to be summed up in general ideas, and to furnish us with those great results which throw light on the sciences of legislation and political economy, and on the vast study of the destiny of the human race. Far, then, from being less inclined to consider history under a philosophic point of view, it seems to have acquired a wider interest in this respect. More than ever, we feel the necessity of tracing events back to their primitive causes, of reducing them to their simplest expression, of penetrating into their remotest effects; and if old chronicles have regained their charm in our eyes, the great combinations of historic philosophy still constitute a pressing necessity of our minds.

Finally, our birth into public life, the institutions that we possess and that we will not lose, that aurora of liberty which, though it arose in the midst of tempests, is not destined to perish therein, the past which we leave behind us, the present with which we are busied, the future which awaits us, in fine, our entire position —all impart to history, considered under the political point of view, the most imperious interest. Before our time, the movement of public life, the game of parties, the war of factions, the struggles of assemblies, all the agitations and developments of power and liberty, were things which men had heard of but had not seen, which they had read of in books but which were not actually existing around the reader. These things have occurred, and are now occurring under our very eyes; every consideration leads us to study them, every circumstance aids us to comprehend them. And not to us alone has political life been restored: it has returned into history, hitherto cold and vague to the minds of those who had not been struck by the real visions of the scenes which it relates. And while regaining our comprehension of history, we have also become aware of the counsels and the lessons which it can furnish us; its ability no longer consists, as formerly, in a general idea, a sort of moral and literary dogma professed by writers rather than adopted and practised by the public. Now, a more or less thorough acquaintance with history, and especially with that of free peoples, is not merely an accomplishment of cultivated minds; it is a necessity to every citizen who feels desirous to take part in the affairs of his country, or merely to appreciate them correctly. And thus this great study now presents itself to us with all the kinds of interest that it is able to offer, because we have in us the ability to consider it under all its aspects, and to seek and to find all that it contains.

Such are the motives which induce me to select the history of the political institutions of England as the subject of this course of lectures. Here, in effect, history considered under its three different aspects, presents itself with the greatest simplicity and richness. Nowhere have the primitive manners of modern peoples been preserved for a longer period, or exercised so decisive an influence upon the institutions of a country. Nowhere do great philosophical considerations spring with greater abundance from the contemplation of events and men. Here, in fine, representative government, the special object of our study, developed without interruption, received into its bosom and fertilized its alliance with the religious movement imparted to Europe in the sixteenth century, and thus became the starting point of the political reformation which is now beginning on the Continent.

It is by no means my intention to relate to you the history of England. I intend merely to consider it under its political point of view; and even under this point of view, we shall not study all the institutions of the kingdom. Representative government is our theme; and we shall therefore follow the history of the Parliament step by step. We shall only refer to judicial, administrative, and municipal institutions in so far as they are connected with representative government, and have contributed either to form it, or to determine its character.

Last year, before entering upon our examination of facts, I attempted to define with precision what we ought to understand by representative government. Before seeking for its existence, I desired to know by what signs we might discern its presence. Now that we are about to study the history of the only representative government which, until our days, has existed with full vitality in Europe, I think it well to recapitulate some of these ideas.

I have said that I had no very high opinion of the division of governments by publicists, into monarchical, aristocratic, and democratic; and that, in my opinion, it was by their essential principle, by their general and internal idea, that governments were characterized and distinguished. The most general idea that we can seek out in a government is its theory of sovereignty, that is, the manner in which it conceives, places, and attributes the right of giving law and carrying it into execution in society.

There are two great theories of sovereignty. One seeks for it and places it in some one of the real forces which exist upon the earth, no matter whether it be the people, the monarch, or the chief men of the people. The other maintains that sovereignty as a right can exist nowhere upon earth, and ought to be attributed to no power, for no earthly power can fully know and constantly desire truth, reason, and justice—the only sources of sovereignty as a right, and which ought also to be the rule of sovereignty in fact. The first theory of sovereignty founds absolute power, whatever may be the form of the government. The second combats absolute power in all its forms, and recognizes its legitimacy in no case. It is not true to say that of these two theories, one or the other reigns exclusively in the various governments of the world. These two theories commingle in a certain measure; for nothing is completely destitute of truth or perfectly free from error. Nevertheless, one or the other always dominates in every form of government, and may be considered as its principle.

The true theory of sovereignty, that is, the radical illegitimacy of all absolute power, whatever may be its name and place, is the principle of representative government.

In fact, in representative government, absolute power, sovereignty as a right, inhere in none of the powers which concur to form the government: they must agree to make the law; and even when they have agreed, instead of accepting forever the absolute power which actually results from their agreement, the representative system subjects this power to the variableness of election. And the electoral power itself is not absolute, for it is confined to the choice of the men who shall have a share in the government.

It is, moreover, the character of that system, which nowhere admits the legitimacy of absolute power, to compel the whole body of citizens incessantly, and on every occasion, to seek after reason, justice, and truth, which should ever regulate actual power. The representative system does this, (1) by discussion, which compels existing powers to seek after truth in common; (2) by publicity, which places these powers when occupied in this search, under the eyes of the citizens; and (3) by the liberty of the press, which stimulates the citizens themselves to seek after truth, and to tell it to power.

Finally, the necessary consequence of the true theory of sovereignty is, that all actual power is responsible. If, in fact, no actual power possesses sovereignty as a right, they are all obliged to prove that they have sought after truth, and have taken it for their rule; and they must legitimize their title by their acts, under penalty of being taxed with illegitimacy. The responsibility of power is, in fact, inherent in the representative system; it is the only system which makes it one of its fundamental conditions.

After having recognised the principle of representative government, we investigated its external characteristics, that is to say, the forms which necessarily accompany the principle, and by which alone it can manifest its existence. These forms we reduced to three: (1) division of powers; (2) election; and (3) publicity. It is not difficult to convince ourselves that these characteristics necessarily flow from the principle of representative government. Indeed, (1) all sole power in fact soon becomes absolute in right. It is therefore necessary that all power in fact should be conscious of dependence. "All unity," says Pascal, "that is not multitude, is tyranny." Hence results the necessity for two Houses of Parliament. If there be only one, the executive power either suppresses it, or falls into so subaltern a condition that there would soon remain only the absolute power of the single House of Parliament. (2) Unless election occurred frequently to place power in new hands, that power which derived its right from itself would soon become absolute in right; this is the tendency of all aristocracies. (3) Publicity, which connects power with society, is the best guarantee against the usurpation of sovereignty as a right by the actual power.

Representative government can neither be established nor developed without assuming, sooner or later, these three characteristics; they are the natural consequences of its principle; but they do not necessarily coexist, and representative government may exist without their union.

This was the case in England. It is impossible not to enquire why representative government prevailed in that country, and not in the other states of the Continent. For, indeed, the Barbarians who settled in Great Britain had the same origin and the same primitive manners as those who, after the fall of the Roman Empire, overran Europe; and it was not in the midst of very different circumstances that they consolidated their dominion in that country.

From the fifth to the twelfth century, we find no more traces of true representative government in England than upon the Continent; its institutions were analogous to those of the other European nations; and we behold in every land the conflict of the three systems of free, feudal, and monarchical institutions.

We cannot fully resolve this question beforehand, and in a general manner. We shall answer it gradually, as we advance in the examination of facts. We shall see by what successive and varied causes political institutions took a different course in England to that which they pursued on the Continent. We may, however, indicate at once the great fact which, from a very early period, determined the character and direction of British institutions.

The first of the great external characteristics of representative government, division of power, is met with in every age, in the government of England. Never was the government concentrated in the hands of the king alone; under the name of the *Wittenagemot,* of the *Council* or *Assembly of the Barons,* and after the reign of Henry III, of the *Parliament,* a more or less numerous and influential assembly, composed in a particular manner, was always associated with the sovereignty. For a long period, this assembly somewhat subserved despotism, and sometimes substituted civil war and anarchy in the place of despotism; but it always interfered in the central government. An independent council, which derived its strength from the individual power of its members, was always adjoined to the royal authority. The English monarchy has always been the government of the king in council, and the king's council was frequently his adversary. The great council of the king became the Parliament.

This is the only essential characteristic of the system of representative government which the government of England presents until the fourteenth century. During the course of this epoch, the division of power, far from efficiently repressing despotism, served only to render it more changeful and more dangerous. The council of barons was no more capable than the king himself, of comprehending and establishing a stable political order and true liberty; these two forces were incessantly in conflict, and their conflict was war, that is to say, the devastation of the country, and the oppression of the mass of the inhabitants. But from this there resulted, in process of time, two decisive facts, from which liberty took its origin; they were these:

1. From the very fact that power was divided, it followed that absolute power, sovereignty as a right, was never attributed to the King, nor supposed to be in itself legitimate. Now, this is the

very principle of representative government; but this principle was far from being understood, or even suspected, philosophically speaking. It was incessantly stifled by force, or else it was lost in the confusion of the ideas of the time regarding divine right, the origin of power, and so forth; but it existed in the depths of the public mind, and became by slow degrees a fundamental maxim. We find this principle formally expressed in the writings of Bracton, Lord Chief Justice under Henry III, and of Fortescue, who held the same office under Henry VI. "The king," says Bracton, "should be subject to no man, but only to God and to the law, for the law makes him king; he can do nothing upon earth but that which, by law, he may do; and that which is said in the *Pandectes*, that that which pleases the king becomes law, is no objection; for we see by the context, that these words do not mean the pure and simple will of the prince, but that which has been determined by the advice of his councils, the king giving the sanction of his authority to their deliberations upon the subject."

"The English monarchy," says Fortescue, "*non solum est regalis, sed legalis et politica potestas*," and he frequently develops this idea. The limitation of powers was, thus, at a very early period, a matter of public right in England; and the legitimacy of sole and absolute power was never recognised. Thus was established and preserved, for better times, the generative principle of all legitimate power as well as of all liberty; and by the virtue of this principle alone was maintained, in the souls of the people, that noble sentiment of right which becomes extinguished and succumbs wherever man finds himself in presence of an unlimited sovereignty, whatever may be its form and name.

2. The division of the supreme power produced yet another result. When the towns had acquired greater wealth and importance, when there had been formed, beyond the circle of the king's immediate vassals, a nation capable of taking part in political life, and which the government found it necessary to treat with consideration, this nation naturally adjoined itself to the great council of the king, which had never ceased to exist.

In order to gain itself a place in the central government, it had no need abruptly to create new institutions; a place was already prepared to receive it, and although its entrance into the national council ere long changed its nature and forms, it at least was not under the necessity of asserting and reanimating its existence. There was a fact capable of receiving extension, and of admitting into its bosom new facts, together with new rights. The British Parliament, in truth, dates only from the formation of the House of Commons; but without the presence and importance of the council of Barons, the House of Commons would, perhaps, never have been formed.

Thus, on the one hand, the permanence of the idea that the sovereignty ought to be limited, and, on the other, the actual division of the central power, were the germs of representative government in England. Until the end of the thirteenth century we met with no other of its characteristics; and the English nation, until that period, was not perhaps actually more free and happy than any of the peoples of the Continent. But the principle of the right of resistance to oppression was already a legal principle in England; and the idea of the supremacy which holds dominion over all others, of the supremacy of the law, was already connected, in the mind of the people and of the jurisconsults themselves, not with any particular person, or with any particular actual power, but with the name of the law itself. Already the law was said to be superior to all other powers; sovereignty had thus, in principle at least, left that material world in which it could not fix itself without engendering tyranny, to place itself in that moral world, in which actual powers ought constantly to seek it. Many favourable circumstances were doubtless necessary to fecundate these principles of liberty in England. But when the sentiment of right lives in the souls of men, when the citizen meets with no power in his country which he is bound to consider as infallible and absolutely sovereign, liberty can never fail to spring up. It has developed in England less universally, less equally, and less reasonably, we venture to believe, then we are permitted to hope will be the case at the present day in our own country; but, in fine, it was born, and increased in growth in that country more than in any other; and the history of its progress, the study of the institutions which served as its guarantees, and of the system of government to which its destinies seem henceforward to link themselves, is at once a great spectacle and a necessary work for us. We shall enter upon it with impartiality, for we can do so without envy.

3

Shakspeare and His Times
Excerpts from Chapter 1

VOLTAIRE was the first person in France who spoke of Shakspeare's genius; and although he spoke of him merely as a barbarian genius, the French public were of the opinion that Voltaire
had said too much in his favor. Indeed, they thought it nothing
less than profanation to apply the words genius and glory to
dramas which they considered as crude as they were coarse.

At the present day, all controversy regarding Shakspeare's
genius and glory has come to an end. No one ventures any longer
to dispute them; but a greater question has arisen, namely,
whether Shakspeare's dramatic system is not far superior to that
of Voltaire.

This question I do not presume to decide. I merely say that
it is now open for discussion. We have been led to it by the
onward progress of ideas. I shall endeavor to point out the
causes which have brought it about; but at present I insist merely
upon the fact itself, and deduce from it one simple consequence,
that literary criticism has changed its ground, and can no longer
remain restricted to the limits within which it was formerly
confined.

Excerpts from chapter 1 of *Shakspeare and His Times* (New York:
Harper & Brothers, 1852), from *Etudes sur Shakspeare—Oeuvres Com-
plète de Shakspeare.*

Literature does not escape from the revolutions of the human mind; it is compelled to follow it in its course—to transport itself beneath the horizon under which it is conveyed; to gain elevation and extension with the ideas which occupy its notice, and to consider the questions which it discusses under the new aspects and novel circumstances in which they are placed by the new state of thought and of society.

My readers will not, therefore, be surprised that, in order properly to appreciate Shakspeare, I find it necessary to make some preliminary researches into the nature of dramatic poetry and the civilization of modern peoples, especially of England. If we did not begin with these general considerations, it would be impossible to keep pace with the perhaps confused but active and urgent ideas which such a subject now arouses in all minds.

A theatrical performance is a popular festival; that it should be so is required by the very nature of dramatic poetry. Its power rests upon the effects of sympathy—of that mysterious force which causes laughter to beget laughter; which bids tears to flow at the sight of tears, and which, in spite of the diversity of dispositions, conditions, and characters, produces the same impression on all upon whom it simultaneously acts. For the proper development of these effects, a crowd must be assembled; those ideas and feelings which would pass languidly from one man to another, traverse the serried ranks of a multitude with the rapidity of lightning; and it is only when large masses of men are collected together that we observe the action of that moral electricity which the dramatic poet calls into such powerful operation.

Dramatic poetry, therefore, could originate only among the people. At its birth it was destined to promote their pleasures; in their festivities it once performed an active part; and with the first songs of Thespis the chorus of the spectators invariably united.

But the people are not slow to perceive that the pleasures with which they can supply themselves are neither the best, nor the only pleasures which they are capable of enjoying. To those classes which spend their days in toil, complete repose seems to be the first and almost the sole condition of pleasure. A momentary suspension of the efforts or privations of daily life, an interval of movement and liberty, a relative abundance; this is all that the people seek to derive from those festivities which they are able to provide for themselves—these are all the enjoyments which it is in their power to procure. And yet these men are born to experience nobler and keener delights; they are possessed of faculties which the monotony of their existence has allowed to lie dormant in inactivity. If these faculties be awakened by a powerful voice; if an animated narrative, or a stirring scene stimulate these drowsy imaginations, these torpid sensibilities, they will gain an activity which they could never have imparted to themselves, but which they will rejoice to receive; and then will arise, without the cooperation of the multitude, but in its presence and for its amusement, new games and new pleasures which will speedily become necessities.

To such festivities as these the dramatic poet invites the assembled people. He undertakes to divert them, but the amusement which he supplies is one of which they would have been ignorant without his assistance. Æschylus relates to his fellow-citizens the victories of Salamis, the anxieties of Atossa, and the grief of Xerxes. He charms the people of Athens, but it is by raising them to a level with emotions and ideas which Æschylus alone could exalt to so high a point; and he communicates to the multitude impressions which they are capable of feeling, but which Æschylus alone is able to awaken. Such is the nature of dramatic poetry; for the people it calls its creations into being, to the people it addresses itself; but it is in order to ennoble their character, to extend and vivify their moral existence, to reveal to them faculties which they unconsciously possess, and to procure for them enjoyments which they eagerly seize, but which they would not even seek after, if a sublime art did not reveal to them their existence by making them minister to their gratification.

And this work the dramatic poet must necessarily pursue; he must elevate and civilize, as it were, the crowd that he summons to hear his performance. How can he act upon the as-

sembled multitude, except by an appeal to the most general and
elevated characteristics of their nature? It is only by going out
of the narrow circle of common life and individual interests that
the imagination becomes exalted and the heart enlarged, that
pleasures become disinterested and the affections generous, and
that men can sympathize in those common emotions the expression of which causes the theatre to resound with transports
of delight. Religion has, therefore, universally been the source
and furnished the primitive materials of dramatic art; at its
origin, it celebrated, among the Greeks, the adventures of
Bacchus, and, in Northern Europe, the mysteries of Christ. This
arises from the fact that, of all human affections, piety most
powerfully unites men in common feelings, because it most
thoroughly detaches them from themselves; it is also less dependent for its development upon the progress of civilization, as
it is powerful and pure even in the most backward state of
society. From its very beginning, dramatic poetry has invoked
the aid of piety, because, of all the sentiments to which it
could address itself, piety was the noblest and the most
universal.

Originating thus among the people and for the people, but
destined to elevate them by affording them delight, the dramatic
art speedily became, in every age, and country, and by reason
of this very characteristic of its nature, the favorite pleasure of
the superior classes.

This was its natural tendency; and in this, also, it has encountered its most dangerous quicksands. More than once, allow-
ing itself to be led astray by its high fortune, dramatic art has
lost or compromised its energy and liberty. When the superior
classes can fully give themselves up to their position, they fall
into the error or misfortune of isolating themselves from their
fellows, and ceasing, as it were, to share in the general nature
of man, and the public interests of society. Those universal feelings, natural ideas, and simple relationships which constitute
the basis of humanity and of life, become changed and enervated in a social condition which consists entirely of exceptions
and privileges. In such a state of society, conventions take

the place of realities, and morals become factitious and feeble. Human destiny ceases to be known under its most salient and general aspects. It has a thousand phases, it leads to a host of impressions and relations of which the higher classes are utterly ignorant, unless they are compelled to enter frequently into the public atmosphere. Dramatic art, when devoted to their pleasure, finds its domain greatly diminished and impoverished; it is invaded by a sort of monotony; events, passions, characters, all those natural treasures which it lays under contribution, no longer supply it with the same originality and wealth. Its independence is imperiled as well as its variety and energy. The habits of elegant society, like those of the multitude, are characterized by their pettiness, and elegant society is much more capable of making a law of this pettiness. It is stimulated by tastes rather than by necessities; it rarely introduces into its pleasures that serious and ingenuous disposition which abandons itself with transport to the impressions which it receives; and it very frequently treats genius as a servant who is bound to please it, and not as a power that is capable of governing it by the enjoyments which it can supply. If the dramatic poet does not possess, in the suffrages of a larger and more simple public, the means of defending himself against the haughty taste of a select coterie —if he cannot arm himself with public approbation, and rely for support upon the universal feelings which he has been able to arouse in all hearts—his liberty is lost; the caprices which he has attempted to satisfy will weigh upon him like a chain, from which he will be unable to free himself; talent, which is entitled to command all, will find itself subject to the minority, and he who ought to guide the taste of the people, will become the slave of fashion.

Such, then, is the nature of dramatic poetry that, in order to produce its most magical effects, and to preserve, during its growth, its liberty as well as its wealth, it must not separate from the people, to whom its earliest efforts were addressed. It languishes if it is transplanted from the soil in which it first took root. Popular at its origin, it must continue to be national, and it must not cease to comprehend beneath its sway, and to charm with its productions, all classes that are capable of experiencing the emotions from which it derives its power.

All ages of society, and all states of civilization are not equally favorable to calling the people to the aid of dramatic poetry, and insuring its prosperity under their influence. It was the happy lot of Greece that the whole nation grew and developed together with literature and the arts, keeping always on a level with their progress, and acting as a competent judge of their glory. That same people of Athens, who had surrounded the chariot of Thespis, thronged to hear the masterpieces of Sophocles and Euripides; and the most splendid triumphs of genius were always, in that city, popular festivals. So brilliant a moral equality has not presided over the destiny of modern nations; their civilization, displaying itself upon a far more extended scale, has undergone many more vicissitudes, and presented much less unity. During more than ten centuries, nothing was easy, general, or simple in our Europe. Religion, liberty, public order, literature—nothing has been developed among us without long-continued effort, in the midst of incessantly renewed struggles, and under the most diversified influences. Amid this mighty and agitated chaos, dramatic poetry did not possess the privilege of an easy and rapid career. It was not its fate to find, almost at its birth, a public at once homogeneous and various, the constituent members of which, both great and small, rich and poor, in fine, all classes of citizens, should be equally eager for, and worthy of its most brilliant solemnities. Neither epochs of great social disorder nor periods of severe necessity are times in which the masses can devote themselves with enthusiasm to the pleasures of the stage. Literature prospers only when it is so intimately united with the tastes, habits, and entire existence of a people as to be regarded at once as an occupation and a festivity, an amusement and a necessity. Dramatic poetry, more than any other branch of literature, depends upon this deep-seated and general union of the arts with society. It is not satisfied with the tranquil pleasures of enlightened approbation, but it requires the quick impulses of passion; it does not seek men in leisure and retirement that it may furnish agreeable occupation for their hours of repose, but it requires men to hasten and throng around it. A certain degree of mental development and simplicity, a certain community of ideas and habits between the different classes of society, greater ardor than fixity of imagination, greater movement of soul than of existence, a strongly excited moral activity destitute of any imperious and determined object, liberty of thought and repose of life—these are the circumstances of which dramatic poetry has need, in order to shine with its full splendor. These circumstances never combined so completely or so harmoniously among modern peoples as among the Greeks. But whenever their leading characteristics have been found to exist, the drama has become elevated; and neither have men of genius been lacking to the public, nor has a public been lacking to men of genius.

The reign of Elizabeth, in England, was one of those decisive epochs, so laboriously attained by modern peoples, which terminate the empire of force and inaugurate the reign of ideas. Original and fruitful epochs are these, when the nations flock to mental enjoyments as to a new kind of gratification, and when thought prepares, in the pleasures of youth, for the discharge of those functions which it will be called upon to exercise at a riper age.

Scarcely recovered from the storms with which it had been ravaged by the alternate successes and reverses of the Red and White Roses, before it was again distracted and exhausted by the capricious tyranny of Henry VIII and the malevolent despotism of Mary, England demanded of Elizabeth, at her accession, nothing but order and peace; and this was precisely what Elizabeth was most disposed to bestow. Naturally prudent and reserved, though haughty and strong-willed, she had been taught by the stern necessities of her youth never to compromise herself. When upon the throne, she maintained her independence by asking little of her people, and staked her policy upon running no risks. Military glory could not seduce a distrustful woman. The sovereignty of the Netherlands, notwithstanding the efforts of the Dutch to induce her to accept it, did not tempt her wary ambition. She resignedly determined to make no attempt to recover

Calais, or to retain Havre; and all her desires of greatness, as well as all the cares of her government, were concentrated upon the direct interests of the country which she had to restore to repose and prosperity.

Surprised at so novel a state of things, the people reveled in it with the intoxication of returning health. Civilization, which had been destroyed or suspended by their dissensions, revived or progressed on every side. Industry brought wealth in its train, and notwithstanding the shackles imposed by the oppressive proceedings of the government, all the historians and all the documents of this period bear testimony to the rapid progress of popular luxury. The chronicler Harrison informs us that he had heard many old men express their surprise at

> the multitude of chimneys lately erected, whereas in their young days there were not above two or three, if so many, in most uplandish towns of the realm (the religious houses and manor-places of their lords always excepted). "Our fathers," they said, "lay full oft upon straw pallets, on rough mats covered only with a sheet, and a good round log under their heads instead of a bolster or pillow; and if the good man of the house had, within seven years after his marriage, purchased a mattress or stock-bed, and thereto a sack of chaff to rest his head upon, he thought himself to be as well lodged as the lord of the town."[1]

Elizabeth ascended the throne, and Shakspeare tells us that the busiest employment of the elves and fairies was to pinch "black and blue" those servants who neglected to cleanse the hearthstone with due regularity. And Harrison informs us that the farmers' houses in his time were well supplied "with three or four featherbeds, as many coverlids and carpets of tapestry, besides a fair garnish of pewter on the cupboard, with a silver saltcellar, a bowl for wine, and a dozen of spoons to furnish up the suit."[2]

More than one generation will pass away before a people will have exhausted the novel enjoyments of such unusual good fortune. The reigns of both Elizabeth and her successor were

---

1. Harrison's "Description of England," prefixed to Holinshed's *Chronicles*, vol. 1, p. 188.
2. Ibid., p. 189.

scarcely sufficient to wear out that taste for comfort and repose which had been fostered by long-continued agitations; and that religious ardor, the explosion of which subsequently revealed the existence of new forces which had lain hid in the bosom of society during the tranquillity of these two reigns, was then spreading itself silently among the masses, without as yet giving birth to any general and decisive movement.

The Reformation, though treated with hostility by the great sovereigns of the Continent, had received from Henry VIII enough encouragement and support to lessen its ambition and retard its progress for a time. The yoke of Rome had been cast off, and monastic life abolished. By thus granting satisfaction to the primary desires of the age, and turning the first blows of the Reformation to the advantage of material interests, Henry VIII deterred many minds from inquiring more thoroughly into the purely theological dogmas of Catholicism, which no longer shocked them by the exhibition of its most obnoxious abuses. Faith, it is true, was in a tottering state, and could no longer cling firmly to disputed doctrines. These doctrines, therefore, were fated one day to fall; but the day of their rejection was delayed. At a time when the Catholic defender of the real presence was burned at the stake for maintaining the supremacy of the Pope, and the Reformer who denied the papal supremacy suffered the same punishment for refusing to admit the real presence, many minds necessarily remained in suspense. Neither of the two conflicting opinions afforded to cowardice, which is so plentifully manifested in difficult times, the refuge of a victorious party. The dogma of political obedience was the only one which docile consciences could adopt with any zeal; and among the sincere adherents of either party, the hopes of triumph which so singular a position allowed each to entertain still kept in activity those timidly courageous individuals whom tyranny is obliged to pursue into their last strongholds, in order to force them to offer any resistance.

The vicissitudes experienced by the religious establishment of England, during the reigns of Edward VI and Mary, tended to maintain this disposition. Anxiety for martyrdom had not time, in either party, to nourish and diffuse itself; and though the party of the Reformation—which was already more influential over the public mind, more persevering in its exertions, and more remarkable for the number and courage of its martyrs—was proceeding evidently toward a final victory, yet the success which it had obtained at the accession of Elizabeth had supplied it rather with leisure to prepare for new conflicts than with power to engage in them at once, and to render them decisive.

Though connected, by her position, with the doctrines of the Reformers, Elizabeth had, in common with the Catholic clergy, a strong taste for pomp and authority. Her first regulations in regard to religious matters were, consequently, of such a character that most of the Catholics felt no repugnance to attend the divine worship with which the Reformers were satisfied; and the establishment of the Anglican Church, which was entrusted to the hands of the existing clergy, met with very little resistance, and at the same time very little encouragement, from the general body of ecclesiastics. Religion continued to be regarded, by a great many persons, as a merely political matter. The disputes of England with the Court of Rome and with Spain, a few internal conspiracies and the severities with which they were repressed, successively created new causes for animosity between the two parties. Religious interest, however, had so little influence over public feeling, that in 1569, Elizabeth, the daughter of the Reformation, but far more precious to her people as the pledge of public repose and prosperity, found most of her Catholic subjects zealous to assist her to crush the Catholic rebellion of a part of the north of England.

For still stronger reasons, they willingly agreed to that joyous forgetfulness of all great subjects of dispute which Elizabeth encouraged them to entertain. It is true that, in the depths of the masses of the people, the Reformation, which had been flattered, but not satisfied, murmured indistinctly; and even that voice which was destined soon to shake all England to its centre was heard gradually rising to utterance. But amid that movement of youthful vigor, which had, as it were, carried away the whole nation, the stern severity of the Reformers was still regarded as importunate, and those who had bestowed on it a passing glance quickly turned their eyes in some more agreeable direction; so that the accents of Puritanism, united with those of liberty, were repressed without effort by a power under whose protection the people had too recently been sheltered to entertain any great fear of its encroachments.

No periods are perhaps more favorable to the fertility and originality of mental productions than those times at which a nation already free, but still ignorant of its own position, ingenuously enjoys what it possesses without perceiving in what it is deficient: times full of ardor, but very easy to please, before rights have been narrowly defined, powers discussed, or restrictions agreed upon. The government and the public, proceeding in their course undisturbed by fears or scruples, exist together without any distrustful observance of each other, and even come into communication but rarely. If, on the one side, power is unlimited, on the other liberty will be great; for both parties will be ignorant of those general forms, those innumerable and minute duties to which actions and minds are more or less subjected by a scientifically constructed despotism, and even by a well-regulated liberty. Thus it was that the age of Richelieu and Louis XIV consciously possessed that amount of liberty which has furnished us with a literature and a drama. At that period of our history, when even the name of public liberties seemed to have been forgotten, and when a feeling for the dignity of man served as the basis neither of the institutions of the country nor of the acts of the government, the dignity of individual positions still existed wherever power had not yet found it necessary to crush it. Beside the forms of servility, we meet with forms, and sometimes even with manifestations of independence. The grand seigneur, though submissive and adoring as a courtier, could nevertheless proudly remember on certain occasions that he was a gentleman. Corneille the citizen could find no terms sufficiently humble to express his gratitude to, and dependence upon, Cardinal Richelieu; but Corneille the poet disdained the authority which assumed to prescribe rules for the guidance of his genius, and defended, against the literary pretensions of an absolute minister, those "secret means of pleasing which he might have found in his art." In fine, men of vigorous mind evaded in a thousand ways the yoke of a still incomplete or inexperienced despotism; and the imagination soared freely in every direction within the range of its flight.

In England, during the reign of Elizabeth, the supreme power, though far more irregular and less skillfully organized than it was in France under Louis XIV, had to treat with much more deeply rooted principles of liberty. It would be a mistake to measure the despotism of Elizabeth by the speeches of her flatterers, or even by the acts of her government. In her still young and inexperienced court, the language of adulation far exceeded the servility of the adulator; and in the country, in which ancient institutions had by no means perished, the government was far from exercising universal sway. In the counties and chief towns, an independent administration maintained habits and instincts of liberty. The queen imposed silence upon the Commons when they pressed her to appoint a successor, or to grant some article of religious liberty. But the Commons had met, and spoken; and the queen, notwithstanding the haughtiness of her refusal, took great care to give no cause for complaints that might have increased the authority of their words. Despotism and liberty, thus avoiding a meeting instead of seeking a battle, manifested themselves without feeling any hatred for each other, with that simplicity of action which prevents those collisions and banishes those bitter feelings which are occasioned on both sides by continual resistance. A Puritan had had his right hand cut off as a punishment for having written a tract against the proposed marriage of Elizabeth to the Duke of Anjou; and immediately after the sentence had been executed, he waved his hat with his left hand, and shouted, "God save the Queen!" When loyalty is thus deeply rooted in the heart of a man exposed to such sufferings for the cause of liberty, liberty in general must necessarily think that it has no great reason for complaint.

This period, then, was deficient in none of the advantages which it was capable of desiring. There was nothing to prevent the minds of the people from indulging freely in all the intoxication natural to thought when it has reached the age of development—an age of follies and miracles, when the imagination revels in its most puerile as well as in its noblest manifestations. Extravagantly luxurious festivities, splendor of dress, addiction to gallantry, ardent conformity to fashion, and sacrifices to favor, employed the wealth and leisure of the courtiers of Elizabeth. More enthusiastic temperaments went to distant lands in search of adventures, which, in addition to the hope of fortune, offered them the livelier pleasure of perilous encounters. Sir Francis Drake sailed forth as a corsair, and volunteers thronged on board his ship; Sir Walter Raleigh announced a distant expedition, and scions of noble houses sold their goods to join his crew. Spontaneous ventures and patriotic enterprises followed each other in almost daily succession; and, far from becoming exhausted by this continual movement, the minds of men received from it fresh vigor and impulse. Thought claimed its share in the supply of pleasures, and became, at the same time, the sustenance of the most serious passions. While the crowd hurried on all sides into the numerous theatres which had been erected, the Puritan, in his solitary meditations, burned with indignation against these pomps of Belial, and this sacrilegious employment of man, the image of God upon earth. Poetic ardor and religious asperity, literary quarrels and theological controversies, taste for festivities and fanaticism for austerities, philosophy and criticism, sermons, pamphlets, and epigrams, appeared simultaneously, and jostled each other in admired confusion. Amid this natural and fantastic conflict of opposite elements, the power of opinion, the feeling and habit of liberty, were silently in process of formation: two forces, brilliant at their first appearance and imposing in their progress, the first-fruits of which belong to any skillful government that is able to use them, but the maturity of which is terrible to any imprudent government that may attempt to reduce them to servitude. The impulse which has constituted the glory of a reign, may speedily become the fever which will precipitate a people into revolution. In the days of Elizabeth, the movement of the public mind summoned England only to festivities; and dramatic poetry sprang into full being under the master-hand of Shakspeare.

Who would not delight to go to the fountainhead of the first inspirations of an original genius; to penetrate into the secret of the causes which guided his nascent powers; to follow him step by step in his progress; and, in a word, to behold the whole inner life of a man who, after having in his own country opened to dramatic poetry the road which she has never since quitted, still reigns preeminent, and with almost undivided sway? Unfortunately, Shakspeare is one of those superior men whose life was but little noticed by his contemporaries, and it has therefore remained obscure to succeeding generations. A few civil registers in which traces of the existence of his family have been preserved, a few traditions connected with his name in the district in which he was born, and the splendid productions of his own genius, are the only means which we possess of supplying the deficiencies of his personal history.

.   .   .   .

Nowhere on the Continent has a taste for poetry been so constant and popular as in Great Britain. Germany has had her Minnesingers, France her Troubadours and *Trouvères;* but these graceful apparitions of nascent poetry rapidly ascended to the superior regions of social order, and vanished before long. The English minstrels are visible, throughout the history of their country, in a position which has been more or less brilliant according to circumstances, but which has always been recognized by society, established by its acts, and determined by its rules. They appear as a regularly organized corporation, with its special business, influence, and rights, penetrating into all ranks of the nation, and associating in the diversions of the people as well as in the festivities of their chiefs. Heirs of the Breton bards and the Scandinavian Scalds, with whom they are incessantly confounded by English writers of the Middle Ages, the minstrels of Old England retained for a considerable length of time a portion of the authority of their predecessors. When afterward subjugated, and quickly deserted, Great Britain did not, like Gaul, receive a universal and profound impression of Roman civilization. The Britons disappeared or retired before the Saxons and Angles; after this period, the conquest of the Saxons by the

Danes, and of the united Danes and Saxons by the Normans, only commingled upon the soil a number of peoples of common origin, of analogous habits, and almost equally barbarous· character. The vanquished were oppressed, but they had not to exhibit their weakness before the brutal manners of their masters; and the victors were not compelled to submit by degrees to the rule of the more polished manners of their new subjects. Among a nation so homogeneous, and throughout the vicissitudes of its destiny, even Christianity did not perform the part which devolved upon it elsewhere. On adopting the faith of Saint Remi, the Franks found in Gaul a Roman clergy, wealthy and influential, who necessarily undertook to modify the institutions, ideas, and manner of life, as well as the religious belief of the conquerors. The Christian clergy of the Saxons were themselves Saxons, long as uncouth and barbarous as the members of their flocks, but never estranged from, or indifferent to, their feelings and recollections. Thus the young civilization of the North grew up, in England, in all the simplicity and energy of its nature, and in complete independence of the borrowed forms and foreign sap which it elsewhere received from the old civilization of the South. This important fact, which perhaps determined the course of political institutions in England, could not fail to exercise great influence over the character and development of her poetry also.

A nation that proceeds in such strict conformity to its first impulse, and never ceases to belong entirely to itself, naturally regards itself with looks of complacency. The feeling of property attaches, in its view, to all that affects it, and the joy of pride to all that it produces. Its poets, when inspired to relate to it its own deeds, and describe its own customs, are certain of never meeting with an ear that will not listen or a heart that will not respond; their art is at once the charm of the lower classes of society, and the honor of the most exalted ranks. More than in any other country, poetry is united with important events in the ancient history of England. It introduced Alfred into the tents of the Danish leaders; four centuries before, it had enabled the Saxon Bardulph to penetrate into the city of York, in which the

Britons held his brother Colgrim besieged; sixty years later, it accompanied Anlaf, king of the Danes, into the camp of Athelstan; and, in the twelfth century, it achieved the honor of effecting the deliverance of Richard Cœur-deLion. These old narratives, and a host of others, however doubtful they may be supposed, prove at least how present to the imagination of the people were the art and profession of the minstrel. A fact of more modern date fully attests the power which these popular poets long exercised over the multitude: Hugh, first Earl of Chester, had decreed, in the foundation deed of the Abbey of St. Werburgh, that the fair of Chester should be, during its whole duration, a place of asylum for criminals, excepting in the case of crimes committed in the fair itself. In the year 1212, during the reign of King John, and at the time of this fair, Ranulph, last Earl of Chester, traveling into Wales, was attacked by the Welsh, and compelled to retire to his castle of Rothelan, in which they besieged him. He succeeded in informing Roger, or John de Lacy, the Constable of Chester, of his position; this nobleman interested the minstrels who had come to the fair in the cause of the earl; and they so powerfully excited, with their songs, the multitude of outlawed persons then collected at Chester beneath the safeguard of the privilege of St. Werburgh, that they marched forth, under the command of young Hugh Dutton, the steward of Lord de Lacy, to deliver the earl from his perilous situation. It was not necessary to come to blows, for the Welsh, when they beheld the approach of this troop, thought it was an army, and raised the siege; and the grateful Ranulph immediately granted, to the minstrels of the county of Chester, various privileges, which they were to enjoy under the protection of the Lacy family, who afterward transferred this patronage to the Duttons and their descendants.[3]

3. During the reign of Elizabeth, when fallen from their ancient splendor, but still of such importance that the law, which would no longer protect them, was obliged to pay attention to them, the minstrels were, by an act of Parliament, classed in the same category with beggars and vagabonds; but an exception was made in favor of those protected by the Dutton family, and they continued freely to exercise their profession and privileges, in honorable remembrance of the service by which they had gained them.

Nor do the chronicles alone bear witness to the number and popularity of the minstrels; from time to time they are mentioned in the acts of the Legislature. In 1315, during the reign of Edward II, the Royal Council, being desirous to suppress vagabondage, forbade all persons, "except minstrels," to stop at the houses of prelates, earls, and barons, to eat and drink; nor might there enter, on each day, into such houses, "more than three or four minstrels of honor," unless the proprietor himself invited a greater number. Into the abodes of persons of humbler rank even minstrels might not enter unless they were invited; and they must then content themselves "with eating and drinking, and with such courtesy" as it should please the master of the house to add thereto. In 1316, while Edward was celebrating the festival of Whitsuntide, at Westminster, with his peers, a woman, "dressed in the manner of minstrels," and mounted on a large horse, caparisoned "according to the custom of minstrels," entered the banqueting hall, rode round the tables, laid a letter before the king, and, quickly turning her horse, went away with a salute to the company. The letter displeased the king, whom it blamed for having lavished liberalities on his favorites to the detriment of his faithful servants; and the porters were reprimanded for having allowed the woman to come in. Their excuse was, "that it was not the custom ever to refuse to minstrels admission into the royal houses." During the reign of Henry VI, we find that the minstrels, who undertook to impart mirth to festivals, were frequently better paid than the priests who came to solemnize them. To the festival of the Holy Cross, at Abingdon, came twelve priests and twelve minstrels; each of the former received "fourpence," and each of the latter "two shillings and fourpence." In 1441, eight priests, from Coventry, who had been invited to Maxtoke Priory to perform an annual service, received two shillings each; but the six minstrels who had been appointed to amuse the assembled monks in the refectory had four shillings apiece, and supped with the sub-prior in the "painted chamber," which was lighted up for the occasion with eight large flambeaux of wax, the expense of which is set down in due form in the accounts of the convent.

Thus, wherever festivities took place, wherever men gathered together for amusement, in convents and fairs, in the public highways and in the castles of the nobility, the minstrels were always present, mixing with all classes of society, and charming, with their songs and tales, the inhabitants of the country and the dwellers in towns, the rich and the poor, the farmers, the monks, and the nobles of high degree. Their arrival was at once an event and a custom, their intervention a luxury and a necessity; at no time, and in no place, could they fail to collect around them an eager crowd; they were protected by the public favor, and Parliament often had them under consideration, sometimes to recognize their rights, but more frequently to repress the abuses occasioned by their wandering life and increasing numbers.

What, then, were the manners of the people who took such enthusiastic delight in these amusements? What leisure had they for the indulgence of their taste? What opportunities, what festive occasions collected these men so frequently together, and provided these popular bards with a multitude ever ready to listen and applaud? That, beneath the brilliant sky of the South, free from the necessity of striving against natural hardships, invited by the mildness of the climate and the genial warmth of the sun to live in the open air beneath the cooling shade of their olive trees, devolving upon their slaves the performance of all laborious duties, and uncontrolled by any domestic habits, the Greeks should have thronged around their rhapsodists, and, at a later period, crowded their open theatres, to yield their imagination to the charm of the simple narratives or pathetic delineations of poetry; or that even in our own day, under the influence of their scorching atmosphere and idle life, the Arabs, gathering round an animated story teller, should spend entire days in following the course of his adventures—all this we can understand and explain; there the sky is not inclement, and material life requires none of those efforts which prevent men from giving themselves up to pleasures of this kind; nor are their institutions opposed to their indulgence in such enjoyments, but all things combine, on the contrary, to render their attainment easy and natural, and to occasion numerous meetings, frequent festivities, and protracted periods of leisure. But it was in a northern climate, beneath the sway of a cold and severe nature, in a society partially subject to the feudal system, and among a people living a difficult and laborious life, that the English minstrels found repeated opportunities for the exercise of their art, and were always sure that a crowd would collect to witness their performance.

The reason for this is, that the habits of England, being formed by the influence of the same causes that led to the establishment of her political institutions, early assumed that character of agitation and publicity which calls for the appearance of a popular poetry. In other countries, the general tendency was to the separation of the various social conditions, and even to the isolation of individuals. In England, every thing combined to bring them into contact and connection. The principle of common deliberation upon matters of common interest, which is the foundation of all liberty, prevailed in all the institutions of England, and presided over all the customs of the country. The freemen of the rural districts and the towns never ceased to meet together for the discussion and transaction of their common affairs. The county courts, the jury, corporate associations, and elections of all kinds, multiplied occasions for meeting, and diffused in every direction the habits of public life. That hierarchical organization of feudalism, which, on the Continent, extended from the poorest gentleman to the most powerful monarch, and was incessantly stimulating the vanity of every man to leave his own sphere and pass into the rank of suzerain, was never completely established in Great Britain. The nobility of the second order, by separating themselves from the great barons, in order to take their place at the head of the commons, returned, so to speak, into the body of the nation, and adopted its manners as well as assumed its rights. It was on his own estate, among his tenants, farmers, and servants, that the gentleman established his importance; and he based it upon the cultivation of his lands and the discharge of those local magistrates which, by placing him in connection with the whole of the population, necessitated the concurrence of public opinion, and provided the adjacent district with a centre

around which it might rally. Thus, while active rights brought
equals into communication, rural life created a bond of union
between the superior and his inferior; and agriculture, by the
community of its interests and labors, bound the whole population together by ties, which, descending successively from class
to class, were in some sort terminated and sealed in the earth,
the immutable basis of their union.

Such a state of society leads to competence and confidence;
and where competence reigns and confidence is felt, the necessity of common enjoyment soon arises. Men who are accustomed
to meet together for business will meet together for pleasure
also; and when the serious life of the land-owner is spent among
his fields, he does not remain a stranger to the joys of the people
who cultivate or surround them. Continual and general festivals
gave animation to the country life of Old England. . . .

Amid these games, festivals, and banquets, at these innumerable friendly meetings, and in this joyous and habitual conviviality (to use the national expression), the minstrels took their place
and sang their songs. The subjects of these songs were the traditions of the country, the adventures of popular heroes as well as
of noble champions, the exploits of Robin Hood against the
sheriff of Nottingham, as well as the conflicts of the Percies with
the Douglas clan. Thus the public manners called for poetry; thus
poetry originated in the manners of the people, and became connected with all the interests, and with the entire existence, of a
population accustomed to live, to act, to prosper, and to rejoice
in common.

How could dramatic poetry have remained unknown to a people of such a character, so frequently assembling together, and
so fond of holidays? We have every reason to believe that it was
more than once introduced into the games of the minstrels. The
ancient writers speak of them under the names of *mimi, jocula-
tores,* and *histriones.* Women were frequently connected with
their bands; and several of their ballads, among others that of
"The Nut-brown Maid," are evidently in the form of dialogue.
The minstrels, however, rather formed the national taste, and
directed it to the drama, than originated the drama itself. The

first attempts at a true theatrical performance are difficult and expensive. The cooperation of a public power is indispensable; and it is only in important and general solemnities that the effect produced by the play can possibly correspond to the efforts of imagination and labor which it has cost. England, like France, Italy, and Spain, was indebted for her first theatrical performances to the festivals of the clergy; only they were, it would appear, of earlier origin in that country than elsewhere. The performance of Mysteries in England can be traced back as far as the twelfth century, and probably originated at a still earlier period. But in France, the clergy, after having erected theatres, were not slow to denounce them. They had claimed the privilege in the hope of being able, by the means of such performances, to maintain or stimulate the conquests of the faith; but ere long they began to dread their effects, and abandoned their employment. The English clergy were more intimately associated with the tastes, habits, and diversions of the people. The Church, also, took advantage of that universal conviviality which I have just described. Was any great religious ceremony to be celebrated? or was any parish in want of funds? A *Church-ale*[4] was announced; the church-wardens brewed some beer, and sold it to the people at the door of the church, and to the rich in the interior of the church itself. Every one contributed his money, presence, provisions, and mirth to the festival; the joy of good works was augmented by the pleasures of good cheer, and the piety of the rich rejoiced to exceed, by their gifts, the price demanded. It often happened that several parishes united to hold the *Church-ale* by turns for the profit of each. The ordinary games followed these meetings; the minstrel, the morris dance, and the performance of Robin Hood, with Maid Marian and the Hobby Horse, were never absent. The seasons of confession, Easter and Whitsuntide, also furnished the Church and the people with periodical opportunities for common rejoicings. Thus familiar with the popular manners, the English clergy, when offering new pleasures to the people, thought less of modi-

4. Also called Whitsun-ale. Beer was so intimately connected with the popular festivals that the word *ale* had become synonymous with *holiday.*

fying them than of turning them to account; and when they perceived the fondness of the people for dramatic performances, whatever the subject might be, they had no idea of renouncing so powerful a means of gaining popularity. In 1378, the choristers of St. Paul's complained to Richard II that certain ignorant fellows had presumed to perform histories from the Old Testament, "to the great prejudice of the clergy." After this period, the Mysteries and Moralities never ceased to be, both in churches and convents, a favorite amusement of the nation, and a leading occupation of the ecclesiastics. At the beginning of the sixteenth century, an Earl of Northumberland, who was a great protector of literature, established, as a rule of his household, that the sole business of one of his chaplains should be to compose interludes. Toward the end of his reign, Henry VIII forbade the Church to continue these performances, which, in the wavering state of his belief, were displeasing to the king, and offended him sometimes as a Catholic and sometimes as a Protestant. But they reappeared after his death, and were sanctioned by such high authority, that the young king, Edward VI, himself composed a piece against the Papists, entitled "The Whore of Babylon," and Queen Mary, in her turn, commanded the performance, in the churches, of popular dramas favorable to Popery. Finally, in 1569, we find the choristers of St. Paul's, "clothed in silk and satin," playing profane pieces in Elizabeth's chapel, in the different royal houses; and they were so well skilled in their profession, that, in Shakspeare's time, they constituted one of the best and most popular troops of actors in London.

Far, therefore, from opposing or seeking to change the taste of the people for theatrical representations, the English clergy hastened to gratify it. Their influence, it is true, gave to the works which they brought on the stage a more serious and moral character than was possessed in other countries by compositions dependent upon the whims of the public, and cursed by the anathemas of the Church. Notwithstanding its coarseness of ideas and language, the English drama, which became so licentious in the reign of Charles II, appears chaste and pure in the middle of the sixteenth century, when compared to the first essays of dramatic composition in France. But it did not the less continue to be popular in its character, ignorant of all scientific regularity, and faithful to the national taste. The clergy would have lost much by endeavoring to suppress theatrical performances. They possessed no exclusive privilege; and numerous competitors vied with them for applause and success. Robin Hood and Maid Marian, the Lord of Misrule and the Hobby Horse, had not yet disappeared. Traveling actors, attached to the service of the powerful nobles, traversed the counties of England under their auspices, and obtained, by favor of a gratuitous performance before the mayor, aldermen, and their friends, the right of exercising their profession in the various towns, the courtyards of inns usually serving as their theatre. As they were in a position to give greater pomp to their exhibitions, and thus to attract a larger number of spectators, the clergy struggled successfully against their rivals, and even maintained a marked predominance, but always upon condition of adapting their representations to the feelings, habits, and imaginative character of the people, who had been formed to a taste for poetry by their own festivals and by the songs of the minstrels.

Such was the condition and tendency of dramatic poetry, when, at the commencement of the reign of Elizabeth, it appeared threatened by a two-fold danger. As it daily became more popular, it at last awakened the anxiety of religious severity and fired the ambition of literary pedantry. The national taste found itself attacked, almost simultaneously, by the anathemas of the Reformers and the pretensions of men of letters.

If these two classes of enemies had united in their opposition to the drama, it would, perhaps, have fallen a victim to their attacks. But while the Puritans wished to destroy it, men of letters only desired to get it into their own hands. It was, therefore, defended by the latter when the former inveighed against its existence. Some influential citizens of London obtained from Elizabeth the temporary suppression of stage plays within the jurisdiction of the civic authorities; but, beyond that jurisdiction, the Blackfriars' Theatre and the court of the Queen still retained their dramatic privileges. The Puritans, by their sermons, may have alarmed some few consciences, and occasioned some few scruples; and perhaps, also, some sudden conversions may here and there have deprived the May day games of the performance of the Hobby Horse, their greatest ornament, and the special object of the wrath of the preachers. But the time of the power of the Puritans had not yet arrived, and, to obtain decisive success, it was too much to have to overcome at once the national taste and the taste of the court.

Elizabeth's court would well have liked to be classical. Theological discussions had made learning fashionable. At that time it was an essential part of the education of a noble lady to be able to read Greek, and to distill strong waters. The known taste of the queen had added to these the gallantries of ancient mythology. "When she paid a visit at the house of any of her nobility," says Warton,

> at entering the hall she was saluted by the Penates, and conducted to her privy-chamber by Mercury. The pages of the family were converted into wood-nymphs, who peeped from every bower; and the footmen gamboled over the lawns in the figure of Satyrs. When she rode through the streets of Norwich, Cupid, at the command of the mayor and aldermen, advancing from a group of gods who had left Olympus to grace the procession, gave her a golden arrow, which, under the influence of such irresistible charms, was sure to wound the most obdurate heart: "a gift," says Holinshed, "which her majesty, now verging to her fiftieth year, received very thankfully."[5]

But the court may strive in vain; it is not the purveyor of its own pleasures; it rarely makes choice of them, invents them even less frequently, and generally receives them at the hands of men who make it their business to provide for its amusement. The empire of classical literature, which was established in France before the foundation of the stage, was the work of men of letters, who derived protection from, and felt justly proud of, the exclusive possession of a foreign erudition which raised them above the rest of the nation. The court of France submitted to the guidance of the men of letters; and the nation at large, un-

5. Warton, *History of English Poetry*, vol. 3, pp. 492, 493.

decided how to act, and destitute of those institutions which might have given authority to its habits and influence to its tastes, formed into groups, as it were, around the court. In England the drama had taken precedence of classic lore; ancient history and mythology found a popular poetry and creed in possession of the means of delighting the minds of the people; and the study of the classics, which became known at a late period, and at first only by the medium of French translations, was introduced as one of those foreign fashions by which a few men may render themselves remarkable, but which take root only when they fall into harmonious accordance with the national taste. The court itself sometimes affected, as evidence of its attainments, exclusive admiration for ancient literature; but as soon as it stood in need of amusement, it followed the example of the general public; and, indeed, it was not easy to pass from the exhibition of a bear-baiting to the pretensions of classical severity, even according to the ideas then entertained regarding it.

.   .   .   .

The first dramatic work which the imagination of Shakspeare truly produced was a comedy; and this comedy will be followed by others: he has at last taken wing, but not as yet toward the realms of tragedy. Corneille also began with comedy, but he was then ignorant of his own powers, and almost ignorant of the drama. The familiar scenes of life had alone presented themselves to his thoughts; and the scenes of his comedies are laid in his native town, in the Galerie du Palais and in the Place Royale. His subjects are timidly borrowed from surrounding circumstances; he has not yet risen above himself, or transcended his limited sphere; his vision has not yet penetrated into those ideal regions in which his imagination will one day roam at will. But Shakspeare is already a poet; imitation no longer trammels his progress; and his conceptions are no longer formed exclusively within the world of his habits. How was it that the frivolous spirit of comedy was his first guide into that poetic world from which he drew his inspiration? Why did not the emotions of tragedy first awaken the powers of so eminently tragic a poet? Was it this circumstance which led Johnson to give this singular opinion: "Shakspeare's tragedy seems to be skill; his comedy to be instinct"?

Assuredly, nothing can be more whimsical than to refuse to Shakspeare the instinct of tragedy; and if Johnson had had any feeling of it himself, such an idea would never have entered his mind. The fact which I have just stated, however, is not open to doubt; it is well deserving of explanation, and has its causes in the very nature of comedy, as it was understood and treated by Shakspeare.

Shakspeare's comedy is not, in fact, the comedy of Molière; nor is it that of Aristophanes, or of the Latin poets. Among the Greeks, and in France, in modern times, comedy was the off-spring of a free but attentive observation of the real world, and its object was to bring its features on the stage. The distinction between the tragic and the comic styles is met with almost in the cradle of dramatic art, and their separation has always become more distinctly marked during the course of their progress. The principle of this distinction is contained in the very nature of things. The destiny and nature of man, his passions and affairs, characters and events—all things within and around us—have their serious and their amusing sides, and may be considered and described under either of these points of view. This two-fold aspect of man and the world has opened to dramatic poetry two careers naturally distinct; but in dividing its powers to traverse them both, art has neither separated itself from realities, nor ceased to observe and reproduce them. Whether Aristophanes attacks, with the most fantastic liberty of imagination, the vices or follies of the Athenians; or whether Molière depicts the absurdities of credulity and avarice, of jealousy and pedantry, and ridicules the frivolity of courts, the vanity of citizens, and even the affectation of virtues, it matters little that there is a difference between the subjects in the delineation of which the two poets have employed their powers; it matters little that one brought public life and the whole nation on the stage, while the other merely described incidents of private life, the interior arrangements of families, and the nonsensicality of individual characters; this difference in the materials of comedy arises from the difference of time, place, and state of civilization. But in both Aristophanes and Molière realities always constitute the substance of the picture. The manners and ideas of their times, the vices and follies of their fellow-citizens—in a word, the nature and life of man—are always the stimulus and nutriment of their poetic vein. Comedy thus takes its origin in the world which surrounds the poet, and is connected, much more closely than tragedy, with external and real facts.

The Greeks, whose mind and civilization followed so regular a course in their development, did not combine the two kinds of composition, and the distinction which separates them in nature was maintained without effort in art. Simplicity prevailed among this people; society was not abandoned by them to a state of conflict and incoherence; and their destiny did not pass away in protracted obscurity, in the midst of contrasts, and a prey to dark and deep uneasiness. They grew and shone in their land just as the sun rose and pursued its course through the skies which overshadowed them. National perils, internal discord, and civil wars agitated the life of a man in those days, without disturbing his imagination, and without opposing or deranging the natural and easy course of his thoughts. The reflex influence of this general harmony was diffused over literature and the arts. Styles of composition spontaneously became distinguished from each other, according to the principles upon which they depended and the impressions which they aspired to produce. The sculptor chiseled isolated statues or small groups, and did not aim at composing violent scenes or vast pictures out of blocks of marble. Æschylus, Sophocles, and Euripides undertook to excite the people by the narration of the mighty destinies of heroes and of kings. Cratinus and Aristophanes aimed at diverting them by the representation of the absurdities of their contemporaries or of their own follies. These natural classifications corresponded with the entire system of social order, with the state of the minds of the age, and with the instincts of public taste—which would have been shocked at their violation, which desired to yield without uncertainty or participation to a single impression or a single pleasure, and which would have rejected all those unnatural mixtures and uncongenial combinations to which their attention had never been called or their judgment accustomed. Thus every art and every style received its free and isolated development within the limits of its proper mission. Thus tragedy and comedy shared man and the world between them, each taking a different domain in the region of realities, and coming by turns to offer to the serious or mirthful consideration of a people who invariably insisted upon simplicity and harmony, the poetic effects which their skill could derive from the materials placed in their hands.

In our modern world, all things have borne another character. Order, regularity, natural and easy development, seem to have been banished from it. Immense interests, admirable ideas, sublime sentiments, have been thrown, as it were, pell-mell with brutal passions, coarse necessities, and vulgar habits. Obscurity, agitation, and disturbance have reigned in minds as well as in states. Nations have been formed, not of freemen and slaves, but of a confused mixture of diverse, complicated classes, ever engaged in conflict and labor; a violent chaos, which civilization, after long-continued efforts, has not yet succeeded in reducing to complete harmony. Social conditions, separated by power, but united in a common barbarism of manners; the germ of loftiest moral truths fermenting in the midst of absurd ignorance; great virtues applied in opposition to all reason; shameful vices maintained and defended with hauteur; an indocile honor, ignorant of the simplest delicacies of honesty; boundless servility, accompanied by measureless pride; in fine, the incoherent assemblage of all that human nature and destiny contain of that which is great and little, noble and trivial, serious and puerile, strong and wretched—this is what man and society have been in our Europe; this is the spectacle which has appeared on the theatre of the world.

In such a state of mind and things, how was it possible for a clear distinction and simple classification of styles and arts to be effected? How could tragedy and comedy have presented and formed themselves isolatedly in literature, when, in reality, they were incessantly in contact, entwined in the same facts, and intermingled in the same actions, so thoroughly, that it was sometimes difficult to discern the moment of passage from one to the other. Neither the rational principle, nor the delicate feeling which separate them, could attain any development in minds which were incapacitated from apprehending them by the disorder and rapidity of different or opposite impressions. Was it proposed to bring upon the stage the habitual occurrences of ordinary life? Taste was as easily satisfied as manners. Those religious performances which were the origin of the European theatre, had not escaped this admixture. Christianity is a popular religion; into the abyss of terrestrial miseries, its divine founder came in search of men, to draw them to himself; its early history is a history of poor, sick, and feeble men; it existed at first for a long while in obscurity, and afterward in the midst of persecutions, despised and proscribed by turns, and exposed to all the vicissitudes and efforts of a humble and violent destiny. Uncultivated imaginations easily seized upon the triviality which might be intermingled with the incidents of this history; the Gospel, the acts of martyrs, and the lives of saints, would have struck them much less powerfully if they had seen only their tragic aspect or their rational truths. The first Mysteries brought simultaneously upon the stage the emotions of religious terror and tenderness, and the buffooneries of vulgar comedy; and thus, in the very cradle of dramatic poetry, tragedy and comedy contracted that alliance which was inevitably forced upon them by the general condition of nations and of minds.

In France, however, this alliance was speedily broken off. From causes which are connected with the entire history of our civilization, the French people have always taken extreme pleasure in drollery. Of this, our literature has from time to time given evidence. This craving for gayety, and for gayety without alloy, early supplied the inferior classes of our countrymen with their comic farces, into which nothing was admitted that had not a tendency to excite laughter. In the infancy of the art, comedy in France may very possibly have invaded the domain of tragedy,

but tragedy had no right to the field which comedy had reserved
to itself; and in the *piteous* Moralities and *pompous* Tragedies
which princes caused to be represented in their palaces, and rec-
tors in their colleges, the trivially comic element long retained
a place which was inexorably refused to the tragic element in
the buffooneries with which the people were amused. We may
therefore affirm that in France comedy, in an imperfect but distinct form, was created before tragedy. At a later period, the
rigorous separation of classes, the absence of popular institutions, the regular action of the supreme power, the establishment of a more exact and uniform system of public order than
existed in any other country, the habits and influence of the court,
and a variety of other causes, disposed the popular mind to maintain that strict distinction between the two styles which was or-
dained by the classical authorities, who held undisputed sway
over our drama. Then arose among us true and great comedy, as conceived by Molière; and as it was in accordance with
our manners, as well as with the rules of the art, to strike out
a new path—as, while adapting itself to the precepts of antiquity,
it did not fail to derive its subjects and coloring from the facts and
personages of the surrounding world, our comedy suddenly rose
to a pitch of perfection which, in my opinion, has never been attained by any other country in any other age. To place himself
in the interior of families, and thereby to gain the immense advantage of a variety of ideas and conditions, which extends the
domain of art without injuring the simplicity of the effects which
it produces; to find in man passions sufficiently strong, and caprices sufficiently powerful to sway his whole destiny, and
yet to limit their influence to the suggestion of those errors which
may make man ridiculous, without ever touching upon those
which would render him miserable; to describe an individual as
laboring under that excess of preoccupation which, diverting
him from all other thoughts, abandons him entirely to the guidance of the idea which possesses him, and yet to throw in his
way only those interests which are sufficiently frivolous to enable
him to compromise them without danger; to depict, in *Tartuffe*,
the threatening knavery of the hypocrite, and the dangerous im-

121

becility of the dupe, in such a manner as merely to divert the
spectator, without incurring any of the odious consequences of
such a position; to give a comic character, in the *Misanthrope*, to
those feelings which do most honor to the human race, by condemning them to confinement within the dimensions of the
existence of a courtier; and thus to reach the amusing by means
of the serious; to extract food for mirth from the inmost recesses
of human nature, and incessantly to maintain the character of
comedy while bordering upon the confines of tragedy—this is
what Molière has done, this is the difficult and original style
which he bestowed upon France; and France alone, in my
opinion, could have given dramatic art this tendency, and
Molière.

Nothing of this kind took place among the English. The
asylum of German manners, as well as of German liberties,
England pursued, without obstacle, the irregular, but natural
course of the civilization which such elements could not fail
to engender. It retained their disorder as well as their energy,
and, until the middle of the seventeenth century, its literature,
as well as its institutions, was the sincere expression of these
qualities. When the English drama attempted to reproduce the
poetic image of the world, tragedy and comedy were not separated. The predominance of the popular taste sometimes carried
tragic representations to a pitch of atrocity which was unknown
in France, even in the rudest essays of dramatic art; and the
influence of the clergy, by purging the comic stage of that excessive immorality which it exhibited elsewhere, also deprived it
of that malicious and sustained gayety which constitutes the
essence of true comedy. The habits of mind which were entertained among the people by the minstrels and their ballads, allowed the introduction, even into those compositions which
were most exclusively devoted to mirthfulness, of some touches
of those emotions which comedy in France can never admit without losing its name, and becoming melodrama. Among truly
national works, the only thoroughly comic play which the English stage possessed before the time of Shakspeare, "Grammer
Gurton's Needle," was composed for a college, and modeled in

accordance with the classic rules. The vague titles given to dramatic works, such as *play, interlude, history,* or even *ballad,* scarcely ever indicate any distinction of style. Thus, between that which was called *tragedy* and that which was sometimes named *comedy,* the only essential difference consisted in the *dénouement,* according to the principles laid down in the fifteenth century by the monk Lydgate, who "defines a comedy to begin with complaint and to end with gladness, whereas tragedy begins in prosperity and ends in adversity."

.   .   .   .

Guizot has been discussing the history of dramatic poetry and how it deals with the question of "the nature and destiny of man." He has just mentioned Racine's Athalie *as flawed but reaching nearly "the ideal of dramatic poetry."*

Though easily attained among the Greeks, whose life and feelings might be summed up in a few large and simple features, this ideal did not present itself to modern nations under forms sufficiently general and pure to receive the application of the rules laid down in accordance with the ancient models. France, in order to adopt them, was compelled to limit its field, in some sort, to one corner of human existence. Our poets have employed all the powers of genius to turn this narrow space to advantage; the abysses of the heart have been sounded to their utmost depth, but not in all their dimensions. Dramatic illusion has been sought as its true source, but it has not been required to furnish all the effects that might have been obtained from it. Shakspeare offers to us a more fruitful and a vaster system. It would be a strange mistake to suppose that he has discovered and brought to light all its wealth. When we embrace human destiny in all its aspects, and human nature in all the conditions of man upon earth, we enter into possession of an inexhaustible treasure. It is the peculiar advantage of such a system, that it escapes, by its extent, from the dominion of any particular genius. We may discover its principles in Shakspeare's works; but he was not fully acquainted with them, nor did he always respect them. He should serve as an example, not as a model. Some men, even of superior talent, have attempted to write plays according to Shakspeare's taste, without perceiving that they were deficient in one important qualification for the task; and that was, to write as he did, to write them for our age, just as Shakspeare's plays were written for the age in which he lived. This is an enterprise, the difficulties of which have hitherto, perhaps, been maturely considered by no one. We have seen how much art and effort was employed by Shakspeare to surmount those which are inherent in his system. They are still greater in our times, and would unveil themselves much more completely to the spirit of criticism which now accompanies the boldest essays of genius. It is not only with spectators of more fastidious taste, and of more idle and inattentive imagination, that the poet would have to contend, who should venture to follow in Shakspeare's footsteps. He would be called upon to give movement to personages embarrassed in much more complicated interests, preoccupied with much more various feelings, and subject to less simple habits of mind, and to less decided tendencies. Neither science, nor reflection, nor the scruples of conscience, nor the uncertainties of thought, frequently encumber Shakspeare's heroes; doubt is of little use among them, and the violence of their passions speedily transfers their belief to the side of their desires, or sets their actions above their belief. Hamlet alone presents the confused spectacle of a mind formed by the enlightenment of society, in conflict with a position contrary to its laws; and he needs a supernatural apparition to determine him to act, and a fortuitous event to accomplish his project. If incessantly placed in an analogous position, the personages of a tragedy conceived at the present day, according to the romantic system, would offer us the same picture of indecision. Ideas now crowd and intersect each other in the mind of man, duties multiply in his conscience, and obstacles and bonds impede his life. Instead of those electric brains, prompt to communicate the spark which they have received—instead of those ardent and simpleminded men, whose projects, like Macbeth's, "will to hand"—the world now presents to the poet minds like Hamlet's, deep in the observation of those inward conflicts which our classical system has derived from a state of society more advanced than that of the time in which Shakspeare lived. So many feelings, interests, and ideas, the necessary consequences of modern civilization, might become, even in their simplest form of expression, a troublesome burden, which it would be difficult to carry through the rapid evolutions and bold advances of the romantic system.

We must, however, satisfy every demand; success itself requires it. The reason must be contented at the same time that the imagination is occupied. The progress of taste, of enlightenment, of society, and of mankind, must serve, not to diminish or disturb our enjoyment, but to render them worthy of ourselves, and capable of supplying the new wants which we have contracted. Advance without rule and art in the romantic system, and you will produce melodrames calculated to excite a passing emotion in the multitude, but in the multitude alone, and for a few days; just as, by dragging along without originality in the classical system, you will satisfy only that cold literary class who are acquainted with nothing in nature which is more important than the interests of versification, or more imposing than the three unities. This is not the work of the poet who is called to power and destined for glory; he acts upon a grander scale, and can address the superior intellects, as well as the general and simple faculties of all men. It is doubtless necessary that the crowd should throng to behold those dramatic works of which you desire to make a national spectacle; but do not hope to become national if you do not unite in your festivities all those classes of persons and minds whose well-arranged hierarchy raises a nation to its loftiest dignity. Genius is bound to follow human nature in all its developments; its strength consists in finding within itself the means for constantly satisfying the whole of the public. The same task is now imposed upon government and upon poetry; both should exist for all, and suffice at once for the wants of the masses and for the requirements of the most exalted minds.

Doubtless stopped in its course by these conditions, the full severity of which will only be revealed to the talent that can comply with them, dramatic art, even in England, where, under the protection of Shakspeare, it would have liberty to attempt any thing, scarcely ventures at the present day to endeavor timidly to follow him. Meanwhile, England, France, and the whole of Europe demand of the drama pleasures and emotions that can no longer be supplied by the inanimate representation of a world that has ceased to exist. The classical system had its origin in the life of its time; that time has passed; its image subsists in brilliant colors in its works, but can no more be reproduced. Near the monuments of past ages, the monuments of another age are now beginning to arise. What will be their form? I can not tell; but the ground upon which their foundations may rest is already perceptible. This ground is not the ground of Corneille and Racine, nor is it that of Shakspeare; it is our own; but Shakspeare's system, as it appears to me, may furnish the plans according to which genius ought now to work. This system alone includes all those social conditions and all those general or diverse feelings, the simultaneous conjunction and activity of which constitute for us, at the present day, the spectacle of human things. Witnesses, during thirty years, of the greatest revolutions of society, we shall no longer willingly confine the movement of our mind within the narrow space of some family event, or the agitations of a purely individual passion. The nature and destiny of man have appeared to us under their most striking and their simplest aspect, in all their extent and in all their variableness. We require pictures in which this spectacle is reproduced, in which man is displayed in his completeness, and excites our entire sympathy. The moral dispositions which impose this necessity upon poetry will not change; but we shall see them, on the contrary, manifesting themselves more plainly, and receiving greater development, day by day. Interests, duties, and a movement common to all classes of citizens, will strengthen among them that chain of habitual relations with which all public feelings connect themselves. Never could dramatic art have taken its subjects from an order of ideas at once more popular and more elevated; never was the connection between the most vulgar interests of man and the principles upon which his highest destinies are dependent, more clearly present to all minds; and the importance of an event may now appear in its pettiest details as well as in its mightiest results. In this state of society, a new dramatic system ought to be established. It should be liberal and free, but not without principles and laws. It should establish itself like liberty, not upon disorder and forgetfulness of every check, but upon rules more severe and more difficult of observance, perhaps, than those which are still enforced to maintain what is called order against what is designated license.

4

The History of the English Revolution Preface

I HAVE published the original memoirs of the English revolution; I now publish its history. Previous to the French revolution, this was the greatest event which Europe had to narrate.

I have no fear of its importance being underrated; our revolution, in surpassing, did not make that of England less great in itself; they were both victories in the same war, and to the profit of the same cause; glory is their common attribute; they do not eclipse, but set off each other. My fear is lest their true character should be mistaken, lest the world should not assign to them that place which is properly theirs in the world's history.

According to an opinion now widely adopted, it would seem as though these two revolutions were unexpected events, which, emanating from principles and conceived in designs unheard of before, threw society out of its ancient and natural course; hurricanes, earthquakes—instances, in a word, of those mysterious phenomena which altogether depart from the ordinary laws of nature, and which burst forth suddenly—blows, as it were, of Providence—it may be to destroy, it may be to renovate. Friends and enemies, panegyrists and detractors, alike adopt this view.

Preface to the First Edition, *The History of the English Revolution*, translated by William Hazlitt (London: H. G. Bohn, 1856), from *L'Histoire de la Révolution d'Angleterre* (1826).

According to the one class, they were glorious events, which brought to light, for the first time, truth, liberty, and justice, before the occurrence of which all was absurdity, iniquity, and tyranny; to which alone the human race owes its terrestrial salvation. According to the other class, they were deplorable calamities, which interrupted a long golden age of wisdom, virtue, and happiness; whose perpetrators proclaimed maxims, put forward pretensions, and committed crimes, till then without parallel: the nations in a paroxysm of madness dashed aside from their accustomed road; an abyss opened beneath their feet.

Thus, whether they exalt or deplore them, whether they bless or curse them, all parties, in considering revolutions, forget all the circumstances, alike isolate them absolutely from the past, alike make them in themselves responsible for the destiny of the world, and load them with anathema or crown them with glory.

It is time to get clear of all such false and puerile declamation. Far from having interrupted the natural course of events in Europe, neither the English revolution nor our own, ever said, wished, or did anything that had not been said, wished, done, or attempted, a hundred times before they burst forth. They proclaimed the illegality of absolute power; the free consent of the people, in reference to laws and taxes, and the right of armed resistance, were elemental principles of the feudal system; and the church has often repeated these words of St. Isidore, which we find in the canons of the fourth council of Toledo: "He is king who rules his people with justice; if he rule otherwise, he shall no longer be king." They attacked prerogative, and sought to introduce greater equality into social order: kings throughout Europe have done the same; and, down to our own times, the various steps in the progress of civil equality have been founded upon the laws and measured by the progress of royalty. They demanded that public offices should be thrown open to the citizens at large, should be distributed according to merit only, and that power should be conferred by election: this is the fundamental principle of the internal government of the church, which not only acts upon it, but has emphatically proclaimed its worth. Whether we consider the general doctrines of the two revolutions, or the results to which they were applied—whether we regard the government of the state, or civil legislation, property or persons, liberty or power—nothing will be found of which the invention originated with them, nothing which is not equally met with, or which, at all events, did not come into existence in periods which are called regular.

Nor is this all: those principles, those designs, those efforts which are attributed exclusively to the English revolution and to our own, not only preceded them by several centuries, but are precisely the same principles, the same efforts, to which society in Europe owes all its progress. Was it by its disorders and its privileges, by its brute force, and by keeping men down beneath its yoke, that the feudal aristocracy took part in the development of nations? No: it struggled against royal tyranny, exercised the right of resistance, and maintained the maxims of liberty. For what have nations blessed kings? Was it for their pretensions to divine right, to absolute power? for their profusion? for their courts? No: kings assailed the feudal system and aristocratical privileges; they introduced unity into legislation, and into the executive administration; they aided the progress of equality. And the clergy—whence does it derive its power? how has it promoted civilization? Was it by separating itself from the people, by taking fright at human reason, by sanctioning tyranny in the name of Heaven? No: it gathered together, without distinction, in its churches, and under the law of God, the great and the small, the poor and the rich, the weak and the strong; it honoured and fostered science, instituted schools, favoured the propagation of knowledge, and gave activity to the mind. Interrogate the history of the masters of the world; examine the influence of the various classes which have decided its destiny; wherever any good shall manifest itself, wherever the lasting gratitude of man shall recognise a great service done to humanity, it will be seen that these were steps towards the object which were pursued by the English revolution and by our own; we shall find ourselves in presence of one of the principles they sought to establish.

Let these mighty events, then, no longer be held forth as

monstrous apparitions in the history of Europe; let us hear no more about their unheard-of pretensions, their infernal inventions. They advanced civilization in the path it has been pursuing for fourteen centuries; they professed the maxims, they forwarded the works to which man has, in all time, owed the development of his nature and the amelioration of his condition; they did that which has been by turns the merit and the glory of the clergy, of the aristocracy, and of kings.

I do not think mankind will much longer persist in absolutely condemning them because they are chargeable with errors, calamities, and crimes. Admit all this to the full: nay, exceed the severity of the condemners, and closely examine their accusations to supply their omissions; then summon them, in their turn, to draw up the list of the errors, the crimes, and the calamities, of those times and those powers which they have taken under their protection: I much doubt whether they will accept the challenge.

It may be asked: in what respect, then, are the two revolutions so distinguishable from any other epoch, that carrying on, as they did, the common work of ages, they merited their name, and changed, in effect, the face of the world? The answer is this:

Various powers have successively predominated in European society, and led by turns the march of civilization. After the fall of the Roman empire and the invasion of the Barbarians, amid the dissolution of all ties, the ruin of all regular power, dominion everywhere fell into the hands of bold brute force. The conquering aristocracy took possession of all things, persons and property, people and land. In vain did a few great men, Charlemagne in France, Alfred in England, attempt to subject this chaos to the unity of the monarchical system. All unity was impossible. The feudal hierarchy was the only form that society would ac-·cept. It pervaded everything, Church as well as State; bishops and abbots became barons, the king was merely chief lord. Yet, rude and unsettled as was this organization, Europe is indebted to it for its first step out of barbarism. It was among the proprietors of fiefs, by their mutual relations, their laws, their customs, their feelings, their ideas, that European civilization began.

They weighed fearfully upon the people. The clergy alone

sought to claim, on behalf of the community, a little reason, justice, and humanity. He who held no place in the feudal hierarchy, had no other asylum than the churches, no other protectors than the priests. Inadequate as it was, yet this protection was immense, for there was none beside. Moreover, the priests alone offered some food to the moral nature of man; to that invincible craving after thought, knowledge, hope, and belief, which overcomes all obstacles and survives all misfortune. The church soon acquired a prodigious power in every part of Europe. Nascent royalty added to its strength by borrowing its assistance. The preponderance passed from the conquering aristocracy to the clergy.

By the cooperation of the church and its own inherent vigour, royalty rose up to a stature above that of its rivals; but the clergy which had aided, now wished to enslave it. In this new danger, royalty called to its assistance sometimes the barons, now become less formidable, more frequently the commons, the people, already strong enough to give good help but not strong enough to demand a high price for their services. By their aid, royalty triumphed in its second struggle, and became in its turn the ruling power, invested with the confidence of nations.

Such is the history of ancient Europe. The feudal aristocracy, the clergy, royalty, by turns possessed it, successively presided over its destiny and its progress. It was to their coexistence and to their struggles that it was, for a long time, indebted for all it achieved of liberty, prosperity, enlightenment; in a word, for the development of its civilization.

In the seventeenth century in England, in the eighteenth in France, all struggle between these three powers had ceased; they lived together in sluggish peace. It may even be said, that they had lost their historical character, and even the remembrance of those efforts, which, of old, constituted their power and their splendour. The aristocracy no longer protected public liberty, nor even its own; royalty no longer laboured to abolish aristocratical privilege; it seemed, on the contrary, to have become favourable to its possesors, in return for their servility. The clergy, a spiritual power, feared the human mind, and no longer able to guide, called upon it, with threats, to check its career. Still civilization followed its course, daily more general and more active. Forsaken by its ancient leaders, astonished at their apathy and at the humour they displayed, and at seeing that less was done for it as its power and its desires grew larger, the people began to think it had better undertake to transact its own affairs itself; and, assuming in its own person all the functions which its former leaders no longer fulfilled, claimed at once of the crown liberty, of the aristocracy equality, of the clergy the rights of human intellect. Then burst forth revolutions.

These did, for the benefit of a new power, what Europe had in other cases already several times witnessed; they gave to society leaders who would and could direct it in its progress. By this title alone had the aristocracy, the church, and royalty by turns enjoyed the preponderance. The people now took possession of it by the same means, in the name of the same necessities.

Such was the true operation, the real characteristics of the English revolution as well as of our own. After having considered them as absolutely alike, it has been said that they had nothing but appearances in common. The first, it has been contended, was political rather than social; the second sought to change at once both society and government; the one sought liberty, the other equality; the one, still more religious than political, only substituted dogma for dogma, a church for a church; the other, philosophical more especially, claimed the full independence of reason: an ingenious comparison, and not without its truth, but well nigh as superficial, as frivolous as the opinion it pretends to correct. While, under the external resemblance of the two revolutions, great differences are perceptible, so, beneath their differences, is hidden a resemblance still more profound. The English Revolution, it is true, from the same causes that brought it forth an age before ours, retained a more decided impress of the ancient social state: there, free institutions, which had their origin in the very depth of barbarism, had survived the despotism they could not prevent; the feudal aristocracy, or at least a portion of it, had united its cause to that of the people;

royalty, even in the days of its supremacy, had never been fully or undisturbedly absolute; the national church had itself begun religious reform, and called forth the daring inquiries of mind. Everywhere, in the laws, the creed, the manners of the people, revolution found its work half accomplished; and from that order of things which it sought to change, came at once assistance and obstacles, useful allies and still powerful adversaries. It thus presented a singular mixture of elements, to all appearance the most contrary, at once aristocratic and popular, religious and philosophical, appealing alternately to laws and theories; now proclaiming a new yoke for conscience, now its entire liberty; sometimes narrowly confined within the limits of facts, at others soaring to the most daring attempts; placed, in short, between the old and new social state, rather as a bridge over which to pass from the one to the other, than as an abyss of separation.

The most terrible unity, on the contrary, pervaded the French revolution; the new spirit alone dominated; and the old system, far from taking its part and its place in the movement, only sought to defend itself against it, and only defended itself for a moment; it was alike without power as without virtue. On the day of the explosion, one fact only remained real and powerful, the general civilization of the country. In this great but sole result, old institutions, old manners, creeds, the memory of the past, the whole national life, had fused themselves and become lost. So many active and glorious ages had produced only France. Hence the immense results of the revolution, and also its immense errors; it possessed absolute power.

Assuredly there is a great difference, and one worthy to be well borne in mind; it strikes us more especially when we regard the two revolutions in themselves as isolated events, detached from general history, and seek to unravel, if I may so express it, their peculiar physiognomy, their individual character. But let them resume their place in the course of ages, and then inquire what they have done towards the development of European civilization, and the resemblance will reappear, will rise above all minor differences. Produced by the same causes, the decay of the feudal aristocracy, the church, and royalty, they both laboured at the same work, the dominion of the public in public affairs; they struggled for liberty against absolute power, for equality against privilege, for progressive and general interests against stationary and individual interests. Their situations were different, their strength unequal; what the one clearly conceived, the other saw but in imperfect outline; in the career which the one fulfilled, the other soon stopped short; on the same battle-field, the one found victory, the other defeat; the sin of the one was contempt of all religious principle, of the other hypocrisy; one was wiser, the other more powerful; but their means and their success alone differed; their tendency, as well as their origin, was the same; their wishes, their efforts, their progress, were directed towards the same end; what the one attempted or accomplished, the other accomplished or attempted. Though guilty of religious persecution, the English revolution saw the banner of religious liberty uplifted in its ranks; notwithstanding its aristocratic alliances, it founded the preponderance of the commons; though especially intent upon civil order, it still called for more simple legislation, for parliamentary reform, the abolition of entails, and of primogenitureship; and though disappointed in premature hopes, it enabled English society to take a great stride out of the monstrous inequality of the feudal system. In a word, the analogy of the two revolutions is such, that the first would never have been thoroughly understood had not the second taken place.

In our days, the history of the English revolution has changed its face. Hume[1] for a long series of years enjoyed the privilege of forming, in accordance with his views, the opinion of Europe; and, notwithstanding the aid of Mirabeau,[2] Mrs. Macauley's declamations had not been able to shake his authority. All at once, men's minds have recovered their natural independence; a

1. The first volume of Hume's History of the House of Stuart appeared in England in 1754, and the second in 1756.
2. Mrs. Macauley's work was to have been a *History of England from the Accession of James the First to the Elevation of the House of Hanover*, but it reaches no further than the fall of James the Second. It was published in England from 1763 to 1783. Of the French translation, sent forth in 1791, under the name of Mirabeau, only two volumes appeared.

crowd of works have attested, not only that this epoch has become once more the object of lively sympathy, but that the narrative and opinions of Hume have ceased to satisfy the imagination and reason of the public. A great orator, Mr. Fox, distinguished writers, Mr. Malcolm Laing, Macdiarmid, Brodie, Lingard, Godwin, &c., hastened to meet this new-roused curiosity. Born in France, the movement could not fail to make its way there; *L'Histoire de Cromwell* by M. Villemain, *L'Histoire de la Révolution de 1688,* by M. Mazure, evidently prove, that neither for us, was Hume sufficient; and I have been able myself, to publish the voluminous collection of the original memoirs of that epoch, without wearying the attention or exhausting the curiosity of readers.

It would little become me to enter here into a detailed examination of these works; but I do not hesitate to assert that, without the French revolution, without the vivid light it threw on the struggle between the Stuarts and the English people, they would not possess the new merits which distinguish them. I need only as a proof, the difference that is to be remarked between those produced by Great Britain, and those which France gave birth to. How great soever the patriotic interest inspired in the mind of the former, by the revolution of 1640, even when they place themselves under the banner of one of the parties which it educed, historical criticism reigns throughout their works; they apply themselves more especially to exact research, to the comparison and cross-questioning of witnesses; what they relate, is to them an old story they thoroughly know, not a drama at which they are present; a period long past, which they pride themselves on being well acquainted with, but in whose bosom they live not. Mr. Brodie fully participates in all the prejudices, distrust, and anger of the bitterest puritans against Charles and the cavaliers; while, to the faults, the crimes of his party, he is wholly blind. But, at least, one would imagine so much passion would produce an animated narrative; that the party exciting so much sympathy in the mind of the writer, would be described with truth and power. Not so: despite the ardour of his predilections, Mr. Brodie studies, but sees not, discusses, but describes not; he admires the popular party, but does not produce it strikingly on the stage; his work is a learned and useful dissertation, not a moral and animated history. Mr. Lingard shares in none of the opinions, none of the affections of Mr. Brodie; he remains impartial between the king and the parliament; he pleads the cause of neither, and makes no attempt to refute the errors of his predecessors; he even boasts of not having opened the work of Hume since he undertook his own; he wrote, he says, with the aid of original documents alone, with the times he wished to describe ever before his eyes, and with the firm resolution of shunning all systematic theory. Does he restore life to history by this impartiality? Not at all: Mr. Lingard's impartiality is, in this case, sheer indifference; a Roman Catholic priest, it matters little to him whether Church of England men or Presbyterians triumph; thus, indifference has helped him no better than passion did Mr. Brodie to penetrate beyond the external, and, so to speak, the material form of events; with him, too, the principal merit is in having carefully examined facts, and collected and disposed them in commendable order. Mr. Malcolm Laing had discerned with more sagacity the political character of the revolution; he shows very well that from the first, without distinctly apprehending its own aim, it sought to displace power, to transfer it to the house of commons, and thus to substitute parliamentary for royal government, and that it could only rest on this basis. But the moral side of the epoch, the religious enthusiasm, the popular passions, the party intrigues, the personal rivalries, all those scenes in which human nature displays itself, when freed from the restraint of old habits and laws, are wanting in his book; it is the report of a clear-sighted judge, but of one who has only resorted to written documents, and has called before him in person neither actors nor witnesses. I might pass in review all the works with which England has been recently enriched on this subject; they would all, on examination, be found to present the same character—a marked revival of interest in this great crisis of the national life, a more attentive study of the facts that relate to it, a keener feeling of its merits, a juster appreciation of its causes and consequences; still it is but meditation and learning applied to the production of works of erudition or philosophy. I seek in vain for that natural sympathy in the writer for his subject that gives to history light and life; and if Hampden or Clarendon were to return to life, I can scarcely believe they would recognise their own times.

I open *L'Histoire de Cromwell* by M. Villemain, and find altogether another scene before me. It is less complete, less learned, less exact than several of the works I have adverted to; but, throughout, there is a quick and keen comprehension of the opinions, the passions, the vicissitudes of revolutions, of public tendencies, and individual character, of the unconquerable nature and the changing forms of parties; the historian's reason teaches him how to appreciate all situations, all ideas; his imagination is moved by all real and deep impressions; his impartiality, somewhat too sceptical if anything, is yet more animated than is frequently even the passion of the exclusive advocates of a cause; and though the revolution only appears in his book confined within the too narrow frame of a biography, it is clearer and more animated than I have met with it elsewhere.

The reason of this is, that, setting aside the advantages of talent, M. Villemain had those of situation. He has viewed and judged the English revolution from the midst of that of France; he found in the men and the events developing themselves beneath his own eyes, the key to those he had to paint; he drew life from his own times and infused it into the times he wished to recal.

I have no desire to carry these reflections further; I have ventured so much only to point out how great is the analogy between the two epochs, and also to explain how a Frenchman may believe that the history of the English revolution has not yet been written in a fully satisfactory manner, and that he may be allowed to attempt it. I have carefully studied nearly all the old and modern works of which it has formed the subject; I did not fear that this study would weaken the sincerity of my own impressions or the independence of my judgment; it seems to me there is too much timidity in dreading so readily least an auxiliary should become a master; too much pride in refusing so absolutely all aid. Yet, and if I do not deceive myself it will easily be recognised, original documents have more peculiarly been my guides. I have nothing to observe here, as to the *Memoirs;* I endeavoured, in the "Notices" I prefixed to my edition of them, clearly to explain their character and worth; those which did not find a place in my *Collection,* though I have made use of them in my *History,* appear to me of too little importance to require remark. As for the collections of official acts and documents, they are very numerous; and, though often explored, still abound in unworked treasures. I have had constantly before me those of Rushworth, Thurloe, the journals of both houses of parliament, the *Parliamentary History,* the old one as well as that of Mr. Cobbett, the *Collection of State Trials,* and a great number of other works of the same kind, which it would be uninteresting to enumerate. I also found in the pamphlets of the time, not only English, but French, some curious information; for the French public was more occupied than is imagined with the English revolution; many pamphlets were published in France for and against it, and the Frondeurs more than once put forward its example, against Mazarin and the court. I must also say, to do justice to a man and a work now too much neglected, that I have often consulted with profit the History of England, by Rapin de Thoyras; and that notwithstanding the inferiority of the writer's talents, the English revolution is perhaps better understood in it, and more completely displayed than in the works of most of its successors.

In conclusion, let me be allowed to express here my gratitude to all those persons who in France and in England, have been good enough to sanction my work in its progress, and to promote it by the most valuable assistance. Amongst others, I owe to the kindness of Sir James Mackintosh, as inexhaustible as his mind and knowledge, suggestions and advice which no one but himself could have given me; and one of those, who, amongst ourselves, are the most versed in the past history as well as in the present state of England, M. Gallois, has thrown open to me, with a kindness I have some right to consider friendship, the treasures of his library and of his conversation.

5

The History of Civilization in Europe

Lecture 1

I AM deeply affected by the reception you give me, and which, you will permit me to say, I accept as a pledge of the sympathy which has not ceased to exist between us, notwithstanding so long a separation.* Alas! I speak as though you, whom I see around me, were the same who, seven years ago, used to assemble within these walls, to participate in my then labors; because I myself am here again, it seems as if all my former hearers should be here also; whereas, since that period, a change, a mighty change, has come over all things. Seven years ago we repaired hither, depressed with anxious doubts and fears, weighed down with sad thoughts and anticipations; we saw ourselves surrounded with difficulty and danger; we felt ourselves dragged on toward an evil which we essayed to avert by calm, grave, cautious reserve, but in vain. Now, we meet together, full of

---

Selections from *The History of Civilization in Europe*, translated by William Hazlitt (London: George Bell & Sons, 1887), from *L'Histoire de la Civilisation en Europe*, lectures given at the Sorbonne, 1828–30.

* Guizot had been expelled from the university in 1822 for the liberal character of his politics and his histories. He was allowed to return to his university post and resume his course in 1828, thanks to the liberal Martignac cabinet. He received a great ovation upon entering the lecture hall after an absence of nearly seven years. The young liberal students of the Sorbonne regarded his return as a great triumph and as a portent of a genuine liberal restoration.—EDITOR.

confidence and hope, the heart at peace, thought free. There is
but one way in which we can worthily manifest our gratitude
for this happy change; it is bringing to our present meetings, our
new studies, the same calm tranquility of mind, the same firm
purpose, which guided our conduct when, seven years ago, we
looked, from day to day, to have our studies placed under rigorous supervision, or, indeed, to be arbitrarily suspended. Good
fortune is delicate, frail, uncertain; we must keep measures with
hope as with fear; convalescence requires well nigh the same
care, the same caution, as the approaches of illness. This care,
this caution, this moderation, I am sure you will exhibit. The
same sympathy, the same intimate conformity of opinions, of
sentiments, of ideas, which united us in times of difficulty and
danger, and which at least saved us from grave faults, will
equally unite us in more auspicious days, and enable us to gather
all their fruits. I rely with confidence upon your coöperation, and
I need nothing more.

The time between this our first meeting and the close of the
year is very limited; that which I myself have had, wherein to
meditate upon the lectures I am about to deliver, has been infinitely more limited still. One great point, therefore, was the
selection of a subject, the consideration of which might best be
brought within the bounds of the few months which remain to
us of this year, within that of the few days I have had for preparation; and it appeared to me that a general review of the modern
history of Europe, considered with reference to the development
of civilization—a general sketch, in fact, of the history of European civilization, of its origin, its progress, its aim, its character,
might suitably occupy the time at our disposal. This, accordingly,
is the subject of which I propose to treat.

I have used the term European civilization, because it is evident that there is an European civilization; that a certain unity
pervades the civilization of the various European states; that,
notwithstanding infinite diversities of time, place and circumstance, this civilization takes its first rise in facts almost wholly
similar, proceeds everywhere upon the same principles, and

tends to produce well nigh everywhere analogous results. There is, then, an European civilization, and it is to the subject of this aggregate civilization that I will request your attention.

Again, it is evident that this civilization cannot be traced back, that its history cannot be derived from the history of any single European state. If, on the one hand, it is manifestly characterized by brevity, on the other, its variety is no less prodigious; it has not developed itself with completeness, in any one particular country. The features of its physiognomy are widespread; we must seek the elements of its history, now in France, now in England, now in Germany, now in Spain.

We of France occupy a favorable position for pursuing the study of European civilization. Flattery of individuals, even of our country, should be at all times avoided: it is without vanity, I think, we may say that France has been the center, the focus of European civilization. I do not pretend, it were monstrous to do so, that she has always, and in every direction, marched at the head of nations. At different epochs, Italy has taken the lead of her, in the arts; England, in political institutions; and there may be other respects under which, at particular periods, other European nations have manifested a superiority to her; but it is impossible to deny, that whenever France has seen herself thus outstripped in the career of civilization, she has called up fresh vigor, has sprung forward with a new impulse, and has soon found herself abreast with, or in advance of all the rest. And not only has this been the peculiar fortune of France, but we have seen that when the civilizing ideas and institutions which have taken their rise in other lands have sought to extend their sphere, to become fertile and general, to operate for the common benefit of European civilization, they have been necessitated to undergo, to a certain extent, a new preparation in France; and it has been from France, as from a second native country, that they have gone forth to the conquest of Europe. There is scarcely any great idea, any great principle of civilization, which, prior to its diffusion, has not passed in this way through France.

And for this reason: there is in the French character something sociable, something sympathetic, something which makes its way with greater facility and effect than does the national genius of any other people; whether from our language, whether from the turn of our mind, of our manners, certain it is that our ideas are more popular than those of other people, present themselves more clearly and intelligibly to the masses and penetrate among them more readily; in a word, perspicuity, sociability, sympathy, are the peculiar characteristics of France, of her civilization, and it is these qualities which rendered her eminently fit to march at the very head of European civilization.

In entering, therefore, upon the study of this great fact, it is no arbitrary or conventional choice to take France as the center of this study; we must needs do so if we would place ourselves, as it were, in the very heart of civilization, in the very heart of the fact we are about to consider.

I use the term *fact*, and I do so purposely; civilization is a fact like any other—a fact susceptible, like any other, of being studied, described, narrated.

For some time past, there has been much talk of the necessity of limiting history to the narration of facts: nothing can be more just; but we must always bear in mind that there are far more facts to narrate, and that the facts themselves are far more various in their nature, than people are at first disposed to believe; there are material, visible facts, such as wars, battles, the official acts of governments; there are moral facts, none the less real that they do not appear on the surface; there are individual facts which have denominations of their own; there are general facts, without any particular designation, to which it is impossible to assign any precise date, which it is impossible to bring within strict limits, but which are yet no less facts than the rest, historical facts, facts which we cannot exclude from history without mutilating history.

The very portion of history which we are accustomed to call its philosophy, the relation of events to each other, the connection which unites them, their causes and their effects—these are all facts, these are all history, just as much as the narratives of battles, and of other material and visible events. Facts of this class it is doubtless more difficult to disentangle and explain; we are more liable to error in giving an account of them, and it is no easy thing to give them life and animation, to exhibit them in clear and vivid colors; but this difficulty in no degree changes their nature; they are none the less an essential element of history.

Civilization is one of these facts; general, hidden, complex fact; very difficult, I allow, to describe, to relate, but which none the less for that exists, which, none the less for that, has a right to be described and related. We may raise as to this fact a great number of questions; we may ask, it has been asked, whether it is a good or an evil? Some bitterly deplore it; others rejoice at it. We may ask, whether it is an universal fact, whether there is an universal civilization of the human species, a destiny of humanity; whether the nations have handed down from age to age, something which has never been lost, which must increase, form a larger and larger mass, and thus pass on to the end of time? For my own part, I am convinced that there is, in reality, a general destiny of humanity, a transmission of the aggregate of civilization; and, consequently, an universal history of civilization to be written. But without raising questions so great, so difficult to solve, if we restrict ourselves to a definite limit of time and space, if we confine ourselves to the history of a certain number of centuries, of a certain people, it is evident that within these bounds, civilization is a fact which can be described, related—which is history. I will at once add, that this history is the greatest of all, that it includes all.

And, indeed, does it not seem to yourselves that the fact civilization is the fact *par excellence*—the general and definitive fact, in which all the others terminate, into which they all resolve themselves? Take all the facts which compose the history of a nation, and which we are accustomed to regard as the elements of its life; take its institutions, its commerce, its industry, its wars, all the details of its government: when we would consider these facts in their aggregate, in their connection, when we would estimate them, judge them, we ask in what they have contributed to the civilization of that nation, what part they have taken in it, what influence they have exercised over it. It is in this way that we not only form a complete idea of them, but measure and appreciate their true value; they are, as it were, rivers, of which we ask what quantity of water it is they contribute to the ocean? For civilization is a sort of ocean, constituting the wealth of a people, and on whose bosom all the elements of the life of that people, all the powers supporting its existence, assemble and unite. This is so true, that even facts, which from their nature are odious, pernicious, which weigh painfully upon nations, despotism, for example, and anarchy, if they have contributed in some way to civilization, if they have enabled it to make an onward stride, up to a certain point we pardon them, we overlook their wrongs, their evil nature; in a word, wherever we recognize civilization, whatever the facts which have created it, we are tempted to forget the price it has cost.

There are, moreover, facts which, properly speaking, we cannot call social; individual facts, which seem to interest the human soul rather than the public life: such are religious creeds and philosophical ideas, sciences, letters, arts. These facts appear to address themselves to man with a view to his moral perfection, his intellectual gratification; to have for their object his internal amelioration, his mental pleasure, rather than his social condition. But, here again, it is with reference to civilization that these very facts are often considered, and claim to be considered.

At all times, in all countries, religion has assumed the glory of having civilized the people; sciences, letters, arts, all the intellectual and moral pleasures, have claimed a share in this glory; and we have deemed it a praise and an honor to them, when we have recognized this claim on their part. Thus, facts the most important and sublime in themselves, independently of all external result, and simply in their relations with the soul of man, increase in importance, rise in sublimity from their affinity with civilization. Such is the value of this general fact, that it gives value to everything it touches. And not only does it give value; there are even occasions when the facts of which we speak, religious creeds, philosophical ideas, letters, arts, are especially considered and judged of with reference to their influence upon civilization; an influence which becomes, up to a certain point and during a certain time, the conclusive measure of their merit, of their value.

What, then, I will ask, before undertaking its history, what, considered only in itself, what is this so grave, so vast, so precious fact, which seems the sum, the expression of the whole life of nations?

I shall take care here not to fall into pure philosophy; not to lay down some ratiocinative principle, and then deduce from it the nature of civilization as a result; there would be many chances of error in this method. And here again we have a fact to verify and describe.

For a long period, and in many countries, the word *civilization* has been in use; people have attached to the word ideas more or less clear, more or less comprehensive; but there it is in use, and those who use it attach some meaning or other to it. It is the general, human, popular meaning of this word that we must study. There is almost always in the usual acceptation of the most general terms more accuracy than in the definitions, apparently more strict, more precise, of science. It is common sense which gives to words their ordinary signification, and common sense is the characteristic of humanity. The ordinary signification of a word is formed by gradual progress and in the constant presence of facts; so that when a fact presents itself which seems to come within the meaning of a known term, it is received into it, as it were, naturally; the signification of the term extends itself, expands, and by degrees the various facts, the various ideas which from the nature of the things themselves men should include under this word, are included.

When the meaning of a word, on the other hand, is determined by science, this determination, the work of one individual, or of a small number of individuals, takes place under the influence of some particular fact which has struck upon the mind. Thus, scientific definitions are, in general, much more narrow, and, hence, much less accurate, much less true, at bottom, than the popular meanings of the terms. In studying as a fact the meaning of the word civilization, in investigating all the ideas which are comprised within it, according to the common sense of mankind, we shall make a much greater progress toward a knowledge of the fact itself than by attempting to give it ourselves a scientific definition, however more clear and precise the latter might appear at first.

I will commence this investigation by endeavoring to place before you some hypotheses: I will describe a certain number of states of society, and we will then inquire whether general instinct would recognize in them the condition of a people civilizing itself; whether we recognize in them the meaning which mankind attaches to the word civilization.

First, suppose a people whose external life is easy, is full of physical comfort; they pay few taxes, they are free from suffering; justice is well administered in their private relations—in a word, material existence is for them altogether happy and happily regulated. But at the same time, the intellectual and moral existence of this people is studiously kept in a state of torpor and inactivity; of, I will not say, oppression, for they do not understand the feeling, but of compression. We are not without instances of this state of things. There has been a great number of small aristocratic republics in which the people have been thus treated like flocks of sheep, well kept and materially happy, but without moral and intellectual activity. Is this civilization? Is this a people civilizing itself?

Another hypothesis: here is a people whose material existence is less easy, less comfortable, but still supportable. On the other hand, moral and intellectual wants have not been neglected, a certain amount of mental pasture has been served out to them; elevated, pure sentiments are cultivated in them; their religious and moral views have attained a certain degree of development; but great care is taken to stifle in them the principle of liberty; the intellectual and moral wants, as in the former case the material wants, are satisfied; each man has meted out to him his portion of truth; no one is permitted to seek it for himself. Immobility is the characteristic of moral life; it is the state into which have fallen most of the populations of Asia; wherever theocratic dominations keep humanity in check; it is the state of the Hindoos, for example. I ask the same question here as before; is this a people civilizing itself?

I change altogether the nature of the hypothesis: here is a people among whom is a great display of individual liberties, but where disorder and inequality are excessive: it is the empire of force and of chance; every man, if he is not strong, is oppressed, suffers, perishes; violence is the predominant feature of the social state. No one is ignorant that Europe has passed through this state. Is this a civilized state? It may, doubtless, contain principles of civilization which will develop themselves by successive degrees; but the fact which dominates in such a society is, assuredly, not that which the common sense of mankind calls civilization.

I take a fourth and last hypothesis: the liberty of each individual is very great, inequality among them is rare, and at all events, very transient. Every man does very nearly just what he pleases, and differs little in power from his neighbor; but there are very few general interests, very few public ideas, very little society— in a word, the faculties and existence of individuals appear and then pass away, wholly apart and without acting upon each other, or leaving any trace behind them; the successive generations leave society at the same point at which they found it: this is the state of savage tribes; liberty and equality are there, but assuredly not civilization.

I might multiply these hypotheses, but I think we have before us enough to explain what is the popular and natural meaning of the word *civilization.*

It is clear that none of the states I have sketched corresponds, according to the natural good sense of mankind, to this term. Why? It appears to me that the first fact comprised in the word civilization (and this results from the different examples I have rapidly placed before you), is the fact of progress, of development; it presents at once the idea of a people marching onward, not to change its place, but to change its condition; of a people who are extending and ameliorating their condition. The idea of progress, of development, appears to me the fundamental idea contained in the word, *civilization.* What is this progress? what this development? Herein is the greatest difficulty of all.

The etymology of the word would seem to answer in a clear and satisfactory manner: it says that it is the perfecting of civil life, the development of society, properly so called, of the relations of men among themselves.

Such is, in fact, the first idea which presents itself to the understanding when the word civilization is pronounced; we at once figure forth to ourselves the extension, the greatest activity, the best organization of the social relations: on the one hand, an increasing production of the means of giving strength and happiness to society; on the other, a more equitable distribution, among individuals, of the strength.

Is this all? Have we here exhausted all the natural, ordinary meaning of the word civilization? Does the fact contain nothing more than this?

It is almost as if we asked: is the human species after all a mere ant-hill, a society in which all that is required is order and physical happiness, in which the greater the amount of labor, and the more equitable the division of the fruits of labor, the more surely is the object attained, the progress accomplished?

Our instinct at once feels repugnant to so narrow a definition of human destiny. It feels at the first glance that the word civilization comprehends something more extensive, more complex, something superior to the simple perfection of the social relations, of social power and happiness.

Fact, public opinion, the generally received meaning of the term, are in accordance with this instinct.

Take Rome in the palmy days of the republic, after the second Punic war, at the time of its greatest virtues, when it was marching to the empire of the world, when its social state was evidently in progress. Then take Rome under Augustus, at the epoch when her decline began, when, at all events, the progressive movement of society was arrested, when evil principles were on the eve of prevailing: yet there is no one who does not think and say that the Rome of Augustus was more civilized than the Rome of Fabricius or of Cincinnatus.

Let us transport ourselves beyond the Alps: let us take the France of the seventeenth and eighteenth centuries: it is evident that, in a social point of view, considering the actual amount and distribution of happiness among individuals, the France of the seventeenth and eighteenth centuries was inferior to some other countries of Europe, to Holland and to England, for example. I believe that in Holland and in England the social activity was greater, was increasing more rapidly, distributing its fruit more fully, than in France, yet ask general good sense, and it will say that the France of the seventeenth and eighteenth centuries was the most civilized country in Europe. Europe has not hesitated in her affirmative reply to the question: traces of this public opinion, as to France, are found in all the monuments of European literature.

We might point out many other states in which the prosperity is greater, is of more rapid growth, is better distributed among individuals than elsewhere, and in which, nevertheless, by the spontaneous instinct, the general good sense of men, the civilization is judged inferior to that of countries not so well portioned out in a purely social sense.

What does this mean; what advantages do these latter countries possess? What is it gives them, in the character of civilized countries, this privilege; what so largely compensates in the opinion of mankind for what they so lack in other respects?

A development other than that of social life has been gloriously manifested by them; the development of the individual, internal life, the development of man himself, of his faculties, his sentiments, his ideas. If society with them be less perfect than elsewhere, humanity stands forth in more grandeur and power. There remain, no doubt, many social conquests to be made; but immense intellectual and moral conquests are accomplished; worldly goods, social rights, are wanting to many men; but many great men live and shine in the eyes of the world. Letters, sciences, the arts, display all their splendor. Wherever mankind beholds these great signs, these signs glorified by human nature, wherever it sees created these treasures of sublime enjoyment, it there recognizes and names civilization.

Two facts, then, are comprehended in this great fact; it subsists on two conditions, and manifests itself by two symptoms: the development of social activity, and that of individual activity; the progress of society and the progress of humanity. Wherever the external condition of man extends itself, vivifies, ameliorates itself; wherever the internal nature of man displays itself with lustre, with grandeur; at these two signs, and often despite the profound imperfection of the social state, mankind with loud applause proclaims civilization.

Such, if I do not deceive myself, is the result of simple and purely commonsense examination of the general opinion of mankind. If we interrogate history, properly so-called, if we examine what is the nature of the great crises of civilization, of those facts which, by universal consent, have propelled it onward, we shall constantly recognize one or other of the two elements I have just described. They are always crises of individual or social development, facts which have changed the internal man, his creed, his manners, or his external condition, his position in his relation with his fellows. Christianity, for example, not merely on its first appearance, but during the first stages of its existence, Christianity in no degree addressed itself to the social state; it announced aloud that it would not meddle with the social state; it ordered the slave to obey his master, it attacked none of the great evils, the great wrongs of the society of that period. Yet who will deny that Christianity was a great crisis of civilization? Why was it so? Because it changed the internal man, creeds, sentiments; because it regenerated the moral man, the intellectual man.

We have seen a crisis of another nature, a crisis which addressed itself, not to the internal man, but to his external condition; one which changed and regenerated society. This also was assuredly one of the decisive crises of civilization. Look through all history, you will find everywhere the same result; you will meet with no important fact instrumental in the development of civilization, which has not exercised one or other of the two sorts of influence I have spoken of.

Such, if I mistake not, is the natural and popular meaning of the term; you have here the fact, I will not say defined, but described, verified almost completely, or, at all events, in its general features. We have before us the two elements of civilization. Now comes the question, would one of these two suffice to constitute it; would the development of the social state, the development of the individual man, separately presented, be civilization? Would the human race recognize it as such, or have the two facts so intimate and necessary a relation between them, that if they are not simultaneously produced, they are notwithstanding inseparable, and sooner or later one brings on the other?

We might, as it appears to me, approach this question on three several sides. We might examine the nature itself of the two elements of civilization, and ask ourselves whether by that alone, they are or are not closely united with, and necessary to each other. We might inquire of history whether they had manifested themselves isolately, apart the one from the other, or whether they had invariably produced the one the other. We may, lastly, consult upon this question the common opinion of mankind— common sense. I will address myself first to common sense.

When a great change is accomplished in the state of a country, when there is operated in it a large development of wealth and power, a revolution in the distribution of the social means, this new fact encounters adversaries, undergoes opposition: this is inevitable. What is the general cry of the adversaries of the change? They say that this progress of the social state does not ameliorate, does not regenerate in like manner, in a like degree, the moral, the internal state of man; that it is a false, delusive progress, the result of which is detrimental to morality, to man. The friends of social development energetically repel this attack; they maintain, on the contrary, that the progress of society necessarily involves and carries with it the progress of morality; that when the external life is better regulated, the internal life is refined and purified. Thus stands the question between the adversaries and partisans of the new state.

Reverse the hypothesis: suppose the moral development in progress: what do the laborers in this progress generally promise? What, in the origin of societies, have promised the religious rulers, the sages, the poets, who have labored to soften and to regulate men's manners? They have promised the amelioration of the social condition, the more equitable distribution of the social means. What, then, I ask you, is involved in these disputes, these promises? What do they mean? What do they imply?

They imply that in the spontaneous, instinctive conviction of mankind, the two elements of civilization, the social development and the moral development, are closely connected together; that at sight of the one, man at once looks forward to the other. It is to this natural instinctive conviction that those who are maintaining or combating one or other of the two developments address themselves, when they affirm or deny their union. It is well understood, that if we can persuade mankind that the amelioration of the social state will be adverse to the internal progress of individuals, we shall have succeeded in decrying and enfeebling the revolution in operation throughout society. On the other hand, when we promise mankind the amelioration of society by means of the amelioration of the individual, it is well understood that the tendency is to place faith in these promises, and it is accordingly made use of with success. It is evidently, therefore, the instinctive belief of humanity, that the movements of civilization are connected the one with the other, and reciprocally produce the one the other.

If we address ourselves to the history of the world, we shall receive the same answer. We shall find that all the great developments of the internal man have turned to the profit of society; all the great developments of the social state to the profit of individual man. We find the one or other of the two facts predominating, manifesting itself with striking effect, and impressing upon the movement in progress a distinctive character. It is, sometimes, only after a very long interval of time, after a thousand obstacles, a thousand transformations, that the second fact, developing itself, comes to complete the civilization which the first had commenced. But if you examine them closely, you will soon perceive the bond which unites them. The march of Providence is not restricted to narrow limits; it is not bound, and it does not trouble itself, to follow out to-day the consequences of the principle which it laid down yesterday. The consequences will come in due course, when the hour for them has arrived, perhaps not till hundreds of years have passed away; though its reasoning may appear to us slow, its logic is none the less true and sound. To Providence, time is as nothing; it strides through time as the gods of Homer through space: it makes but one step, and ages have vanished behind it. How many centuries, what infinite events passed away before the regeneration of the moral man by Christianity exercised upon the regeneration of the social state its great and legitimate influence. Yet who will deny that it any the less succeeded?

If from history we extend our inquiries to the nature itself of the two facts which constitute civilization, we are infallibly led to the same result. There is no one who has not experienced this in his own case. When a moral change is operated in man, when he acquires an idea, or a virtue, or a faculty, more than he had before—in a word, when he develops himself individually, what is the desire, what the want, which at the same moment takes possession of him? It is the desire, the want, to communicate the new sentiment to the world about him, to give realization to his thoughts externally. As soon as a man acquires any thing, as soon as his being takes in his own conviction a new development, assumes an additional value, forthwith he attaches to this new development, this fresh value, the idea of possession; he feels himself impelled, compelled, by his instinct, by an inward voice, to extend to others the change, the amelioration, which has been accomplished in his own person. We owe the great reformers solely to this cause; the mighty men who have changed the face of the world, after having changed themselves, were urged onward, were guided on their course, by no other want than this. So much for the alteration which is operated in the internal man; now to the other. A revolution is accomplished in the state of society; it is better regulated, rights and property are more equitably distributed among its members—that is to say, the aspect of the world becomes purer and more beautiful, the action of government, the conduct of men in their mutual relations, more just, more benevolent. Do you suppose that this improved aspect of the world, this amelioration of external facts, does not react upon the interior of man, upon humanity? All that is said

as to the authority of examples, of customs, of noble models, is
founded upon this only; that an external fact, good, well-regulated, leads sooner or later, more or less completely, to an internal
fact of the same nature, the same merit; that a world better
regulated, a world more just, renders man himself more just; that
the inward is reformed by the outward, as the outward by the
inward; that the two elements of civilization are closely connected the one with the other; that centuries, that obstacles of all
sorts, may interpose between them; that it is possible they may
have to undergo a thousand transformations in order to regain
each other; but sooner or later they will rejoin each other: this
is the law of their nature, the general fact of history, the instinctive faith of the human race.

I think I have thus—not exhausted the subject, very far from
it—but, exhibited in a well-nigh complete, though cursory manner, the fact of civilization; I think I have described it, settled
its limits, and stated the principal and fundamental questions
to which it gives rise. I might stop here; but I cannot help touching upon a question which meets me at this point; one of those
questions which are not historical questions, properly so called;
which are questions, I will not call them hypothetical, but con-
jectural; questions of which man holds but one end, the other end
being permanently beyond his reach; questions of which he cannot make the circuit, nor view on more than one side; and yet
questions not the less real, not the less calling upon him for
thought; for they present themselves before him, despite of himself, at every moment.

Of those two developments of which we have spoken, and
which constitute the fact of civilization, the development of
society on the one hand and of humanity on the other, which is
the end, which is the means? Is it to perfect his social condition,
to ameliorate his existence on earth, that man develops himself,
his faculties, sentiments, ideas, his whole being? Or rather, is not
the amelioration of the social condition, the progress of society,
society itself, the theatre, the occasion, the *mobile,* of the development of the individual, in a word, is society made to serve the
individual, or the individual to serve society? On the answer to

this question inevitably depends that whether the destiny of man is purely social; whether society drains up and exhausts the whole man; or whether he bears within him something intrinsic —something superior to his existence on earth.

A man, whom I am proud to call my friend, a man who has passed though meetings like our own to assume the first place in assemblies less peaceable and more powerful: a man, all whose words are engraven on the hearts of those who bear them, M. Royer-Collard, has solved this question according to his own conviction, at least, in his speech on the Sacrilege Bill. I find in that speech these two sentences:

> Human societies are born, live and die, on the earth; it is there their destinies are accomplished. . . . But they contain not the whole man. After he has engaged himself to society, there remains to him the noblest part of himself, those high faculties by which he elevates himself to God, to a future life, to unknown felicity in an invisible world. . . . We, persons individual and identical, veritable beings endowed with immortality, we have a different destiny from that of states.[1]

I will add nothing to this; I will not undertake to treat the question itself; I content myself with stating it. It is met with at the history of civilization: when the history of civilization is completed, when there is nothing more to say as to our present existence, man inevitably asks himself whether all is exhausted, whether he has reached the end of all things? This then is the last, the highest of all those problems to which history of civilization can lead. It is sufficient for me to have indicated its position and its grandeur.

From all I have said it is evident that the history of civilization might be treated in two methods, drawn from two sources, considered under two different aspects. The historian might place himself in the heart of the human mind for a given period, a series of ages, or among the determinate people; he might study, describe, relate all the events, all the transformations, all the revolutions which had been accomplished in the internal man;

1. *Opinion de M. Royer-Collard sur le Projet de Loi relatif au Sacrilege,* pp. 7, 17.

and when he should arrive at the end he would have a history of civilization among the people, and in the period he had selected. He may proceed in another manner: instead of penetrating the internal man, he may take his stand—he may place himself in the midst of the world; instead of describing the vicissitudes of the ideas, the sentiments of the individual being, he may describe external facts, the events, the changes of the social state. These two portions, these two histories of civilization are closely connected with each other; they are the reflection, the image of each other. Yet, they may be separated; perhaps, indeed, they ought to be so, at least at the onset, in order that both the one and the other may be treated of in detail, and with perspicuity. For my part I do not propose to study with you the history of civilization in the interior of the human soul; it is the history of external events of the visible and social world that I shall occupy myself with. I had wished, indeed, to exhibit to you the whole fact of civilization, such as I can conceive it in all its complexity and extent, to set forth before you all the high questions which may arise from it. At present I restrict myself; mark out my field of inquiry within narrower limits; it is only the history of the social state that I purpose investigating.

We shall begin by seeking all the elements of European civilization in its cradle at the fall of the Roman Empire; we will study with attention society, such as it was, in the midst of those famous ruins. We will endeavor, not to resuscitate, but to place its elements side by side, and when we have done so, we will endeavor to make them move and follow them in their developments through the fifteen centuries which have elapsed since that epoch.

I believe that when we have got but a very little way into this study, we shall acquire the conviction that civilization is as yet very young; that the world has by no means as yet measured the whole of its career. Assuredly human thought is at this time very far from being all that it is capable of becoming; we are very far from comprehending the whole future of humanity: let each of us descend into his own mind, let him interrogate himself as to the utmost possible good he has formed a conception of and hopes for; let him then compare his idea with what actually exists in the world; he will be convinced that society and civilization are very young; that notwithstanding the length of the road they have come, they have incomparably further to go. This will lessen nothing of the pleasure that we shall take in the contemplation of our actual condition. As I endeavor to place before you the great crises in the history of civilization in Europe during the last fifteen centuries, you will see to what a degree, even up in our own days, the condition of man has been laborious, stormy, not only in the outward and social state, but inwardly in the life of the soul. During all those ages, the human mind has had to suffer as much as the human race; you will see that in modern times, for the first time, perhaps, the human mind has attained a state, as yet very imperfect, but still a state in which reigns some peace, some harmony. It is the same with society; it has evidently made immense progress, the human condition is easy and just, compared with what it was previously; we may almost when thinking of our ancestors apply to ourselves the verses of Lucretius:

Suave mari magno, turbantibus æquora ventis,
E terrâ magnum alterius spectare laborem.[2]

We may say of ourselves, without too much pride, as Sthenelus in Homer:

Ημεῖς τοὶ τ ̓ λτερων μεγ᾽ ἀμείνονες εὐχόμεθ᾽ εἶναι.[3]

Let us be careful, however, not to give ourselves up too much to the idea of our happiness and amelioration, or we may fall into two grave dangers, pride and indolence; we may conceive an over-confidence in the power and success of the human mind, in our own enlightenment, and, at the same time, suffer ourselves to become enervated by the luxurious ease of our condition. It ap-

2. " 'Tis pleasant, in a great storm, to contemplate, from a safe position on shore, the perils of some ships tossed about by the furious winds and the stormy ocean."
3. "Thank Heaven, we are infinitely better than those who went before us."

pears to me that we are constantly fluctuating between a tendency to complain upon light grounds, on the one hand, and to be content without reason, on the other. We have a susceptibility of spirit, a craving, an unlimited ambition in the thought, in our desire, in the movement of the imagination; but when it comes to the practical work of life, when we are called upon to give ourselves any trouble, to make any sacrifices, to use any efforts to attain the object; our arms fall down listlessly by our sides, and we give the matter up in despair, with a facility equaled only by the impatience with which we had previously desired its attainment. We must beware how we allow ourselves to yield to either of these defects. Let us accustom ourselves duly to estimate beforehand the extent of our force, our capacity, our knowledge; and let us aim at nothing which we feel we cannot attain legitimately, justly, regularly, and with unfailing regard to the principles upon which our civilization itself rests. We seem at times tempted to adopt the principles which, as a general rule, we assail and hold up to scorn—the principles, the right of the strongest of barbarian Europe; the brute force, the violence, the downright lying which were matters of course, of daily occurrence, four or five hundred years ago. But when we yield for a moment to this desire, we find in ourselves neither the perseverance nor the savage energy of the men of that period, who, suffering greatly from their condition, were naturally anxious, and incessantly essaying, to emancipate themselves from it. We, of the present day, are content with our condition; let us not expose it to danger by indulging in vague desires, the time for realizing which has not come. Much has been given to us, much will be required of us; we must render to posterity a strict account of our conduct; the public, the government, all are now subjected to discussion, examination, responsibility. Let us attach ourselves firmly, faithfully, undeviatingly, to the principles of our civilization—justice, legality, publicity, liberty; and let us never forget, that while we ourselves require, and with reason, that all things shall be open to our inspection and inquiry, we ourselves are under the eye of the world, and shall, in our turn, be discussed, be judged.

Lecture 2

In meditating the plan of the course with which I propose to present you, I am fearful lest my lectures should possess the double inconvenience of being very long, by reason of the necessity of condensing much matter into little space, and, at the same time, of being too concise.

I dread yet another difficulty, originating in the same cause: the necessity, namely, of sometimes making affirmations without proving them. This is also the result of the narrow space to which I find myself confined. There will occur ideas and assertions of which the confirmation must be postponed. I hope you will pardon me for sometimes placing you under the necessity of believing upon my bare word. I come even now to an occasion of imposing upon you this necessity.

I have endeavored, in the preceding lecture, to explain the fact of civilization in general, without speaking of any particular civilization, without regarding circumstance of time and place, considering the fact in itself, and under a purely philosophical point of view. I come today to the history of European civilization; but before entering upon the narrative itself, I wish to make you acquainted, in a general manner, with the particular physiognomy of this civilization; I desire to characterize it so clearly to you, that it may appear to you perfectly distinct from all other civilizations which have developed themselves in the world. This I am going to attempt, more than which I dare not say; but I can only affirm it, unless I could succeed in depicting European society with such faithfulness that you should instantly recognize it as a portrait. But of this I dare not flatter myself.

When we regard the civilizations which have preceded that of modern Europe, whether in Asia or elsewhere, including even Greek and Roman civilization, it is impossible not to be struck by the unity which pervades them. They seem to have emanated from a single fact, from a single idea; one might say that society has attached itself to a solitary dominant principle, which has determined its institutions, its customs, its creeds, in one word, all its developments.

In Egypt, for instance, it was the theocratic principle which pervaded the entire community; it reproduced itself in the customs, in the monuments, and in all that remains to us of Egyptian civilization. In India, you will discover the same fact; there is still the almost exclusive dominion of the theocratic principle. Elsewhere you will meet with another organizing principle—the domination of a victorious caste; the principle of force will here alone possess society, imposing thereupon its laws and its character. Elsewhere society will be the expression of the democratic principle; it has been thus with the commercial republics which have covered the coasts of Asia Minor and of Syria, in Ionia, in Phoenicia. In short, when we contemplate ancient civilizations, we find them stamped with a singular character of unity in their institutions, their ideas and their manners; a sole, or at least, a strongly preponderating force governs and determines all.

I do not mean to say that this unity of principle and form in the civilization of these states has always prevailed therein. When we go back to their earlier history, we find that the various powers which may develop themselves in the heart of a society, have often contended for empire. Among the Egyptians, the Etruscans, the Greeks themselves, etc., the order of warriors, for example, has struggled against that of the priests; elsewhere, the spirit of clanship has struggled against that of free association; the aristocratic against the popular system, etc. But it has generally been in prehistorical times that such struggles have occurred; and thus only a vague recollection has remained of them.

The struggle has sometimes reproduced itself in the course of the existence of nations; but, almost invariably, it has soon been terminated; one of the powers that disputed for empire has soon gained it, and taken sole possession of the society. The war has always terminated by the, if not exclusive, at least largely preponderating, domination of some particular principle. The coexistence and the combat of different principles have never, in the history of these peoples, been more than a transitory crisis, an accident.

The result of this has been a remarkable simplicity in the majority of ancient civilizations. This simplicity has produced different consequences. Sometimes, as in Greece, the simplicity of the social principle has led to a wonderfully rapid development; never has any people unfolded itself in so short a period with such brilliant effect. But after this astonishing flight, Greece seemed suddenly exhausted; its decay, if it was not so rapid as its rise, was nevertheless strangely prompt. It seems that the creative force of the principle of Greek civilization was exhausted; no other has come to renew it.

Elsewhere, in Egypt and in India, for instance, the unity of the principle of civilization has had a different effect; society has fallen into a stationary condition. Simplicity has brought monotony; the country has not been destroyed, society has continued to exist, but motionless, and as if frozen.

It is to the same cause that we must attribute the character of tyranny which appeared in the name of principle and under the most various forms, among all the ancient civilizations. Society belonged to an exclusive power, which would allow of the existence of none other. Every differing tendency was proscribed and hunted down. Never has the ruling principle chosen to admit beside it the manifestation and action of a different principle.

This character of unity of civilization is equally stamped upon literature and the works of the mind. Who is unacquainted with the monuments of Indian literature, which have lately been distributed over Europe? It is impossible not to see that they are all cast in the same mold; they seem all to be the result of the same fact, the expression of the same idea; works of religion or morals, historical traditions, dramatic and epic poetry, everywhere the same character is stamped; the productions of the mind bear the same character of simplicity and of monotony which appears in events and institutions. Even in Greece, in the center of all the riches of the human intellect, a singular uniformity reigns in literature and in the arts.

It has been wholly otherwise with the civilization of modern Europe. Without entering into details, look upon it, gather together your recollections: it will immediately appear to you varied, confused, stormy; all forms, all principles of social organization co-exist therein; powers spiritual and temporal; elements theocratic, monarchical, aristocratic, democratic; all orders, all social arrangements mingle and press upon one another; there are infinite degrees of liberty, wealth, and influence. These various forces are in a state of continual struggle among themselves, yet no one succeeds in stifling the others, and taking possession of society. In ancient times, at every great epoch, all societies seemed cast in the same mold: it is sometimes pure monarchy, sometimes theocracy or democracy, that prevails; but each, in its turn, prevails completely. Modern Europe presents us with examples of all systems, of all experiments of social organization; pure or mixed monarchies, theocracies, republics, more or less aristocratic, have thus thrived simultaneously, one beside the other: and, notwithstanding their diversity, they have all a certain resemblance, a certain family likeness, which it is impossible to mistake.

In the ideas and sentiments of Europe there is the same variety, the same struggle. The theocratic, monarchic, aristocratic, and popular creeds, cross, combat, limit, and modify each other. Open the boldest writings of the middle ages; never there is an idea followed out to its last consequences. The partisans of absolute power recoil suddenly and unconsciously before the results of their own doctrine; they perceive around them ideas and influences which arrest them, and prevent them from going to extremities. The democrats obey the same law. On neither part exists that imperturbable audacity, that blind determination of logic, which show themselves in ancient civilizations. The sentiments offer the same contrasts, the same variety; an energetic love of independence, side by side with a great facility of submission; a singular faithfulness of man to man, and, at the same time, an uncontrollable wish to exert free will, to shake off every yoke, and to live for one's self, without caring for any other. The souls of men are as different, as agitated as society.

The same character discovers itself in modern literature. We cannot but agree that, as regards artistic form and beauty, they are very much inferior to ancient literature; but, as regards depth of sentiment and of ideas, they are far more rich and vigorous. We see that the human soul has been moved upon a greater number of points, and to a greater depth. Imperfection of form results from this very cause. The richer and more numerous the materials, the more difficult it is to reduce them to a pure and simple form. That which constitutes the beauty of a composition, of that which we call form in works of art, is clearness, simplicity, and a symbolic unity of workmanship. With the prodigious diversity of the ideas and sentiments of European civilization, it has been much more difficult to arrive at this simplicity, this clearness.

On all sides then this predominant character of modern civilization discovers itself. It has no doubt had this disadvantage, that, when we consider separately such or such a particular development of the human mind in letters, in the arts, in all directions in which it can advance, we usually find it inferior to the corresponding development in ancient civilizations; but, on the other hand, when we regard it in the aggregate, European civilization shows itself incomparably richer than any other; it has displayed at one and the same time many more different developments. Consequently you find that it has existed fifteen centuries, and yet is still in a state of continuous progression; it has not advanced nearly so rapidly as the Greek civilization, but its progress has never ceased to grow. It catches a glimpse of the vast career which lies before it, and day after day it shoots forward more rapidly, because more and more of freedom attends its movements. While in other civilizations the exclusive, or at least the excessively preponderating dominion of a single principle, of a single form, has been the cause of tyranny, in modern Europe the diversity of elements which constitute the social order, the impossibility under which they have been placed of excluding each other, have given birth to the freedom which prevails in the present day. Not having been able to exterminate each other, it has become necessary that various principles should exist together—that they should make between them a sort of compact. Each has agreed to undertake that portion of the development which may fall to its share; and while elsewhere the predominance of a principle produced tyranny, in Europe liberty has been the result of the variety of the elements of civilization and of the state of struggle in which they have constantly existed.

This constitutes a real and an immense superiority; and if we investigate yet further, if we penetrate beyond external facts into the nature of things, we shall discover that this superiority is legitimate, and acknowledged by reason as well as proclaimed by facts. Forgetting for a moment European civilization, let us turn our attention to the world in general, on the general course of terrestrial things. What character do we find? How goes the world? It moves precisely with this diversity and variety of elements, a prey to this constant struggle which we have remarked in European civilization. Evidently it has not been permitted to any single principle, to any particular organization, to any single idea, or to any special force, that it should possess itself of the world, molding it once for all, destroying all other influences, to reign therein exclusively.

Various powers, principles and systems mingle, limit each other, and struggle without ceasing, in turn predominating or predominated over, never entirely conquered or conquering. A variety of forms, of ideas, and of principles, then, struggles, their efforts after a certain unity, a certain ideal which perhaps can never be attained, but to which the human race tends by freedom and work; these constitute the general condition of the world: like the course of things in the world, it is neither narrow, exclusive, nor stationary. For the first time, I believe, the character of specialty has vanished from civilization; for the first time it is developed as variously, as richly, as laboriously, as the great drama of the universe.

European civilization has entered, if we may so speak, into the eternal truth, into the plan of Providence; it progresses according to the intentions of God. This is the rational account of its superiority.

I am desirous that this fundamental and distinguishing character of European civilization should continue present to your minds during the course of our labors. At present I can only make the affirmation: the development of facts must furnish the proof. It will, nevertheless, you will agree, be a strong confirmation of my assertion, if we find, even in the cradle of our civilization, the causes and the elements of the character which I have just attributed to it: if, at the moment of its birth, at the moment of the fall of the Roman Empire, we recognize in the state of the world, in the facts that, from the earliest times, have concurred to form European civilization, the principle of this agitated but fruitful diversity which distinguishes it. I am about to attempt this investigation. I shall examine the condition of Europe at the fall of the Roman Empire, and seek to discover, from institutions, creeds, ideas, and sentiments, what were the elements bequeathed by the ancient to the modern world. If, in these elements, we shall already find impressed the character which I have just described, it will have acquired with you, from this time forth, a high degree of probability.

First of all, we must clearly represent to ourselves the nature of the Roman Empire, and how it was formed.

Rome was, in its origin, only a municipality, a corporation. The government of Rome was merely the aggregate of the institutions which were suited to a population confined within the walls of a city: these were municipal institutions, that is their distinguishing character.

This was not the case with Rome only. If we turn our attention to Italy, at this period, we find around Rome nothing but towns. That which was then called a people was simply a confederation of towns. The Latin people was a confederation of Latin towns. The Etruscans, the Samnites, the Sabines, the people of Græcia Magna, may all be described in the same terms.

There was, at this time, no country—that is to say, the country was wholly unlike that which at present exists; it was cultivated, as was necessary, but it was uninhabited. The proprietors of lands were the inhabitants of the towns. They went forth to superintend their country properties, and often took with them a certain number of slaves; but that which we at present call the country, that thin population—sometimes in isolated habitations, sometimes in villages—which everywhere covers the soil, was a fact almost unknown in ancient Italy.

When Rome extended herself, what did she do? Follow history, and you will see that she conquered or founded towns; it was against towns that she fought, with towns that she contracted alliances; it was also into towns that she sent colonies. The history of the conquest of the world by Rome is the history of the conquest and foundation of a great number of towns. In the East, the extention of Roman dominion does not carry altogether this aspect: the population there was otherwise distributed than in the West—it was much less concentrated in towns. But as we have to do here with the European population, what occurred in the East is of little interest to us.

Confining ourselves to the West, we everywhere discover the fact to which I have directed your attention. In Gaul, in Spain, you meet with nothing but towns. At a distance from the towns, the territory is covered with marshes and forests. Examine the character of the Roman monuments, of the Roman roads. You have great roads, which reach from one city to another; the multiplicity of minor roads, which now cross the country in all directions, was then unknown; you have nothing resembling that countless number of villages, country seats and churches, which have been scattered over the country since the middle ages. Rome has left us nothing but immense monuments, stamped with the municipal character, and destined for a numerous population collected upon one spot. Under whatever point of view you consider the Roman world, you will find this almost exclusive preponderance of towns, and the social nonexistence of the country.

This municipal character of the Roman world evidently rendered unity, the social bond of a great state, extremely difficult to establish and maintain. A municipality like Rome had been able to conquer the world, but it was much less easy to govern and organize it. Thus, when the work appeared completed, when all the West, and a great part of the East, had fallen under Roman domination, you behold this prodigious number of cities, of little states, made for isolation and independence, disunite, detach themselves, and escape, so to speak, in all directions. This was one of the causes which rendered necessary the Empire, a form of government more concentrated, more capable of holding together elements so slightly coherent. The Empire endeavored to introduce unity and combination into this scattered society. It succeeded up to a certain point. It was between the reigns of Augustus and Diocletian that, at the same time that civil legislation developed itself, there became established the vast system of administrative despotism which spread over the Roman world a network of functionaries, hierarchically distributed, well linked together, both among themselves and with the imperial court, and solely applied to rendering effective in society the will of power, and in transferring to power the tributes and energies of society.

And not only did this system succeed in rallying and in holding together the elements of the Roman world, but the idea of despotism, of central power, penetrated minds with a singular facility. We are astonished to behold rapidly prevailing throughout this ill-united assemblage of petty republics, this association of municipalities, a reverence for the imperial majesty alone, august and sacred. The necessity of establishing some bond between all these portions of the Roman world must have been very pressing, to insure so easy an access to the mind for the faith and almost the sentiments of despotism.

It was with these creeds, with this administrative organization, and with the military organization which was combined with it, that the Roman Empire struggled against the dissolution at work inwardly, and against the invasion of the barbarians from without. It struggled for a long time, in a continual state of decay, but always defending itself. At last a moment came in which dissolution prevailed: neither the skill of despotism nor the indifference of servitude sufficed to support this huge body. In the fourth century it everywhere disunited and dismembered itself; the barbarians entered on all sides; the provinces no longer resisted, no longer troubled themselves concerning the general destiny. At this time a singular idea suggested itself to some of the emperors: they desired to try whether hopes of general liberty, a confederation—a system analogous to that which, in the present day, we call representative government—would not better defend the unity of the Roman Empire than despotic administration. Here is a rescript of Honorius and Theodosius, the younger, addressed, in the year A.D. 418, to the prefect of Gaul, the only purpose of which was to attempt to establish in the south of Gaul a sort of representative government, and, with its aid, to maintain the unity of the empire.

> Rescript of the Emperors Honorius and Theodosius the younger, addressed, in the year 418, to the prefect of the Gauls, sitting in the town of Arles.

> Honorius and Theodosius, Augusti, to Agricola, prefect of the Gauls:

> Upon the satisfactory statement that your Magnificence has made to us, among other information palpably advantageous to the state, we decree the force of law in perpetuity to the following ordinances, to which the inhabitants of our seven provinces will owe obedience, they being such that they themselves might have desired and demanded them. Seeing that persons in office, or special deputies from motives of public or private utility, not only from each of the provinces, but also from every town, often present themselves before your Magnificence, either to render accounts or to treat of things relative to the interest of proprietors, we have judged that it would be a seasonable and profitable thing that, from the date of the present year, there should be annually, at a fixed time, an assemblage held in the metropolis— that is, in the town of Arles, for the inhabitants of the seven provinces. By this institution we have in view to provide equally for general and particular interests. In the first place, by the meeting of the most notable of the inhabitants in the illustrious presence of the prefect, if motives of public order have not called him elsewhere, the best possible information may be gained upon every subject under deliberation. Nothing of that which will have been treated of and decided upon, after a ripe consideration, will escape the knowledge of any of the provinces, and those who shall not have been present at the assembly will be bound to follow the same rules of justice and equity. Moreover, in ordaining that an annual assembly be held in the city of Constantine,[4] we believe that we are doing a thing not only advantageous to the public good, but also adapted to multiply social relations. Indeed, the city is so advantageously situated, strangers come there in such numbers, and it enjoys such an extensive commerce,

4. Constantine the Great had a singular liking for the town of Arles. It was he who established there the seat of the Gaulish prefecture; he desired also that it should bear his name, but custom prevailed against his wish.

that everything finds its way there which grows or is manufactured in other places. All admirable things that the rich East, perfumed Arabia, delicate Assyria, fertile Africa, beautiful Spain, valiant Gaul produce, abound in this place with such profusion, that whatever is esteemed magnificent in the various parts of the world seems there the produce of the soil. Besides, the junction of the Rhone with the Tuscan sea approximates and renders almost neighbors those countries which the first traverses, and the second bathes in its windings. Thus, since the entire earth places at the service of this city all that it has most worthy—since the peculiar productions of all countries are transported hither by land, by sea, and by the course of rivers, by help of sails, of oars, and of wagons—how can our Gaul do otherwise than behold a benefit in the command which we give to convoke a public assembly in a city, wherein are united, as it were, by the gift of God, all the enjoyments of life, and all the facilities of commerce?

The illustrious prefect Petronius,[5] through a laudable and reasonable motive, formerly commanded that this custom should be observed; but as the practice thereof was interrupted by the confusion of the times, and by the reign of usurpers, we have resolved to revive it in vigor by the authority of our wisdom. Thus, then, dear and beloved cousin Agricola, your illustrious Magnificence, conforming yourself to our present ordinance, and to the custom established by your predecessors, will cause to be observed throughout the provinces the following rules:

"Let all persons who are honored with public functions, or who are proprietors of domains, and all judges of provinces, be informed that, each year, they are to assemble in council in the city of Arles, between the ides of August and those of September, the days of convocation and of sitting being determined at their pleasure.

"Novem Populinia and the second Aquitaine, being the most distant provinces, should their judges be detained by indispensable occupations, may send deputies in their place, according to custom.

"Those who shall neglect to appear at the place assigned and at the time appointed, shall pay a fine, which, for the judges, shall be five pounds of gold, and three pounds for the members of the *curiæ*[6] and other dignitaries."

We propose, by this means, to confer great advantages and favor on the inhabitants of our provinces. We feel, also, assured

5. Petronius was prefect of the Gauls between the years 402 and 408.
6. The municipal bodies of Roman towns were called *curiæ,* and the members of those bodies, who were very numerous, were called *curiales.*

of adding to the ornaments of the city of Arles, to the fidelity of which we are so much indebted, according to our brother and patrician.[7]

Given on the 15th of the calends of May; received at Arles on the 10th of the calends of June.

The provinces and the towns refused the benefit; no one would nominate the deputies, no one would go to Arles. Centralization and unity were contrary to the primitive character of that society; the local and municipal spirit reappeared everywhere, and the impossibility of reconstituting a general society or country became evident. The towns confined themselves, each to its own walls and its own affairs, and the empire fell because none wished to be of the empire, because citizens desired to be only of their own city. Thus we again discover, at the fall of the Roman Empire, the same fact which we have detected in the cradle of Rome, namely, the predominance of the municipal form and spirit. The Roman world had returned to its first condition; towns had constituted it; it dissolved; and towns remained.

In the municipal system we see what ancient Roman civilization has bequeathed to modern Europe; that system was very irregular, much weakened and far inferior, no doubt, to what it had been in earlier times; but, nevertheless, the only real, the only constituted system which had outlived all the elements of the Roman world.

When I say *alone* I make a mistake. Another fact, another idea equally survived: the idea of the empire, the name of emperor, the idea of imperial majesty, of an absolute and sacred power attached to the name of emperor. These are the elements which Rome has transmitted to European civilization; upon one hand, the municipal system, its habits, rules, precedents, the principle of freedom; on the other, a general and uniform civil legislation, the idea of absolute power, of sacred majesty, of the emperor, the principle of order and subjection.

But there was formed at the same time, in the heart of the Roman society, a society of a very different nature, founded upon

7. Constantine, the second husband of Placidius, whom Honorius had chosen for colleague in 421.

totally different principles, animated by different sentiments, a society which was about to infuse into modern European society elements of a character wholly different; I speak of the *Christian church*. I say the Christian church, and not Christianity. At the end of the fourth and at the beginning of the fifth century Christianity was no longer merely an individual belief, it was an institution; it was constituted; it had its government, a clergy, an hierarchy calculated for the different functions of the clergy, revenues, means of independent action, rallying points suited for a great society, provincial, national and general councils, and the custom of debating in common upon the affairs of the society. In a word, Christianity, at this epoch, was not only a religion, it was also a church.

Had it not been a church I cannot say what might have happened to it amid the fall of the Roman Empire. I confine myself to simply human considerations; I put aside every element which is foreign to the natural consequences of natural facts: had Christianity been, as in the earlier times, no more than a belief, a sentiment, an individual conviction, we may believe that it would have sunk amidst the dissolution of the empire and the invasion of the barbarians. In later times, in Asia and in all the north of Africa, it sunk under an invasion of the same nature, under the invasion of the Moslem barbarians; it sunk then, although it subsisted in the form of an institution, or constituted church. With much more reason might the same thing have happened at the moment of the fall of the Roman Empire. There existed, at that time, none of those means by which, in the present day, moral influences establish themselves or offer resistence, independently of institutions; none of those means whereby a pure truth, a pure idea obtains a great empire over minds, governs actions and determines events. Nothing of the kind existed in the fourth century to give a like authority to ideas and to personal sentiments. It is clear that a society strongly organized and strongly governed was indispensable to struggle against such a disaster, and to issue victorious from such a storm. I do not think that I say more than the truth in affirming that at the end of the fourth and the commencement of the fifth centuries it was the Christian church that saved Christianity; it was the church with its institutions, its magistrates and its power, that vigorously resisted the internal dissolution of the empire and barbarism; that conquered the barbarians and became the bond, the medium and the principle of civilization between the Roman and barbarian worlds. It is, then, the condition of the church rather than that of religion, properly so called, that we must look to in order to discover what Christianity has, since then, added to modern civilization, and what new elements it has introduced therein. What was the Christian church at that period?

When we consider, always under a purely human point of view, the various revolutions which have accomplished themselves during the development of Christianity, from the time of its origin up to the fifth century; if, I repeat, we consider it simply as a community and not as a religious creed, we find that it passed through three essentially different states.

In the very earliest period, the Christian society presents itself as a simple association of a common creed and common sentiments; the first Christians united to enjoy together the same emotions, and the same religious convictions. We find among them no system of determinate doctrines, no rules, no discipline, no body of magistrates.

Of course, no society, however newly born, however weakly constituted it may be, exists without a moral power which animates and directs it. In the various Christian congregations there were men who preached, taught and morally governed the congregation, but there was no formal magistrate, no recognized discipline; a simple association caused by a community of creed and sentiments was the primitive condition of the Christian society.

In proportion as it advanced—and very speedily, since traces are visible in the earliest monuments—a body of doctrines, of rules, of discipline, and of magistrates, began to appear; one kind of magistrates were called πρεσβυτεροι, or *ancients*, who became the priests; another, επισηοποι, or inspectors, or superintendents, who became bishops; a third διηονοι, or deacons, who were charged with the care of the poor, and with the distribution of alms.

It is scarcely possible to determine what were the precise functions of these various magistrates; the line of demarcation was probably very vague and variable, but what is clear is that an establishment was organized. Still, a peculiar character prevails in this second period: the preponderance and rule belonged to the body of the faithful. It was the body of the faithful which prevailed, both as to the choice of functionaries, and as to the adoption of discipline, and even doctrine. The church government and the Christian people were not as yet separated. They did not exist apart from, and independently of, one another; and the Christian people exercised the principal influence in the society.

In the third period all was different. A clergy existed who were distinct from the people; a body of priests who had their own riches, jusisdiction, and peculiar constitution; in a word, an entire government, which in itself was a complete society, a society provided with all the means of existence, independently of the society to which it had reference, and over which it extended its influence. Such was the third stage of the constitution of the Christian church; such was the form in which it appeared at the beginning of the fifth century. The government was not completely separated from the people; there has never been a parallel kind of government, and less in religious matters than in any others; but in the relations of the clergy to the faithful, the clergy ruled almost without control.

The Christian clergy had moreover another and very different source of influence. The bishops and the priests became the principal municipal magistrates. You have seen, that of the Roman Empire there remained, properly speaking, nothing but the municipal system. It had happened, from the vexations of despotism and the ruin of the towns, that the *curiales*, or members of the municipal bodies, had become discouraged and apathetic; on the contrary, the bishops, and the body of priests, full of life and zeal, offered themselves naturally for the superintendence and direction of all matters. We should be wrong to reproach them for this, to tax them with usurpation; it was all in the natural course of things; the clergy alone were morally strong and animated; they became everywhere powerful. Such is the law of the universe.

The marks of this revolution are visible in all the legislation of the emperors at this period. If you open the code, either of Theodosius or of Justinian, you will find numerous regulations which remit municipal affairs to the clergy and the bishops. Here are some of them:

> With respect to the yearly affairs of cities, whether they concern the ordinary revenues of the city, either from funds arising from the property of the city, or from private gifts or legacies, or from any other source; whether public works, or depots of provisions, or aqueducts, or the maintenance of baths, or ports, or the construction of walls or towers, or the repairing of bridges or roads, or trials in which the city may be engaged in reference to public or private interests, we ordain as follows: The very pious bishop, and three notables chosen from among the first men of the city, shall meet together; they shall, each year, examine the works done; they shall take care that those who conduct them, or who have conducted them, shall regulate them with precision, render their accounts, and show that they have duly performed their engagements in· the administration, whether of the public monuments, or of the sums appointed for provisions or baths, or of expenses in the maintenance of roads, aqueducts, or any other work. (*Cod. Just.* 1.1, tit. 4, *de episcopali audientia,* § 26.)

> With regard to the guardianship of young persons of the first or second age, and of all those for whom the law appoints guardians, if their fortune does not exceed 500 *aurei,* we ordain that the nomination of the president of the province shall not be waited for, as this gives rise to great expenses, particularly if the said president does not reside in the city in which it is necessary to provide the guardianship. The nomination of guardians shall in such case be made by the magistrate of the city . . . in concert with the very pious bishop and other person or persons invested with public offices, if there be more than one. (Ibid., § 30.)

> We desire that the defenders of the cities, being well instructed in the holy mysteries of the orthodox faith, be chosen and instituted by the venerable bishops, the priests, the notables, the proprietors, and the *curiales.* As regards their installation, it shall be

referred to the glorious power of the pretorian prefect, in order that their authority may have infused into it more solidity and vigor from the letters of admission of his Magnificence. (Ibid., 1.1, tit. 55, *de defensoribus*, § 8.)

I might cite a great number of other laws, and you would everywhere meet with the fact which I have mentioned: between the municipal system of the Romans, and that of the middle ages, the municipal-ecclesiastic system interposed; the preponderance of the clergy in the affairs of the city succeeded that of the ancient municipal magistrates, and preceded the organization of the modern municipal corporations.

You perceive what prodigious power was thus obtained by the Christian church, as well by its own constitution as by its influence upon the Christian people, and by the part which it took in civil affairs. Thus, from that epoch, it powerfully assisted in forming the character and furthering the development of modern civilization. Let us endeavor to sum up the elements which it from that time introduced into it.

And first of all there was an immense advantage in the presence of a moral influence, of a moral power, of a power which reposed solely upon convictions and upon moral creeds and sentiments, amidst the deluge of material power which at this time inundated society. Had the Christian church not existed, the whole world must have been abandoned to purely material force. The church alone exercised a moral power. It did more: it sustained, it spread abroad the idea of a rule, of a law superior to all human laws. It proposed for the salvation of humanity the fundamental belief that there exists, above all human laws, a law which is denominated, according to periods and customs, sometimes reason, sometimes the divine law, but which, everywhere and always, is the same law under different names.

In short, with the church originated a great fact, the separation of spiritual and temporal power. This separation is the source of liberty of conscience; it is founded upon no other principle but that which is the foundation of the most perfect and extended freedom of conscience. The separation of temporal and spiritual power is based upon the idea that physical force has neither right nor influence over souls, over conviction, over truth. It flows from the distinction established between the world of thought and the world of action, between the world of internal and that of external facts. Thus this principle of liberty of conscience for which Europe has struggled so much, and suffered so much, this principle which prevailed so late, and often, in its progress, against the inclination of the clergy, was enunciated, under the name of the separation of temporal and spiritual power, in the very cradle of European civilization; and it was the Christian church which, from the necessity imposed by its situation of defending itself against barbarism, introduced and maintained it.

The presence, then, of a moral influence, the maintenance of a divine law, and the separation of the temporal and spiritual powers, are the three grand benefits which the Christian church in the fifth century conferred upon the European world.

Even at that time, however, all its influences were not equally salutary. Already, in the fifth century, there appeared in the church certain unwholesome principles, which have played a great part in the development of our civilization. Thus, at this period, there prevailed within it the separation of governors and the governed, the attempt to establish the independence of governors as regards the governed, to impose laws upon the governed, to possess their mind, their life, without the free consent of their reason and of their will. The church, moreover, endeavored to render the theocratic principle predominant in society, to usurp the temporal power, to reign exclusively. And when it could not succeed in obtaining temporal dominion, in inducing the prevalence of the theocratic principle, it allied itself with temporal princes, and, in order to share, supported their absolute power at the expense of the liberty of the people.

Such were the principles of civilization which Europe, in the fifth century, derived from the church and from the Empire. It was in this condition that the barbarians found the Roman world, and came to take possession of it. In order to fully understand all the elements which met and mixed in the cradle of our civilization, it only remains for us to study the barbarians.

When I speak of the barbarians, you understand that we have nothing to do here with their history; narrative is not our present business. You know that at this period the conquerors of the Empire were nearly all of the same race; they were all Germans, except some Sclavonic tribes, the Alani, for example. We know also that they were all in pretty nearly the same stage of civilization. Some difference, indeed, might have existed between them in this respect, according to the greater or less degree of connection which the different tribes had had with the Roman world. Thus, no doubt the Goths were more advanced, possessed milder manners than the Franks. But in considering matters under a general point of view, and in their results as regards ourselves, this original difference of civilization among the barbarous people is of no importance.

It is the general condition of society among the barbarians that we need to understand. But this is a subject with which, at the present day, it is very difficult to make ourselves acquainted. We obtain, without much difficulty, a comprehension of the Roman municipal system, of the Christian church; their influence has been continued up to our own days. We find traces of it in numerous institutions and actual facts; we have a thousand means of recognizing and explaining them. But the customs and social condition of the barbarians have completely perished. We are compelled to make them out either from the earliest historical monuments, or by an effort of the imagination.

There is a sentiment, a fact which, before all things, it is necessary that we should well understand in order to represent faithfully to one's self the barbaric character: the pleasure of individual independence; the pleasure of enjoying one's self with vigor and liberty, amidst the chances of the world and of life; the delights of activity without labor; the taste for an adventurous career, full of uncertainty, inequality and peril. Such was the predominating sentiment of the barbarous state, the moral want which put in motion these masses of human beings. In the present day, locked up as we are in so regular a society, it is difficult to represent this sentiment to one's self with all the power which it exercised over the barbarians of the fourth and fifth centuries. There is only one work which, in my opinion, contains this characteristic of barbarism stamped in all its energy —*The History of the Conquest of England by the Normans*, of M. Thierry, the only book wherein the motives, tendencies and impulses which actuate men in a social condition, bordering on barbarism, are felt and reproduced with a really Homeric faithfulness. Nowhere else do we see so well the nature of a barbarian and of the life of a barbarian. Something of this sort is also found, though, in my opinion, in a much lower degree, with much less simplicity, much less truth, in Cooper's romances upon the savages of America. There is something in the life of the American savages, in the relations and the sentiments they bear with them in the middle of the woods, that recalls, up to a certain point, the manners of the ancient Germans. No doubt these pictures are somewhat idealized, somewhat poetic; the dark side of the barbaric manners and life is not presented to us in all its grossness. I speak not only of the evils induced by these manners upon the social state, but of the internal and individual condition of the barbarian himself. There was within this passionate need of personal independence something more gross and more material than one would be led to conceive from the work of M. Thierry; there was a degree of brutality and of apathy which is not always exactly conveyed by his recitals. Nevertheless, when we look to the bottom of the question, notwithstanding this alloy of brutality, of materialism, of dull, stupid selfishness, the love of independence is a noble and a moral sentiment, which draws its power from the moral nature of man; it is the pleasure of feeling one's self a man, the sentiment of personality, of human spontaneity, in its free development.

It was through the German barbarians that this sentiment was introduced into European civilization; it was unknown in the Roman world, unknown in the Christian church, and unknown in almost all the ancient civilizations. When you find liberty in ancient civilizations, it is political liberty, the liberty of the citizen: man strove not for his personal liberty but for his liberty as a citizen: he belonged to an association, he was devoted to an association, he was ready to sacrifice himself to an association. It was the same with the Christian church: a sentiment of strong attachment to the Christian corporation, of devotion to its laws, and a lively desire to extend its empire; or rather, the religious sentiment induced a reaction of man upon himself, upon his soul, an internal effort to subdue his own liberty, and to submit himself to the will of his faith. But the sentiment of personal independence, a love of liberty displaying itself at all risks, without any other motive but that of satisfying itself; this sentiment, I repeat, was unknown to the Roman and to the Christian society. It was by the barbarians that it was brought in and deposited in the cradle of modern civilization, wherein it has played so conspicuous a part, has produced such worthy results, that it is impossible to help reckoning it as one of its fundamental elements.

There is a second fact, a second element of civilization, for which we are equally indebted to the barbarians: this is military clientship; the bond which established itself between individuals, between warriors, and which, without destroying the liberty of each, without even in the beginning destroying, beyond a certain point, the equality which almost completely existed between them, nevertheless founded an hierarchical subordination, and gave birth to that aristocratical organization which afterward became feudalism. The foundation of this relation was the attachment of man to man, the fidelity of individual to individual, without external necessity, and without obligation based upon the general principles of society. In the ancient republics you see no man attached freely and especially to any other man; they were all attached to the city. Among the barbarians it was between individuals that the social bond was formed; first by the relation of the chief to his companion, when they lived in the condition of a band wandering over Europe; and later, by the relation of suzerain to vassal. This second principle, which has played so great a part in the history of modern civilization, this devotion of man to man, came to us from the barbarians; it is from their manners that it has passed into ours.

I ask you, was I wrong in saying at the beginning that modern civilization, even in its cradle, had been as varied, as agitated and as confused as I have endeavored to describe it to you in the general picture I have given you of it? Is it not true that we have now discovered, at the fall of the Roman Empire, almost all the elements which unite in the progressive development of our civilization? We have found, at that time, three wholly different societies: the municipal society, the last remains of the Roman Empire, the Christian society, and the barbaric society. We find these societies very variously organized, founded upon totally different principles, inspiring men with wholly different sentiments; we find the craving after the most absolute independence side by side with the most complete submission; military patronage side by side with ecclesiastical dominion; the spiritual and temporal powers everywhere present; the canons of the church, the learned legislation of the Romans, the almost unwritten customs of the barbarians; everywhere the mixture, or rather the co-existence of the most diverse races, languages, social situations, manners, ideas and impressions. Herein I think we have a sufficient proof of the faithfulness of the general character under which I have endeavored to present our civilization to you.

No doubt this confusion, this diversity, this struggle, have cost us very dear; these have been the cause of the slow progress of Europe, of the storms and sufferings to which she has been a prey. Nevertheless, I do not think we need regret them. To people, as well as to individuals, the chance of the most complete and varied development, the chance of an almost unlimited progress in all directions compensates of itself alone for all that it may cost to obtain the right of casting for it. And all things considered, this state, so agitated, so toilsome, so violent, has availed much more than the simplicity with which other civilizations present themselves; the human race has gained thereby more than it has suffered.

. . . .

Lecture 4
We have studied the condition of Europe after the fall of the Roman empire, in the first period of modern history, the barbarous. We have seen that, at the end of this epoch, and at the

commencement of the tenth century, the first principle, the first system that developed itself and took possession of European society, was the feudal system; we have seen that feudalism was the firstborn of barbarism. It is, then, the feudal system which must now be the object of our study.

I scarcely think it necessary to remind you that it is not the history of events, properly speaking, which we are considering. It is not my business to recount to you the destinies of feudalism. That which occupies us is the history of civilization; this is the general and hidden fact which we seek under all the external facts which envelop it.

Thus, events, social crises, the various states through which society has passed, interests us only in their relations to the development of civilization; we inquire of them solely in what respects they have opposed or assisted it, what they have given to it, and what they have refused it. It is only under this point of view that we are to consider the feudal system.

In the commencement of these lectures we defined the nature of civilization; we attempted to investigate its elements; we saw that it consisted, on the one hand, in the development of man himself, of the individual, of humanity; on the other hand, in that of his external condition, in the development of society. Whenever we find ourselves in the presence of an event, of a system, or of a general condition of the world, we have this double question to ask of it, what has it done for or against the development of man, for or against the development of society?

You understand beforehand, that, during our investigations, it is impossible that we should not meet upon our way most important questions of moral philosophy. When we desire to know in what an event or a system has contributed to the development of man and of society, it is absolutely needful that we should be acquainted with the nature of the true development of society and of man; that we should know what developments are false and illegitimate, perverting instead of ameliorating, causing a retrogressive instead of a progressive movement.

We shall not seek to escape from this necessity. Not only should we thereby mutilate and lower our ideas and the facts, but the actual state of the world imposes upon us the necessity of freely accepting this inevitable alliance of philosophy and history. This is precisely one of the characteristics, perhaps the essential characteristic of our epoch. We are called upon to consider, to cause to progress together, science and reality, theory and practice, right and fact. Up to our times, these two powers have existed separately; the world has been accustomed to behold science and practice following different roads, without recognising each other, or, at least, without meeting. And when doctrines and general ideas have desired to amalgamate with events and influence the world, they have only succeeded under the form and by means of the arm of fanaticism. The empire of human societies, and the direction of their affairs, have hitherto been shared between two kinds of influences: upon one hand, the believers, the men of general ideas and principles, the fanatics; on the other, men strangers to all rational principles, who govern themselves merely according to circumstances, practitioners, freethinkers, as the seventeenth century called them. This condition of things is now ceasing; neither fanatics nor freethinkers will any longer have dominion. In order now to govern and prevail with men, it is necessary to be acquainted with general ideas and circumstances; it is necessary to know how to value principles and facts, to respect virtue and necessity, to preserve oneself from the pride of fanatics, and the not less blind scorn of freethinkers. To this point have we been conducted by the development of the human mind and the social state: upon one hand, the human mind, exalted and freed, better comprehends the connexion of things, knows how to look around on all sides, and makes use of all things in its combinations; on the other hand, society has perfected itself to that degree, that it can be compared with the truth; that facts can be brought into juxtaposition with principles, and yet, in spite of their still great imperfections, not inspire by the comparison invincible discouragement or distaste. I shall thus obey the natural tendency, convenience, and the necessity of our times, in constantly passing from the examination of circumstances to that of ideas, from an exposition of facts to a question of doctrines. Perhaps, even, there is in the actual disposition of men's minds, another reason in favour of this method. For some time past a confirmed taste, I might say a sort of predilection, has manifested itself among us, for facts, for practical views, for the positive aspect of human affairs. We have been to such an extent a prey to the despotism of general ideas, of theories; they have, in some respects, cost us so dear, that they are become the objects of a certain degree of distrust. We like better to carry ourselves back to facts, to special circumstances, to applications. This is not to be regretted; it is a new progress, a great step in knowledge, and towards the empire of truth; provided always that we do not allow ourselves to be prejudiced and carried away by this disposition; that we do not forget that truth alone has a right to reign in the world; that facts have no value except as they tend to explain, and to assimilate themselves more and more to the truth; that all true greatness is of thought; and that all fruitfulness belongs to it. The civilization of our country has this peculiar character, that it has never wanted intellectual greatness; it has always been rich in ideas; the power of the human mind has always been great in French society; greater, perhaps, than in any other. We must not lose this high privilege; we must not fall into the somewhat subordinate and material state which characterizes other societies. Intelligence and doctrines must occupy in the France of the present day, at least the place which they have occupied there hitherto.

We shall, then, by no means avoid general and philosophical questions; we shall not wander in search of them, but where facts lead us to them, we shall meet them without hesitation or embarassment. An occasion of doing so will more than once present itself, during the consideration of the feudal system in its relations to the history of European civilization.

A good proof that, in the tenth century, the feudal system was necessary, was the only possible social state, is the universality of its establishment. Wherever barbarism ceased, everything took the feudal form. At the first moment, men saw in it only the triumph of chaos; all unity, all general civilization vanished; on all sides they beheld society dismembering itself; and, in its stead, they beheld a number of minor, obscure, isolated, and incoherent societies erect themselves. To contemporaries, this appeared the dissolution of all things, universal anarchy. Consult the poets and the chroniclers of the time; they all believed themselves at the end of the world. It was, nevertheless, the beginning of a new and real society, the feudal, so necessary, so inevitable, so truly the only possible consequence of the anterior state, that all things entered into it and assumed its form. Elements, the most foreign to this system, the church, municipalities, royalty, were compelled to accommodate themselves to it; the churches became suzerains and vassals, cities had lords and vassals, royalty disguised itself under the form of suzerainship. All things were given in fief, not only lands, but certain rights, the right, for instance, of felling in forests, and of fishing; the churches gave in fief their perquisites, from their revenues from baptisms, the churchings of women. Water and money were given in fief. Just as all the general elements of society entered into the feudal frame, so the smallest details, and the most trifling facts of common life, became a part of feudalism.

In beholding the feudal form thus taking possession of all things, we are tempted to believe, at first, that the essential and vital principle of feudalism everywhere prevailed. But this is a mistake. In borrowing the feudal form, the elements and institutions of society which were not analogous to the feudal system, did not renounce their own nature or peculiar principles. The feudal church did not cease to be animated and governed, at bottom, by the theocratic principle; and it laboured unceasingly, sometimes in concert with the royal power, sometimes with the pope, and sometimes with the people, to destroy this system, of which, so to speak it wore the livery. It was the same with royalty and with the corporations; in the one the monarchical, in the other the democratical principle, continued, at bottom, to predominate. Notwithstanding their feudal livery, these various elements of European society constantly laboured to deliver themselves from a form which was foreign to their true nature, and to assume that which corresponded to their peculiar and vital principle.

Having shown the universality of the feudal form, it becomes very necessary to be on our guard against concluding from this the universality of the feudal principle, and against studying feudalism indifferently, whenever we meet with its physiognomy. In order to know and comprehend this system thoroughly, to unravel and judge of its effects in reference to modern civilization, we must examine it where the form and principle are in harmony; we must study it in the hierarchy of lay possessors of fiefs, in the association of the conquerors of the European territory. There truly resided feudal society; thereupon we are now to enter.

I spoke just now of the importance of moral questions, and of the necessity of not avoiding them. But there is a totally opposite kind of consideration, which has generally been too much neglected; I mean the material condition of society, the material changes introduced into mankind's method of existing, by a new fact, by a revolution, by a new social state. We have not always sufficiently considered these things; we have not always sufficiently inquired into the modifications introduced by these great crises of the world, into the material existence of men, into the material aspect of their relations. These modifications have more influence upon the entire society than is supposed. Who does not know how much the influence of climates has been studied, and how much importance was attached to it by Montesquieu? If we regard the immediate influence of climate upon men, perhaps it is not so extensive as has been supposed; it is, at all events, very vague and difficult to be appreciated. But the indirect influence of climate, that which, for example, results from the fact, that, in a warm country, men live in the open air, while, in a cold country, they shut themselves up in their houses; that, in one case, they nourish themselves in one manner, in the other, in another, these are facts of great importance, facts which by the simple difference of material life, act powerfully upon civilization. All great revolutions lead to modifications of this sort in the social state, and these are very necessary to be considered.

The establishment of the feudal system produced one of these modifications, of unmistakeable importance; it altered the distribution of the population over the face of the land. Hitherto the masters of the soil, the sovereign population, had lived united in more or less numerous masses of men, whether sedentarily in cities, or wandering in bands through the country. In consequence of the feudal system, these same men lived isolated, each in his own habitation, and at great distances from one another. You will immediately perceive how much influence this change was calculated to exercise upon the character and course of civilization. The social preponderance, the government of society, passed suddenly from the towns to the country; private property became of more importance than public property; private life than public life. Such was the first and purely material effect of the triumph of feudal society. The further we examine into it, the more will the consequence of this single fact be unfolded to our eyes.

Let us investigate this society in itself, and see what part it has played in the history of civilization. First of all, let us take feudalism in its most simple, primitive, and fundamental element; let us consider a single possessor of a fief in his domain, and let us see what will become of all those who form the little society around him.

He establishes himself upon an isolated and elevated spot, which he takes care to render safe and strong: there he constructs what he will call his castle. With whom does he establish himself? With his wife and children; perhaps some freemen, who have not become proprietors, attach themselves to his person, and continue to live with him, at his table. These are the inhabitants of the interior of the castle. Around and at its foot, a little population of colonists and serfs gather together, who cultivate the domains of the possessor of the fief. In the centre of this lower population religion plants a church; it brings hither a priest. In the early period of the feudal system, this priest was commonly at the same time the chaplain of the castle and the pastor of the village; by and by these two characters separated; the village had its own pastor, who lived there, beside his church. This, then, was the elementary feudal society, the feudal molecule, so to speak. It is this element that we have first of all to examine. We will demand of it the double question which should be asked of all our facts: What has resulted from it in favour of the development, (1) of man himself, (2) of society?

We are perfectly justified in addressing this double question to the little society which I have just described, and in placing faith in its replies; for it was the type and faithful image of the entire feudal society. The lord, the people on his domains, and the priest; such is feudalism upon the great as well as the small scale, when we have taken from it royalty and the towns, which are distinct and foreign elements.

The first fact that strikes us in contemplating this little society, is the prodigious importance which the possessor of the fief must have had, both in his own eyes, and in the eyes of those who surrounded him. The sentiment of personality, of individual liberty, predominated in the barbaric life. But here it was wholly different; it was no longer only the liberty of the man, of the warrior; it was the importance of the proprietor, of the head of the family, of the master, that came to be considered. From this situation an impression of immense superiority must have resulted; a superiority quite peculiar, and very different from everything that we meet with in the career of other civilizations. I will give the proof of this. I take in the ancient world some great aristocratical position, a Roman patrician, for instance: like the feudal lord, the Roman patrician was head of a family, master, superior. He was, moreover, the religious magistrate, the pontiff in the interior of his family. Now, his importance as a religious magistrate came to him from without; it was not a purely personal and individual importance; he received it from on high; he was the delegate of the Divinity; the interpreter of the religious creed. The Roman patrician was, besides, the member of a corporation which lived united on the same spot, a member of the senate; this again was an importance which came to him from without, from his corporation, a received, a borrowed importance. The greatness of the ancient aristocrats, associated as it was with a religious and political character, belonged to the situation, to the corporation in general, rather than to the individual. That of the possessor of the fief was purely individual; it was not derived from any one; all his rights, all his power, came to him from himself. He was not a religious magistrate; he took no part in a senate; it was in his person that all his importance resided; all that he was, he was of himself, and in his own name. What a mighty influence must such a situation have exerted on its occupant! What individual haughtiness, what prodigious pride—let us say the word—what insolence, must have arisen in his soul! Above himself there was no superior of whom he was the representative or interpreter; there was no equal near him; no powerful and general law which weighed upon him; no external rule which influenced his will; he knew no curb but the limits of his strength and the presence of danger. Such was the necessary moral result of this situation upon the character of man.

I now proceed to a second consequence, mighty also, and too little noticed, namely, the particular turn taken by the feudal family spirit.

Let us cast a glance over the various family systems. Take first of all the patriarchal system of which the Bible and oriental records offer the model. The family was very numerous; it was a tribe. The chief, the patriarch, lived therein in common with his children, his near relations, the various generations which united themselves around him, all his kindred, all his servants; and not only did he live with them all, but he had the same interests, the same occupations, and he led the same life. Was not this the condition of Abraham, of the patriarchs, and of the chiefs of the Arab tribes, who will reproduce the image of the patriarchal life?

Another family system presents itself, namely, the *clan*, a petty society, whose type we must seek for in Scotland or Ireland. Through this system, very probably, a large portion of the European family has passed. This is no longer the patriarchal family. There is here a great difference between the situation of the chief and that of the rest of the population. They did not lead the same life: the greater portion tilled and served; the chief was idle and warlike. But they had a common origin; they all bore the same name; and their relations of kindred, ancient traditions, the same recollections, the same affections, established a moral tie, a sort of equality between all the members of the clan.

These are the two principal types of the family society presented by history. But have we here the feudal family? Obviously not. It seems, at first, that the feudal family bears some relation to the clan; but the difference is much greater than the resemblance. The population which surrounded the possessor of the fief were totally unconnected with him; they did not bear his name; between them and him there was no kindred, no bond, moral or historical. Neither did it resemble the patriarchal family. The possessor of the fief led not the same life, nor did he engage in the same occupations with those who surrounded him; he was an idler and a warrior, whilst the others were labourers. The feudal family was not numerous; it was not a tribe; it reduced itself to the family, properly so called, namely, to the wife and children; it lived separated from the rest of the population, shut up in the castle. The colonists and serfs made no part of it; the origin of the members of this society was different, the inequality of their situation immense. Five or six individuals, in a situation at once superior to and estranged from the rest of the society: that was the feudal family. It was of course invested with a peculiar character. It was narrow, concentrated, and constantly called upon to defend itself against, to distrust, and, at least, to isolate itself from, even its retainers. The interior life, domestic manners, were sure to become predominant in such a system. I am aware that the brutality of the passions of a chief, his habit of spending his time in warfare or the chase, were a great obstacle to the development of domestic manners. But this would be conquered; the chief necessarily returned home habitually; he always found there his wife and children, and these well nigh only; these would alone constitute his permanent society—they would alone share his interests, his destiny. Domestic life necessarily, therefore, required great sway. Proofs of this abound. Was it not within the bosom of the feudal family that the importance of women developed itself? In all the ancient societies, I do not speak of those where the family spirit did not exist, but of those wherein it was very powerful, in the patriarchal life, for instance, women did not hold at all so considerable a place as they acquired in Europe under the feudal system.

It was to the development and necessary preponderance of domestic manners in feudalism, that they chiefly owed this change, this progress in their condition. Some have desired to trace the cause to the peculiar manners of the ancient Germans; to a national respect which, it is said, they bore towards women amidst their forests. Upon a sentence of Tacitus, German patriotism has built I know not what superiority, what primitive and uneradicable purity of German manners, as regards the relations of the two sexes. Mere fancies! Phrases similar to that of Tacitus, concerning sentiments and usages analogous to those of the ancient Germans, are to be found in the recitals of a crowd of observers of savage or barbarous people. There is nothing primitive therein, nothing peculiar to any particular race. It was in the effects of a strongly marked social position, in the progress and preponderance of domestic manners, that the importance of women in Europe originated; and the preponderance of domestic manners became, very early, an essential characteristic of the feudal system.

A second fact, another proof of the empire of domestic life, equally characterises the feudal family: I mean the hereditary spirit, the spirit of perpetuation, which evidently predominated therein. The hereditary spirit is inherent in the family spirit; but nowhere has it so strongly developed itself as under the feudal system. This resulted from the nature of the property with which the family was incorporated. The fief was unlike other properties: it constantly demanded a possessor to defend it, serve it, acquit himself of the obligations inherent in the domain, and thus maintain it in its rank amidst the general association of the masters of the soil. Thence resulted a sort of identification between the actual possessor of the fief and the fief itself, and all the series of its future possessors.

This circumstance greatly contributed to fortify and make closer the family ties, already so powerful by the very nature of the feudal family.

I now issue from the seignorial dwelling, and descend amidst the petty population that surrounds it. Here all things wear a different aspect. The nature of man is so good and fruitful, that when a social situation endures for any length of time, a certain moral tie, sentiments of protection, benevolence, and affection, inevitably establish themselves among those who are thus approximated to one another, whatever may be the conditions of approximation. It happened thus with feudalism. No doubt, after a certain time, some moral relations, some habits of affection, became contracted between the colonists and the possessor of the fief. But this happened in spite of their relative position, and not by reason of its influence. Considered in itself, the position was radically wrong. There was nothing morally in common between the possessor of the fief and the colonists; they constituted part of his domain; they were his property; and under this name, property, were included all the rights which, in the present day, are called rights of public sovereignty, as well as the rights of private property, the right of imposing laws, of taxing, and punishing, as well as that of disposing of and selling. As far as it is possible that such should be the case where men are in presence of men, between the lord and the cultivators of his lands there existed no rights, no guarantees, no society.

Hence, I conceive, the truly prodigious and invincible hatred with which the people at all times have regarded the feudal system, its recollections, its very name. It is not a case without example for men to have submitted to oppressive despotisms, and to have become accustomed to them; nay, to have willingly accepted them. Theocratic and monarchical despotisms have more than once obtained the consent, almost the affections, of the population subjected to them. But feudal despotism has always been repulsive and odious; it has oppressed the destinies, but never reigned over the souls of men. The reason is, that in theocracy and monarchy, power is exercised in virtue of certain words which are common to the master and to the subject; it is the representative, the minister of another power superior to all human power; it speaks and acts in the name of the Divinity or of a general idea, and not in the name of man himself, of man alone. Feudal despotism was altogether different; it was the power of the individual over the individual; the dominion of the personal and capricious will of a man. This is, perhaps, the only tyranny which, to his eternal honour, man will never willingly accept. Whenever, in his master, he beholds a mere man, from the moment that the will which oppresses him appears a merely human and individual will, like his own, he becomes indignant, and supports the yoke wrathfully. Such was the true and distinguishing character of feudal power; and such was also the origin of the antipathy which it has ever inspired.

The religious element which was associated with it was little calculated to ease the burden. I do not conceive that the influence of the priest, in the little society which I have just described, was very great, nor that he succeeded much in legitimating the relations of the inferior population with the lord. The church has exerted a very great influence upon European civilization, but this it has done by proceedings of a general character, by changing, for instance, the general dispositions of men. When we enter closely into the petty feudal society, properly so called, we find that the influence of the priest, between the colonists and the lord, scacely amounted to anything. Most frequently he was himself rude and subordinate as a serf, and very little in condition or disposition to combat the arrogance of the lord. No doubt, called, as he was, to sustain and develop somewhat of moral life in the inferior population, he was dear and useful to it on this account; he spread through it somewhat of consolation and of life; but, I conceive, he could and did very little to alleviate its destiny.

. . . .

Lecture 7

We have conducted, down to the twelfth century, the history of the two great elements of civilization, the feudal system and the church. It is the third of these fundamental elements, I mean the communes, which we now have to trace likewise down to the twelfth century, confining ourselves to the same limits which we have observed in the other two.

We shall find ourselves differently situated with regard to the communes, from what we were with regard to the church or the feudal system. From the fifth to the twelfth century, the feudal system and the church, although at a later period they experienced new developments, showed themselves almost complete, and in a definitive state; we have watched their birth, increase, and maturity. It is not so with communes. It was only at the end of the epoch which now occupies us, in the eleventh and twelfth centuries, that they take up any position in history; not but that before then they had a history which was deserving of study; nor is it that there were not long before this epoch traces of their existence; but it was only at the eleventh century that they became evidently visible upon the great scene of the world, and as an important element of modern civilization. Thus, in the feudal system and the church, from the fifth to the twelfth century, we have seen the effects born and developed from the causes. Whenever, by way of induction or conjecture, we have deduced certain principles and results, we have been able to verify them by an inquiry into the facts themselves. As regards the communes, this facility fails us; we are present only at their birth. At present I must confine myself to causes and origins. What I say concerning the effects of the existence of the communes, and their influence in the course of European civilization, I shall say in some measure by way of anticipation. I cannot invoke the testimony of contemporaneous and known facts. It is at a later period, from the twelfth to the fifteenth century, that we shall see the communes taking their development, the institution bearing all its fruit, and history proving our assertions. I dwell upon this difference of situation in order to anticipate your objections against the incompleteness and prematurity of the picture which I am about to offer you. I will suppose, that in 1789, at the time of the commencement of the terrible regeneration of France, a bourgeois of the twelfth century had suddenly appeared among us, and that he had been given to read, provided he knew how, one of the pamphlets which so powerfully agitated mind; for example, the pamphlet of M. Sieyès, *What Is the Third Estate?* His eyes fall upon this sentence, which is the foundation of the pamphlet: "The third estate is the French nation, less the nobility and the clergy." I ask you, what would be the effect of such a phrase upon the mind of such a man? Do you suppose he would understand it? No, he could not understand the words, *the French nation,* because they would represent to him no fact with which he was acquainted, no fact of his age; and if he understood the phrase, if he clearly saw in it this sovereignty attributed to the third estate above all society, of a verity it would appear to him mad, impious, such would be its contradiction to all that he had seen, to all his ideas and sentiments.

Now, ask this astonished bourgeois to follow you; lead him to one of the French communes of this epoch, to Rheims, Beauvais, Laon, or Noyon; a different kind of astonishment would seize him: he enters a town; he sees neither towers, nor ramparts, nor bourgeois militia; no means of defence; all is open, all exposed to the first comer, and the first occupant. The bourgeois would doubt the safety of this commune; he would think it weak and ill-secured. He penetrates into the interior, and inquires what is passing, in what manner it is governed, and what are its inhabitants. They tell him, that beyond the walls there is a power which taxes them at pleasure, without their consent; which convokes their militia, and sends it to war, without their voice in the matter. He speaks to them of magistrates, of the mayor, and of the aldermen; and he hears that the bourgeois do not nominate them. He learns that the affairs of the commune are not decided in the commune; but that a man belonging to the king, an intendant, administers them, alone and at a distance. Furthermore, they will tell him that the inhabitants have not the right of assembling and deliberating in common upon matters which concern them; that they are never summoned to the public place by the bell of their church. The bourgeois of the twelfth century would be confounded. First, he was stupified and dismayed at the grandeur and importance that the communal nation, the third estate, attributed to itself; and now he finds it on its own hearthstone, in a state of servitude, weakness, and nonentity, far worse than anything which he had experienced. He passes from one spectacle to another utterly different, from the view of a sovereign bourgeoisie to that of one entirely powerless. How would you have him comprehend this—reconcile it, so that his mind be not overcome.

Let us, bourgeois of the nineteenth century, go back to the twelfth, and be present at an exactly corresponding double spectacle. Whenever we regard the general affairs of a country, its state, government, the whole society, we shall see no bourgeois, hear speak of none; they interfere in nothing, and are quite unimportant. And not only have they no importance in the state, but if we would know what they think of their situation, and how they speak of it, and what their position in regard to their relation with the government of France in general is in their own eyes, we shall find in their language an extraordinary timidity and humility. Their ancient masters, the lords, from whom they forced their franchises, treat them, at least in words, with a haughtiness which confounds us; but it neither astonishes nor irritates them.

Let us enter into the commune itself; let us see what passes there. The scene changes; we are in a kind of fortified place defended by armed bourgeois: these bourgeois tax themselves, elect their magistrates, judge and punish, and assemble for the purpose of deliberating upon their affairs. All come to these assemblies; they make war on their own account against their lord; and they have a militia. In a word, they govern themselves; they are sovereigns. This is the same contrast which, in the France of the eighteenth century, so much astonished the bourgeois of the twelfth; it is only the parts that are changed. In the latter, the bourgeois nation is all, the commune nothing; in the former, the bourgeoisie is nothing, the commune everything.

Assuredly, between the twelfth and the eighteenth century, many things must have passed—many extraordinary events, and many revolutions have been accomplished, to bring about, in the existence of a social class, so enormous a change. Despite this change, there can be no doubt but that the third estate of 1789 was, politically speaking, the descendant and heir of the corporations of the twelfth century. This French nation, so haughty and ambitious, which raises its pretensions so high, which so loudly proclaims its sovereignty, which pretends not only to regenerate and govern itself, but to govern and regenerate the world, undoubtedly descends, principally at least, from the bourgeois who obscurely though courageously revolted in the twelfth century, with the sole end of escaping in some corner of the land from the obscure tyranny of the lords.

Most assuredly it is not in the state of the communes in the twelfth century that we shall find the explanation of such a metamorphosis: it was accomplished and had its causes in the events which succeeded it from the twelfth to the eighteenth century; it is there that we shall meet it in its progression. Still the origin of the third estate has played an important part in its history; although we shall not find there the secret of its destiny, we shall, at least, find its germ: for what it was at first is again found in what it has become, perhaps, even to a greater extent than appearances would allow of our presuming. A picture, even an incomplete one, of the state of the communes in the twelfth century, will, I think, leave you convinced of this.

The better to understand this state, it is necessary to consider the communes from two principal points of view. There are two great questions to resolve: the first, that of the enfranchisement of the communes itself—the question how the revolution was operated, and from what causes—what change it brought into the situation of the bourgeois, what effect it has had upon society in general, upon the other classes, and upon the state. The second question relates only to the government of the communes, the internal condition of the enfranchised towns, the relations of the bourgeois among themselves, and the principles, forms, and manners which dominated in the cities.

It is from these two sources, on the one hand, from the change introduced into the social condition of the bourgeois, and on the other, from their internal government and their communal condition, that all their influence upon modern civilization originated. There are no facts produced by this influence, but which should be referred to one or other of these causes. When, therefore, we shall have summed them up, when we thoroughly understand, on one side, the enfranchisement of the communes, and on the other, the government of the communes, we shall be in possession, so to speak, of the two keys to their history.

Lastly, I shall say a word concerning the various state of the communes throughout Europe. The facts which I am about to place before you do not apply indifferently to all the communes of the twelfth century, to the communes of Italy, Spain, England, or France; there are certainly some which belong to all, but the differences are great and important. I shall point them out in passing; we shall again encounter them in a later period of civilization, and we will then investigate them more closely.

To understand the enfranchisement of the communes, it is necessary to recal to your minds what was the state of the towns from the fifth to the eleventh century—from the fall of the Roman empire down to the commencement of the communal revolution. Here, I repeat, the differences were very great; the state of the towns varied prodigiously in the various countries of Europe; still there are general facts which may be affirmed of almost all towns; and I shall try to confine myself to them. When I depart from this restriction, what I say more especially will apply to the communes of France, and particularly to the communes of the north of France, beyond the Rhone and the Loire. These will be the prominent points in the picture which I shall attempt to trace.

After the fall of the Roman empire, from the fifth to the tenth century, the condition of the towns was one neither of servitude nor liberty. One runs the same risk in the employment of words, that I spoke of the other day in the painting of men and events. When a society and a language has long existed, the words take a complete, determined, and precise sense, a legal and official sense, in a manner. Time has introduced into the sense of each term a multitude of ideas, which arise the moment that it is pronounced, and which, not belonging to the same date, are not applicable alike to all times. For example, the words *servitude* and *liberty* call to our minds in the present day ideas infinitely more precise and complete than the corresponding facts of the eighth, ninth, or tenth centuries. If we say that, at the eighth century, the towns were in a state of liberty, we say far too much;

in the present day we attach a sense to the word *liberty,* which does not represent the fact of the eighth century. We shall fall into the same error if we say that the towns were in a state of servitude, because the word implies an entirely different thing from the municipal facts of that period.

I repeat that, at that time, the towns were neither in a state of servitude nor liberty; they suffered all the ills which accompany weakness; they were a prey to the violence and continual depredations of the strong; but yet, despite all these fearful disorders, despite their impoverishment and depopulation, the towns had preserved, and did still preserve a certain importance: in most of them there was a clergy, a bishop, who by the great exercise of power and his influence upon the population, served as a connecting link between them and their conquerors, and thus maintained the town in a kind of independence, and covered it with the shield of religion. Moreover, there remained in the towns many wrecks of Roman institutions. One meets at this epoch (and many facts of this nature have been collected by M.M. de Savigny and Hullman, Mademoiselle de Lézardière, etc.) with frequent convocations of the senate, of the curia; there is mention made of public assemblies and municipal magistrates. The affairs of the civil order, wills, grants, and a multitude of acts of civil life, were legalised in the curia by its magistrates, as was the case in the Roman municipality. The remains of urban activity and liberty, it is true, gradually disappeared. Barbarism, disorder, and always increasing misfortunes, accelerated the depopulation. The establishment of the masters of the land in the rural districts, and the growing preponderance of agricultural life, were new causes of decay to the towns. The bishops themselves, when they had entered the frame of feudalism, placed less importance on their municipal existence. Finally, when feudalism had completely triumphed, the towns, without falling into the servitude of serfs, found themselves entirely in the hands of a lord, inclosed within some fief, and robbed of all the independence which had been left to them, even in the most barbarous times, in the first ages of the invasion. So that from the fifth century, down to the time of the complete organization of feudalism, the condition of the towns was always upon the decline.

When once feudalism was thoroughly established, when each man had taken his place, and was settled upon his land, when the wandering life had ceased, after some time the towns again began to acquire some importance, and to display anew some activity. It is, as you know, with human activity as with the fecundity of the earth; from the time that commotion ceases, it reappears and makes everything germinate and flourish. With the least glimpse of order and peace, man takes hope, and with hope goes to work. It was thus with the towns; the moment that feudalism was a bit settled, new wants sprang up among the fief-holders, a certain taste for progress and amelioration; to supply this want, a little commerce and industry reappeared in the towns of their domain; riches and population returned to them; slowly, it is true, but still they returned. Among the circumstances which contributed thereto, one, I think, is too little regarded; this is the right of sanctuary in the churches. Before the communes had established themselves, before their strength and their ramparts enabled them to offer an asylum to the afflicted population of the country, when as yet they had no safety but that afforded by the church, this sufficed to draw into the towns many unhappy fugitives. They came to shelter themselves in or around the church; and it was not only the case with the inferior class, with serfs and colons, who sought safety, but often with men of importance, rich outlaws. The chronicles of the time are filled with examples of this nature. One sees men, formerly powerful themselves, pursued by a more powerful neighbour, or even by the king himself, who abandon their domains, carrying with them all they can, shut themselves up within a town, and putting themselves under the protection of the church, become bourgeois. These kind of refugees have not been, I think, without their influence upon the progress of the towns; they introduced into them riches, and elements of a superior population to the mass of their inhabitants. Besides, who knows not, that when once an association is in part formed, men flock to it, both because they find more safety, and also for the mere sake of that sociability which never leaves them.

By the concurrence of all these causes, after the feudal government was in some manner regulated, the towns regained a little strength. Their security, however, did not return to them in the same proportion. The wandering life had ceased, it is true, but the wandering life had been for the conquerors, for the new proprietors of the soil, a principal means of satisfying their passions. When they had wished to pillage, they made an excursion, they went abroad to seek another fortune, another domain. When each was nearly established, when it became necessary to renounce this conquering vagrancy, there was no cessation of their avidity, their inordinate wants, nor their violent desires. Their weight, then, fell on the people nearest at hand, upon the towns. Instead of going abroad to pillage, they pillaged at home. The extortions of the nobility upon the bourgeois were redoubled from the commencement of the tenth century. Whenever the proprietor of a domain in which a town was situated had any fit of avarice to satisfy, it was upon the bourgeois that he exercised his violence. This, above all, was the epoch in which the complaints of the bourgeoise against the absolute want of security of commerce, burst forth. The merchants, after having made their journeys, were not permitted to enter their towns in peace; the roads and approaches were incessantly beset by the lord and his followers. The time at which industry was recommencing, was exactly that in which security was most wanting. Nothing can irritate a man more than being thus interfered with in his work, and despoiled of the fruits which he had promised himself from it. He is far more annoyed and enraged than when harassed in an existence which has been some time fixed and monotonous, when that which is carried from him has not been the result of his own activity, has not excited in his bosom all the pleasures of hope. There is, in the progressive movement towards fortune of a man or a population, a principle of resistance against injustice and violence far more energetic than in any other situation.

This, then, was the position of the towns during the tenth century; they had more strength, more importance, more riches, and more interests to defend. At the same time, it was more than ever necessary to defend them, because this strength, these interests, these riches, became an object of envy to the lords. The danger and evil increased with the means of resisting them. Moreover, the feudal system gave to all those who participated in it the example of continued resistance; it never presented to the mind the idea of an organized government, capable of ruling and quelling all by imposing its single intervention. It offered, on the contrary, the continuous spectacle of the individual will refusing submission. Such, for the most part, was the position of the possessors of fiefs towards their superiors, of the lesser lords towards the greater; so that at the moment when the towns were tormented and oppressed, when they had new and most important interests to sustain, at that moment they had before their eyes a continual lesson of insurrection. The feudal system has rendered one service to humanity, that of incessantly showing to men the individual will in the full display of its energy. The lesson prospered: in spite of their weakness, in spite of the infinite inequality of condition between them and their lords, the towns arose in insurrection on all sides.

It is difficult to assign an exact date to this event. It is generally said, that the enfranchisement of the communes commenced in the eleventh century; but, in all great events, how many unhappy and unknown efforts occur, before the one which succeeds! In all things, to accomplish its designs, Providence lavishly expends courage, virtues, sacrifices, in a word, man himself; and it is only after an unknown number of unrecorded labours, after a host of noble hearts have succumbed in discouragement, convinced that their cause is lost, it is only then that the cause triumphs. It doubtless happened thus with the communes. Doubtless, in the eighth, ninth, and tenth centuries, there were many attempts at resistance, and movements towards enfranchisement, which not only were unsuccessful, but of which the memory remained alike without glory or success. It is true, however, that these attempts have influenced posterior events; they reanimated and sustained the spirit of liberty, and prepared the way for the great insurrection of the eleventh century.

I say designedly, insurrection. The enfranchisement of the communes in the eleventh century was the fruit of a veritable insurrection, and a veritable war, a war declared by the population of the towns against their lords. The first fact which is always met with in such histories, is the rising of the bourgeois, who arm themselves with the first thing that comes to hand; the expulsion of the followers of the lord who have come to put in force some extortion; or it is an enterprise against the castle; these are always the characteristics of the war. If the insurrection fails, what is done by the conqueror? He orders the destruction of the fortifications raised by the citizens, not only round the town but round each house. One sees at the time of the confederation, after having promised to act as a commune, and after taking the oath of mutual aid, the first act of the citizen is to fortify himself within his house. Some communes, of which at this day the name is entirely obscure, as, for example, the little commune of Vézelay in Nivernais, maintained a very long and energetic struggle against their lord. Victory fell to the abbot of Vézelay; he immediately enjoined the demolition of the fortifications of the bourgeois' houses; the names of many are preserved, whose fortified houses were thus immediately destroyed.

Let us enter the interior of the habitations of our ancestors; let us study the mode of their construction and the kind of life which they suggest; all is devoted to war, all has the character of war.

This is the construction of a bourgeois' house in the twelfth century, as far as we can follow it out: there were generally three floors, with one room upon each floor; the room on the ground floor was the common room, where the family took their meals; the first floor was very high up, by way of security; this is the most remarkable characteristic of the construction. On this floor was the room which the bourgeois and his wife inhabited. The house was almost always flanked by a tower at the angle, generally of a square form; another symptom of war, a means of defence. On the second floor was a room, the use of which is doubtful, but which probably served for the children, and the rest of the family. Above, very often, was a small platform, evidently intended for a place of observation. The whole construction of the house suggests war. This was the evident character, the true name of the movement which produced the enfranchisement of the communes.

When war has lasted a certain time, whoever may be the belligerent powers, it necessarily leads to peace. The treaties of peace between the communes and their adversaries were the charters. The commune charters are mere treaties of peace between the bourgeois and their lord.

The insurrection was general. When I say *general,* I do not mean that there was union or coalition between all the bourgeois in a country: far from it. The situation of the communes was almost everywhere the same; they were everywhere a prey to the same danger, afflicted with the same evil. Having acquired almost the same means of resistance and defence, they employed them at nearly the same epoch. Example, too, may have done something, and the success of one or two communes may have been contagious. The charters seem sometimes to have been drawn after the same pattern; that of Noyon, for example, served as a model for those of Beauvais, St. Quentin, etc. I doubt, however, whether example had so much influence as has been supposed. Communications were difficult and rare, and hearsay vague and transient; it is more likely that the insurrection was the result of a similar situation, and of a general and spontaneous movement. When I say, general, I mean to say that it took place almost everywhere; for, I repeat, that the movement was not unanimous and concerted, all was special and local: each commune was insurgent against its lord upon its own account; all passed in its own locality.

The vicissitudes of the struggle were great. Not only did success alternate, but even when peace seemed established, after the charter had been sworn to by each party, it was violated and eluded in every way. The kings played a great part in the alternations of this struggle. Of this I shall speak in detail when I treat the royalty itself. Its influence in the movement of communal enfranchisement has been sometimes praised, perhaps too highly; sometimes, I think, too much undervalued, and some times denied. I shall confine myself at present to saying that it frequently interfered, sometimes invoked by the communes and sometimes by the lords; that it has often played contrary parts; that it has acted sometimes on one principle, sometimes on another; that it has unceasingly changed its intentions, designs, and conduct; but that, upon the whole, it has done much, and with more of good than of evil effect.

Despite these vicissitudes, despite the continual violations of the charters, the enfranchisement of the communes was consummated in the twelfth century. All Europe, and especially France, which for a century had been covered with insurrections, was covered with charters more or less favourable; the corporations enjoyed them with more or less security, but still they enjoyed them. The fact prevailed, and the right was established.

Let us now attempt to discover the immediate results of this great fact, and what changes it introduced into the condition of the bourgeois, in the midst of society.

In the first place, it changed nothing, at least not in the commencement, in the relations of the bourgeois with the general government of the country—with what we of the present day call the state; they interfered no more in it than heretofore: all remained local, inclosed within the limits of the fief.

One circumstance, however, should modify this assertion; a bond now began to be established between the bourgeois and the king. At times, the bourgeois had invoked the aid of the king against their lord, or his guarantee, when the charter was promised or sworn to. At other times, the lords had invoked the judgment of the king between themselves and the bourgeois. At the demand of either one or other of the parties in a multitude of different causes, royalty had interfered in the quarrel; from thence resulted a frequent relation, and sometimes a rather intimate one, between the bourgeois and the king. It was by this relation that the bourgeois approached the centre of the state, and began to have a connexion with the general government.

Notwithstanding that all remained local, a new and general

class was created by the enfranchisement. No coalition had existed between the bourgeois; they had, as a class, no common and public existence. But the country was filled with men in the same situation, having the same interests, and the same manners, between whom a certain bond and unity could not fail of being gradually established, which should give rise to the *bourgeoisie*. The formation of a great social class, the bourgeoisie, was the necessary result of the local enfranchisement of the bourgeois.

It must not be imagined that this class was at this time that which it has since become. Not only has its situation changed, but its elements were entirely different: in the twelfth century it consisted almost entirely of merchants, traders carrying on a petty commerce, and of small proprietors either of land or houses, who had taken up their residence in the town. Three centuries after, the bourgeoisie included besides, lawyers, physicians, learned men of all sorts, and all the local magistrates. The bourgeoisie was formed gradually, and of very different elements; as a general thing, in its history no account is given of its succession or diversity. Wherever the bourgeoisie is spoken of, it seems to be supposed that at all epochs it was composed of the same elements. This is an absurd supposition. It is perhaps in the diversity of its composition at different epochs of history that we should look for the secret of its destiny. So long as it did not include magistrates nor men of letters, so long as it was not what it became in the sixteenth century, it possessed neither the same importance nor the same character in the state. To comprehend the vicissitudes of its fortune and power, it is necessary to observe in its bosom the successive rise of new professions, new moral positions, and a new intellectual state. In the twelfth century, I repeat, it was composed of only the small merchants, who retired into the towns after having made their purchases and sales, and of the proprietors of houses and small domains who had fixed their residence there. Here we see the European bourgeois class in its first elements.

The third great consequence of the enfranchisement of the communes was the class struggle, a struggle which constitutes the fact itself, and which fills modern history. Modern Europe

was born from the struggle of the various classes of society. Elsewhere, as I have already observed, this struggle led to very different results: in Asia, for example, one class completely triumphed,
and the government of castes succeeded to that of classes,
and society sunk into immobility. Thank God, none of this has
happened in Europe. Neither of the classes has been able to
conquer or subdue the others; the struggle, instead of becoming a principle of immobility, has been a cause of progress; the
relations of the principal classes among themselves, the necessity
under which they found themselves of combating and yielding
by turns; the variety of their interests and passions, the desire
to conquer without the power to satisfy it; from all this has
arisen perhaps the most energetic and fertile principle of the development of European civilization. The classes have incessantly
struggled; they detested each other; an utter diversity of situation, of interests, and of manners, produced between them a
profound moral hostility: and yet they have progressively approached nearer, come to an understanding, and assimilated;
every European nation has seen the birth and development in
its bosom of a certain universal spirit, a certain community of
interests, ideas, and sentiments, which have triumphed over
diversity and war. In France, for example, in the seventeenth and
eighteenth centuries, the social and moral separation of the
classes was still very profound; yet the fusion was advancing;
still, without doubt, at that time there was a veritable French
nation, not an exclusive class, but which embraced them all, and
in which all were animated by a certain sentiment in common,
having a common social existence, strongly impressed, in a word,
with nationality. Thus, from the bosom of variety, enmity, and
war, has arisen in modern Europe the national unity so striking
in the present day, and which tends to develop and refine itself,
from day to day, with still greater brilliancy.

Such are the great external, apparent, and social effects of the
revolution which at present occupies us. Let us investigate its
moral effects, what changes it brought about in the soul of the
bourgeois themselves, what they became, what, in fact, they
necessarily became morally in their new situation.

There is a fact by which it is impossible not to be struck while contemplating the relation of the bourgeois towards the state in general, the government of the state, and the general interests of the country, not only in the twelfth century, but also in subsequent ages; I mean the prodigious timidity of the citizens, their humility, the excessive modesty of their pretensions as to the government of the country, and the facility with which they contented themselves. Nothing is seen among them of the true political spirit, which aspires to influence, reform, and govern; nothing which gives proof or boldness of thought, or grandeur of ambition: one might call them sensible-minded, honest, freed men.

There are but two sources in the sphere of politics from which greatness of ambition or firmness of thought can arise. It is necessary to have either the feeling of immense importance, of great power exercised upon the destiny of others, and in a vast extent— or else it is necessary to bear within oneself a feeling of complete individual independence, a confidence in one's own liberty, a conviction of a destiny foreign to all will but that of the man himself. To one or other of these two conditions seem to belong boldness of thought, greatness of ambition, the desire of acting in an enlarged sphere, and of obtaining great results.

Neither one nor the other of these conditions entered into the condition of the bourgeois of the middle ages. These, as you have just seen, were only important to themselves; they exercised no sensible influence beyond their own town, or upon the state in general. Nor could they have any great sentiment of individual independence. It was in vain that they conquered, in vain that they obtained a charter. The bourgeois of a town, in comparing himself with the inferior lord who dwelt near him, and who had just been conquered, was not the less sensible of his extreme inferiority; he was not filled with the haughty sentiment of independence which animated the proprietor of the fief; he held not his portion of liberty from himself alone, but from his association with others; a difficult and precarious succour. Hence that character of reserve, of timidity of spirit, of retiring modesty, and humility of language, even in conjunction with a firmness of conduct, which is so deeply imprinted in the life of the citizens, not only in the twelfth century, but even of their descendants. They had no taste for great enterprises; and when fate forced them into such, they were uneasy and embarrassed; the responsibility annoyed them; they felt that they were out of their sphere of action, and wished to return to it; they therefore treated on moderate terms. Thus one finds in the course of European history, especially of France, that the bourgeoisie has been esteemed, considered, flattered, and even respected, but rarely feared; it has rarely produced upon its adversaries an impression of a great and haughty power, of a truly political power. There is nothing to be surprised at in this weakness of the modern bourgeoisie; its principal cause lay in its very origin, and in the circumstances of its enfranchisement, which I have just placed before you. A high ambition, independent of social conditions, enlargement and firmness of political thought, the desire to participate in the affairs of the country, the full consciousness of the greatness of man as man, and of the power which belongs to him, if he is capable of exercising it, these are in Europe sentiments and dispositions entirely modern, the fruit of modern civilization, the fruit of that glorious and powerful universality which characterizes it, and which cannot fail of insuring to the public an influence and weight in the government of the country, which were always wanting, and necessarily so, to the bourgeois our ancestors.

On the other hand, they acquired and displayed, in the struggle of local interests which they had to maintain in their narrow stage, a degree of energy, devotedness, perseverance, and patience, which has never been surpassed. The difficulty of the enterprise was such, and such the perils which they had to strive against, that a display of unexampled courage was necessary. In the present day, a very false idea is formed of the life of the bourgeois in the twelfth and thirteenth centuries. You have read in one of the novels of Walter Scott, *Quentin Durward*, the representation he has given of the burgomaster of Liége; he has made of him a regular bourgeois in a comedy, fat, indolent, without experience or boldness, and wholly occupied in passing his life easily. Whereas, the bourgeois of this period always had a coat of mail upon their breast, a pike in their hand; their life was as temptestuous, as warlike, and as hardy, as that of the lords with whom they fought. It was in these continual perils, in struggling against all the difficulties of practical life, that they acquired that manly character, and that obstinate energy, which is, in a measure, lost in the soft activity of modern times.*

None of these social or moral effects of the enfranchisement of the communes had attained their development in the twelfth century; it is in the following centuries that they distinctly appeared, and are easily discernable. It is certain, however, that the germ was laid in the original situation of the communes, in the manner of their enfranchisement, and the place then taken by the bourgeois in society. I was, therefore, right in placing them before you alone. Let us now investigate the interior of the commune of the twelfth century; let us see how it was governed, what principles and facts dominated in the relations of the bourgeois among themselves.

You will recollect that in speaking of the municipal system, bequeathed by the Roman empire to the modern world, I told you that the Roman empire was a great coalition of municipalities, formerly sovereign municipalities like Rome itself. Each of these towns had originally possessed the same existence as Rome, had once been a small independent republic, making peace and war, and governing itself as it thought proper. In proportion as they became incorporated with the Roman empire, the rights which constitute sovereignty, the right of peace and war, the right of legislation, the right of taxation, etc., fled each town and centred in Rome. There remained but one sovereign municipal-

---

* The original report of Guizot's lectures indicates that at this point the students broke out into applause. Guizot made considerable efforts to try to avoid this kind of demonstration; he made a point of constantly urging his students to receive his lectures in a detached and scientific spirit. However, this evocation of the heroic nature of the medieval bourgeois is an example of how Guizot's lectures did seem to contain much direct political meaning. This passage was much commented upon at the time, containing as it does a most explicit presentation of the middle class as the great heroic and wonder-working class in history.—EDITOR.

ity, Rome, reigning over a large number of municipalities which had now only a civil existence. The municipal system changed its character; and instead of being a political government and a system of sovereignty, it became a mode of administration. This was the great revolution which was consummated under the Roman empire. The municipal system became a mode of administration, was reduced to the government of local affairs, and the civic interests of the city. This was the condition in which the towns and their institutions were left at the fall of the Roman empire. In the midst of the chaos of barbarism, all ideas, as well as facts, were in utter confusion; all the attributes of sovereignty and of the administration were confounded. These distinctions were no longer attended to. Affairs were abandoned to the course of necessity. There was a sovereign or an administrator, in each locality, according to circumstances. When the towns rose in insurrection, to recover some security, they took upon themselves the sovereignty. It was not, in any way, for the purpose of following out a political theory, nor from a feeling of their dignity; it was that they might have the means of resisting the lords against whom they rebelled that they appropriated to themselves the right of levying militia, of taxation for the purposes of war, of themselves nominating their chiefs and magistrates; in a word, of governing themselves. The government in the interior of the towns was the means of defence and security. Thus sovereignty reentered the municipal system, from which it had been eradicated by the conquests of Rome. The communes again became sovereign. We have here the political character of their enfranchisement.

It does not follow, that this sovereignty was complete. It always retained some trace of external sovereignty: sometimes the lord preserved to himself the right of sending a magistrate into the town, who took for his assessors the municipal magistrates; sometimes he possessed the right of receiving certain revenues; elsewhere, a tribute was secured to him. Sometimes the external sovereignty of the community lay in the hands of the king.

The communes themselves having entered within the frame of feudalism, had vassals, became suzerains, and by virtue of this title partly possessed themselves of the sovereignty which was inherent in the lord paramount. This caused a confusion between the rights which they had from their feudal position, and those which they had conquered by their insurrections; and under this double title the sovereignty belonged to them.

Thus we see, as far as can be judged from very deficient monuments, how government was administered, at least in the early ages, in the interior of a commune. The totality of the inhabitants formed the assembly of the commune; all those who had sworn the commune oath (and whoever lived within the walls was obliged to do so) were convoked by the ringing of a bell to the general assembly. It was there that they nominated the magistrates. The number and form of the magistracy were very various. The magistrates being once nominated, the assembly was dissolved, and the magistrates governed almost alone, somewhat arbitrarily, and without any other responsibility than that of the new elections, or popular riots, which were the chief mode of responsibility in those times.

You see that the internal organization of communes reduced itself to two very simple elements; the general assembly of the inhabitants, and a government invested with an almost arbitrary power, under the responsibility of insurrections and riots. It was impossible, principally from the state of manners, to establish a regular government, with veritable guarantees for order and duration. The greater portion of the population of the communes was in a state of ignorance, brutality, and ferocity, which it would have been very difficult to govern. After a short time, there was almost as little security in the interior of the commune as there had formerly been in the relations between the bourgeois and the lord. There was formed, however, very quickly a superior bourgeoisie. You easily comprehend the causes. The state of ideas and of social relations led to the establishment of industrial professions, legally constituted corporations. The system of privilege was introduced into the interior of communes, and from this a great inequality ensued. There was shortly everywhere a certain number of rich and important bourgeois, and a working population more or less numerous, which, in spite of its inferiority, had an important influence in the affairs of the commune. The communes were then divided into a high bourgeoisie, and a population subject to all the errors and vices of a populace. The superior bourgeoisie found itself pressed between the immense difficulty of governing the inferior population, and the incessant attempts of the ancient master of the commune, who sought to re-establish his power. Such was its situation, not only in France but in all Europe, down to the sixteenth century. This perhaps has been the chief means of preventing the corporations, in most European nations, and especially in France, from possessing all the important political influence which they might otherwise have had. Two principles carried on incessant warfare within them; in the inferior population, a blind, unbridled, and ferocious spirit of democracy; and, as a consequence, in the superior population, a spirit of timidity at making agreements, an excessive facility of conciliation, whether in regard to the king, the ancient lords, or in re-establishing some peace and order in the interior of the commune. Each of these principles could not but tend to deprive the corporation of any great influence in the state.

All these effects were not visible in the twelfth century; still, however one might foresee them in the very character of the insurrection, in the manner of its commencement, and in the condition of the various elements of the communal population.

Such, if I mistake not, are the principal characteristics and the general results of the enfranchisement of the communes and of their internal government. I forewarn you, that these facts were neither so uniform nor so universal as I have broadly represented them. There is great diversity in the history of communes in Europe. For example, in Italy and in the south of France, the Roman municipal system dominated; there was not nearly so much diversity and inequality here as in the north, and the communal organization was much better, either by reason of the Roman traditions, or from the superior condition of the population. In the north, the feudal system prevailed in the communal existence; there, all was subordinate to the struggle against the lords. The communes of the south were more occupied with their internal organization, amelioration, and progress; they thought only of becoming independent republics. The destiny of the northern communes, in France particularly, showed themselves more and more incomplete, and destined for less fine developments. If we glance at the communes of Germany, Spain, and England, we shall find in them other differences. I shall not enter into these details; we shall remark some of them as we advance in the history of civilization. In their origin, all things are nearly confounded under one physiognomy; it is only by successive developments that variety shows itself. Then commences a new development which urges society towards free and high unity, the glorious end of all the efforts and wishes of the human race.

Lecture 8

I have not as yet explained to you the complete plan of my course. I commenced by indicating its object; I then passed in review European civilization without considering it as a whole, without indicating to you at one and the same time the point of departure, the route, and the port, the commencement, the middle, and the end. We have now, however, arrived at an epoch when this entire view, this general sketch of the region which we survey, has become necessary. The times which have hitherto occupied us in some measure explain themselves, or are explained by immediate and evident results. Those upon which we are about to enter would not be understood, nor even would they excite any lively interest, unless they are connected with even the most indirect and distant of their consequences.

In so extensive a study, moments occur when we can no longer consent to proceed, while all before us is unknown and dark; we wish not only to know whence we have come and where we are, but also to what point we tend. This is what we now feel. The epoch to which we are approaching is not intelligible, nor can its importance be appreciated except by the relations which unite it to modern times. Its true meaning is not evident until a later period.

We are in possession of almost all the essential elements of

European civilization. I say almost, because as yet I have not spoken to you of royalty. The decisive crisis of the development of royalty did not take place until the twelfth or even thirteenth century; it was not until then that the institution was really constituted, and that it began to occupy a definite place in modern society. I have, therefore, not treated of it earlier; it will form the subject of my next lecture. With this exception, I repeat, we have before us all the great elements of European civilization: you have beheld the birth of feudal aristocracy, of the church, the communes; you have seen the institutions which should correspond to these facts; and not only the institutions, but also the principles and ideas which these facts should raise up in the mind. Thus, while treating of feudalism, you were present at the cradle of the modern family, at the hearth of domestic life; you have comprehended, in all its energy, the sentiment of individual independence, and the place which it has held in our civilization. With regard to the church, you have seen the purely religious society rise up, its relations with the civil society, the theocratical principle, the separation of the spiritual and temporal powers, the first blows of persecutions, and the first cries of the liberty of conscience. The rising communes have shown you glimpses of an association founded upon altogether other principles than those of feudalism and the church, the diversity of the social classes, their struggles, the first and profound characteristics of modern bourgeois manners, timidity of spirit side by side with energy of soul, the demagogue spirit side by side with the legal spirit. In a word, all the elements which have contributed to the formation of European society, all that it has been, and, so to speak, all that it has suggested, have already met your view.

Let us now transport ourselves to the heart of modern Europe: I speak not of existing Europe, after the prodigious metamorphoses which we have witnessed, but of Europe in the seventeenth and eighteenth centuries. I ask you, do you recognise the society which we have just seen in the twelfth century? What a wonderful difference! I have already dwelt upon this difference as regards the communes: I afterwards tried to make you sensible of how little the third estate of the eighteenth century resembled that of the twelfth. If we make the same essay upon feudalism and the church, we shall be struck with the same metamorphosis. There was no more resemblance between the nobility of the court of Louis XV and the feudal aristocracy, or between the church of Cardinal de Bernis and that of the Abbé Suger, than between the third estate of the eighteenth century and the bourgeoisie of the twelfth century. Between these two epochs, although already in possession of all its elements, society was entirely transformed.

I wish to establish clearly the general and essential character of this transformation. From the fifth to the twelfth century, society contained all that I have described. It possessed kings, a lay aristocracy, a clergy, bourgeoisie, labourers, religious and civil powers—in a word, the germs of everything which is necessary to form a nation and a government, and yet there was neither government nor nation. Throughout the epoch upon which we are occupied, there was nothing bearing a resemblance to a people, properly so called, nor to a veritable government, in the sense which the words have for us in the present day. We have encountered a multitude of particular forces, of special facts, and local institutions; but nothing general or public; no policy, properly so called, nor no true nationality.

Let us regard, on the contrary, the Europe of the seventeenth and eighteenth centuries; we shall everywhere see two leading figures present themselves upon the scene of the world, the government, and the people. The action of a universal power upon the whole country, and the influence of the country upon the power which governs it, this is society, this is history: the relations of the two great forces, their alliance, or their struggle, this is what history discovers and relates. The nobility, the clergy, and the bourgeois, all these particular classes and forces, now only appear in a secondary rank, almost like shadows effaced by those two great bodies, the people and its government.

This, if I mistake not, is the essential feature which distinguishes modern from primitive Europe; this is the metamorphosis which was accomplished from the thirteenth to the sixteenth centuries.

216

It is, then, from the thirteenth to the sixteenth century, that is to say, in the period which we are about to enter upon, that the secret of this must be sought for; it is the distinctive character of this epoch that it was employed in converting primitive Europe into modern Europe; and hence its historical importance and interest. If it is not considered from this point of view, and unless we everywhere seek what has arisen from it, not only will it not be understood, but we shall soon be weary of, and annoyed by it. Indeed, viewed in itself, and apart from its results, it is a period without character, a period when confusion continues to increase, without our being able to discover its causes, a period of movement without direction, and of agitation without result. Royalty, nobility, clergy, bourgeoisie, all the elements of social order seem to turn in the same circle, equally incapable of progress or repose. They make attempts of all kinds, but all fail; they attempt to settle governments, and to establish public liberties; they even attempt religious reforms, but nothing is accomplished —nothing perfected. If ever the human race has been abandoned to a destiny, agitated and yet stationary, to labour incessant, yet barren of effect, it was between the thirteenth and the fifteenth centuries that such was the physiognomy of its condition and its history.

I know of but one work in which this physiognomy is truly shown; the *Histoire des ducs de Bourgogne*, by M. de Barante. I do not speak of the truth which sparkles in the descriptions of manners, or in the detailed recital of facts, but of that universal truth which makes the entire book a faithful image, a sincere mirror of the whole epoch, of which it at the same time shows the movement and the monotony.

Considered, on the contrary, in its relation to that which follows, as the transition from the primitive to the modern Europe, this epoch brightens and becomes animated; we discover in it a totality, a direction, and a progress; its unity and interest consist in the slow and secret work which is accomplished in it.

The history of European civilization may then be summed up into three grand periods. First, a period which I shall call the period of origins, of formation—a time when the various ele-

217

ments of our society freed themselves from the chaos, took being, and showed themselves under their native forms with the principles which animated them. This period extended nearly to the twelfth century. Second, the second period is a time of essay, of trial, of grouping; the various elements of the social order drew near each other, combined, and, as it were, felt each other, without the power to bring forth anything general, regular, or durable. This state was not ended, properly speaking, till the sixteenth century. Third, the period of development, properly so called, when society in Europe took a definite form, followed a determined tendency, and progressed rapidly and universally towards a clear and precise end. This commenced at the sixteenth century, and now pursues its course.

Such appears to me to be the spectacle of European civilization in its whole, and such I shall endeavour to represent it to you. It is the second period that we enter upon now. We have to seek in it the great crises and determinative causes of the social transformation which has been the result of it.

The crusades constitute the first great event which presents itself to us, which, as it were, opens the epoch of which we speak. They commenced at the eleventh century, and extended over the twelfth and thirteenth. Of a surety, a great event; for since it was completed, it has not ceased to occupy philosophic historians; even before reading the account of it, all have foreseen that it was one of those events which change the condition of the people, and which it is absolutely necessary to study in order to comprehend the general course of facts.

The first characteristic of the crusades is their universality; the whole of Europe joined in them—they were the first European event. Previously to the crusades, Europe had never been excited by one sentiment, or acted in one cause; there was no Europe. The crusades revealed Christian Europe. The French formed the van of the first army of crusaders; but there were also Germans, Italians, Spaniards, and English. Observe the second, the third crusade; all the Christian nations engaged in it. Nothing like it had yet been seen.

This is not all: just as the crusades form an European event, so in each country do they form a national event. All classes of society were animated with the same impression, obeyed the same idea, abandoned themselves to the same impulse. Kings, lords, priests, bourgeois, countrymen, all took the same part, the same interest in the crusades. The normal unity of nations was shown—a fact as novel as the European unity.

When such events happen in the infancy of a people, at a time when men act freely and spontaneously, without premeditation, without political intention or combination, one recognises therein what history calls heroic events—the heroic age of nations. In fact, the crusades constitute the heroic event of modern Europe—a movement at once individual and general, national, and yet unregulated.

That such was really their primitive character is verified by all documents, proved by all facts. Who were the first crusaders that put themselves in motion? Crowds of the populace, who set out under the guidance of Peter the Hermit, without preparation, without guides, and without chiefs, followed rather than guided by a few obscure knights; they traversed Germany, the Greek empire, and dispersed or perished in Asia Minor.

The superior class, the feudal nobility, in their turn became eager in the cause of the crusade. Under the command of Godefroi de Bouillon, the lords and their followers set out full of ardour. When they had traversed Asia Minor, a fit of indifference and weariness seized the chiefs of the crusaders. They cared not to continue their route; they united to make conquests and establish themselves. The common people of the army rebelled; they wished to go to Jerusalem—the deliverance of Jerusalem was the aim of the crusade; it was not to gain principalities for Raimond de Toulouse, nor for Bohemond, nor for any other, that the crusaders came. The popular, national, and European impulsion was superior to all individual wishes; the chiefs had not sufficient ascendancy over the masses to subdue them to their interests. The sovereigns, who had remained strangers to the first crusade, were at last carried away by the movement, like the people. The great crusades of the twelfth century were commanded by kings.

I pass at once to the end of the thirteenth century. People still spoke in Europe of the crusades, they even preached them with ardour. The popes excited the sovereigns and the people—they held councils to call attention to the Holy Land; but no one went there—it was no longer cared for. Something had passed into the European spirit and European society that put an end to the crusades. There were still some private expeditions. A few lords, a few bands, still set out for Jerusalem; but the general movement was evidently stopped; and yet it does not appear that either the necessity or the facility of continuing it had disappeared. The Moslems triumphed more and more in Asia. The Christian kingdom founded at Jerusalem had fallen into their hands. It was necessary to reconquer it; there were greater means of success than they had at the commencement of the crusades; a large number of Christians were established, and still powerful, in Asia Minor, Syria, and Palestine. They were better acquainted with the means of travelling and acting. Still nothing could revive the crusades. It was clear that the two great forces of society— the sovereigns on one side and the people on the other—were averse to it.

It has often been said that this was lassitude—that Europe was tired of thus falling upon Asia. We must come to an understanding upon this word *lassitude,* which is so often used upon similar occasions; it is strangely inexact. It is not possible that human generations can be weary with what they have never taken part in; weary of the fatigues undergone by their forefathers. Weariness is personal, it cannot be transmitted like a heritage. Men in the thirteenth century were not fatigued by the crusades of the twelfth: they were influenced by another cause. A great change had taken place in ideas, sentiments, and social conditions. There were no longer the same wants and desires. They no longer thought or wished the same things. It is these political or moral metamorphoses, and not weariness, which explain the different conduct of successive generations. The pretended lassitude which is attributed to them is a false metaphor.

Two great causes, one moral and the other social, threw Europe into the crusades. The moral cause, as you know, was the impulsion of religious sentiment and creeds. Since the end of the seventh century, Christianity had been struggling against Mohammedanism; it had conquered it in Europe after being dangerously menaced; it had succeeded in confining it to Spain. Thence also it still constantly strove to expel it. The crusades have been represented as a kind of accident, as an event unforeseen, unheard of, born solely of the recitals of pilgrims on their return from Jerusalem, and of the preachings of Peter the Hermit. It was nothing of the kind. The crusades were the continuation, the zenith of the grand struggle which had been going on for four centuries between Christianity and Mohammedanism. The theatre of this struggle had been hitherto in Europe; it was now transported into Asia. If I put any value upon those comparisons and parallels, into which some people delight at times to press, suitably, or not, historical facts, I might show you Christianity running precisely the same career in Asia, and undergoing the same destiny as Mohammedanism in Europe. Mohammedanism was established in Spain, and had there conquered and founded a kingdom and principalities. The Christians did the same in Asia. They there found themselves, with regard to Mohammedans, in the same situation as the latter in Spain with regard to the Christians. The kingdom of Jerusalem and the kingdom of Granada correspond to each other. But these similitudes are of little importance. The great fact is the struggle of the two social and religious systems; and of this the crusades was the chief crisis. In that lies their historical character, the connecting link which attaches them to the totality of facts.

There was another cause, the social state of Europe in the eleventh century, which no less contributed to their outburst. I have been careful to explain why, between the fifth and the eleventh century, nothing general could be established in Europe. I have attempted to show how everything had become local, how states, existences, minds, were confined within a very limited horizon. It was thus feudalism had prevailed. After some time, an horizon so restricted did not suffice; human thought and activity desired to pass beyond the circle in which they had been confined. The wandering life had ceased, but not the inclination of its excitement and adventures. The people rushed into the crusades as into a new existence, more enlarged and varied, which at one time recalled the ancient liberty of barbarism, at others opened out the perspective of a vast future.

Such, I believe, were the two determining causes of the crusades of the twelfth century. At the end of the thirteenth century, neither of these causes existed. Men and society were so much changed, that neither the moral impulsion nor the social need which had precipitated Europe upon Asia, was any longer felt. I do not know if many of you have read the original historians of the crusades, or whether it has ever occurred to you to compare the contemporaneous chroniclers of the first crusades, with those at the end of the twelfth and thirteenth centuries; for example, Albert d'Aix, Robert the Monk, and Raymond d'Agiles, who took part in the first crusade, with William of Tyre and James de Vitry. When we compare these two classes of writers, it is impossible not to be struck by the distance which separates them. The first are animated chroniclers, full of vivid imagination, who recount the events of the crusades with passion. But they are, at the same time, men of very narrow minds, without an idea beyond the little sphere in which they have lived; strangers to all science, full of prejudices, and incapable of forming any judgment whatever upon what passes around them, or upon the events which they relate. Open, on the contrary, the history of the crusades by William of Tyre: you will be surprised to find almost an historian of modern times, a mind developed, extensive and free, a rare political understanding of events, completeness of views, a judgment bearing upon causes and effects. James de Vitry affords an example of a different kind of development; he is a scholar, who not only concerns himself with what has reference to the crusades, but also occupies himself with manners, geography, ethnography, natural history; who observes and describes the country. In a word, between the chroniclers of the first crusades and the historians of the last, there is an immense interval, which indicates a veritable revolution in mind.

This revolution is above all seen in the manner in which each speaks of the Mohammedans. To the first chroniclers, and consequently to the first crusaders, of whom the first chroniclers are but the expression, the Mohammedans are only an object of hatred. It is evident that they knew nothing of them, that they weighed them not, considered them not, except under the point of view of the religious hostility which existed between them; we discover no trace of any social relation; they detested and fought them, and that was all. William of Tyre, James de Vitry, and Bernard the Treasurer, speak quite differently of the Mussulmans: one feels that, although fighting them, they do not look upon them as mere monsters; that to a certain point they have entered into their ideas; that they have lived with them; that there is a sort of relation, and even a kind of sympathy established between them. William of Tyre warmly eulogises Noureddin—Bernard the Treasurer, Saladin. They even go so far as to compare the manners and conduct of the Mussulmans with those of the Christians; they take advantage of the Mussulmans to satirize the Christians, as Tacitus painted the manners of the Germans in contrast with the manners of the Romans. You see how enormous the change between the two epochs must have been, when you find in the last, with regard to the enemies of the Christians, to those against whom the crusades were directed, a liberty and impartiality of spirit which would have filled the first crusaders with surprise and indignation.

This, then, was the first and principal effect of the crusades, a great step towards the enfranchisement of mind, a great progress towards more extensive and liberal ideas. Commenced in the name and under the influence of religious creeds, the crusades removed from religious ideas, I will not say their legitimate influence, but the exclusive and despotic possession of the human mind. This result, doubtless altogether unforeseen, was born of many causes. The first is evidently the novelty, extension, and variety of the spectacle which was opened to the view of the crusaders. It happened with them as with travellers. It is a common saying that the mind of travellers becomes enlarged; that the habit of observing various nations and manners, and different opinions, extends the ideas, and frees the judgment from old prejudices. The same fact was accomplished among these travelling nations who were called crusaders: their minds were opened and elevated, by seeing a multitude of different things, and by observing other manners than their own. They also found themselves in juxtaposition with two civilizations, not only different from their own, but more advanced; the Greek on the one hand, and the Mohammedan on the other. There can be no doubt that the Greek society, although enervated, perverted, and falling into decay, had upon the crusaders the effect of a more advanced, polished, and enlightened society than their own. The Mohammedan society afforded them a spectacle of the same nature. It is curious to observe in the old chronicles the impression which the crusaders made upon the Mussulmans; these latter regarded them at first as barbarians, as the rudest, most ferocious, and most stupid class of men they had ever seen. The crusaders, on their part, were struck with the riches and elegance of manners of the Mussulmans. To this first impression succeeded frequent relations between the two people. These extended and became much more important than is generally supposed. Not only had the Christians of the east habitual relations with the Mussulmans, but the west and the east became acquainted, visited and mixed with each other. It is not long since that one of those scholars who honour France in the eyes of Europe, M. Abel Rémusat, discovered the existence of relations between the Mongol emperors and the Christian kings. Mongol ambassadors were sent to the Frank kings, to Saint Louis among others, to treat for an alliance with them, and to recommence the crusades in the common interest of the Mongols and the Christians against the Turks. And not only were diplomatic and official relations thus established between the sovereigns; frequent and various national relations were formed. I quote the words of M. Abel Rémusat.

Many Italian, French, and Flemish monks, were charged with diplomatic missions to the Great Khan. Mongols of distinction came to Rome, Barcelona, Valencia, Lyons, Paris, London, Northampton; and a Franciscan of the kingdom of Naples was archbishop of Pekin. His successor was a professor of theology of the faculty of Paris. But how many others, less known, were drawn after these, either as slaves, or attracted by the desire for gain, or guided by curiosity into countries till then unknown! Chance has preserved the names of some: the first who came to visit the king of Hungary, on the part of the Tartars, was an Englishman, banished from his country for certain crimes, and who, after wandering all over Asia, ended by taking service among the Mongols. A Flemish shoemaker met in the depths of Tartary a woman from Metz, named Paquette, who had been carried off from Hungary; a Parisian goldsmith, whose brother was established at Paris, upon the great bridge; and a young man from the environs of Rouen, who had been at the taking of Belgrade. He saw, also, Russians, Hungarians, and Flemings. . . . The idea of another hemisphere ceased to present itself as a paradox void of all probability, when our own became better known; and it was in searching for the Zipangri of Marco Polo that Christopher Columbus discovered the New World.[8]

You see, by the facts which led to the impulsion of the crusades, what, at the thirteenth and fourteenth centuries, was the new and vast world which was thrown open to the European mind. There can be no doubt but that this was one of the most powerful causes of development, and of the freedom of mind which shone forth at the end of this great event.

There is another cause which merits observation. Down to the time of the crusades, the court of Rome, the centre of the church, had never been in communication with the laity, except through the medium of ecclesiastics, whether legates sent from the court of Rome, or the bishops and the entire clergy. There had always been some laymen in direct relation with Rome; but, taken all together, it was through the ecclesiastics that she communicated with the people. During the crusades, on the contrary, Rome became a place of passage to the greater part of the crusaders, both in going and in returning. Numbers of the laity viewed her policy and manners, and could see how much of personal interest influenced religious controversy. Doubtless this new knowledge inspired many minds with a hardihood till then unknown.

When we consider the state of minds in general, at the end of the crusades, and particularly in ecclesiastical matters, it is

8. Abel Rémusat, *Mémoires sur les Relations Politiques des Princes Chrétiens avec les Empereurs Mongols*, Deuxième Mémoire, pp. 154–57.

impossible not to be struck by one singular fact: religious ideas experienced no change; they had not been replaced by contrary or even different opinions. Yet minds were infinitely more free; religious creeds were no longer the only sphere in which it was brought into play; without abandoning them, it began to separate itself from them, and carry itself elsewhere. Thus, at the end of the thirteenth century, the moral cause which had determined the crusades, which at least was its most energetic principle, had vanished; the moral state of Europe was profoundly modified.

The social state had undergone an analogous change. Much investigation has been expended upon what was the influence of the crusades in this respect; it has been shown how they reduced a large number of fief-holders to the necessity of selling them to their sovereigns, or of selling charters to the communes in order to procure the means of following the crusade. It has been shown that by their mere absence, many of the lords must have lost the greater portion of their power. Without entering into the details of this inquiry, we may, I think, resolve into a few general facts, the influence of the crusades upon the social state.

They greatly diminished the number of petty fiefs and small domains, of inferior fief-holders; and they concentred property and power in a smaller number of hands. It is with the commencement of the crusades that we see the formation and augmentation of large fiefs, and great feudal existences.

I have often regretted that there is no map of France divided into fiefs, as there is of its division into departments, arrondissements, cantons, and parishes, in which all the fiefs should be marked, with their extent and successive relations and changes. If we were to compare, with the aid of such a map, the state of France before and after the crusades, we should see how many fiefs had vanished, and to what a degree the great and middle fiefs had increased. This was one of the most important facts to which the crusades led.

Even where the petty proprietors preserved their fiefs, they no longer lived as isolated as formerly. The great fief-holders became so many centres, around which the smaller ones converged, and near to which they passed their lives. It had become necessary, during the crusades, for them to put themselves in the train of the richest and most powerful, to receive succour from him; they had lived with him, partaken of his fortune, gone through the same adventures. When the crusaders returned home, this sociability, this habit of living near to the superior lord, remained fixed in their manners. Thus as we see the augmentation of the great fiefs after the crusades, so we see the holders of those fiefs holding a much more considerable court in the interior of their castles, having near them a larger number of gentlemen who still preserved their small domains, but did not shut themselves up within them.

The extension of the great fiefs and the creation of a certain number of centres of society, in place of the dispersion which formerly existed, are the two principal effects brought about by the crusades in the heart of feudalism.

As to the bourgeois, a result of the same nature is easily perceptible. The crusades created the great communes. Petty commerce and industry did not suffice to create communes such as the great towns of Italy and Flanders were. It was commerce on a great scale, maritime commerce, and especially that of the east, which gave rise to them; it was the crusades which gave to maritime commerce the most powerful impulsion it had ever received.

Upon the whole, when we regard the state of society at the end of the crusades, we find that this movement of dissolution, of the dispersion of existences and influences, this movement of universal localization, if such a phrase be permitted, which had preceded this epoch, had ceased, by a movement with an exactly contrary tendency, by a movement of centralization. All now tended to approximation. The lesser existences were either absorbed in the greater, or were grouped around them. It was in this direction that society advanced, that all its progress was made.

You now see, why, towards the end of the thirteenth and fourteenth centuries, neither people nor sovereigns any longer desired the crusades; they had no longer either the need or desire for them; they had been cast into them by the impulsion of the religious spirit, and by the exclusive domination of religious

227

ideas upon the whole existence; this domination had lost its energy. They had sought, too, in the crusades a new life, more extensive and more varied; they now began to find it in Europe itself, in the progress of social relations. It was at this epoch the career of political aggrandizement opened itself to kings. Wherefore seek kingdoms in Asia, when they had them to conquer at their own doors? Philip Augustus went to the crusades against his will: what could be more natural? He had to make himself king of France. It was the same with the people. The career of riches opened before their eyes; they renounced adventures for work. For the sovereigns, the place of adventures was supplied by policy; for the people, by work on a great scale. One single class of society still had a taste for adventure: this was that portion of feudal nobility who, not being in a condition to think of political aggrandizement, and not liking work, preserved their ancient condition and manners. They therefore continued to rush to the crusades, and attempted their revival.

Such, in my opinion, are the great and true effects of the crusades: on one side, the extension of ideas, the enfranchisement of mind; on the other, the aggrandizement of existences, and a large sphere opened to activity of all kind: they produced at once a greater degree of individual liberty, and of political unity. They aided the independence of man and the centralization of society. Much has been asked as to the means of civilization—which they directly imported from the east; it has been said that the chief portion of the great discoveries which, in the fourteenth and fifteenth centuries, called forth the development of European civilization—the compass, printing, gunpowder—were known in the east, and that the crusaders may have brought them thence. This, to a certain point, is true. But some of these assertions are disputable. That which is not disputable is this influence, this general effect of the crusades upon the mind on one hand, and upon society on the other hand; they drew European society from a very straightened track, and led it into new and infinitely more extensive paths; they commenced that transformation of the various elements of European society into governments and peoples, which is the character of modern civilization. About the same time, royalty, one of those institutions which have most powerfully contributed to this great result, developed itself. Its history, from the birth of modern states down to the thirteenth century, will form the subject of my next lecture.

Lecture 9

In our last lecture, I attempted to determine the essential and distinctive character of modern European society, as compared with primitive European society; I believe that we discovered in this fact, that all the elements of the social state, at first numerous and various, reduce themselves to two: on one hand the government, and on the other, the people. Instead of encountering the feudal nobility, the clergy, the kings, bourgeois, and serfs, as the dominant powers and chief actors in history, we find in modern Europe but two great figures which alone occupy the historic scene, the government and the country.

If such is the fact in which European civilization terminates, such also is the end to which we should tend, and to which our researches should conduct us. It is necessary that we should see this grand result take birth, and progressively develop and strengthen itself. We are entered upon the epoch in which we may arrive at its origin: it was, as you have seen, between the twelfth and the sixteenth century that the slow and concealed work operated in Europe which has led our society to this new form and definitive state. We have likewise studied the first great event, which, in my opinion, evidently and powerfully impelled Europe in this direction, that is, the crusades.

About the same epoch, almost at the moment that the crusades broke out, that institution commenced its aggrandizement, which has, perhaps, contributed more than anything to the formation of modern society, and to that fusion of all the social elements into two powers, the government and the people; royalty.

It is evident that royalty has played a prodigious part in the history of European civilization; a single glance at facts suffices to convince one of it; we see the development of royalty marching with the same step, so to speak, at least for a long period, as that of society itself; the progress is mutual.

And not only is the progress mutual, but whenever society advances towards its modern and definitive character, royalty seems to extend and prosper; so that when the work is consummated, when there is no longer any, or scarcely any other important or decisive influence in the great states of Europe, than that of the government and the public, royalty is the government.

And it has thus happened, not only in France, where the fact is evident, but also in the greater portion of European countries: a little earlier or a little later, under somewhat different forms, the same result is offered us in the history of society in England, Spain, and Germany. In England, for example, it was under the Tudors, that the ancient, peculiar and local elements of English society were perverted and dissolved, and gave place to the system of public powers; this also was the time of the greatest influence of royalty. It was the same in Germany, Spain, and all the great European states.

If we leave Europe, and if we turn our view upon the rest of the world, we shall be struck by an analogous fact; we shall everywhere find royalty occupying an important position, appearing as, perhaps, the most general and permanent of institutions, the most difficult to prevent, where it did not formerly exist, and the most difficult to root out where it had existed. From time immemorial it has possessed Asia. At the discovery of America, all the great states there were found with different combinations, subject to the monarchical system. When we penetrate into the interior of Africa, wherever we meet with nations in any way extensive, this is the prevailing system. And not only has royalty penetrated everywhere, but it has accommodated itself to the most diverse situations, to civilization and to barbarism, to manners the most pacific, as in China, for example, and to those in which war, in which the military spirit dominate. It has alike established itself in the heart of the system of castes, in the most rigorously classified societies, and in the midst of a system of equality, in societies which are utter strangers to all legal and permanent classification. Here despotic and oppressive, there favourable to civilization and even to liberty, it seems like a head which may be placed upon a multitude of different bodies, a fruit that will spring from the most dissimilar germs.

In this fact, we may discover many curious and important consequences. I will take only two. The first is, that it is impossible such a result should be the fruit of mere chance, of force or usurpation alone; it is impossible but that there should be a profound and powerful analogy between the nature of royalty, considered as an institution, and the nature, whether of individual man, or of human society. Doubtless, force is intermixed with the origin of the institution; doubtless, force has taken an important part in its progress; but when we meet with such a result as this, when we see a great event developing and reproducing itself during the course of many centuries, and in the midst of such different situations, we cannot attribute it to force. Force plays a great part, and an incessant one, in human affairs; but it is not their principle, their *primum mobile;* above force and the part which it plays, there hovers a moral cause which decides the totality of things. It is with force in the history of societies, as with the body in the history of man. The body surely holds a high place in the life of man, but still it is not the principle of life. Life circulates within it, but it does not emanate from it. So it is with human societies; whatever part force takes therein, it is not force which governs them, and which presides supremely over their destinies; it is ideas and moral influences, which conceal themselves under the accidents of force, and regulate the course of the society. It is a cause of this kind, and not force, which gave success to royalty.

A second fact, and one which is no less worthy of remark, is the flexibility of the institution, its faculty of modifying, and adapting itself to a multitude of different circumstances. Mark the contrast: its form is unique, permanent, and simple; it does not offer that prodigious variety of combinations which we see in other institutions, and yet it applies itself to societies which the least resemble it. It must evidently allow of great diversity, and must attach itself, whether in man himself or in society, to many different elements and principles.

It is from not having considered the institution of royalty in its whole extent; from not having on the one hand penetrated to its peculiar and fixed principle, which, whatever may be the circumstances to which it applies itself, is its very essence and being—and on the other, from not having estimated all the varieties to which it lends itself, and all the principles with which it may enter into alliance; it is, I say, from not having considered royalty under this vast and twofold point of view, that the part taken by it in the history of the world has not been always comprehended, that its nature and effects have often been misconstrued.

This is the work which I wish to go through with you, and in such a manner as to take an exact and complete estimate of the effects of this institution in modern Europe, whether they have flowed from its own peculiar principles or the modifications which it has undergone.

There can be no doubt that the force of royalty, that moral power which is its true principle, does not reside in the sole and personal will of the man momentarily king; there can be no doubt that the people, in accepting it as an institution, philosophers in maintaining it as a system, have not intended or consented to accept the empire of the will of a man, essentially narrow, arbitrary, capricious, and ignorant.

Royalty is quite a distinct thing from the will of a man, although it presents itself in that form; it is the personification of the sovereignty of right, of that will, essentially reasonable, enlightened, just, and impartial, foreign and superior to all individual wills, and which in virtue of this title has a right to govern them. Such is the meaning of royalty in the minds of nations, such the motive for their adhesion.

Is it true that there is a sovereignty of right, a will which possesses the right of governing men? It is quite certain that they believe so; because they seek, and constantly have sought, and indeed cannot but seek, to place themselves under its empire. Conceive to yourselves the smallest assembly of men, I will not say a people: conceive that assembly under the submission to a sovereign who is only so *de facto*, under a force which has no right except that of force, which governs neither according to reason, justice, nor truth; human nature revolts at such a supposition—it must have right to believe in. It is the supremacy of right which it seeks, that is the only power to which man consents to submit. What is history but the demonstration of this universal fact? What are the greater portion of the struggles which take place in the life of nations, but an ardent effort towards the sovereignty of right, so that they may place themselves under its empire? And not only nations but philosophers believe in its existence, and incessantly seek it. What are all the systems of political philosophy, but the search for the sovereign of right? What is it that they treat of, but the question of knowing who has a right to govern society? Take the theocratical, monarchical, aristocratical, or democratical systems, all of them boast of having discovered wherein the sovereignty of right resides; all promise to society that they will place it under the rule of its legitimate master. I repeat, this is the end alike of all the works of philosophers, of all efforts of nations.

How should they but believe in the sovereignty of right? How should they but be constantly in search of it? Take the most simple suppositions; let there be something to accomplish, some influence to exercise, whether upon society in its whole, or upon a number of its members, or upon a single individual; there is evidently always a rule for this action, a legitimate will to follow and apply. Whether you penetrate into the smallest details of social life, or whether you elevate yourselves to the greatest events, you will everywhere encounter a truth to be proved, or a just and reasonable idea to be passed into reality. This is the sovereign of right, towards which philosophers and nations have never ceased and never can cease to aspire.

Up to what point can the sovereignty of right be represented in a general and permanent manner by a terrestrial force or by a human will? How far is such a supposition necessarily false and dangerous? What should be thought in particular of the personification of the sovereignty of right under the image of royalty? Upon what conditions, within what limits is this personification admissible? Great questions, which I have not to treat of here, but which I could not resist pointing out, and upon which I shall say a word in passing.

I affirm, and the merest common sense will acknowledge, that the sovereignty of right completely and permanently can appertain to no one; that all attribution of the sovereignty of right to any human power whatsoever, is radically false and dangerous. Hence arises the necessity for the limitation of all powers, whatever their names or forms may be; hence the radical illegitimacy of all absolute power, whether its origin be from conquest, inheritance, or election. People may differ as to the best means of seeking the sovereign of right; they may vary as to place and times; but in no place, no time, can any legitimate power be the independent possessor of this sovereignty.

This principle being laid down, it is no less certain that royalty, in whatever system it is considered, presents itself as the personification of the sovereign of right. Listen to the theocratical system: it will tell you that kings are the image of God upon earth; this is only saying that they are the personification of sovereign justice, truth, and goodness. Address yourself to the jurisconsults; they will tell you that the king is the living law; that is to say, the king is the personification of the sovereign of right, of the just law, which has the right of governing society. Ask royalty itself, in the system of pure monarchy; it will tell you that it is the personification of the State, of the general interest. In whatever alliance and in whatever situation you consider it, you will always find it summing itself up in the pretension of representing and reproducing the sovereign of right, alone capable of legitimately governing society.

There is no occasion for astonishment in all this. What are the characteristics of the sovereign of right, the characteristics derivable from his very nature? In the first place he is unique; since there is but one truth, one justice, there can be but one sovereign of right. He is permanent, always the same; truth never changes. He is placed in a superior situation, a stranger to all the vicissitudes and changes of this world; his part in the world is, as it were, that of a spectator and judge. Well! it is royalty which externally reproduces, under the most simple form, that which appears its most faithful image, these rational and natural characteristics of the sovereign of right. Open the work in which M. Benjamin Constant has so ingeniously represented royalty as a neutral and moderating power, raised above the accidents and struggles of social life, and only interfering at great crises. Is not this, so to speak, the attitude of the sovereign of right in the government of human things? There must be something in this idea well calculated to impress the mind, for it has passed with singular rapidity from books to facts. One sovereign made it in the constitution of Brazil the very foundation of his throne; there royalty is represented as a moderating power, raised above all active powers, as a spectator and judge.

Under whatever point of view you regard this institution, as compared with the sovereign of right, you will find that there is a great external resemblance, and that it is natural for it to have struck the minds of men. Accordingly, whenever their reflection or imagination turned with preference towards the contemplation or study of the nature of the sovereign of right, and his essential characteristics, they have inclined towards royalty. As, in the time of the preponderance of religious ideas, the habitual contemplation of the nature of God led mankind towards the monarchical system, so when the jurisconsults dominated in society, the habit of studying, under the name of the law, the nature of the sovereign of right, was favourable to the dogma of his personification in royalty. The attentive application of the human mind to the contemplation of the nature of the sovereignty of right when no other causes have interfered to destroy the effect, has always given force and credit to royalty, which presents its image.

Moreover, there are times peculiarly favourable to this personification: these are the times when individual powers display themselves in the world with all their risks and caprices; times when egotism dominates in individuals, whether from ignorance and brutality, or from corruption. Then society, abandoned to the contests of personal wills, and unable to raise itself by their free concurrence to a common and universal will, passionately long for a sovereign to whom all individuals may be forced to submit; and the moment any institution, bearing any one of the characteristics of the sovereignty of right, presented itself, and promised its empire to society, society rallied round it with eager earnestness, like outlaws taking refuge in the asylum of a church. This is what has been seen in the disorderly youth of nations, such as we have surveyed. Royalty is admirably adapted to epochs of vigorous and fruitful anarchy, so to speak, when so-ciety desires to form and regulate itself, without knowing how to do so by the free concord of individual wills. There are other times when, from directly opposite causes, it has the same recommendation. Why did the Roman empire, so nearly in a state of dissolution at the end of the republic, subsist for nearly fifteen centuries afterwards, under the name of that empire, which, after all, was but a continual decay, a lengthened agony? Royalty alone could produce such an effect; that alone could hold together a society which selfishness incessantly tended to destroy. The imperial power struggled for fifteen centuries against the ruin of the Roman world.

Thus there are times when royalty alone can retard the dissolution of society, and times when it alone accelerates its formation. And in both these cases, it is because it represents more clearly and powerfully than any other form the sovereignty of right, that it exercises this power upon events.

From whatever point of view you may consider this institution, and at whatever epoch, you will acknowledge then that its essential characteristic, its moral principle, its true and inmost meaning is the image, the personification, the presumed interpreter of this unique, superior, and essentially legitimate will, which alone has the right of governing society.

Let us now regard royalty from the second point of view, that is to say, in its flexibility, in the variety of parts which it has played, and the effects which it has produced; it is necessary that we should give the reason for these features, and determine their causes.

Here we have an advantage; we can immediately enter upon history, and upon our own history. By a concourse of singular circumstances, it has happened, that in modern Europe royalty has assumed every character under which it has shown itself in the history of the world. If I may be allowed to use an arithmetical expression, European royalty is the sum total of all possible species of royalty. I will run over its history from the fifth to the twelfth century; you will see how various are the aspects under which it presents itself, and to what an extent we shall everywhere find this character of variety, complication, and conflict which belongs to all European civilization.

In the fifth century, at the time of the great German invasion, two royalties are present; the barbarian and the imperial royalty, that of Clovis and that of Constantine; both differing essentially in principles and effects. Barbaric royalty is essentially elective; the German kings were elected, although their election did not take place with the same forms which we are accustomed to attach to the idea; they were military chiefs, who were bound to make their power freely acceptable to a large number of companies who obeyed them as being the most brave and the most able among them. Election is the true source of barbaric royalty, its primitive and essential characteristic.

Not that this characteristic in the fifth century was not already a little modified, or that different elements had not been introduced into royalty. The various tribes had had their chiefs for a certain time; some families had raised themselves to more trust, consideration, and riches than others. Hence a commencement of inheritance; the chief was now mostly elected out of these families. This was the first differing principle which became associated with the dominant principle of election.

Another idea, another element, had also already penetrated into barbaric royalty: this was the religious element. We find among some of the barbarous nations, among the Goths, for example, that the families of their kings descended from the families of their gods, or from those heroes of whom they had made gods, such as Odin. This is the situation of the kings of Homer, who sprang from gods or demigods, and by reason of this title were the objects of a kind of religious veneration, despite their limited power.

Such, in the fifth century, was barbaric royalty, already varying and fluctuating, although its primitive principle still dominated.

I take imperial, Roman royalty; this is a totally different thing; it is the personification of the state, the heir of the sovereignty and majesty of the Roman people. Consider the royalty of Augustus and Tiberius; the emperor is the representative of the senate, the comitia, and the whole republic; he succeeded them, and they are summed up in his person. Who would not recognise this in the modesty of language of the first emperors; of those, at least, who were men of sense, and understood their situation? They felt themselves in the presence of the late sovereign people who had abdicated in their favour; they addressed them as their representatives and ministers. But, in fact, they exercised the whole power of the people, and that with the most formidable intensity. It is easy for us to understand such a transformation; we have ourselves witnessed it; we have seen the sovereignty pass from the people to a man; that is the history of Napoleon. He also was the personification of the sovereign people; he unceasingly repeated to it, "Who like me has been elected by eighteen millions of men? Who like me is the representative of the people?" And when upon one side of his coinage we read, *The French Republic*, and upon the other, *Napoleon, Empereur*, what does this mean, if not the fact which I have described, the people become king?

Such was the fundamental character of imperial royalty, which it preserved for the first three centuries of the empire. It was not till Diocletian that it took its definitive and complete form. It was then, however, upon the point of undergoing a great change; a new royalty had almost appeared. Christianity laboured for three centuries to introduce the religious element into society. It was under Constantine that it met with success, not in making it the prevalent fact, but in making it play an important part. Here royaly presents itself under a different aspect; its origin is not earthly; the prince is not the representative of the public sovereignty; he is the image of God, his representative and delegate. Power came down to him from above, while in imperial royalty it came from below. These are two utterly different situations, and have entirely different results. The rights of liberty, political guarantees are difficult to combine with the principle of religious royalty; but the principle itself is elevated, moral, and salutary. Let us see the idea which was formed of the prince in the seventh century, in the system of religious royalty. I take it from the canons of the councils of Toledo.

The king is called king because he governs justly. If he act with justice, he legitimately possesses the name of king; if he act with injustice, he miserably loses it. Our fathers, therefore, said, with good reason: *Rex ejus, eris si recta facis, si autem non facis non eris.* The two principal royal virtues are justice and truth.

The royal power is bound, like the people, to respect the laws . . . Obedience to the will of Heaven, gives to us and to our subjects wise laws, which our greatness and that of our successors is bound to obey, as well as the whole population of our kingdom. . . .

God, the creator of all things, in disposing the structure of the human body, has raised the head on high, and has willed that the nerves of all the members should proceed therefrom. And he has placed in the head the torch of the eyes, to the end that from thence may be viewed all things that might be prejudicial. He has established the power of intellect, charging it to govern all the members, and wisely to regulate their action. . . . It is first necessary, then, to regulate what relates to princes, to watch over their safety, and to protect their life, and then to order what relates to the people; so that in guaranteeing, as is fitting, the safety of kings, they at the same time guarantee, and more effectually, that of the people.[9]

But, in the system of religious royalty, another element, quite different from that of royalty itself, almost always introduced itself. A new power took its place by the side of it, a power nearer to God, to the source whence royalty emanates, than royalty itself: this was the clergy, the ecclesiastical power which interposed itself between God and kings, and between kings and the people; so that royalty, the image of divinity, ran a chance of falling to the rank of an instrument of the human interpreters of the divine will. This was a new cause of diversity in the destinies and effects of the institution.

9. *Forum Judicum* 1.2, tit. 1.2, 4.

Here, then, we see, what in the fifth century were the various royalties which manifested themselves upon the ruins of the Roman empire: the barbaric royalty, the imperial royalty, and the rising religious royalty. Their fortunes were as various as their principles.

In France, under the first race, barbaric royalty prevailed; there were many attempts of the clergy to impress upon it the imperial or religious character; but election in the royal family, with some mixture of inheritance and religious ideas, remained dominant. In Italy, among the Ostrogoths, imperial royalty superseded the barbarian customs. Theodoric asserted himself the successor of the emperors. You need only read Cassiodorus, to acknowledge this character of his government.

In Spain, royalty appeared more religious than elsewhere; as the councils of Toledo were, I will not say the masters, but the influencing power, the religious character dominated, if not in the government, properly so called, of the Visigoth kings, at least, in the laws with which the clergy inspired them, and the language which it made them speak.

In England, among the Saxons, barbarian manners subsisted almost entire. The kingdoms of the Heptarchy were merely the domains of various bands, having each its chief. The military election is more evident there than elsewhere. Anglo-Saxon royalty is the most perfect type of barbaric royalty.

Thus from the fifth to the twelfth century, three kinds of royalty manifested themselves at the same time, in general facts; one or other of them prevailed, according to circumstances, in each of the different states of Europe.

The chaos was such at this epoch, that nothing universal or permanent could be established; and, from one vicissitude to another, we arrive at the eighth century, without royalty having anywhere taken a definitive character. Towards the middle of the eighth century, with the triumph of the second race of the Frank kings, events generalized themselves and became clearer; as they were accomplished upon a greater scale, they were better understood, and led to more results. You will shortly see the different royalties distinctly succeed and combine with each other.

At the time when the Carlovingians replace the Merovingians, a return of barbaric royalty is visible; election again appears. Pepin causes himself to be elected at Soissons. When the first Carlovingians give the kingdoms to their sons they take care to have them accepted by the chief persons in the states assigned them; when they make a partition, they wish it to be sanctioned in the national assemblies. In a word, the elective principle, under the form of public acceptation, reassumes some reality. You bear in mind, that this change of dynasty was like a new invasion of the Germans in the west of Europe, and brought back some shadow of their ancient institutions and manners.

At the same time we see the religious principle introduced more clearly into royalty, and playing therein a more important part. Pepin was acknowledged and crowned by the pope. He had need of religious sanction; it had already a great power, and he courted it. Charlemagne took the same precaution; religious royalty was developing. Still under Charlemagne this character did not dominate; imperial royalty was evidently what he attempted to resuscitate. Although he closely allied himself to the clergy, and made use of them, he was not their instrument. The idea of a great state, of a great political unity, the resurrection of the Roman empire, was the favourite idea, the dream of Charlemagne's reign. He died, and was succeeded by Louis le Debonnaire. Every one knows what character the royal power instantly assumed; the king fell into the hands of the clergy, who censured, deposed, reestablished, and governed him; religious royalty, late subordinate, seemed on the point of being established.

Thus, from the middle of the eighth to the middle of the ninth century, the diversity of three kinds of royalty manifested itself in important, closely connected, and palpable events.

After the death of Louis le Debonnaire, in the dissolution into which Europe fell, the three species of royalty disappeared almost simultaneously; all became confusion. After some time, when the feudal system prevailed, a fourth royalty presented itself, different from any that we have yet seen; this was feudal royalty. This is confused, and very difficult to define. It has been said that the king in the feudal system was sovereign of sovereigns, lord of lords, that he held by sure ties, from one class to another, the entire society; that in calling around him his vassals, then the vassals of his vassals, he called the whole nation, and truly showed himself a king. I do not deny that this was the theory of feudal royalty; but it is a mere theory, which has never governed facts. That general influence of the king by the means of an hierarchical organization, those ties which united royalty to the entire feudal society, are the dreams of publicists. In fact, the greater part of the feudal lords were at this epoch entirely independent of royalty; a large number scarcely knew the name, and had little or no connexion with it. All the sovereignties were local and independent: the title of king, borne by one of the feudal lords, expressed rather a remembrance than a fact.

This was the state of royalty during the course of the tenth and eleventh centuries. In the twelfth, with the reign of Louis le Gros, the aspect of things began to change. We more often find the king spoken of; his influence penetrated into places where hitherto he had never made way; his part in society became more active. If we seek by what title, we shall recognise none of the titles of which royalty had hitherto been accustomed to avail itself. It was not as the heir of the emperors, or by the title of imperial royalty, that it aggrandized itself and assumed more coherence; nor was it in virtue of election, nor as the emanation of divine power. All trace of election had disappeared, the hereditary principle of succession had become definitely established; and although religion sanctioned the accession of kings, the minds of men did not appear at all engrossed with the religious character of the royalty of Louis le Gros. A new element, a character hitherto unknown, produced itself in royalty; a new royalty commenced.

I need not repeat that society was at this epoch in a prodigious disorder, a prey to unceasing violence. Society had in itself no means of striving against this deplorable state, of regaining any regularity or unity. The feudal institutions, those parliaments of barons, those seigneurial courts, all those forms under which, in modern times, feudalism has been represented as a systematic and organised regime, all this was devoid of reality, of power; there was nothing there which could reestablish order or justice; so that, amidst this social desolation, none knew to whom to have recourse for the reparation of any great injustice, or to remedy any great evil, or in any way to constitute anything resembling a state. The name of king remained; a lord bore it, and some few addressed themselves to him. The various titles under which royalty had hitherto presented itself, although they did not exercise any great control, were still present to many minds, and on some occasions were recognised. It sometimes happened that they had recourse to the king to repress any scandalous violence, or to reestablish something like order in any place near to his residence, or to terminate any difference which had long existed; he was sometimes called upon to interfere in matters not strictly within his jurisdiction; he interfered as the protector of public order, as arbitrator and redresser of wrongs. The moral authority which remained attached to his name, by degrees attracted to him this power.

Such is the character which royalty began to take under Louis le Gros, and under the administration of Suger. Then, for the first time, we see in the minds of men the idea, although very incomplete, confused, and weak, of a public power, foreign to the powers which possessed society, called to render justice to those who were unable to obtain it by ordinary means, capable of establishing, or, at least, of commanding order; the idea of a great magistrate, whose essential character was that of maintaining or reestablishing peace, of protecting the weak, and of ending differences which none others could decide. This is the entirely new character under which, dating from the twelfth century, royalty presented itself in Europe, and especially in France. It was neither as a barbarous royalty, a religious royalty, nor as an imperial royalty, that it exercised its empire; it possessed only a limited, incomplete, and accidental power, the power, as it were (I know of no expression more exact), of a great justice of peace for the whole nation.

This is the true origin of modern royalty; this, so to speak, is its vital principle; that which has been developed in the course of its career, and which, I do not hesitate in saying, has brought about its success. At the different epochs of history, we see the different characters of royalty reappear; we see the various royalties which I have described attempting by turns to regain the preponderance. Thus the clergy has always preached religious royalty; jurisconsults laboured to resuscitate imperial royalty; and the nobles have sometimes wished to revive elective royalty, or the feudal. And not only have the clergy, jurisconsults, and nobility, striven to make dominant in royalty such or such a character; it has itself made them all subservient to the aggrandizement of its power; kings have sometimes represented themselves as the delegates of God, sometimes as the successors of the emperors, according to the need or inclination of the moment; they have illegitimately availed themselves of these various titles, but none of them has been the veritable title of modern royalty, or the source of its preponderating influence. It is, I repeat, as the depositary and protector of public order, of universal justice, and common interest—it is under the aspect of a great magistracy, the centre and union of society—that it has shown itself to the eyes of the people, and has appropriated their strength by obtaining their adhesion.

You will see, as we advance, this characteristic of modern European royalty, which commenced at the twelfth century, under the reign of Louis le Gros, strengthen and develop itself, and became, so to speak, its political physiognomy. It is through it that royalty has contributed to the great result which characterizes European societies in the present day, namely, the reduction of all social elements into two, the government and the country.

Thus, at the termination of the crusades, Europe entered the path which was to conduct it to its present state; and royalty took its appropriate part in the great transformation. In our next lecture we shall study the different attempts made at political organization, from the twelfth to the sixteenth century, with a view to maintain, by regulating it, the order, then almost in ruin. We shall consider the efforts of feudalism, of the church, and even of the communes, to constitute society after its ancient principles, and under its primitive forms, and thus defend themselves against the general metamorphosis which was in preparation.

Lecture 14
In my last lecture I endeavoured to determine the true character and political meaning of the English revolution. We have seen that it was the first shock of the two great facts to which all the civilization of primitive Europe reduced itself in the course of the sixteenth century, namely, pure monarchy, on one hand, and free inquiry on the other; those two powers came to strife for the first time in England. Attempts have been made to infer from this fact the existence of a radical difference between the social state of England and that of the continent; some have pretended that no comparison was possible between countries of destinies so different; they have affrmed that the English people had existed in a kind of moral isolation analogous to its material situation.

It is true that there had been an important difference between English civilization, and the civilization of the continental states —a difference which we are bound to calculate. You have already, in the course of my lectures, been enabled to catch a glimpse of it. The development of the different principles and elements of society occurred in England simultaneously, and, as it were, abreast; at least, far more so than upon the continent. When I attempted to determine the peculiar physiognomy of European civilization as compared with the ancient and Asiatic civilizations, I showed you the first varied, rich, and complex; that it never fell under the dominion of an exclusive principle; that therein the various elements of the social state were modified, combined, and struggled with each other, and had been constantly compelled to agree and live in common. This fact, the general characteristic of European civilization, has above all characterized the English civilization; it was in England that this character developed itself with the most continuity and obviousness; it was there that the civil and religious orders, aristocracy, democracy, royalty, local and central institutions, moral and political developments, progressed and increased together, pell-mell, so to speak, and if not with an equal rapidity, at least always within a short distance of each other. Under the reign of the Tudors, for instance, in the midst of the most brilliant progress of pure monarchy, we see the democratical principle, the popular power, arising and strengthening itself at the same time. The revolution of the seventeenth century burst forth; it was at the same time religious and political. The feudal aristocracy appeared here in a very weakened condition, and with all the symptoms of decline: nevertheless, it was ever in a position to preserve a place and play an important part therein, and to take its share in the results. It is the same with the entire course of English history: never has any ancient element completely perished; never has any new element wholly triumphed, or any special principle attained to an exclusive preponderance. There has always been a simultaneous development of different forces, a compromise between their pretensions and their interests.

Upon the continent, the progress of civilization has been much less complex and complete. The various elements of society—the religious and civil orders—monarchy, aristocracy, and democracy, have developed themselves, not together and abreast, but in succession. Each principle, each system has had, after a certain manner, its turn. Such a century belongs, I will not say exclusively, which would be saying too much, but with a very marked preponderance, to feudal aristocracy, for example; another belongs to the monarchical principle; a third to the democratic system.

Compare the French with the English middle ages, the eleventh, twelfth, and thirteenth centuries of our history with the corresponding centuries beyond the channel; you will find that at this period, in France, feudalism was almost absolutely sovereign, while royalty and the democratical principle were next to nullities. Look to England: it is, indeed, the feudal aristocracy which predominates; but royalty and democracy were nevertheless powerful and important.

Royalty triumphed in England under Elizabeth, as in France under Louis XIV; but how many precautions was it obliged to take; to how many restrictions—now from the aristocracy, now from the democracy, did it submit! In England, also, each system and each principle has had its day of power and success; but never so completely, so exclusively as upon the continent; the conqueror has always been compelled to tolerate the presence of his rivals, and to allow each his share.

With the differences in the progress of the two civilizations, are connected advantages and disadvantages, which manifest themselves, in fact, in the history of the two countries. There can be no doubt, for instance, but that this simultaneous development of the different social elements greatly contributed to carry England, more rapidly than any other of the continental states, to the final aim of all society—namely, the establishment of a government at once regular and free. It is precisely the nature of a government to concern itself for all interests and all powers, to reconcile them, and to induce them to live and prosper in common; now, such, beforehand, by the concurrence of a multitude of causes, was the disposition and relation of the different elements of English society: a general and somewhat regular government had therefore less difficulty in becoming constituted there. So, the essence of liberty is the manifestation and simultaneous action of all interests, rights, powers, and social elements. England was therefore much nearer to its possession than the majority of other states. For the same reasons, national good sense, the comprehension of public affairs, necessarily formed themselves there more rapidly than elsewhere; political good sense consists in knowing how to estimate all facts, to appreciate them, and render to each its share of consideration; this, in England, was a necessity or the social state, a natural result of the course of civilization.

On the other hand, in the continental states, each system, each principle having had its turn, having predominated after a more complete and more exclusive manner, its development was wrought upon a larger scale, and with more grandeur and brilliancy. Royalty and feudal aristocracy, for instance, came upon the continental stage with far greater boldness, extension, and freedom. Our political experiments, so to speak, have been broader and more finished: the result of this has been that political ideas (I speak of general ideas, and not of good sense applied to the conduct of affairs) and political doctrines have risen higher, and displayed themselves with much more rational vigour. Each system having, in some measure, presented itself alone, and having remained a long time upon the stage, men have been enabled to consider it in its entirety, to mount up to its first principles, to follow it out into its last consequences, and fully to unfold its theory. Whoever attentively observes the English character, must be struck with a twofold fact—on the one hand, with the soundness of its good sense and its practical ability; on the other, with its lack of general ideas, and its disdain for theoretical questions. Whether we open a work upon English history, upon jurisprudence, or any other subject, it is rarely that we find the grand reason of things, the fundamental reason. In all things, and especially in the political sciences, pure doctrine, philosophy, and science, properly so called, have prospered much better on the Continent than in England; their flights have, at least, been far more powerful and bold; and we cannot doubt but that the different developments of civilization in the two countries have greatly contributed to this result.

For the rest, whatever we may think of the advantages or disadvantages which this difference has entailed, it is a real and incontestable fact, the fact which most deeply distinguishes England from the continent. But it does not follow, because the different principles and social elements have been there developed more simultaneously, here more successively, that, at bottom, the path and the goal have not been one and the same. Considered in their entirety, the continent and England have traversed the same grand phases of civilization; events have, in either, followed the same course, and the same causes have led to the same effects. You have been enabled to convince yourselves of this fact from the picture which I have placed before you of civilization up to the sixteenth century, and you will equally recognise it in studying the seventeenth and eighteenth centuries. The development of free inquiry, and that of pure monarchy, almost simultaneous in England, accomplished themselves upon the continent at long intervals; but they did accomplish themselves, and the two powers, after having successively preponderated with splendour, came equally, at last, to blows. The general path of societies, considering all things, has thus been the same, and though the points of difference are real, those of resemblance are more deeply seated. A rapid sketch of modern times will leave you in no doubt upon this subject.

Glancing over the history of Europe in the seventeenth and eighteenth centuries, it is impossible not to perceive that France has advanced at the head of European civilization. At the beginning of this work I have already insisted upon this fact, and I have endeavoured to point out its cause. We shall now find it more striking than ever.

The principle of pure monarchy, of absolute royalty, predominated in Spain under Charles V and Philip II, before developing in France under Louis XIV. In the same manner the principle of free inquiry had reigned in England in the seventeenth century, before developing in France in the eighteenth. Nevertheless, pure monarchy and free inquiry came not from Spain and England to take possession of the world. The two principles, the two systems remained, in a manner, confined to the countries in which they had arisen. It was necessary that they should pass through France in order that they might extend their conquests; it was necessary that pure monarchy and free inquiry should become French in order to become European. This communicative character of French civilization, this social genius of France, which has displayed itself at all periods, was thus more than ever manifest at the period with which we now occupy ourselves. I will not further insist upon this fact; it has been developed to you with as much reason as brilliance in other lectures wherein you have been called upon to observe the influence of

French literature and philosophy in the eighteenth century.* You have seen that philosophic France possessed more authority over Europe, in regard to liberty, than even free England. You have seen that French civilization showed itself far more active and contagious than that of any other country. I need not, therefore, pause upon the details of this fact, which I mention only in order to rest upon it my right to confine my picture of modern European civilization to France alone. Between the civilization of France and that of the other states of Europe at this period, there have, no doubt, been differences, which it would have been necessary to bear in mind, if my present purpose had been a full and faithful exposition of the history of those civilizations; but I must go on so rapidly that I am compelled to omit entire nations and ages, so to speak. I choose rather to concentrate your attention for a moment upon the course of French civilization, an image, though imperfect, of the general course of things in Europe.

The influence of France in Europe, during the seventeenth and eighteenth centuries, presents itself under very different aspects. In the former, it was French government that acted upon Europe, and advanced at the head of general civilization. In the latter it was no longer to the government, but France herself, that the preponderance belonged. In the first case, it was Louis XIV and his court, afterwards France and her opinion, that governed minds and attracted attention. In the seventeenth century there were peoples who, as peoples, appeared more prominently upon the scene, and took a greater part in events, than the French people. Thus during the thirty years war, the German nation, in the English revolution, the English people,

* When Guizot was restored to his post at the Sorbonne in 1828, he joined his two friends and collaborators Victor Cousin and Abel Villemain. These three then became that famous liberal trio of professors between the years 1828 and 1830. Their courses were so arranged that they would lecture on different days of the week in order that the students who listened to Guizot's history lectures could also attend Cousin's course in philosophy and Villemain's class in literature. Since these three courses were in effect the core of the modern curriculum, most of the students did attend all three, so that Guizot could with confidence refer to the work of his colleagues.—EDITOR.

played, in their own destinies, a much greater part than was played, at this period, by the French, in theirs. So, also, in the cighteenth century, there were governments stronger, of greater consideration, and more to be dreaded, than the French government. No doubt Frederick II, Catherine II, and Maria Theresa, had more influence and weight in Europe than Louis XV; nevertheless, at both periods it was France that was at the head of European civilization, placed there, first, by its government, afterwards, by itself; now by the political action of its masters, now by its peculiar intellectual development.

In order to fully understand the predominant influence in the course of civilization in France, and therefore in Europe, we must study, in the seventeenth century, French government, in the eighteenth, French society. We must change the plan and the drama according as time alters the stage and the actors.

When we occupy ourselves with the government of Louis XIV, when we endeavour to appreciate the causes of his power and influence in Europe, we scarcely think of anything but his renown, his conquests, his magnificence, and the literary glory of his time. It is to external causes that we apply ourselves, and attribute the European preponderance of the French government. But I conceive that this preponderance had deeper and more serious foundations. We must not believe that it was simply by means of victories, *fêtes*, or even masterworks of genius, that Louis XIV and his government, at this epoch, played the part which it is impossible to deny them.

Many of you may remember, and all of you have heard speak of the effect which the consular government produced in France twenty-nine years ago, and of the condition in which it found our country. Without, was impending foreign invasion, and continual disasters were occurring in our armies; within, was an almost complete dissolution of power and of the people; there were no revenues, no public order; in a word, society was prostrate, humiliated, and disorganised: such was France on the advent of the consulate government. Who does not recall the prodigious and felicitous activity of this government, that activity which, in a little time, secured the independence of the land, revived national honour, reorganized the administration, remodelled the legislation, and, after a manner, regenerated society under the hand of power?

Well, the government of Louis XIV, when it commenced, did something analogous to this for France; with great difference of times, proceedings, and forms, it pursued and attained nearly the same results.

Recal to your memory the state into which France was fallen after the government of Cardinal Richelieu, and during the minority of Louis XIV: the Spanish armies always on the frontiers, sometimes in the interior; continual danger of an invasion; internal dissensions urged to extremity, civil war, the government weak and discredited at home and abroad. Society was perhaps in a less violent, but still sufficiently analogous state to ours, prior to the eighteenth *Brumaire*. It was from this state that the government of Louis XIV extricated France. His first victories had the effect of the victory of Marengo: they secured the country, and retrieved the national honour. I am about to consider this government under its principal aspects—in its wars, in its external relations, in its administration, and in its legislation; and you will see, I imagine, that the comparison of which I speak, and to which I attach no puerile importance (for I think very little of the value of historical parallels), you will see, I say, that this comparison has a real foundation, and that I have a right to employ it.

First of all let us speak of the wars of Louis XIV. The wars of Europe have originated, as you know, and as I have often taken occasion to remind you, in great popular movements. Urged by necessity, caprice, or any other cause, entire populations, sometimes numerous, sometimes in simple bands, have transported themselves from one territory to another. This was the general character of European wars until the crusades, at the end of the thirteenth century.

At that time began a species of wars scarcely less different from modern wars than the above. These were the distant wars, undertaken no longer by the people, but by governments, which went at the head of their armies to seek states and adventures afar off. They quitted their countries, abandoned their own territories, and plunged, some into Germany, others into Italy, and others into Africa, with no other motives than personal caprice. Almost all the wars of the fifteenth and even a part of the sixteenth century were of this description. What interest—I speak not of a legitimate interest—but what possible motive had France that Charles VIII should possess the kingdom of Naples? This evidently was a war dictated by no political consideration: the king conceived that he had a personal right to the kingdom of Naples, and with a personal aim and to satisfy his personal desire, he undertook the conquest of a distant country, which was in no way adapted for annexation to his kingdom; which, on the contrary, did nothing but compromise his power externally, and internally, his repose. It was the same with the expedition of Charles the Fifth to Africa. The latest war of this kind was the expedition of Charles XII against Russia. The wars of Louis XIV had no such character; they were the wars of a regular government, fixed in the centre of its states, and labouring to make conquests around it, to extend or consolidate its territory; in a word, they were political wars.

They may have been just or unjust; they may have cost France too dearly; there are a thousand reasons which might be adduced against their morality and their excess; but they bear a character incomparably more rational than the antecedent wars: they were no longer undertaken for whim or adventure; they were dictated by some serious motive; it was some natural limit that it seemed desirable to attain; some population speaking the same language that they aimed at annexing; some point of defence against a neighbouring power, which it was thought necessary to acquire. No doubt personal ambition had a share in these wars; but examine one after another of the wars of Louis XIV, particularly those of the first part of his reign, and you will find that they had truly political motives; and that they were conceived for the interest of France, for obtaining power, and for the country's safety.

The results are proofs of the fact. France of the present day is still, in many respects, what the wars of Louis XIV have made it.

The provinces which he conquered, Franche-Comté, Flanders, and Alsace, remain yet incorporated with France. There are sensible as well as senseless conquests: those of Louis XIV were of the former species; his enterprises have not the unreasonable and capricious character which, up to his time, was so general; a skilful, if not always just and wise policy, presided over them.

Leaving the wars of Louis XIV, and passing to the consideration of his relations with foreign states, of his diplomacy, properly so called, I find an analogous result. I have insisted upon the occurrence of the birth of diplomacy in Europe at the end of the fifteenth century. I have endeavoured to show how the relations of governments and states between themselves up to that time accidental, rare, and transitory, became at this period more regu-• lar and enduring; how they took a character of great public interest; how, in a word, at the end of the fifteenth, and during the first half of the sixteenth century, diplomacy came to play an immense part in events. Nevertheless, up to the seventeenth century, it had not been, truly speaking, systematic; it had not led to long alliances, or to great, and above all, durable combinations, directed, according to fixed principles, towards a constant aim, with that spirit of continuity which is the true character of established governments. During the course of the religious revolution, the external relations of states were almost completely under the power of the religious interest; the Protestant and Catholic leagues divided Europe. It was in the seventeenth century, after the treaty of Westphalia, and under the influence of the government of Louis XIV, that diplomacy changed its character. It then escaped from the exclusive influences of the religious principle; alliances and political combinations were formed upon other considerations. At the same time it became much more systematic, regular, and constantly directed towards a certain aim, according to permanent principles. The regular origin of this system of balance in Europe belongs to this period. It was under the government of Louis XIV that the system, together with all the considerations attached to it, truly took possession of European policy. When we investigate what was the general idea in regard to this subject, what was the predominating principle of the policy of Louis XIV, I believe that the following is what we discover:

I have spoken of the great struggle between the pure monarchy of Louis XIV, aspiring to become universal monarchy, and civil and religious liberty, and the independence of states, under the direction of the prince of Orange, William III. You have seen that the great fact of this period was the division of the powers under these two banners. But this fact was not then estimated as we estimate it now; it was hidden and unknown even to those who accomplished it; the suppression of the system of pure monarchy and the consecration of civil and religious liberty was, at bottom, the necessary result of the resistance of Holland and its allies to Louis XIV; but the question was not thus openly enunciated between absolute power and liberty. It has been often said that the propagation of absolute power was the predominant principle of the diplomacy of Louis XIV; but I do not believe it. This consideration played no very great part in his policy, until latterly, in his old age. The power of France, its preponderance in Europe, the humbling of rival powers, in a word, the political interest and strength of the state, was the aim which Louis XIV constantly pursued, whether in fighting against Spain, the emperor of Germany, or England; he acted far less with a view to the propagation of absolute power than from a desire for the power and aggrandizement of France and of its government. Among many proofs, I will adduce one which emanates from Louis XIV himself. In his Memoirs, under the year 1666, if I remember right, we find a note nearly in these words:

> I have had, this morning, a conversation with Mr. Sidney, an English gentleman, who maintained to me the possibility of reanimating the republican party in England. Mr. Sidney demanded from me, for that purpose, 400,000 livres. I told him that I could give no more than 200,000. He induced me to summon from Switzerland another English gentleman, named Ludlow, and to converse with him of the same design.

And, accordingly, we find among the Memoirs of Ludlow, about the same date, a paragraph to this effect:

I have received from the French government an invitation to go to Paris, in order to speak of the affairs of my country; but I am distrustful of that government.

And Ludlow remained in Switzerland.

You see that the diminution of the royal power in England was, at this time, the aim of Louis XIV. He fomented internal dissensions, and laboured to resuscitate the republican party, to prevent Charles II from becoming too powerful in his country. During the embassy of Barillon in England, the same fact constantly reappears. Whenever the authority of Charles seemed to obtain the advantage, and the national party seemed on the point of being crushed, the French ambassador directed his influence to this side, gave money to the chiefs of the opposition, and fought, in a word, against absolute power, when that became a means of weakening a rival power to France. Whenever you attentively consider the conduct of external relations under Louis XIV, it is with this fact that you will be the most struck.

You will also be struck with the capacity and skill of French diplomacy at this period. The names of M.M. de Torcy, d'Avaux, de Bonrepos, are known to all well-informed persons. When we compare the despatches, the memoirs, the skill and conduct of these counsellors of Louis XIV with those of Spanish, Portuguese, and German negotiators, we must be struck with the superiority of the French ministers; not only as regards their earnest activity and their application to affairs, but also as regards their liberty of spirit. These courtiers of an absolute king judged of external events, of parties, of the requirements of liberty, and of popular revolutions, much better even than the majority of the English ministers themselves at this period. There was no diplomacy in Europe, in the seventeenth century, which appears equal to the French, except the Dutch. The ministers of John de Witt and of William of Orange, those illustrious chiefs of the party of civil and religious liberty, were the only ministers who seemed in condition to wrestle with the servants of the great and absolute king.

You see, then, that whether we consider the wars of Louis XIV, or his diplomatic relations, we arrive at the same results.

We can easily conceive that a government which conducted its wars and negotiations in this manner, should have assumed a high standing in Europe, and presented itself therein, not only as dreadworthy, but as skilful and imposing.

Let us now consider the interior of France, the administration and legislation of Louis XIV; we shall there discern new explanations of the power and splendour of his government.

It is difficult to determine with any degree of precision what we ought to understand by *administration* in the government of a state. Nevertheless, when we endeavour to investigate this fact, we discover, I believe, that, under the most general point of view, administration consists in an aggregate of means destined to propel, as promptly and certainly as possible, the will of the central power through all parts of society, and to make the force of society, whether consisting of men or money, return again, under the same conditions, to the central power. This, if I mistake not, is the true aim, the predominant characteristic of administration. Accordingly we find that in times when it is above all things needful to establish unity and order in society, administration is the chief means of attaining this end, of bringing together, of cementing, and of uniting incoherent and scattered elements. Such, in fact, was the work of the administration of Louis XIV. Up to this time, there had been nothing so difficult, in France as in the rest of Europe, as to effect the penetration of the action of the central power into all parts of society, and to gather into the bosom of the central power the means of force existing in society. To this end Louis XIV laboured, and succeeded, up to a certain point; incomparably better, at least, than preceding governments had done. I cannot enter into details: just run over, in thought, all kinds of public services, taxes, roads, industry, military administration, all the establishments which belong to whatsoever branch of administration; there is scarcely one of which you do not find either the origin, development, or great amelioration under Louis XIV. It was as administrators that the greatest men of his time, Colbert and Louvois, displayed their genius and exercised their ministry. It was by the excellence of its administration that his government acquired a generality, decision, and consistency which were wanting to all the European governments around him.

Under the legislative point of view, this reign presents to you the same fact. I return to the comparison which I have already made use of, to the legislative activity of the consular government, to its prodigious work of revising and generally recasting the laws. A work of the same nature took place under Louis XIV. The great ordinances which he promulgated, the criminal ordinance, the ordinances of procedure, commerce, the marine, waters, and woods, are true codes, which were constructed in the same manner as our codes, discussed in the council of state, some of them under the presidency of Lamoignon. There are men whose glory consists in having taken part in this labour and this discussion, M. Pussort, for instance. If we were to consider it in itself, we should have much to say against the legislation of Louis XIV; it was full of vices, which now fully declare themselves, and which no one can deny; it was not conceived in the interest of true justice and of liberty, but in the interest of public order, and for giving more regularity and firmness to the laws. But even that was a great progress; and we cannot doubt but that the ordinances of Louis XIV, so very superior to anything preceding them, powerfully contributed to advance French society in the career of civilization.

You see that under whatever point of view we regard this government, we very soon discover the source of its power and influence. It was the first government that presented itself to the eyes of Europe as a power sure of its position, which had not to dispute its existence with internal enemies—tranquil as to its dominions and the people, and intent only on governing. Up to that time, all European governments had been unceasingly thrown into wars, which deprived them of security as well as leisure, or had been so beset with parties and internal enemies, that they were compelled to spend their time in fighting for their lives. The government of Louis XIV appeared as the first which applied itself solely to the conduct of affairs, as a power at once definitive and progressive; which was not afraid of innovating, because it could count upon the future. There have, in fact, existed very few governments of such an innovating spirit. Compare it with a government of the same nature, with the pure monarchy of Philip II in Spain; it was more absolute than that of Louis XIV, and yet far less regular and less tranquil. But how did Philip II succeed in establishing absolute power in Spain? By stifling the activity of the country, by refusing to it every species of amelioration, by rendering the condition of Spain completely stationary. The government of Louis XIV, on the contrary, showed itself active in all kinds of innovations, favourable to the progress of letters, of arts, of riches, and, in a word, of civilization. These are the true causes of its preponderance in Europe; a preponderance such that it became upon the continent, during the whole of the seventeenth century, the type of government, not only for sovereigns, but even for nations.

And now we inquire—and it is impossible to help doing so—how it happened that a power, thus brilliant, and, judging from the facts which I have placed before you, thus well established, so rapidly fell into decline? how, after having played such a part in Europe, it became, in the next century, so inconsistent, weak, and inconsiderable? The fact is incontestable. In the seventeenth century the French government was at the head of European civilization; in the eighteenth century it disappeared; and it was French society, separated from its government, often even opposed to it, that now preceded and guided the European world in its progress.

It is here that we discover the incorrigible evil and the infallible effect of absolute power. I will not go into any detail concerning the faults of the government of Louis XIV; he committed many: I will speak neither of the war of the Spanish succession, nor of the revocation of the edict of Nantes, nor of excessive expenses, nor of many other of the fatal measures that compromised his fortunes. I will take the merits of the government as I have described them. I will agree that perhaps there has never existed an absolute power more fully recognised by its age and nation, nor one which has rendered more real services to the civilization of its country and of Europe in general. But, by the very fact that this government had no other principle than absolute power, and reposed upon no other base than this, its decline became sudden and well merited. What France, under Louis XIV, essentially wanted, was political institutions and forces, independent, subsisting of themselves, and, in a word, capable of spontaneous action and resistance. The ancient French institutions, if they merited that name, no longer existed: Louis XIV completed their ruin. He took no care to endeavour to replace them by new institutions; they would have cramped him, and he did not choose to be cramped. All that appeared conspicuous at that period was will, and the action of central power. The government of Louis XIV was a great fact, a fact powerful and splendid, but without roots. Free institutions are a guarantee, not only of the wisdom of governments, but also of their duration. No system can endure except by means of institutions. When absolute power has endured, it has been supported by true institutions, sometimes by the division of society into strongly distinct castes, sometimes by a system of religious institutions. Under the reign of Louis XIV institutions were wanting to power as well as to liberty. In France, at this period, nothing guaranteed either the country against the illegitimate actions of the government, or the government itself against the inevitable action of time. Thus we see the government helping on its own decay. It was not Louis XIV alone who was becoming aged and weak at the end of his reign: it was the whole absolute power. Pure monarchy was as much worn out in 1712 as was the monarch himself: and the evil was so much the more grave, as Louis XIV had abolished political morals as well as political institutions. There are no political morals without independence. He alone who feels that he has a strength of his own is always capable either of serving or opposing power. Energetic characters disappear with independent situations, and dignity of soul alone gives birth to security of rights.

This, then, is the state in which Louis XIV left France and power: a society in full development of riches, power, and all kinds of intellectual activity; and, side by side with this progressive society, a government essentially stationary, having no means of renewing itself, of adapting itself to the movement of its people; devoted, after half a century of the greatest splendour, to immobility and weakness, and already, during the life of its founder, fallen into a decline which seemed like dissolution. Such was the condition of France at the conclusion of the seventeenth century, a condition which impressed the epoch that followed with a direction and a character so different.

I need hardly say that the onward impulse of the human mind, that free inquiry was the predominating feature, the essential fact of the eighteenth century. You have already heard much concerning this fact from this chair; already you have heard that powerful epoch characterised by a philosophical orator, and by that of an eloquent philosopher. I cannot pretend, in the short space of time which remains to me, to trace all the phases of the great moral revolution which then accomplished itself. I would, nevertheless, fain not leave you without calling your attention to some characteristics which have been too little remarked upon.

The first—one which strikes me most, and which I have already mentioned—is the, so to speak, almost complete disappearance of the government in the course of the eighteenth century, and the appearance of the human mind as the principal and almost the only actor.

Except in that which is connected with external relations under the ministry of the Duc de Choiseul, and in certain great concessions made to the general tendency of opinion, for instance, in the American war; except, I say, in some events of this nature, perhaps there has scarcely ever been so inactive, apathetic, and inert a government as was the French government of this period. Instead of the energetic, ambitious government of Louis XIV, which appeared everywhere, and put itself at the head of everything, you have a government which laboured only to hide itself, to keep itself in the background, so weak and compromised did it feel itself to be. Activity and ambition had passed over wholly to the people. It was the nation, which, by its opinion and its intellectual movement, mingled itself with all things, interfered in all, and, in short, alone possessed moral authority, which is the only true authority.

A second characteristic which strikes me, in the condition of the human mind in the eighteenth century, is the universality of free inquiry. Up to that time, and particularly in the seventeenth century, free inquiry had been exercised within a limited and partial field; it had had for its object sometimes religious questions, sometimes religious and political questions together, but it did not extend its pretensions to all subjects. In the eighteenth century, on the contrary, the character of free inquiry is universality; religion, politics, pure philosophy, man and society, moral and material nature, all at the same time became the object of study, doubt, and system; ancient sciences were overturned, new sciences were called into existence. The movement extended itself in all directions, although it had emanated from one and the same impulse.

This movement, moreover, had a peculiar character; one which, perhaps, is not to be met elsewhere in the history of the world: it was purely speculative. Up to that time, in all great human revolutions, action had commingled itself with speculation. Thus, in the sixteenth century, the religious revolution began with ideas, with purely intellectual discussions, but it very soon terminated in events. The heads of intellectual parties soon became the heads of political parties; the realities of life were mixed with the labour of the understanding. Thus, too, it happened in the seventeenth century, in the English revolution. But in France, in the eighteenth century, you find the human spirit exercising itself upon all things, upon ideas which, connecting themselves with the real interests of life, seemed calculated to have the most prompt and powerful influence upon facts. Nevertheless, the leaders and actors of these great discussions remained strangers to all species of practical activity—mere spectators, who observed, judged, and spoke, without ever interfering in events. At no other time has the government of facts, of external realities, been so completely distinct from the government of minds. The separation of the spiritual and temporal orders was never completely real in Europe until the eighteenth century. For the first time, perhaps, the spiritual order developed wholly apart from the temporal order: an important fact, and one which exercised a prodigious influence upon the course of events. It gave to the ideas of the time a singular character of ambition and inexperience; never before had philosophy aspired so strongly to rule the world, never had philosophy been so little acquainted with the world. It became necessary one day to get down to the facts; for the intellectual movement to pass into external events; and as they had been totally separated, their meeting was the more difficult, the shock far more violent.

How can we now be surprised with another character of the condition of the human mind at this epoch, I mean its prodigious boldness? Up to that time its greatest activity had always been confined by certain barriers; the mind of man had always existed amidst facts, whereof some inspired it with caution, and, to a certain extent, checked its movements. In the eighteenth century, I should be at a loss to say what external facts the human mind respected, or what external facts exercised any empire over it: it hated or despised the entire social state. It concluded, therefore, that it was called upon to reform all things; it came to consider itself a sort of creator; institutions, opinions, manners, society, and man himself, all seemed to require reform, and human reason charged itself with the enterprise. What audacity equal to this had ever before been imagined by it!

Such was the power which, in the course of the eighteenth century, confronted what still remained of the government of Louis XIV. You perceive that it was impossible to avoid the occurrence of a shock between these two so unequal forces. The predominant fact of the English revolution, the struggle between free inquiry and pure monarchy, was now also to burst forth in France. No doubt the differences were great, and these necessarily perpetuated themselves in the results; but, at bottom, the general conditions were similar, and the definitive event had the same meaning.

I do not pretend to exhibit the infinite consequences of this struggle. The time for concluding this course of lectures has arrived; I must check myself. I merely desire, before leaving you, to call your attention to the most grave, and, in my opinion, the most instructive fact which was revealed to us by this great struggle. This is the danger, the evil, and the insurmountable vice of absolute power, whatever form, whatever name it may bear, and towards whatever aim it may direct itself. You have seen that the government of Louis XIV perished by almost this cause only. Well, the power which succeeded it, the human mind, the true sovereign of the eighteenth century, suffered the same fate; in its turn, it possessed an almost absolute power; it, in its turn, placed an excessive confidence in itself. Its onward impulse was beautiful, good, most useful; and were it necessary that I should express a definitive opinion, I should say that the eighteenth century appears to me to have been one of the greatest ages of history, that which, perhaps, has done the greatest services for humanity, that which has in the greatest degree aided its progress, and rendered that progress of the most general character: were I asked to pronounce upon it as a public administration, I should pronounce in its favour. But it is not the less true that, at this epoch, the human mind, possessed of absolute power, became corrupted and misled by it; holding established facts and former ideas in an illegitimate disdain and aversion; an aversion which carried it into error and tyranny. The share of error and tyranny, indeed, which mingled itself with the triumph of human reason, at the end of this century, a portion which we cannot conceal from ourselves, was very great, and which we must proclaim and not deny; this portion of error and tyranny was chiefly the result of the extravagance into which the mind of man had been thrown, at this period, by the extension of his power.

It is the duty, and, I believe, it will be the peculiar merit of our times, to know that all power, whether intellectual or temporal, whether belonging to governments or peoples, to philosophers or ministers, whether exercising itself in one cause or in another, bears within itself a natural vice, a principle of weakness and of abuse which ought to render it limited. Now nothing but the general freedom of all rights, all interests, and all opinions, the free manifestation and legal coexistence of all these forces, can ever restrain each force and each power within its legitimate limits, prevent it from encroaching on the rest, and, in a word, cause the real and generally profitable existence of free inquiry. Herein consists for us the grand lesson of the struggle which occurred at the end of the eighteenth century, between absolute temporal power and absolute spiritual power.

I have now arrived at the term which I proposed to myself. You remember that my object, in commencing this course, was to present you with a general picture of the development of European civilization, from the fall of the Roman empire to our own days. I have traversed this career very rapidly, and without being able to inform you, far from it, of all that was important, or to bring proofs of all that I have said. I have been compelled to omit much, and often to request you to believe me upon my word. I hope, nevertheless, that I have attained my aim, which was to mark the grand crises in the development of modern society. Allow me yet one word more.

I endeavoured, in the beginning, to define civilization, and to describe the fact which bears this name. Civilization seemed to me to consist of two principal facts: the development of human society, and that of man himself; on the one hand, political and social development; on the other, internal and moral development. I have confined myself so far to the history of society. I have presented civilization only under the social point of view; and have said nothing of the development of man himself. I have not endeavoured to unfold to you the history of opinions, of the moral progress of humanity. I propose, when we meet again, to confine myself especially to France, to study with you the history of French civilization, to study it in detail, and under its various aspects. I shall endeavour to make you acquainted, not only with the history of society in France, but also with that of man; to be present with you at the progress of institutions, of opinions, and of intellectual works of all kinds; and to arrive thus at a complete understanding of the development of our glorious country, in its entirety. In the past as well as in the future, our country may well lay claim to our tenderest affections.

6

The History of Civilization in France

First Series

Lecture 1

Many of you will call to mind the nature and aim of a course of lectures which were brought to a close some months since. That course was cursory and of a general nature. I then attempted, in a very short period of time, to place before you an historical view of European civilization. I hastened, as it were, from point to point, confining myself strictly to general facts and assertions, at the risk of being sometimes misunderstood and perhaps discredited.

Necessity, as you know, imposed this method upon me; but in spite of this necessity I should have been much pained by the inconveniences which arose from it, had I not foreseen that in a future course I should be enabled to remedy it; and had I not proposed to myself, at the time, to complete, at some future period, the outline which I then traced, and of leading you to the general results which I placed before you, by the same path which I myself had followed, an attentive and complete study of the facts. Such is the end at which I now aim.

Selections from *The History of Civilization in France,* translated by William Hazlitt (New York: Appleton Century and Crofts, 1864), from *L'Histoire de la Civilisation en France,* lectures delivered at the Sorbonne, 1828–30.

The History of Civilization in France

Two methods offer themselves as tending to the attainment of the proposed end. I might either recommence the course of last summer, and review the general history of European civilization in its whole extent, by giving in detail that which it was impossible to give in mass, and by again passing over with more leisurely steps that ground which before was gone over in almost breathless haste. Or I might study the history of civilization in a single great country, in one of the principal European nations in which it has been developed, and thus, by confining the field of my researches, be the better enabled thoroughly to explore it.

The first method seemed to offer serious inconveniences. It would be very difficult, if not impossible, to maintain any unity in a history with so extensive a range, and which, at the same time should be perfect in all its details. We discovered last summer, that there was a true unity running through European civilization; but this unity is only visible in general actions and grand results. We must ascend the highest mountain before the petty inequalities and diversities of the surface will become invisible, and before we can discover the general aspect, and the true and essential nature of the entire country. When we quit general facts and wish to look into particulars, the unity vanishes, the diversities again appear, and in the variety of occurrences one loses sight of both causes and effects; so that to give a detailed history, and still to preserve some harmony, it is absolutely necessary to narrow the field of inquiry.

There is also another great objection to this method, in the immense extent and diversity of knowledge which it presupposes and requires both in the speaker and his audience. Those who wish to trace with moderate accuracy the course of European civilization should have a sufficiently intimate acquaintance, not only with the events which have passed among each people, with their history, but likewise with their language, literature, and philosophy, in short, with all phases of their career; a work which is evidently almost impossible, and certainly so in the time which we could spend upon it.

It appears to me, that by studying the history of civilization in one great European nation, I shall arrive more quickly at the desired result. The unity of the narrative will then, indeed, be compatible with details; there is in every country a certain national harmony, which is the result of the community of manners, laws, language, and events, and this harmony is imprinted in the civilization. We may pass from fact to fact without losing sight of the whole picture. And lastly, though I will not say that it can easily be done, it is yet possible to combine the knowledge necessary for such a work.

I have therefore decided upon this second method, upon that of abandoning the general history of European civilization, in all the nations which have contributed thereto, and confining myself to the civilization of one country, which if we note the differences between it and other countries, may become, for our purpose, an image of the whole destiny of Europe.

The choice of method being once made, that of a nation easily follows; I have taken the history and civilization of France. I shall certainly not deny having experienced a sensation of pleasure while making this choice. No one will deny that the emotions of patriotism are legitimate, provided they be sanctioned by truth and reason. Some there are, in the present day, who seem to fear that patriotism suffers much from the enlargement of ideas and sentiments, arising from the actual state of European civilization; they predict that it will become enervated, and lose itself in cosmopolitism. I cannot share such fears. In the present day, it will be with patriotism as with all human actions, feelings and opinions. It is condemned, I admit, incessantly to undergo the test of publicity, of inquiry and discussion; it is condemned no longer to remain a mere prejudice, habit, or a blind and exclusive passion; it must give a reason for itself. It will be oppressed by this necessity no more than any natural and legitimate feelings are; on the contrary, it will become refined and elevated. These are the tests to which it must submit, and it will soar above them. I can truly say, if any other history in Europe had appeared to me greater, more instructive, or better suited to represent the general course of civilization than that of France, I should have chosen it. But I have reasons for selecting France; independently of the special interest which its history has for us, France has long since been proclaimed by all Europe the most civilized of its nations. Whenever the opinion of the struggle has not been between the national self-love, when one seeks the true and disinterested opinion of people in the ideas and actions wherein it manifests itself indirectly, without taking the form of a controversy, we find that France is acknowledged to be the country in which civilization has appeared in its most complete form, where it has been most communicative, and where it has most forcibly struck the European imagination.

And we must not suppose, that the superiority of this country is solely attributable to the amenity of our social relations, to the gentleness of our manners, or to that easy and animated life which people so often come to seek among us. There can be no doubt that it partly arises from these attributes; but the fact of which I speak has more profound and universal causes: it is not a fashion, as might have been supposed when the question was concerning the civilization of the age of Louis XIV, neither is it a popular ebullion, as a view of our own times would lead us to suppose. The preference which the disinterested opinion of Europe accords to French civilization is philosophically just; it is the result of an instinctive judgment, doubtless in some measure confused, but well based, upon the essential elements and general nature of civilization.

You will call to mind the definition of civilization I attempted to give in the commencement of the former course of lectures. I there sought to discover what ideas attach themselves to this word in the common sense of men. It appeared to me, on a reference to general opinion, that civilization essentially consists of two principles: the improvement of the exterior and general condition of man, and that of his inward and personal nature; in a word, in the improvement both of society and of humanity.

And it is not these two principles of themselves, which constitute civilization; to bring it to perfection, their intimate and rapid union, simultaneousness, and reciprocal action, are absolutely necessary. I showed that if they do not always arrive conjointly— that if, at one time, the improvement of society, and at another, that of individual man, progresses more quickly or extends further, they are not the less necessary the one to the other; they excite each other, and sooner or later will amalgamate. When one progresses for any length of time without the other, and when their union is long interrupted, a feeling of regret, and of a painful hiatus and incompleteness, seizes the spectators. If an important social improvement, a great progress in material well being is manifested among a people without being accompanied by intellectual improvement, or an analogous progression in mind; the social improvement seems precarious, inexplicable, and almost unjust. One asks what general ideas have produced and justified it, or to what principles it attaches itself. One wishes to assure oneself that it will not be limited to particular generations, to a single country; but that it will spread and communicate itself, and that it will fill every nation. And how can social improvement spread and communicate itself but by ideas, upon the wings of doctrines? Ideas alone mock at distance, pass over oceans, and everywhere make themselves received and comprehended. Besides, such is the noble nature of humanity, that it cannot see a great improvement in material strength, without aspiring to the moral strength which should be joined with it and direct it; something subordinate remains imprinted on social improvement, as long as it bears no fruit but mere physical prosperity, as long as it does not raise the mind of man to the level of his condition.

So, on the other hand, if any great intellectual improvement appears, unaccompanied by a social progress, one feels uneasy and surprised. It seems as if we saw a beautiful tree devoid of fruit, or a sun bringing with it neither heat nor fertility. One feels a kind of disdain for ideas thus barren and not seizing upon the external world. And not only do we feel a disdain for them, but in the end we doubt their reasonable legitimacy and truth; one is tempted to believe them chimerical, when they show themselves powerless and incapable of governing human condition. So powerfully is man impressed with the feeling that his business upon earth is to transform the ideal into the actual, to reform and regulate the world which he inhabits according to the truth he conceives; so closely are the two great elements of civilization, social and intellectual development, bound to one another, so

270

true is it that its perfection consists, not only in their union, but in their simultaneousness, and in the extent, facility, and rapidity with which they mutually evoke and produce themselves.

Let us now endeavour to regard from this point of view the several nations of Europe: let us investigate the particular characteristics of the civilization in each particular case, and inquire how far these characteristics coincide with that essential, fundamental, and sublime fact which now constitutes for us the perfection of civilization. We shall thus discover which of the various kinds of European civilization is the most complete, and the most conformable to the general type of civilization, and, consequently, which possesses the best right to our attention, and best represents the history of Europe.

I begin with England. English civilization has been especially directed towards social perfection; towards the amelioration of the external and public condition of men; towards the amelioration, not only of their material but also of their moral condition; towards the introduction of more justice, more prosperity into society; towards the development of right as well as of happiness.

Nevertheless, all things considered, in England the development of society has been more extensive and more glorious than that of humanity; social interests and social facts have, in England, maintained a more conspicuous place, and have exercised more power than general ideas: the nation seems greater than the individual. This is so true, that even the philosophers of England, men who seem devoted by their profession to the development of pure intelligence—as Bacon, Locke, and the Scottish philosophers—belong to what one may call the practical school of philosophy; they concern themselves, above all things, with direct and positive results; they trust themselves neither to the flights of the imagination, nor to the deductions of logic: theirs is the genius of common sense. I turn to the periods of England's greatest intellectual activity, the periods when ideas and mental movements occupied the most conspicuous place in her history: I take the political and religious crisis of the sixteenth and seventeenth centuries. No man is ignorant of the mighty movement which was going on at that time in England. Can any one, however, tell me of any great philosophical system, of any great general doctrines since become law in Europe, which were born of this movement? It has had immense and admirable results; it has established rights, manners; it has not only powerfully influenced social relations, it has influenced the souls of men; it has made sects and enthusiasts, but it has hardly exalted or extended—at all events, directly—the horizon of the human mind; it has not ignited one of those great intellectual torches which illuminate an entire epoch. Perhaps in no country have religious creeds possessed, nor at the present day do they possess, more power than in England; but they are, above all things, practical; they exert a great influence over the conduct, happiness, and sentiments of individuals; but they have few general and mental results, results which address themselves to the whole of the human race. Under whatever point of view you regard this civilization, you will discover this essentially practical and social character. I might investigate this development in a more extended degree; I might review every class of English society, and I should everywhere be struck with the same fact. In literature, for instance, practical merit still predominates. There is no one who will say that the English are skilful at composing a book, the artistical and rational arrangement of the whole, in the distribution of the parts, in executing, so as to strike the imagination of the reader with that perfection of art and form, which, above all things, gratifies the understanding. The purely intellectual aim in works of genius is the weak point of English writers, whilst they excel in the power of persuasion by the lucidity of their expositions, by frequently returning to the same ideas, by the evidence of good sense, in short, by all the ways of leading to practical effects.

The same character is seen, even in the English language. It is not a language rationally, uniformly, and systematically constructed; it borrows words on all sides, from the most various sources, without troubling itself about maintaining any symmetry or harmony. Its essential want is that logical beauty which is seen in the Greek and Latin languages: it has an appearance of coarseness and incoherence. But it is rich, flexible, fitted for general adaptation, and capable of supplying all the wants of man in the external course of life. Everywhere the principle of utility and application dominates in England, and constitutes at once the physiognomy and the force of its civilization.

From England I shall pass to Germany. The development of civilization has been slow and tardy; the brutality of German manners has been proverbial throughout Europe for centuries. Still when, under this apparent grossness, one seeks the comparative progress of the two fundamental elements of civilization, we find that, in Germany, intellectual development has always surpassed and left behind social development, that the human spirit has there prospered much more than the human condition.

Compare the intellectual state of the German reformers at the sixteenth century—Luther, Melanchthon, Butzer, and many others—compare, I say, the development of mind which is shown in their works with the contemporaneous manners of the country. What a disparity! In the seventeenth century, place the ideas of Leibnitz, the studies of his disciples, and the German universities, by the side of the manners which prevailed, not only among the people, but also among the superior classes; read, on one side, the writings of the philosophers, and, on the other, the memoirs which paint the court of the Elector of Brandenburg or Bavaria. What a contrast! When we arrive at our own times, this contrast is yet more striking. It is a common saying in the present day, that beyond the Rhine, ideas and facts, the intellectual and the real orders, are almost entirely separated. No one is ignorant of what has been the activity of spirit in Germany for the last fifty years; in all classes, in philosophy, history, general literature, or poetry, it has advanced very far. It may be said that it has not always followed the best path; one may contest part of the results at which it has arrived; yet concerning its energy and extensive development it is impossible to dispute. But assuredly the social state and public condition have not advanced at the same pace. Without doubt, there also progress and amelioration have been made; but it is impossible to draw a comparison between the two facts. Thus, the peculiar character of all works in Germany, in poetry, philosophy, or history, is a non-acquaintance with the external world, the absence of the feeling of reality. One perceives, in reading them, that life and facts have exercised but little influence upon the authors, that they have not preoccupied their imagination; they have lived retired within themselves, by turns enthusiasts or logicians. Just as the practical genius everywhere shows itself in England, so the pure intellectual activity is the dominant feature of German civilization.

In Italy we shall find neither one nor the other of these characters. Italian civilization has been neither essentially practical as that of England, nor almost exclusively speculative as that of Germany; in Italy, neither great development of individual intelligence, nor social skill and ability have been wanting; the Italians have flourished and excelled at one and the same time in the pure sciences, the arts and philosophy, as well as in practical affairs and life. For some time, it is true, Italy seems to have stopped in both of these progressions; society and the human mind seem enervated and paralysed; but one feels, upon looking closely, that this is not the effect of an inward and national incapacity; it is from without that Italy is weighed down and impeded; she resembles a beautiful flower that wishes to blossom, but is compressed in every part by a cold and rude hand. Neither intellectual nor political capacity has perished in Italy; it wants that which it has always wanted, and which is everywhere one of the vital conditions of civilization—it wants faith, the faith in truth. I wish to make myself correctly understood, and not to have attributed to my words a different sense from that which I intend to convey. I mean here, by faith, that confidence in truth, which not only causes it to be held as truth, and which satisfies the mind, but which gives men a confidence in right to reign over the world, to govern facts, and in its power to succeed. It is by this feeling that, once having possession of truth, man feels called upon to introduce it into external facts, to reform them, and to regulate them according to reason. Well, it is this which is almost universally wanted in Italy; she has been fertile in great minds, and in universal ideas; she has been filled with men of rare practical ability, versed in the knowledge of all conditions of external life, and in the art of conducting and managing society; but these two classes of men and facts have remained strangers to each other. The men of universal ideas, the speculative spirits, have not believed in the duty, perhaps not even in the right, of influencing society; although confident in the truth of their principles, they have doubted their power. Men of action, on the other hand, the masters of society, have held small account of universal ideas; they have scarcely ever felt a desire to regulate, according to fixed principles, the facts which came under their dominion. Both have acted as if it was desirable merely to know the truth, but as if it had no further influence, and demanded nothing more. It is this, alike in the fifteenth century and in later times, that has been the weak side of the civilization in Italy; it is this which has struck with a kind of barrenness both its speculative genius and its practical ability; here the two powers have not lived in reciprocal confidence, in correspondence, in continual action and reaction.

There is another great country of which, indeed, I speak more out of consideration and respect for a noble and unhappy nation, than from necessity; I mean Spain. Neither great minds nor great events have been wanting in Spain; understanding and human society have at times appeared there in all their glory; but these are isolated facts, cast here and there throughout Spanish history, like palm trees on a desert. The fundamental character of civilization, its continued and universal progress, seems denied in Spain, as much to the human mind as to society. There has been either solemn immobility, or fruitless revolutions. Seek one great idea, or social amelioration, one philosophical system or fertile institution, which Spain has given to Europe; there are none such: this nation has remained isolated in Europe; it has received as little from it as it has contributed to it. I should have reproached myself, had I wholly omitted its name; but its civilization is of small importance in the history of the civilization of Europe.

You see that the fundamental principle, the sublime fact of general civilization, the intimate and rapid union, and the harmonious development of ideas and facts, in the intellectual and real orders, has been produced in neither of the great countries at which we have glanced. Something is essentially wanting in all of them to complete civilization; neither of them offers us the complete image, the pure type of civilization in all its conditions, and with all its great characteristics.

In France it is different. In France, the intellectual and social development have never failed each other. Here society and man have always progressed and improved, I will not say abreast and equally, but within a short distance of each other. By the side of great events, revolutions, and public ameliorations, we always find in this country universal ideas and corresponding doctrines. Nothing has passed in the real world, but the understanding has immediately seized it, and thence derived new riches; nothing within the dominion of understanding, which has not had in the real world, and that almost always immediately, its echo and result. Indeed, as a general thing, in France, ideas have preceded and impelled the progress of the social order; they have been prepared in doctrines, before being accomplished in things, and in the march of civilization mind has always taken the lead. This two-fold character of intellectual activity and practical ability, of meditation and application, is shown in all the great events of French history, and in all the great classes of French society, and gives them an aspect which we do not find elsewhere.

At the commencement of the twelfth century, for example, burst forth the great movement for the enfranchisement of the communes, a great step in social condition; at the same time was manifested a vivid aspiration after freedom of thought. Abelard was contemporary with the citizens of Laon and Vézelay. The first great struggle of free-thought against absolute power in the intellectual order, is contemporaneous with the struggle of the citizens for public liberty. These two movements, it is true, were apparently foreign to each other; the philosophers had a very ill opinion of the insurgent bourgeois, whom they treated as barbarians; and the bourgeois, in their turn, when they heard them spoken of, regarded the philosophers as heretics. But the double progress is not the less simultaneous.

Quit the twelfth century; take one of the establishments which have played the most conspicuous part in the history of mind in France, the University of Paris. No one is ignorant of what have been its scientific labors, dating from the thirteenth century; it was the first establishment of the kind in Europe. There was no other in the same age which had so important and active a political existence. The University of Paris is associated with the policy of kings, and with all the struggles of the French clergy against the court of Rome, and those of the clergy against the temporal power; ideas developed themselves, and doctrines were established in its bosom; and it strove almost immediately to propagate them in the external world. It was the principles of the University of Paris which served as the standard of the reformers at the councils of Constance and Basle; which were the origin of, and sustained the Pragmatic Sanction of Charles VII.

Intellectual activity and positive influence have for centuries been inseparable in this great school. Let us pass to the sixteenth century, and glance at the history of the Reformation in France; it has here a distinguishing character; it was more learned, or, at least, as learned as elsewhere, and more moderate and reasonable. The principal struggle of erudition and doctrine against the Catholic church was sustained by the French Reformers; it was either in France or Holland, and always in French, that so many philosophical, historical, and polemical works were written in this cause; it is certain, that at this epoch, neither in Germany nor in England, was there so much spirit and learning employed; the French Reformation, too, was a stranger to the flights of the German anabaptists and the English sectarians; it was seldom it was wanting in practical prudence, and yet one cannot doubt the energy and sincerity of its creed, since for so long a period it withstood the most severe reverses.

In modern times, in the seventeenth and eighteenth centuries, the intimate and rapid union of ideas with facts, and the development both of society and of man as an individual, are so evident, that it is needless to insist upon them.

We see, then, four or five great epochs, and four or five grand events, in which the particular character of French civilization is shown. Let us take the various classes of our society; let us regard their manners and physiognomy, and we shall be struck with the same fact. The clergy of France is both learned and active, it is connected with all intellectual works and all worldly affairs as reasoner, scholar, administrator; it is, as it were, neither exclusively devoted to religion, science, nor politics, but is constantly occupied in combining and conciliating them all. The French philosophers also present a rare mixture of speculation and practical knowledge; they meditate profoundly and boldly; they seek the pure truth, without any view to its application; but they always keep up a sympathy with the external world, and with the facts in the midst of which they live; they evaluate themselves to the greatest height, but without ever losing sight of the earth. Montaigne, Descartes, Pascal, Bayle, almost all the great French philosophers, are neither pure logicians nor enthusiasts. Last summer, in this place, you heard their eloquent interpreter[1] characterize the genius of Descartes, who was at the same time a man of science and a man of the world. "Clear, firm, resolved, and daring, he thought in his study with the same intrepidity with which he fought under the walls of Prague;" having an inclination alike for the movement of life and for the activity of thought. Our philosophers have not all of them possessed the same genius, nor experienced the same adventurous destiny as Descartes; but almost all of them, at the same time that they sought truth, have comprehended the world. They were alike capable of observing and of meditating.

Finally, in the history of France, what is the particular trait which characterizes the only class of men who have there taken a truly public part, the only men who have attempted to thoroughly bring the country within its administration, and to give a legal government to the nation, the French magistracy and the bar, the parliaments and all that surrounds them? Is it not essentially this mixture of learning and practical wisdom, this respect for ideas and facts, for science and its application? Wherever pure knowledge is exercised, in erudition, philosophy, literature, or history, everywhere you encounter the parliaments and the French bar; they take part, at the same time, in all affairs, both

1. M. Villemain.

public and private; and they have had a hand in all the real and positive interests of society.

From whatever point of view we regard France, we shall discover this two-fold character. The two essential principles of civilization are there developed in a strict correspondence. There man has never been wanting in individual greatness; nor has his individual greatness been devoid of public importance and utility. Much has been said, especially latterly, of good sense as a distinguishing trait of French genius. This is true; but it is not a purely practical good sense, merely calculated to succeed in its enterprises; it is an elevated and philosophical good sense, which penetrates to the roots of ideas, and comprehends and judges them in all their bearings, while at the same time it attends to external facts. This good sense is reason; the French mind is at the same time reasoning and reasonable.

To France, then, must be ascribed this honour, that her civilization has reproduced more faithfully than any other the general type and fundamental idea of civilization. It is the most complete, the most veritable, and, so to speak, the most civilized of civilizations. This it is that has given her the first rank in the disinterested opinion of Europe. France has proved herself at once intelligent and powerful, rich in ideas, and in the means of giving effect to those ideas. She has addressed herself at once to the intellect of the nations, and to their desire for social amelioration; she has aroused at once imagination and ambition; she has manifested a capability of discovering the truth, and of making it prevail. By this double title, she has rendered herself popular, for this is the double want of humanity.

We are, then, fully entitled to regard civilization in France as having the first claim on our attention, as being the most important in itself, the most fruitful of consequences. In studying it, we must earnestly regard it under the double aspect I have indicated, of social development and of intellectual development; we must closely watch the progress of ideas, of mind, of the interior individual man, and of his exterior and general condition. Considering it upon this principle, there is not in the general history of Europe any great event, any great question which we shall not meet with in our own. We shall thus attain the historical and scientific object which we proposed to ourselves; we shall be constantly present at the spectacle of European civilization, without being ourselves lost in the number and variety of the scenes and actors.

But we have before us, as I conceive, something more, and something more important than a spectacle, or even than study; unless I am altogether mistaken, we seek something beyond mere information. The course of civilization, and in particular that of the civilization of France, has raised a great problem, a problem peculiar to our own time, in which all futurity is interested, not only our own future but that of humanity at large, and which we, we of the present generation, are, perhaps, especially called upon to solve.

What is the spirit which now prevails in the intellectual world, which presides over the search after truth, in whatever direction truth is sought? A spirit of rigorous reserve, of strict, cautious prudence, a scientific spirit, a philosophical spirit pursuing a philosophical method. It is a spirit which carefully observes facts, and only admits generalization slowly, progressively, concurrently with the ascertainment of facts. This spirit has, for more than a half century past, manifestly prevailed in the conduct of the sciences which occupy themselves in the material world; it has been the cause of their progress, the source of their glory; and now, every day it infuses itself more and more deeply into the sciences of the moral world, into politics, history, philosophy. In every direction the scientific method is extending and establishing itself; in every direction the necessity is more and more felt of taking facts as the basis and rule of our proceedings; and we all fully understand that facts constitute the subject matter of science, and that no general idea can be of any real value, unless it be founded upon, and supported throughout its progress by facts. Facts are now in the intellectual order, the power in authority.

In the real order, in the social world, in the government, in the public administration, in political economy, we perceive a different tendency; there prevails the empire of ideas, of reasoning, of general principles, of what is called theory. Such is evidently the feature of the great revolution which has developed itself in our time, of all the labours of the eighteenth century; and the feature is not merely one characterizing a crisis, a period of transient agitation; it is the permanent, regular, calm characteristic of the social state which is now establishing, or, at all events, announcing itself in every direction—a social state, which has its basis on discussion and publicity, that is to say, on the empire of public reason, on the empire of doctrines, of convictions common to all the members of the society. On the one hand, then, never before have facts held so large a place in science; on the other, never before have ideas played so leading a part in the outer world.

Matters were very different a hundred years ago: then, in the intellectual order, in science properly so called, facts were but slightly consulted, but little respected; reason and imagination gave themselves full career, and men yielded without hesitation to the wildest impulses of hypothesis, dashing on recklessly, with no other guide than the thread of deduction. In the political order, on the contrary, in the real world, facts were all powerful, were admitted without a doubt or a murmur, as the authority alike *de jure* and *de facto*. Men complained, indeed, of particular facts, but scarcely ever ventured to contest them; sedition itself was more common in those times than freedom of thought. He who should have claimed for an idea, though in the name of truth itself, any place in the affairs of this world, would have had reason to repent of his temerity.

The course of civilization, then, has reversed the former order of things: it has established the empire of facts where once the free movement of mind dominated, and raised ideas to the throne once filled exclusively by facts.

This proposition is so true, that the result stated forms a marked feature in the reproaches of which modern civilization is made the object. Whenever the adversaries of that civilization speak of the actual condition of the human mind, of the direction of its labours, they charge it with being hard, dry, narrow. This rigorous positive method, this scientific spirit, cramps, say they, the ideas, freezes up the imagination, takes from the understanding its breadth, its freedom, confines, materializes it. When the question turns upon the actual state of societies, upon what societies are attempting, are effecting, these same men exclaim, "Out upon chimeras! Place no faith in theories: it is facts alone which should be studied, respected, valued; it is experience alone which should be believed." So that modern civilization is accused at once of dryness and of dreamy reverie, of hesitation and of precipitation, of timidity and of temerity. As philosophers, we creep along the earth; as politicians, we essay the enterprise of Icarus, and we shall undergo the same fate.

It is this double reproach, or rather this double danger, which we have to repel. We are called upon, in fact, to solve the problem which has occasioned it. We are called upon to confirm, more and more, in the intellectual order, the empire of facts— in the social order, the empire of ideas; to govern our reason more and more according to reality, and reality according to our reason; to maintain at once the strictness of the scientific method, and the legitimate empire of the intellect. There is nothing incongruous or inconsistent in this, far from it; it is, on the contrary, the natural, necessary result of the position of man, as a spectator of the world, and of his mission as an actor in its mighty drama. I take nothing for granted here, I make no comment; I merely describe what I see before me. We are thrown into the midst of a world which we neither invented nor created; we find it before us, we look at it, we study it: we must needs take it as a fact, for it subsists out of us, independently of us; it is with facts our mind exercises itself; it has only facts for materials; and when it comes to the general laws resulting from them, the general laws themselves are facts like any others. So much for our position as spectators. As actors, we proceed in a different way: when we have observed external facts, our acquaintance with these develops in us ideas which are of a nature superior to them; we feel ourselves called upon to reform, to perfect, to regulate that which is; we feel ourselves capable of acting upon the world, of extending therein the glorious empire of reason. This is the mission of man:

as spectator, he is subject to facts; as actor, he takes possession of them, and impresses upon them a more regular, a more perfect form. I was justified, then, in saying that there is nothing incongruous, nothing self-contradictory in the problem which we have to solve. It is quite true, however, that there is a double danger involved in this double task: it is quite true, that in studying facts, the understanding may be overwhelmed by them; that it may become depressed, confined, materialized; it may conceive that there are no other facts than those which strike us at first glance, which present themselves directly, obviously before us, which make themselves palpable to the senses; a great and grievous error: there are facts, facts so remote as to be obscure, facts vast, sublime, most difficult to compass, to observe, to describe, but which are none the less facts, and facts which man is, none the less, absolutely called upon to study and to know. If he fail to make himself acquainted with them, if he forget them, the character of his thought will be inevitably and prodigiously lowered, and all the learning which he may possess will bear the impress of that abasement. On the other hand, it is quite possible for intellectual ambition, in its action upon the real world, to be carried away, to become excessive, chimerical; to lose itself in its eagerness to extend too far and too rapidly the empire of its ideas over external things. But this double danger itself proves the double mission whence it originates; and this mission must be accomplished, the problem must be solved, for the actual condition of civilization lays it down with perfect clearness, and will not permit it to be lost sight of. Henceforth, whosoever, in the search after truth, shall depart from the scientific method, will not be in a position to take the study of facts as the basis of intellectual development; and whosoever, in administering the affairs of society, shall refuse the guidance of general principles and ideas, of doctrines, will assuredly achieve no permanent success, will find himself without any real power; for power and success, whether rational or social, now wholly depend upon the conformity of our labours with these two laws of human activity, with these two tendencies of civilization.

This is not all; we have still a far different problem to solve.

Of the two which I have laid down, the one is scientific and the other social; the one concerns pure intelligence, the study of truth; the other applies the results of this study to the external world. There is a third, which arises equally from the present state of civilization, and the solution of which is equally prescribed to us; a moral problem which refers not to science, not to society, but to the internal development of each of us to the merit, the worth of the individual man.

In addition to the other reproaches of which, as I have said, our civilization is made the object, it is accused of exercising a baleful effect upon our moral nature. Its opponents say, that by its everlastingly disputative spirit, by its mania for discussing and weighing everything, for reducing everything to a precise and definite value, it freezes, dries up, narrows the human soul; that the result of its setting up a pretension to universal infallibility, of its assumption of a superiority to all illusion, all impulse of the thought, of its affecting to know the real value of all things, will be that man will become severally disgusted with all the rest of the world, will become absorbed in self. Further, it is said, that owing to the tranquil ease of life in our times, to the facility and amenity of social relations, to the security which prevails throughout society, men's minds become effeminate, enervated; and that thus, at the same time that we acquire the habit of looking only to oneself, one acquires also a habit of requiring all things for oneself, a disposition to dispense with nothing, to sacrifice nothing, to suffer nothing. In a word, it is asserted that selfishness on the one hand, and captious effeminacy on the other, the dry hardness of manners, and their puerile enervation, are the natural matter-of-course results of the actual condition of civilization; that high-souled devotion and energy, at once the two great powers and the two great virtues of man, are wanting, and will be more and more wanting, in the periods which we call civilized, and more especially in our own.

It were easy, I think, to repel this double reproach, and to establish (1) the general proposition, that the actual condition of civilization, considered thoroughly and as a whole, by no means as a matter of moral probability, induces as its results selfishness and effeminacy; (2) the fact that neither devotion nor energy have been found to be wanting, in time of need, to the civilized members of modern times. But this were a question which would carry us too far. It is true, the actual state of civilization imposes upon moral devotion and energy, as upon patriotism, as upon all the noble thoughts and feelings of man, an additional difficulty. These great faculties of our nature have hitherto often manifested themselves somewhat fortuitously, in a manner characterized by no reflection, by no reference to motives; so to speak, at random. Henceforth they will be bound to proceed only upon the basis of reason; legitimacy of motives, and utility of results will be required of them. Doubtless, this is an additional weight for nature to raise up ere she can manifest herself in all her grandeur; but she will raise it up. Never yet has human nature been wanting to herself, never has she failed of that which circumstances have required at her hands; the more has been asked of her, the more she has given. Her revenue ever more than keeps pace with her expenditure. Energy and devotion will derive from other sources, will manifest themselves under other forms. Doubtless, we possess not fully as yet those general ideas, those innate convictions which must inspire the qualities I speak of; the faith which corresponds with our manners is as yet weak, shadowy, tottering; the principles of devotion and energy which were in action in past times are now without effect, for they have lost our confidence. It must be our task to seek out until we discover principles of a character to take strong hold of us, to convince our minds and to move our hearts at one and the same time. These will inspire devotion and energy; these will keep our minds in that state of disinterested activity, of simple, unsophisticated steadfastness which constitutes moral health. The same progress of events which imposes the necessity of doing this upon us, will supply us with the means of doing it.

In the study, then, upon which we are about to enter, we have to aim at far more than the mere acquisition of knowledge; intellectual development cannot, may not remain an isolated fact. We are imperatively called upon to derive from it, for our country, new materials of civilization; for ourselves, a moral regeneration.

Science is a beautiful thing, undoubtedly, and of itself well worth all the labour that man may bestow upon it; but it becomes a thousand times grander and more beautiful when it becomes a power; when it becomes the parent of virtue. This, then, is what we have to do in the course of these lectures: to discover the truth; to realise it out of ourselves in external facts, for the benefit of society; in ourselves, to convert it into a faith capable of inspiring us with disinterestedness and moral energy, the force and dignity of man in this world. This is our triple task; this the aim and object of our labour; a labour difficult of execution and slow of progress, and which success, instead of terminating, only extends. But in nothing, perhaps, is it given to man ever to arrive at the goal he has proposed to himself; his glory is in advancing towards it.

Lecture 7

We approach successively the various sources of our civilization. We have already studied, on one side, what we call the Roman element, the civil Roman society; on the other, the Christian element, the religious society. Let us now consider the barbaric element, the German society.

Opinions are very various concerning the importance of this element, concerning the part and share of the Germans in modern civilization; the prejudices of nation, of situation, of class, have modified the idea which each has formed of it.

The German historians, the feudal publicists, M. de Boulainvilliers, for example, have in general attributed too extensive an influence to the barbarians; the bourgeois publicists, as the Abbé Dubos, have, on the contrary, too much reduced it, in order to give far too large a part to Roman society; according to the ecclesiastics, it is to the church that modern civilization is the most indebted. Sometimes political doctrines have alone determined the opinion of the writer; the Abbé de Mably, all devoted as he was to the popular cause, and despite his antipathy for the feudal system, insists strongly upon the German origins, because he thought to find there more institutions and principles of liberty than anywhere else. I do not wish to treat at present of this question; we shall treat of it, it will be resolved as we advance in the history of French civilization. We shall see from epoch to epoch what part each of its primitive elements has there played, what each has brought and received in their combination. I shall confine myself to asserting beforehand the two results to which I believe this study will conduct us: First, that the state of the barbaric element in modern civilization has, in general, been made a great deal too much of. Second, its true share has not been given it: too great an influence upon our society has been attributed to the Germans, to their institutions, to their manners; what they have truly exercised has not been attributed to them; we do not owe to them all that has been done in their name; we do owe to them what seems not to proceed from them.

Until this two-fold result shall arise under our eyes, from the progressive development of facts, the first condition, in order to appreciate with accuracy the share of the Germanic element in our civilization, is to correctly understand what the Germans really were at the time when it commenced, when they themselves concurred in its formation; that is to say, before their invasion and their establishment on the Roman territory; when they still inhabited Germany in the third and fourth centuries. By this alone shall we be enabled to form an exact idea of what they brought to the common work, to distinguish what facts are truly of German origin.

This study is difficult. The monuments where we may study the barbarians before the invasion are of three kinds; first, the Greek or Roman writers, who knew and described them from their first appearance in history up to this epoch; that is to say, from Polybius, about one hundred and fifty years before Christ, down to Ammianus Marcellinus, whose work stops at the year of our Lord 378. Between these two eras a crowd of historians, Livy, Cæsar, Strabo, Pomponius Mela, Pliny, Tacitus, Ptolemy, Plutarch, Florus, Pausanias, etc., have left us information, more or less detailed, concerning the German nations; secondly, writings and documents posterior to the German invasion, but which relate or reveal anterior facts; for example, many Chronicles, the Barbaric laws, Salic, Visigoth, Burgundian, etc.; thirdly, the recollection and national traditions of the Germans themselves concerning their fate and their state in the ages anterior to the invasion, reascending up to the first origin and their most ancient history.

At the mere mention of these documents, it is evident that very various times and states are comprehended in them. The Roman and Greek writers, for example, embrace a space of five hundred years, during which Germany and her nations were presented to them in the most different points of view. Then came the first expeditions of the wandering Germans, especially that of the Teutones and the Cimbrians. Rather later, dating from Cæsar and Augustus, the Romans, in their turn, penetrated into Germany; their armies passed the Rhine and the Danube, and saw the Germans under a new aspect and in a new state. Lastly, from the third century, the Germans fell upon the Roman empire, which repelling and admitting them alternately, came to know them far more intimately, and in an entirely different situation from what they had done hitherto. Who does not perceive that, during this interval, through so many centuries and events, the barbarians and the writers who described them, the object and the picture, must have prodigiously varied?

The documents of the second class are in the same case: the barbaric laws were drawn up some time after the invasion; the most ancient portion of the law of the Visigoths belonged to the last half of the fifth century; the Salic law may have been written first under Clovis, but the digest which we have of it is of a far posterior epoch; the law of the Burgundians dates from the year 517.

They are all, therefore, in their actual form, much more modern than the barbaric society which we wish to study. There can be do doubt but that they contain many facts, that they often describe a social state anterior to the invasion; there can be no doubt but that the Germans, transported into Gaul, retained much of their ancient customs, their ancient relations. But there can also be no doubt here that, after the invasion, Germanic society was profoundly modified, and that these modifications had passed into laws; the law of the Visigoths and that of the

Burgundians are much more Roman than barbarian; three fourths of the provisions concern facts which could not have arisen until after these nations were established upon Roman soil. The Salic law is more primitive, more barbaric; but still, I believe it may be proved that, in many parts—among others, in that concerning property—it is of more recent origin. Like the Roman historians, the German laws evidence very various times and states of society.

According to the documents of the third class, the national traditions of the Germans, the evidence is still more striking: the subjects of these traditions are almost all facts, so far anterior as probably to have become almost foreign to the state of these nations at the third and fourth centuries; facts which had concurred to produce this state and which may serve to explain it, but which no longer constituted it. Suppose, that, in order to study the state of the highlanders of Scotland fifty years ago, one had collected their still living and popular traditions, and had taken the facts which they express as the real elements of Scottish society in the eighteenth century: assuredly the illusion would be great and fruitful of error. It would be the same and with much greater reason, with regard to the ancient German traditions; they coincide with the primitive history of the Germans, with their origin, their religious filiation, their relations with a multitude of nations in Asia, on the borders of the Black Sea, of the Baltic Sea; with events, in a word, which, doubtless, had powerfully tended to bring about the social state of the German tribes in the third century, and which we must closely observe, but which were then no longer facts but only causes.

You see that all the monuments that remain to us of the state of the barbarians before the invasion, whatever may be their origin and their nature, Roman or German, traditions, chronicles, or laws, refer to times and facts very far removed from one another, and among which it is very difficult to separate what truly belongs to the third and fourth centuries. The fundamental error, in my opinion, of a great number of German writers, and sometimes of the most distinguished, is not having sufficiently attended to this circumstance: in order to picture German society and manners at this epoch, they have drawn their materials pell-mell from the three sources of documents I have indicated, from the Roman writers, from the barbaric laws, from the national traditions, without troubling themselves with the difference of times and situations, without observing any moral chronology. Hence arises the incoherence of some of these pictures, a singular mixture of mythology, of barbarism, and of rising civilization, of fabulous, heroic, and semi-political ages, without exactitude and without order in the eyes of the more severe critic, without truth for the imagination.

I shall endeavour to avoid this error; it is with the state of the Germans, a little before the invasion, that I desire to occupy you; that is what it imports us to know, for it was that which was real and powerful at the time of the amalgamation of the nations, that which exercised a true influence upon modern civilization. I shall in no way enter into the examination of the German origins and antiquities; I shall in no way seek to discover what were the relations between the Germans and the nations and religions of Asia; whether their barbarism was the wreck of an ancient civilization, nor what might be, under barbaric forms, the concealed features of this original society. The question is an important one; but it is not ours, and I shall not stop at it. I would wish, too, never to transfer into the state of the Germans, beyond the Rhine and the Danube, facts which belong to the Germans established upon Gaulish soil. The difficulty is extreme. Before having passed the Danube or the Rhine, the barbarians were in relation with Rome; their condition, their manners, their ideas, their laws, had perhaps already submitted to its influence. How separate, amidst notices so incomplete, so confused, these first results of foreign importation? How decide with precision what was truly Germanic, and what already bore a Roman stamp? I shall attempt this task; the truth of history absolutely requires it.

The most important document we possess concerning the state of the Germans, between the time when they began to be known in the Roman world, and that in which they conquered it, is incontestably the work of Tacitus. Two things must be here carefully distinguished: on one side, the facts which Tacitus has collected and described; on the other, the reflections which he mixes with them, the colour under which he presents them, the judgment which he gives of them. The facts are correct: there are many reasons for believing that the father of Tacitus, and perhaps himself, had been procurator of Belgium; he could thus collect detailed information concerning Germany; he occupied himself carefully in doing so; posterior documents almost all prove the material accuracy of his descriptions. With regard to their moral hue, Tacitus has painted the Germans, as Montaigne and Rousseau the savages, in a fit of ill humour against his country: his book is a satire on Roman manners, the eloquent sally of a philosophical patriot, who is determined to see virtue, wherever he does not happen to find the disgraceful effeminacy and the learned depravation of an old society. Do not suppose, however, that everything is false, morally speaking, in this work of anger —the imagination of Tacitus is essentially vigorous and true; when he wishes simply to describe German manners, without allusion to the Roman world, without comparison, without deducing any general consequence therefrom, he is admirable, and one may give entire faith, not only to the design, but to the colouring of the picture. Never has the barbaric life been painted with more vigour, more poetical truth. It is only when thoughts of Rome occur to Tacitus, when he speaks of the barbarians with a view to shame his fellow-citizens; it is then only that his imagination loses its independence, its natural sincerity, and that a false colour is spread over his pictures.

Doubtless, a great change was brought about in the state of the Germans, between the end of the first century, the epoch in which Tacitus wrote, and the times bordering on the invasion; the frequent communications with Rome could not fail of exercising a great influence upon them, attention to which circumstance has too often been neglected. Still the groundwork of the book of Tacitus was true at the end of the fourth as in the first century. Nothing can be a more decisive proof of it than the accounts of Ammianus Marcellinus, a mere soldier, without imagination, without instruction, who made war against the Germans, and whose brief and simple descriptions coincide almost everywhere with the lively and learned colours of Tacitus. We may, therefore, for the epoch which occupies us, give almost entire confidence to the picture *of the manners of the Germans.*

If we compare this picture with the description of the ancient social state of the Germans, lately given by able German writers, we shall be surprised by the resemblance. Assuredly the sentiment which animates them is different; it is with indignation and sorrow at corrupted Rome that Tacitus describes the simple and vigorous manners of the barbarians; it is with pride and complaisance that the modern Germans contemplate it; but from these diverse causes rises a single and identical fact; like Tacitus, nay, far more than Tacitus, the greater part of the Germans paint ancient Germany, her institutions, her manners, in the most vivid colours; if they do not go so far as to represent them as the ideal of society, they at least defend them from all imputation of barbarism. According to them: first, the agricultural or sedentary life prevailed there, even before the invasion, over the wandering life; the institutions and ideas which create landed property were already very far advanced; second, the guarantees of individual liberty, and even security, were efficacious; third, manners were indeed violent and coarse, but at bottom the natural morality of man was developed with simplicity and grandeur; family affections were strong, characters lofty, emotions profound, religious doctrines high and powerful; there was more energy and moral purity than is found under more elegant forms, in the heart of a far more extended intellectual development.

When this cause is maintained by ordinary minds, it abounds in strange assumptions and ridiculous assertions. Heinrich, the author of an esteemed *History of Germany,* will not have it that the ancient Germans were addicted to intoxication;[2] Meiners, in his *History of the Female Sex,* maintains that women have never been so happy nor so virtuous as in Germany, and that before the arrival of the Franks, the Gauls knew not how either to respect or to love them.[3]

2. *Reichsgeschichte,* vol. 1, p. 69.
3. *Geschichte des Weiblichen Geschlechts,* vol. 1, p. 198.

I shall not dwell upon these puerilities of learned patriotism; I should not even have touched upon them, if they were not the consequence, and as it were, the excrescence of a system, maintained by very distinguished men, and which, in my opinion, destroys the historical and poetical idea which is formed of the ancient Germans. Considering things at large, and according to mere appearances, the error seems to me evident.

How can it be maintained, for example, that German society was well nigh fixed, and that the agricultural life dominated there, in the presence of the very fact of migrations, of invasions, of that incessant movement which drew the Germanic nations beyond their territory? How can we give credit to the empire of manorial property, and of the ideas and institutions which are connected with it, over men who continually abandoned the soil in order to seek fortune elsewhere? And mark, that it was not only on the frontiers that this movement was accomplished; the same fluctuation reigned in the interior of Germany; tribes incessantly expelled, displaced, succeeded one another: some paragraphs from Tacitus will abundantly prove this:

The Batavians were formerly a tribe of the Catti; internal divisions forced them to retire into the islands of the Rhine, where they formed an alliance with the Romans. (Tacitus, *de Moribus Germanorum,* c. 29)

In the neighbourhood of the Tencteres were formerly the Bructeres; it is said, however, that now the Chamaves and the Angrivarians possess the district, having, in concert with the adjoining tribes, expelled and entirely extirpated the ancient inhabitants. (Ibid., c. 32)

The Marcomannians are the most eminent for their strength and military glory; the very territory they occupy is the reward of their valour, they having dispossessed its former owners, the Boians. (Ibid., c. 42)

Even in time of peace the Cattians retain the same ferocious aspect, never softened with an air of humanity. They have no house to dwell in, no land to cultivate, no domestic cares to employ them. Wherever they chance to be, they live upon the produce they find, and are lavish of their neighbours' substance, till

old age incapacitates them for these continuous struggles. (Ibid.,
c. 31)

> The tribes deem it an honourable distinction to have their
> frontiers devastated, to be surrounded with immense deserts.
> The regard it as the highest proof of valour for their neighbours
> to abandon their territories out of fear of them, moreover, they
> have thus an additional security against sudden attacks. (Cæsar,
> *de Bello Gallico*, 6.23)

Doubtless, since the time of Tacitus, the German tribes, more
or less, had made some progress; still, assuredly, the fluctuation,
the continual displacement had not ceased, since the invasion
became daily more general and more pressing.

Hence, if I mistake not, partly proceeds the difference which
exists between the point of view of the Germans and our own.
There was, in fact, at the fourth century, among many German
tribes or confederations, among others with the Franks and Saxons, a commencement of the sedentary, agricultural life; the
whole nation was not addicted to the wandering life. Its composition was not simple; it was not an unique race, a single social
condition. We may there recognise three classes of men: first,
freemen, men of honour or nobles, proprietors; second, the *lidi,
liti, lasi,* etc., or labourers, men attached to the soil, who cultivated it for masters; third, slaves properly so called. The existence of the first two classes evidently indicate a conquest; the
class of freemen was the nation of conquerors, who had obliged
the ancient population to cultivate the soil for them. This was an
analogous fact to that which, at a later period, in the Roman
empire, gave rise to the feudal system. This fact was accomplished at various epochs, and upon various points, in the interior
of Germany. Sometimes the proprietors and the labourers—the
conquerors and the conquered—were of different races; sometimes it was in the bosom of the same race, between different
tribes, that the territorial subjection took place; we see Gaulish or
Belgian colonies submit to German colonies, Germans to Slavonians, Slavonians to Germans, Germans to Germans. Conquest
was generally effected upon a small scale, and remained exposed

to many vicissitudes; but the fact itself cannot be disputed; many passages in Tacitus positively express it:

> The slaves, in general, are not arranged in their several employments in household affairs, as is the practice at Rome. Each has his separate habitation or home. The master considers him as an agrarian dependent, who is obliged to furnish, by way of rent, a certain quantity of grain, of cattle, or of wearing apparel. The slave does this, and there his servitude ends. All domestic matters are managed by the master's own wife and children. To punish a slave with stripes, to load him with chains, or condemn him to hard labour, is unusual. (*De Moribus Germanorum,* c. 25)

Who does not recognise in this description, ancient inhabitants of the territory, fallen under the yoke of conquerors?

The conquerors in the earliest ages, at least, did not cultivate. They enjoyed the conquest—sometimes abandoned to a profound idleness, sometimes excited with a profound passion for war, hunting, and adventures. Some distant expedition tempted them; all were not of the same inclination— they did not all go; a party set off under the conduct of some famous chief; others remained, preferring to guard their first conquests, and continued to live upon the labour of the ancient inhabitants. The adventurous party sometimes returned laden with booty, sometimes pursued its course, and went to a distance to conquer some province of the empire, perhaps found some kingdom. It was thus that the Vandals, the Suevi, the Franks, the Saxons, were dispersed; thus we find these nations overrunning Gaul, Spain, Africa, Britain, establishing themselves there, beginning states, while the same names are always met with in Germany—where, in fact, the same people still live and act. They were parcelled out: one part abandoned themselves to the wandering life; another was attached to the sedentary life, perhaps only waiting the occasion or temptation to set out in its turn.

Hence arises the difference between the point of view of the German writers, and that of our own; they more especially were acquainted with that portion of the German tribes which remained upon the soil, and was more and more addicted to the agricultural and sedentary life; we, on the contrary, have been naturally led to consider chiefly the portion which followed the wandering life, and which invaded western Europe. Like the learned Germans, we speak of the Franks, the Saxons, the Suevi, but not of the same Suevi, the same Saxons, the same Franks; our researches, our words, almost always refer to those who passed the Rhine, and it is in the state of wandering bands that we have seen them appear in Gaul, in Spain, in Britain, etc. The assertions of the Germans, chiefly allude to the Saxons, the Suevi, the Franks who remained in Germany; and it is in the state of conquering nations, it is true, but fixed, or almost fixed in certain parts of the land, and beginning to lead the life of proprietors, that they are exhibited by almost all the ancient monuments of local history. The error of these scholars, if I mistake not, is in carrying the authority of these monuments too far back—too anterior to the fourth century—of attributing too remote a date to the sedentary life, and to the fixedness of the social state in Germany; but the error is much more natural and less important than it would be on our part.

With regard to ancient German institutions, I shall speak of them in detail when we treat especially of the barbarian laws, and more especially of the Salic law. I shall confine myself at present to the characterizing, in a few words, their state at the epoch which occupies us.

At that time, we find among the Germans the seeds of the three great systems of institutions which, after the fall of the Roman empire, contested for Europe. We find there: first, assemblies of freemen, where they debate upon the common interests, public enterprises, all the important affairs of the nation; second, kings, some by hereditary title, and sometimes invested with a religious character, others by title of election, and especially bearing a warlike character; third, the aristocratical patronage, whether of the warlike chief over his companions, or of the proprietor over his family and labourers. These three systems, these three modes of social organization and of government may be seen in almost all the German tribes before the invasion; but none of them are real, efficacious. Properly speaking, there are no free institutions, monarchies, or aristocracies, but merely the principle to which they relate, the germ from whence they may arise. Everything is abandoned to the caprice of individual wills. Whenever the assembly of the nation, or the king, or the lord, wished to be obeyed, the individual must either consent, or disorderly brute force obliged him. This is the free development and the contest between individual existences and liberties; there was no public power, no government, no state.

With regard to the moral condition of the Germans at this epoch, it is very difficult to estimate it. It has been made the text of infinite declamations for or against civilization of savage life; primitive independence or developed society; natural simplicity or scientific enlightenment; but we are without documents enabling us to estimate the true nature of these generalities. There exists, however, one great collection of facts, posterior, it is true, to the epoch of which we are speaking, but which yet presents a sufficiently faithful image of it; this is the *Histoire des Francs*, by Gregory of Tours, unquestionably, of all others, the work which furnishes us with the most information, which throws the clearest light upon the moral state of the barbarians; not that the chronicler made it any part of his plan, but, in the ordinary course of his narrative, he relates an infinite number of private anecdotes, of incidents of domestic life, in which the manners, the social arrangements, the moral state, in a word, the man of his period, are exhibited to us more clearly than in any other work we possess.

It is here that we may contemplate and understand this singular mixture of violence and deceit, of improvidence and calculation, of patience and bursts of passion; this egoism of interest and of passion, mixed with the indestructible empire of certain ideas of duty, of certain disinterested sentiments: in a word, that chaos of our moral nature which constitutes barbarism; a state of things very difficult to describe with precision, for it has no general and fixed feature, no one decided principle; there is no proposition we can make it, which we are not compelled the next instant to modify, or altogether to throw aside. It is humanity, strong and active, but abandoned to the impulse of its reckless propensities, to the incessant mobility of its wayward fancies, to the gross imperfection of its knowledge, to the incoherence of its ideas, to the infinite variety of the situations and accidents of its life.

It were impossible to penetrate far enough into such a state, and reproduce its image, by the mere aid of a few dry and mutilated chronicles, of a few fragments of old poems, of a few unconnected paragraphs of old laws.

I know but of one way of attaining anything like a correct idea of the social and moral state of the German tribes—it is to compare them with the tribes who, in modern times, in various parts of the globe, in North America, in the interior of Africa, in the North of Asia, are still almost in the same degree of civilization, and lead very nearly the same life. The latter have been observed more nearly, and described in greater detail; fresh accounts of them reach us every day. We have a thousand facilities for regulating and completing our ideas with respect to them; our imagination is constantly excited, and at the same time rectified, by the narratives of travellers. By closely and critically observing these narratives, by comparing and analyzing the various circumstances, they become for us as it were a mirror, in which we raise up and reproduce the image of the ancient Germans. I have gone through this task; I have followed, step by step, the work of Tacitus, seeking throughout my progress, in voyages and travels, in histories, in national poetry, in all the documents which we possess concerning the barbarous tribes in the various parts of the world, facts analogous to those described by the Roman writer. I will lay before you the principal features of this comparison, and you will be astonished at the resemblance between the manners of the Germans and those of the more modern barbarians—a resemblance which sometimes extends into details where one would have had not the slightest idea of finding it.

·   ·

Guizot constructed a table comparing the German barbarian as described by Tacitus to primitive tribes as depicted in contem-

porary sources, including Robertson's definition of American Indians in his History of America; *the last three examples are given here.*

They yield to gambling with such ardour, that when they have lost everything else, they place their own liberty on the hazard of the die. (Tacitus, *De Moribus Germanorum*, c. 24)

The Americans play for their furs, their domestic utensils, their clothes, their arms, and when all is lost, we often see them risk, at a single blow, their liberty. (Robertson, *History of America*, vol. 2, pp. 459–61)

It was not in order to succeed in love, or to please, that they decked themselves, but in order to give themselves a gigantic and terrible appearance, as they might have decked themselves to go before their enemies. (Ibid., c. 38)

When the Iroquois choose to paint their faces it is to give themselves a terrible air, with which they hope to intimidate their enemies; it is also for this reason that they paint themselves black when they go to war. (*Memoir on the Iroquois*, in *Variétés Litteraires*, vol. 1, p. 472)

From the age of early manhood they allow their hair and beard to grow, until they have killed an enemy. (Ibid., c. 31)

After the Indians are twenty years old they allow their hair to grow. (*Lett. edif.*, vol. 8, p. 261)

The custom of scalping, or taking off the hair of their enemies, so common among the Americans, was also practised among the Germans: this is the *decalvare* mentioned in the laws of the Visigoths; the *capillos et cutem detrahere*, still in use among the Franks towards the year 879, according to the annals of Fulda; the *hettinan* of the Anglo-Saxons, etc. (Adelung, *Ancient History of the Germans*, p. 303)

Here are numerous citations; I might extend them much more, and might almost always place, side by side with the most trifling assertion of Tacitus concerning the Germans, an analogous assertion of some modern traveller or historian, concerning some one of the barbarous tribes at present dispersed over the face of the globe.

You see what is the social condition which corresponds to that of ancient Germany: what, then, must we think of those magnificent descriptions which have so often been drawn? Precisely that which we should think of Cooper's romances, as pictures of the condition and manners of the savages of North America. There is, without doubt, in these romances and in some of the works in which the Germans have attempted to depict their wild ancestors, a sufficiently vivid and true perception of certain parts and certain periods of barbarous society and life—of its independence, for instance; of the activity and indolence which it combines; of the skilful energy which man therein displays against the obstacles and perils wherewith material nature besieges him; of the monotonous violence of his passions, etc. But the picture is very incomplete—so incomplete that the truth of even what it represents is often much changed by it. That Cooper, in writing of the Mohicans or the Delawares, and that the German writers, in describing the ancient Germans, should allow themselves to represent all things under their poetic aspect —that, in their descriptions, the sentiments and circumstances of barbarous life should become exalted to their ideal form—is very natural, and, I willingly admit, is very legitimate: the ideal is the essence of poetry—history itself is partial to it; and perhaps it is the only form under which times gone by can be duly represented. But the ideal must also be true, complete, and harmonious; it does not consist in the arbitrary and fanciful suppression of a large portion of the reality to which it corresponds. Assuredly, the songs which bear the name of Homer, form an ideal picture of Greek society; nevertheless, that society is therein reproduced in a complete state, with the rusticity and ferocity of its manners, the coarse simplicity of its sentiments, and its good and bad passions, without any design of particularly drawing forth or celebrating such or such of its merits and its advantages, or of leaving in the shade its vices and its evils.

This mixture of good and evil, of strong and weak—this coexistence of ideas and sentiments apparently contradictory—this variety, this incoherence, this unequal development of human nature and human destiny—is precisely the condition which is the most rife with poetry, for through it we see to the bottom of things, it is the truth concerning man and the world; and in the ideal pictures which poetry, romance, and even history, make of it, this so various and yet harmonious whole ought to be found, for without it the true ideal will be wanting, no less than the reality. Now it is into this fault that the writers of whom I speak have always fallen; their pictures of savage man and of savage life are essentially incomplete, formal, factitious, and wanting in simplicity and harmony. One fancies that one sees melodramatic barbarians and savages, who present themselves to display their independence, their energy, their skill, or such and such a portion of their character and destiny, before the eyes of spectators who, at once greedy of, but worn out with, excitement, still take pleasure in qualities and adventures foreign to the life they themselves lead, and to the society by which they are surrounded. I know not whether you are struck, as I am, with the defects of the imagination in our times. Upon the whole, it seems to me that it lacks nature, facility, and extension; it does not take a large and simple view of things in their primitive and real elements; it arranges them theatrically, and mutilates them under the pretence of idealizing them. It is true that I find, in the modern descriptions of ancient German manners, some scattered characteristics of barbarism, but I can discover nothing therefrom of what barbarous society was as a whole.

If I were obliged to sum up that which I have now said upon the state of the Germans before the invasion, I confess I should be somewhat embarrassed. We find therein no precise and well defined traits which may be detached and distinctly exhibited; no fact, no idea, no sentiment had as yet attained to its development, or as yet presented itself under a determinate form; it was the infancy of all things, of the social and moral states, of institutions, of relations, of man himself; everything was rough and confused. There are, however, two points to which I think I ought to direct your attention.

First, at the opening of modern civilization, the Germans influenced it far less by the institutions which they brought with them from Germany, than by their situation itself, amidst the Roman world. They had conquered it: they were, at least upon the spot where they had established themselves, masters of the population and of the territory. The society which formed itself after this conquest, arose rather from this situation, from the new life led by the conquerors in their relations with the conquered, than from the ancient German manners.

Second, that which the Germans especially brought into the Roman world was the spirit of individual liberty, the need, the passion for independence and individuality. To speak properly, no public power, no religious power, existed in ancient Germany; the only real power in this society, the only power that was strong and active in it, was the will of man; each one did what he chose, at his own risk and peril.

The system of force, that is to say, of personal liberty, was at the bottom of the social state of the Germans. Through this it was that their influence became so powerful upon the modern world. Very general expressions border always so nearly upon inaccuracy, that I do not like to risk them. Nevertheless, were it absolutely necessary to express in few words the predominating characters of the various elements of our civilization, I should say, that the spirit of legality, of regular association, came to us from the Roman world, from the Roman municipalities and laws. It is to Christianity, to the religious society that we owe the spirit of morality, the sentiment and empire of rule, of a moral law, of the mutual duties of men. The Germans conferred upon us the spirit of liberty, of liberty such as we conceive of and are acquainted with in the present day, as the right and property of each individual, master of himself, of his actions, and of his fate, so long as he injures no other individual. This is a fact of universal importance, for it was unknown to all preceding civilizations: in the ancient republics, the public power disposed of all things; the individual was sacrificed to the citizen. In the societies where the religious principle predominated, the believer belonged to his God, not to himself. Thus, man hitherto had always been absorbed in the church or in the state. In modern Europe, alone, has he existed and developed himself on his own account and in his own way, charged, no doubt, charged continually, more and more heavily with toils and duties, but finding in himself his aim and his right. It is to German manners that we must trace this distinguishing characteristic of our civilization. The fundamental idea of liberty, in modern Europe, came to it from its conquerors.

Lecture 8

We are now in possession of the two primitive and fundamental elements of French civilization; we have studied, on the one hand, Roman civilization, on the other, German society, each in itself, and prior to their apposition. Let us endeavour to ascertain what happened in the moment at which they touched together, and became confounded with one another; that is to say, to describe the condition of Gaul after the great invasion and settlement of the Germans.

I should wish to assign to this description a somewhat precise date, and to inform you, beforehand, to what age and to what territory it especially belongs. The difficulty of doing this is great. Such, at this epoch, was the confusion of things and minds, that the greater part of the facts have been transmitted to us without order and without date, particularly general facts, those connected with institutions, with the relations of the different classes, in a word, with the social condition; facts which, by nature, are the least apparent and the least precise. They are omitted or strangely confused in contemporary monuments; we must, at every step, guess at and restore their chronology. Happily, the accuracy of this chronology is of less importance at this epoch than at any other. No doubt, between the sixth and eighth centuries, the state of Gaul must have changed; relations of men, institutions and manners must have been modified; less, however, than we might be tempted to believe. The chaos was extreme, and chaos is essentially stationary. When all things are disordered and confounded to this degree, they require much time for unravelling and rearranging themselves; much time is needed for each of the elements to return to its place, to reenter its right path, to place itself again in some measure under the direction and motive force of the special principle which should govern its development. After the settlement of the barbarians upon the Roman soil, events and men revolved for a long time in the same circle, a prey to a movement more violent than progressive. Thus, from the sixth to the eighth century, the state of Gaul changed less, and the strict chronology of general facts is of less importance than we might naturally presume from the length of the interval. Let us, nevertheless, endeavour to determine, within certain limits, the epoch of which we are now to trace the picture.

The true Germanic people who occupied Gaul were the Burgundians, the Visigoths, and the Franks. Many other people, many other single bands, of Vandals, Alani, Suevi, Saxons, etc., wandered over its territory; but of these, some only passed over it, and the others were rapidly absorbed by it; these are partial incursions which are without any historical importance. The Burgundians, the Visigoths, and the Franks, alone deserve to be counted among our ancestors. The Burgundians definitively established themselves in Gaul between the years 406 and 413; they occupied the country between the Jura, the Saône, and the Durance; Lyon was the centre of their dominion. The Visigoths, between the years 412 and 450, spread themselves over the provinces bounded by the Rhone, and even over the left bank of the Rhone to the south of the Durance, the Loire, and the Pyrenees: their king resided at Toulouse. The Franks, between the years 481 and 500, advanced in the north of Gaul, and established themselves between the Rhine, the Scheldt, and the Loire, without including Brittany and the western portions of Normandy; Clovis had Soissons and Paris for his capitals. Thus, at the end of the fifth century, was accomplished the definitive occupation of the territory of Gaul by the three great German tribes.

The condition of Gaul was not exactly the same in its various parts, and under the dominion of these three nations. There were remarkable differences between them. The Franks were far more foreign, German, and barbarous, than the Burgundians and the Goths. Before their entrance into Gaul, these last had had ancient relations with the Romans; they had lived in the eastern empire, in Italy; they were familiar with the Roman manners and population. We may say almost as much for the Burgundians. Moreover, the two nations had long been Christians. The Franks, on the contrary, arrived from Germany in the condition of pagans and enemies. Those portions of Gaul which they occupied became deeply sensible of this difference, which is described with truth and vivacity in the seventh of the *Letters upon the History of France*, of M. Augustin Thierry. I am inclined, however, to believe that it was less important than has been commonly supposed. If I do not err, the Roman provinces differed more among themselves than did the nations which had conquered them. You have already seen how much more civilized was southern than northern Gaul, how much more thickly covered with population, towns, monuments, and roads. Had the Visigoths arrived in as barbarous a condition as that of the Franks, their barbarism would yet have been far less visible and less powerful in Gallia Narbonensis and in Aquitania; Roman civilization would much sooner have absorbed and altered them. This, I believe, is what happened; and the different effects which accompanied the three conquests resulted rather from the differences of the conquered than from that of the conquerors.

Besides, this difference, sensible so long as we confine ourselves to a very general view of things, becomes effaced, or at least very difficult to be perceived, when we go farther on with the study of the society. It may be said that the Franks were more barbarous than the Visigoths; but, that being said, we must stop. In what consisted the positive differences between the two peoples, in institutions, ideas, and relations of classes? No precise record contains an answer to this question. Finally, the difference of condition in the provinces of Gaul, that difference, at least, which was referable to their masters, soon disappeared or became greatly lessened. About the year 534, the country of the Burgundians fell under the yoke of the Franks: between the years

507 and 542, that of the Visigoths became subject to nearly the same fate. In the middle of the sixth century, the Frankish race had spread itself and obtained dominion throughout Gaul. The Visigoths still possessed a part of Languedoc, and still disputed the possession of some towns at the foot of the Pyrenees; but, properly speaking, Brittany excepted, the whole of Gaul was, if not governed, at least overrun by the Franks.

It is with the Gaul of this epoch that I desire to make you acquainted; it is the state of Gaul about the last half of the sixth century, and, above all, of Frankish Gaul, that I shall now endeavour to describe. Any attempt to assign a more precise date to this description would be vain and fertile in errors. No doubt there was still, at this epoch, much variety in the condition of the Gaulish provinces; but I shall attempt to estimate it no farther, remaining satisfied with having warned you of its existence.

It seems to me that people commonly form to themselves a very false idea of the invasion of the barbarians, and of the extent and rapidity of its effects. You have, in your reading upon this subject, often met with the words *inundation, earthquake, conflagration.* These are the terms which have been employed to characterize this revolution. I think that they are deceptive, that they in no way represent the manner in which this invasion occurred, nor its immediate results. Exaggeration is natural to human language; words express the impressions which man receives from facts, rather than the facts themselves; it is after having passed through the mind of man, and according to the impressions which they have produced thereupon, that facts are described and named. But the impression is never the complete and faithful image of the fact. In the first place, it is individual, which the fact is not; great events, the invasion of a foreign people, for instance, are related by those who have been personally affected, as victims, actors, or spectators: they relate the event as they have seen it; they characterize it according to what they have known or undergone. He who has seen his house or his village burnt, will, perhaps, call the invasion a conflagration; to the thought of another, it will be found arrayed in the form of a deluge or an earthquake. These images are true, but are of a truth which, if I may so express myself, is full of prejudice and egoism; they reproduce the impressions of some few men; they are not expressions of the fact in its entire extent, nor of the manner in which it impressed the whole of the country.

Such, moreover, is the instinctive poetry of the human mind, that it receives from facts an impression which is livelier and greater than are the facts themselves; it is its tendency to extend and ennoble them; they are for it but matter which it fashions and forms, a theme upon which it exercises itself, and from which it draws, or rather over which it spreads beauties and effects which were not really there. Thus, a double and contrary cause fills language with illusion; under a material point of view, facts are greater than man, and he perceives and describes only that which strikes him personally; under the moral point of view, man is greater than facts; and, in describing them, he lends them something of his own greatness.

This is what we must never forget in studying history, particularly in reading contemporary documents; they are at once incomplete and exaggerated; they omit and amplify: we must always distrust the impression conveyed by them, both as too narrow and as too poetical; we must both add to and take from it. Nowhere does this double error appear more strongly than in the narratives of the Germanic invasion; the words by which it has been described in no way represent it.

The invasion, or rather, the invasions, were events which were essentially partial, local, and momentary. A band arrived, usually far from numerous; the most powerful, those who found kingdoms, as the band of Clovis, scarcely numbered from 5,000 to 6,000 men; the entire nation of the Burgundians did not exceed 60,000 men. It rapidly overran a limited territory; ravaged a district; attacked a city, and sometimes retreated, carrying away its booty, and sometimes settled somewhere, always careful not to disperse itself too much. We know with what facility and promptitude such events accomplish themselves and disappear. Houses are burnt, fields are devastated, crops carried off, men killed or led away prisoners: all this evil over, at the end of a few days the waves close, the ripple subsides, individual sufferings are forgotten, society returns, at least in appearance, to its former state. This was the condition of things in Gaul during the fourth century.

But we also know that the human society, that society which we call a people, is not a simple juxtaposition of isolated and fugitive existence: were it nothing more, the invasions of the barbarians would not have produced the impression which the documents of the epoch depict; for a long while the number of places and men that suffered therefrom was far inferior to the number of those who escaped. But the social life of each man is not concentrated in the material space which is its theatre, nor in the passing moment; it extends itself to all the relations which he has contracted upon different points of the land; and not only to those relations which he has contracted, but also to those which he might contract, or can even conceive the possibility of contracting; it embraces not only the present, but the future; man lives in a thousand places which he does not inhabit, in a thousand moments which, as yet, are not; and if this development of his life is cut off from him, if he is forced to confine himself to the narrow limits of his material and actual existence, to isolate himself in space and time, social life is mutilated and society is no more.

And this was the effect of the invasions, of those apparitions of barbarous hordes, short, it is true, and limited, but reviving without cessation, everywhere possible, and always imminent: they destroyed, first, all regular, habitual, and easy correspondence between the various parts of the territory; second, all security, all sure prospect of the future; they broke the ties which bound together the inhabitants of the same country, the moments of the same life, they isolated men, and the days of each man. In many places, and for many years, the aspect of the country might remain the same; but the social organization was attacked, the members no longer held together, the muscles no longer played, the blood no longer circulated freely or surely in the veins: the disease appeared sometimes at one point, sometimes at another: a town was pillaged, a road rendered impassable, a bridge destroyed; such or such a communication ceased; the culture of the land became impossible in such or such a district: in a word, the organic harmony, the general activity of the social body, were each day fettered and disturbed; each day dissolution and paralysis made some new advance.

Thus was Roman society destroyed in Gaul; not as a valley is ravaged by a torrent, but as the most solid body is disorganised by the continual infiltration of a foreign substance. Between all the members of the state, between all the moments of the life of each man, the barbarians continually intruded themselves. I lately endeavoured to paint to you the dismemberment of the Roman empire, the impossibility under which its masters found themselves of holding together the different parts, and how the imperial administration was obliged to retire spontaneously from Britain, from Gaul, incapable of resisting the dissolution of that vast body. What occurred in the Empire occurred equally in each province; as the Empire had suffered disorganization, so did each province; the cantons, the towns detached themselves, and returned to a local and isolated existence. The invasion operated everywhere in the same manner, and everywhere produced the same effects. All the ties by which Rome had been enabled, after so many efforts, to combine together the different parts of the world; that great system of administration, of imposts, of recruiting, of public works, of roads, had not been able to support itself. There remained of it nothing but what could subsist in an isolated and local condition, that is to say, nothing but the wrecks of the municipal system. The inhabitants shut themselves up in the towns, where they continued to govern themselves nearly as they had done of old, with the same rights, by the same institutions. A thousand circumstances prove this concentration of society in towns; here is one which has been little noticed. Under the Roman administration, it is the governors of provinces, the consuls, the correctors, the presidents who fill the scene, and reappear continually in the laws and history; in the sixth century, their names become much more rare; we, indeed, still meet with dukes and counts, to whom the government of the provinces was confided; the barbarian kings strove to inherit the Roman administration, to preserve the same officers, and to induce their power to flow in the same channels; but they succeeded only very incompletely, and with great disorder; their dukes were rather military chiefs than administrators. It is manifest that the governors of provinces had no longer the same importance, and no longer played the same part; the governors of towns now filled history; the majority of these counts of Chilperic, of Gontran, of Theodebert, whose exactions are related by Gregory of Tours, are counts of towns established within their walls, and by the side of their bishop. I should exaggerate were I to say that the province disappeared, but it became disorganized, and lost all consistency, and almost all reality. The towns, the primitive elements of the Roman world, survived almost alone amidst its ruin. The rural districts became the prey of the barbarians; it was there that they established themselves with their men; it was there that they were about to introduce by degrees totally new institutions, and a new organization, but till then the rural districts will occupy scarcely any place in society, they will be but the theatre of excursions, pillages, and misery.

Even within the towns the ancient society was far from maintaining itself strong and entire. Amidst the movement of the invasions, the towns were regarded above all as fortresses; the population shut themselves therein to escape from the hordes which ravaged the country. When the barbarous immigration was somewhat diminished, when the new people had planted themselves upon the territory, the towns still remained fortresses: in place of having to defend themselves against the wandering hordes, they had to defend themselves against their neighbours, against the greedy and turbulent possessors of the surrounding country. There was therefore little security behind those weak ramparts. Towns are unquestionably centres of population and of labour, but under certain conditions; under the condition, on the one hand, that the country population cultivate for them; on the other, that an extended and active commerce consume the products of the citizen's labour. If agriculture and commerce decay, towns must decay; their prosperity and their power cannot be isolated. Now you have just seen into what a condition the rural districts of Gaul had fallen in the sixth century; the towns were able to escape for some time, but from day to day the evil threatened to conquer them. Finally, it did conquer them, and very soon this last wreck of the Empire seemed stricken with the same weakness, and a prey to the same dissolution.

Such, in the sixth century, were the general effects of the invasion and establishment of the barbarians upon Roman society; that was the condition in which they had placed it. Let us now inquire, what was the consequence of these facts, with regard to the second element of modern civilization, the German society itself?

A great mistake lies at the bottom of most of the researches which have been made upon this subject. The institutions of the Germans have been studied in Germany, and then transported just as they were into Gaul, in the train of the Germans. It has been assumed that the German society was in much the same condition after as before the conquest; and persons have reasoned from this postulate in determining the influence of the conquest, and in assigning to it its part in the development of modern civilization. Nothing can be more false and more deceptive. The German society was modified, defaced, dissolved, by the invasion, no less than the Roman society. In this great commotion a wreck was all that remained to each; the social organization of the conquerors perished like that of the conquered.

Two societies—at bottom perhaps more like each other than has been supposed, distinct, nevertheless—subsisted in Germany: first, the society of the colony or tribe, tending to a sedentary condition, and existing upon a limited territory, which it cultivated by means of labourers and slaves; second, the society of the warfaring horde, accidentally grouped around some famous chief, and leading a wandering life. This manifestly results from the facts which I have already described to you.

To the first of these two societies, to the tribes, are, in a certain measure, applicable those descriptions of the condition of the ancient Germans by modern Germans, concerning which I have already spoken. When, in fact, a tribe, small in number as were all the tribes, occupied a limited territory; when each head of a family was established upon his domain, in the midst of his people, the social organization which has been described by these writers might well exist, if not completely, and effectively, at least in the rough sketch; the assembly of proprietors, of heads of families, decided upon all matters; each horde had its own assembly; justice was dispensed to them by the freemen themselves, under the direction of the aged; a kind of public polity might arise between the confederate hordes; free institutions were then under the form in which we meet them in the infancy of nations.

The organization of the warfaring band was different; another principle presided in it, the principle of the patronage of the chief, of aristocratic clientship, and military subordination. It is with regret that I make use of these last words; they are ill suited to barbarian hordes; yet, however barbarian men may be, a kind of discipline necessarily introduces itself between the chief and his warriors; and in this case there must assuredly exist more arbitrary authority, more forced obedience, than in associations which have not war for their object. The German warfaring band therefore contained a political element that was not possessed by the tribe. At the same time, however, its freedom was great: no man engaged therein against his will; the German was born within his tribe, and thus belonged to a situation which was not one of his choice; the warrior chose his chief and his companions, and undertook nothing but with the consent of his own free will. Besides, in the bosom of the warfaring band, the inequality was not great between the chiefs and their men; there was nothing more than the natural inequality of strength, skill, or courage; an inequality which afterwards becomes fruitful, and which produces sooner or later immense results, but which, at the outset of society, displays itself only in very narrow limits. Although the chief had the largest share of the booty, although he possessed more horses and more arms, he was not so superior in riches to his companions as to be able to dispose of them without their consent; each warrior entered the association with his strength and his courage, differing very little from the others, and at liberty to leave it whenever he pleased.

Such were the two primitive German societies: what did they become by the fact of the invasion? What change did it necessarily work upon them? By ascertaining this alone it is that we can learn what German society truly was after its transplantation to the Roman soil.

The characteristic fact, the grand result of the invasion, as regards the Germans, was their change to the condition of proprietors, the cessation of the wandering life, and the definitive establishment of the agricultural life.

This fact accomplished itself gradually, slowly, and unequally; the wandering life continued for a long time in Gaul, at least it so continued for a great number of the Germans. Nevertheless, when we have estimated all these delays and disorders, we see that, in the end, the conquerors became proprietors, that they attached themselves to the soil, that landed property was the essential element of the new social state.

What were the consequences of this single fact, as regards the regulation of the warfaring band and of the tribe?

As to the tribe, remember what I have told you of the manner of its territorial establishment in Germany, of the manner in which the villages were constructed and disposed. The population was not condensed therein; each family, each habitation was isolated and surrounded with a plot of cultivated ground. It is thus that nations, who have only arrived at this degree of civilization, arrange themselves, even when they lead a sedentary life.

When the tribe was transplanted to the soil of Gaul, the habitations became yet further dispersed; the chiefs of families established themselves at a much greater distance from one another; they occupied vast domains; their houses afterwards became castles. The villages which formed themselves around them were no longer peopled with men who were free, who were their equals, but with labourers who were attached to their lands. Thus, in its material relations, the tribe became dissolved by the single fact of its new establishment.

You may easily guess what effect this single change was calculated to exert upon its institutions. The assembly of freemen, wherein all things were debated, was now got together with

313

much greater difficulty. So long as they had lived near to one another, there was no need of any great art, or wise combinations, in order that they might treat in common of their affairs; but when a population is scattered, in order that the principles and forms of free institutions may remain applicable to it, great social development is necessary, riches, intelligence, in short, a thousand things are necessary, which were wanting to the German horde, transported suddenly to a territory far more extensive than that which it had hitherto occupied. The system which regulated its existence in Germany now perished. In looking over the most ancient German laws—those of the Allemanni, Boii, and Franks—we see that, originally, the assembly of freemen in each district was held very frequently, at first, every week, and afterwards, every month. All questions were carried before it; judgments were given there, and not only criminal, but also civil judgments: almost all acts of civil life were done in its presence, as sales, donations, etc. When once the tribe was established in Gaul, the assemblies became rare and difficult; so difficult, that it was necessary to employ force to make the freemen attend: this is the object of many legal decrees. And if you pass suddenly from the fourth to the middle of the eighth century, you find that at this last epoch there were in each county but three assemblies of freemen in the year: and these not regularly kept, as is proved by some of Charlemagne's laws.

If other proofs were necessary, here is one which deserves to be noticed. When the assemblies were frequent, freemen, under the name of *rachimburgi, arhimanni, boni homines,* and in various forms, decided upon affairs. When they no longer attended, it became necessary, upon urgent occasions, to supply their places; and thus we see, at the end of the eighth century, the freemen replaced in judicial functions by permanent judges. The *scabini,* or sheriffs of Charlemagne, were regular judges. In each county, five, seven, or nine freemen were appointed by the count, or other local magistrate, and charged to present themselves at the assembly of the country to decide upon cases. The primitive institutions had become impracticable, and the judicial power passed from the people to the magistrates.

Such was the state into which the first element of German society, the colony or tribe, fell after the invasion and under its influence. Politically speaking, it was disorganised, as Roman society had been. As to the warfaring band, facts accomplished themselves in another way, and under a different form, but with the same results.

When a band arrived anywhere, and took possession of the land, or of a portion of it, we must not believe that this occupation took place systematically, or that the territory was divided by lots, and that each warrior received one, proportionate to his importance or his rank. The chiefs of the band, or the different chiefs who were united in it, appropriated to themselves vast domains. The greater part of the warriors who had followed them continued to live around them, with them, and at their table, without possessing any property which belonged especially to them. The band did not dissolve into individuals of whom each became a proprietor; the most considerable warriors entered almost alone into this situation. Had they dispersed themselves, in order that each might establish himself upon a piece of the territory, their safety amidst the original population would have been compromised; it was necessary that they should remain united in groups. Moreover, it was by the life in common that the pleasures of the barbarians, gaming, the chase, and banquets, could alone subsist. How could they have resigned themselves to isolation? Isolation is only supportable in a laborious condition; man cannot remain idle and alone. Now, the barbarians were essentially idle; they therefore required to live together, and many companions remained about their chief, leading upon his domains pretty nearly the same life which they had led before in his train. But from these circumstances it arose that their relative situation was completely altered. Very soon a prodigious inequality sprang up between them: their inequality no longer consisted in some personal difference of strength or of courage, or in a more or less considerable share of cattle, slaves, or valuable goods. The chief, become a great proprietor, disposed of many of the means of power; the others were always simple warriors; and the more the ideas of property established and extended themselves in men's minds, the more was inequality, with its effects, developed. At this period we find a great number of freemen falling by degrees into a very inferior position. The laws speak constantly of freemen, of Franks living upon the lands of another, and reduced almost to the situation of labourers.[4] The band, regarded as a peculiar society, reposed upon two facts—the voluntary association of the warriors in order to lead in common a wandering life, and their equality. These two facts perished in the results of the invasion. On one hand, the wandering life ended—on the other, inequality introduced itself, and increased from day to day, among the sedentary warriors.

The progressive parcelling out of lands, during the three centuries after the invasion, did not change this result. All of you have heard of the benefices that the king, or the great chiefs who occupied a vast territory, distributed to their men, to attach them to their service, or to recompense them for services done. This practice, in proportion as it extended, produced, upon what remained of the warfaring band, effects analogous to those which I have pointed out to you. On one hand, the warrior upon whom the chief had conferred the benefice, departed to inhabit it —a new source of isolation and individuality; on the other, this warrior had usually a certain number of men attached to him; or he sought and found men who would come to live with him upon his domain—a new source of inequality. Such were the general effects of the invasion upon the two ancient Germanic societies, the tribe and the wandering band. They became equally disorganized, and entered upon totally different situations, upon totally new relations. In order to bind them among themselves anew, in order to form society anew, and to deduce from that society a government, it became necessary to have recourse to other principles, to other institutions. Dissolved, like Roman society, German society, in like manner, furnished to the society which followed it nothing but wrecks.

I hope that these expressions, *society dissolved, society which perished*, do not mislead you, and that you understand them in

4. Guizot, *Essais sur l'Histoire de France,* pp. 109–11.

their right sense. A society never dissolves itself, but because a new society is fermenting and forming in its bosom, the concealed work is there going on which tends to separate its elements, in order to arrange them under new combinations. Such a disorganization shows that facts are changed, that the relations and dispositions of men are no longer the same; that other principles and other forms are ready to assume the predominance. Thus, in affirming that, in the sixth century, ancient society, Roman as well as German, was dissolved in Gaul by the results of the invasion, we say that, by the same causes, at the same epoch, and upon the same ground, modern society began.

We have no means of explaining or clearly contemplating this first labour; the original sources, the original creation, is profoundly concealed, and does not manifest itself outwardly until later, when it has already made considerable progress. Nevertheless, it is possible to foresee it; and it is important that you should know, at once, what was fermenting and being formed beneath this general dissolution of the two elements of modern society; I will endeavour to give you an idea of this in few words.

The first fact of which we catch a glimpse at this period, is a certain tendency to the development of royalty. Persons have often praised barbarian at the expense of modern royalty, wrongfully, as I think: in the fourth and in the seventeenth centuries this word expresses two institutions, two powers which are profoundly different from each other. There were, indeed, among the barbarians, some germs of hereditary royalty, some traces of a religious character inherent in certain families descended from the first chiefs of the nations, from heroes become gods. There can, however, be no doubt but that choice, election, was the principal source of royalty, and that the character of warlike chiefs predominates in the barbarous kings.

When they were transplanted to the Roman territory, their situation changed. They found there a place which was empty, namely, that of the emperors. Power, titles, and a machine of government with which the barbarians were acquainted, and of which they admired the splendour and soon appreciated the efficacy, were there; they were, of course, strongly tempted to appropriate these advantages. Such, indeed, was the aim of all their efforts. This fact appears everywhere: Clovis, Childebert, Gontran, Chilperic, Clotaire, laboured incessantly to assume the names and to exercise the rights of the Empire; they wished to distribute their dukes and their counts as the emperors had distributed their consuls, their correctors, and their presidents; they tried to reestablish all that system of taxes, enlistment, and administration which had fallen into ruin. In a word, barbaric royalty, narrow and crude as it was, endeavoured to develop itself, and fill, in some measure the enormous frame of imperial royalty.

For a long while the course of things was not favourable to it, and its first attempts were attended with little success; nevertheless, we may see, from the beginning, that something of the imperial royalty will remain, and that the new royalty will by and by gather a portion of that imperial inheritance, the whole of which it desired to appropriate at the first; immediately after the invasion, it became less warlike, more religious, and more politic than it had hitherto been, that is to say, it assumed more of the character of the imperial royalty. Here, if I mistake not, is the first great fact of that labour which was about to give birth to the new society; that fact is not clearly manifest as yet, but glimpses of it are easily to be caught.

The second great fact is the birth of the territorial aristocracy. Property, for a long time after the settlement of the barbarians, seemed uncertain, fluctuating and confused, passing from one hand to another with surprising rapidity. Nevertheless, it is clear that it prepared to become fixed in the same hands, and to regulate itself. Benefices tend to become hereditary; and, in spite of the obstacles which oppose it, the principle of inheritance prevails therein more and more. At the same time there arose between the possessors of the benefices that hierarchical organization which afterwards became the feudal system. We must not transport into the sixth and seventh centuries the feudalism of the thirteenth; nothing like it then existed; the disorder of property and personal relations was infinitely greater than under the feudal system; nevertheless all things concurred, on the one hand, to render property fixed; on the other, to constitute the society of the proprietors according to a certain hierarchy. As we have seen royalty dawning from the end of the sixth century, so, likewise, we may discover, from that period, the dawn of feudalism.

Finally, a third fact also developed during this epoch. I have engaged your attention with the state of the church; you have seen what power it had, and how it was, so to speak, the sole living remnant of Roman society. When the barbarians were established, let us see in what situation the church found itself, or, at least, what that situation soon became. The bishops were, as you know, the natural chiefs of the towns; they governed the people in the interior of each city, they represented them in the presence of the barbarians, they were their magistrates within, and their protectors without. The clergy were therefore deeply rooted in the municipal system, that is to say, in all that remained of Roman society. And they very soon struck root in other directions; the bishops became the counsellors of the barbarous kings; they counselled them upon the conduct which they ought to observe towards the vanquished people, upon the course they ought to take in order to become the heirs of the Roman emperors. They had far more experience and political intelligence than the barbarians, who came fresh from Germany; they had the love of power, they had been accustomed to serve and to profit by it. They were thus the counsellors of the nascent royalty, while they remained the magistrates and patrons of the still surviving municipality.

Behold them connected on the one hand with the people, on the other with thrones. But this was not all; a third position now opened itself to them; they became great proprietors; they entered into that hierarchical organization of manorial property which, as yet, scarcely existed but in tendency; they laboured to occupy, and soon succeeded in occupying, a considerable place therein. So that at this epoch, while yet the new society was in its first rudiments, the church was already connected with all its parts, was everywhere in good repute and powerful; a sure sign that it would be the first to attain dominion; as happened.

Such were the three great facts—obscure as yet, but visible—by which the new social order announced itself, at the end of the sixth and the beginning of the seventh century. It is, I believe, impossible to mistake them; but, in recognising them, we must remember that neither of them had as yet taken the position and the form which it was to retain. All things were still mixed and confused to such a degree, that it must have been impossible for the shrewdest sight to have discerned any of the characteristics of the future. I have already had occasion to say, and in your studies you had opportunities of becoming convinced, that there exists no modern system, no pretension to power, which has not discovered grounds for its legitimacy in these beginnings of our society. Royalty regards itself as the only heir of the Roman empire. The feudal aristocracy asserts that, at that time, it possessed the entire country, men and lands; the towns affirm that they succeeded to all the rights of the Roman municipalities; the clergy, that they then shared all power. This singular epoch has lent itself to all the requirements of party spirit, to all the hypotheses of science; it has furnished arguments and arms to nations, to kings, to grandees, to priests, to liberty as well as to aristocracy, to aristocracy as well as to royalty.

The fact is, it carried all things in its bosom, theocracy, monarchy, oligarchy, republics, mixed constitutions; and all things in a state of confusion which has allowed each to see all that it chose to see therein. The obscure and irregular fermentation of the wrecks of former society, German as well as Roman, and the first labours of their transformation into elements of the new society, constituted the true condition of Gaul during the sixth and seventh centuries, and this is the only character we can assign to it.

Lecture 20

We enter into a second great epoch of the history of French civilization, and as we enter, at the first step, we encounter a great man. Charlemagne was neither the first of his race, nor the author of its elevation. He received an already established power from his father Pepin. I have attempted to make you understand the causes of this revolution and its true character. When Charlemagne became king of the Franks, it was accomplished; he had no need even to defend it. He, however, has given his name to the second dynasty; and the instant one speaks of it, the instant one thinks of it, it is Charlemagne who presents himself before the mind as its founder and chief. Glorious privilege of a great man! No one disputes that Charlemagne had a right to give name to his race and age. The homage paid to him is often blind and undistinguishing; his genius and glory are extolled without discrimination or measure; yet, at the same time, persons repeat, one after another, that he founded nothing, accomplished nothing; that his empire, his laws, all his works, perished with him. And this historical commonplace introduces a crowd of moral commonplaces on the ineffectualness and uselessness of great men, the vanity of their projects, the little trace which they leave in the world, after having troubled it in all directions.

Is this true? Is it the destiny of great men to be merely a burden and a useless wonder to mankind? Their activity so strong, and so brilliant, can it have no lasting result? It costs much to be present at the spectacle; the curtain fallen, will nothing of it remain? Should we regard these powerful and glorious chiefs of a century and a people, merely as a sterile scourge, or at very best, as a burdensome luxury? Charlemagne, in particular, should he be nothing more?

At the first glance, the commonplace might be supposed to be a truth. The victories, conquests, institutions, reforms, projects, all the greatness and glory of Charlemagne, vanished with him; he seemed a meteor suddenly emerging from the darkness of barbarism, to be as suddenly lost and extinguished in that of feudality. There are other such examples in history. The world has more than once seen, we ourselves have seen an empire like it, one which took pleasure in being compared to that of Charlemagne, and had a right so to be compared; we have likewise seen it fall away with a man.

But we must beware of trusting these appearances. To understand the meaning of great events, and measure the agency and influence of great men, we need to look far deeper into the matter.

The activity of a great man is of two kinds; he performs two parts; two epochs may generally be distinguished in his career. First, he understands better than other people the wants of his time; its real, present exigences; what, in the age he lives in, society needs, to enable it to subsist and attain its natural development. He understands these wants better than any other person of his time, and knows better than any other how to wield the powers of society, and direct them skilfully towards the realization of this end. Hence proceed his power and glory; it is in virtue of this, that as soon as he appears he is understood, accepted, followed; that all give their willing aid to the work which he is performing for the benefit of all.

But he does not stop here. When the real wants of his time are in some degree satisfied, the ideas and the will of the great man proceed further. He quits the region of present facts and exigencies; he gives himself up to views in some measure personal to himself; he indulges in combinations more or less vast and specious, but which are not, like his previous labours, founded on the actual state, the common instincts, the determined wishes of society, but are remote and arbitrary. He aspires to extend his activity and influence indefinitely, and to possess the future as he has possessed the present. Here egoism and illusion commence. For some time, on the faith of what he has already done, the great man is followed in his new career; he is believed in and obeyed; men lend themselves to his fancies; his flatterers and his dupes even admire and vaunt them as his sublimest conceptions. The public, however, in whom a mere delusion is never of any long continuance, soon discovers that it is impelled in a direction in which it has no desire to move. At first the great man had enlisted his high intelligence and powerful will in the service of the general feeling and wish; he now seeks to employ the public force in the service of his individual ideas and desires; he is attempting things which he alone wishes or understands. Hence disquietude first, and then uneasiness; for a time he is still followed, but sluggishly and reluctantly; next he is censured and complained of; finally, he is abandoned and falls; and all which he alone had planned and desired, all the merely personal and arbitrary part of his work, perishes with him.

I shall avoid no opportunity of borrowing from our age the torch which it offers, in this instance, in order to enlighten a time so distant and obscure. The fate and name of Napoleon at present belong to history. I shall not feel the least embarrassed in speaking of it, and speaking of it freely.*

Every one knows that at the time when he seized the power in France, the dominant, imperious want of our country was security—without, national independence; inwardly, civil life. In the revolutionary troubles, the external and internal destiny, the state and society, were equally compromised. To replace the new France in the European confederation, to make her avowed and accepted by the other states, and to constitute her within in a peaceable and regular manner—to put her, in a word, into the possession of independence and order, the only pledges of a long future, this was the desire, the general thought of the country. Napoleon understood and accomplished it.

This finished, or nearly so, Napoleon proposed to himself a thousand others: potent in combinations, and of an ardent imagination, egoistical and thoughtful, machinator and poet, he, as it were, poured out his activity in arbitrary and gigantic projects, children of his own—solitary, foreign to the real wants of our time, and of our France. She followed him for some time, and at great cost, in this path which she had not selected; a day came when she would follow no further, and the emperor found himself alone, and the empire vanished, and all things returned to their proper condition, to their natural tendency.

---

* This curiously apologetic way of introducing the name of Napoleon must be understood in the context of Restoration politics. In the year 1828, with Charles X on the throne, the subject of Napoleon was still a very delicate one. Teaching in a national university system from which he had already been purged once before, Guizot had to be careful. His mention of Napoleon, which was in fact an act of political and intellectual courage, created a sensation in the audience and was much commented on at the time.—EDITOR.

It is an analogous fact which the reign of Charlemagne offers us at the ninth century. Despite the immense difference of time, situation, form, even groundwork, the general phenomenon is similar: these two parts of a great man, these two epochs of his career, are found in Charlemagne as in Napoleon. Let us endeavour to state them.

Here I encounter a difficulty which has long pre-occupied me, and which I do not hope to have completely surmounted. At the commencement of the course, I engaged to give you a general history of France. I have not recounted events to you; I have sought only general results, the concatenation of causes and effects, the progress of civilization, concealed under the external scenes of history; as regards the scenes themselves, I had taken it for granted that you know them. Hitherto I have cared little to know if you had taken this precaution; under the Merovingian race, events, properly so called, are of rare occurrence—so monotonous, that it is less necessary to regard them closely: general facts only are important, and they may, up to a certain point, be brought to light and understood without an exact knowledge of the details. Under the reign of Charlemagne, it is entirely different: wars, political vicissitudes of all kinds, are numerous and brilliant; they occupy an important place, and general facts are concealed far behind the special facts which occupy the front of the scene. History, properly so called, envelops and covers the history of civilization. The latter will not be clear to you unless the former is presented to you; I cannot give you an account of events, and yet you require to know them.

. . . .

Three essential characteristics appear in Charlemagne: he may be considered under three principal points of view: first, as a warrior and a conqueror; second, as an administrator and legislator; third, as a protector of sciences, letters, arts, of intellectual development in general. He exercised a great power, outwardly by force, inwardly by government and laws; he desired to act, and in fact did act, upon mankind itself, upon the human mind as upon society. I shall endeavour to make you understand him in these three respects, by presenting to you . . . the facts which relate to him, and from which the history of civilization may be deduced. . . . [There were], in all, fifty-three expeditions, namely,

1 against the Aquitani
18 against the Saxons
5 against the Lombards
7 against the Arabs of Spain
1 against the Thuringians
4 against the Avares
2 against the Bretons
1 against the Bavarians
4 against the Slavonians beyond the Elbe
5 against the Saracens in Italy
3 against the Danes
2 against the Greeks

Without counting numerous other small expeditions, of which no distinct and positive monuments are left.

From this table alone it is clearly seen that these wars did not the least resemble those of the first race; they are not the dissensions of tribe against tribe, of chief against chief; expeditions undertaken with a view of establishment or pillage; they are systematic and political wars, inspired by an intention of government, commanded by a certain necessity.

What is this system? What is the meaning of these expeditions? You have seen various German nations—Goths, Burgundians, Franks, Lombards, etc.—established upon the Roman territory. Of all these tribes or confederations, the Franks were the strongest, and occupied the central position in the new establishment. They were not united among themselves by any political tie; they incessantly made war. Still, in some respects, and whether they knew it or not, their situation was similar, and their interests common.

You have seen that, from the beginning of the eighth century, these new masters of western Europe, the Roman-Germans, were pressed on the northeast, along the Rhine and the Danube, by new German, Slavonian, and other tribes proceeding to the same territory; on the south by the Arabs spread on all the coasts of the Mediterranean; and that thus a two-fold movement of invasion menaced with imminent fall the states which were just rising out of the ruins of the Roman empire.

Now let us see what was the work of Charlemagne in this situation: he rallied against this two-fold invasion, against the new assailants who crowded upon the various frontiers of the empire, all the recently established inhabitants of his territory, ancient or modern, Romans or Germans. Follow the course of his wars. He begins by definitively subduing, on one side, the Roman population, who still attempted to free themselves from the barbarian yoke, as the Aquitani in the south of Gaul; on the other, the later-arrived German population, the establishment of whom was not consummated, as the Lombards in Italy, etc. He snatched them from the various impulses which animated them, united them all under the domination of the Franks, and turned them against the two-fold invasion, which, on the northeast and south, menaced all alike. Seek a dominant fact which shall be common to all the wars of Charlemagne; reduce them all to their simple expression: you will see that their true meaning is, that they are the struggle of the inhabitants of the ancient empire, conquering or conquered, Romans or Germans, against the new invaders.

They are thus essentially defensive wars, brought about by a triple interest of territory, race, and religion. The interest of territory was especially prominent in expeditions against the nations of the right bank of the Rhine, for the Saxons and Danes were Germans, like the Franks and the Lombards: there were Frankish tribes among them, and some learned men think that many pretended Saxons may have been only Franks, established in Germany. There was, therefore, no diversity of race; it was merely in defence of the territory that war took place. The interest of territory and the interest of race were united against the wandering nations beyond the Elbe, or on the banks of the Danube, against the Slavonians and the Avares. Against the Arabs, who inundated the south of Gaul, there was interest of territory, of race, and of religion, all together. Thus did the various causes of war variously combine; but, whatever might be the combinations, it was always the German Christians and Romans, who defended their nationality, their territory, and their religion against nations of another origin or creed, who sought a soil to conquer. All their wars have this character—all are derived from this triple necessity.

Charlemagne had in no way reduced this necessity to a general idea or theory; but he understood and faced it: great men rarely do otherwise. He faced it by conquest; defensive war took the offensive form; he carried the struggle into the territory of nations who wished to invade his own; he laboured to reduce the foreign races, to extirpate the hostile creeds. Hence arose his mode of government, and the foundation of his empire: offensive war and conquest required this vast and formidable unity.

At the death of Charlemagne, the conquests cease, the unity disappears, the empire is dismembered and falls to pieces; but is it true that nothing remained, that the warlike exploits of Charlemagne were absolutely sterile, that he achieved nothing, founded nothing? There is but one way to resolve this question; it is, to ask ourselves if, after Charlemagne, the countries which he had governed found themselves in the same situation as before; if the two-fold invasions which, on the north and on the south, menaced their territory, their religion, and their race, recommenced after being thus suspended; if the Saxons, Slavonians, Avares, Arabs, still kept the possessors of the Roman soil in perpetual disturbance and anxiety. Evidently it was not so; true, the empire of Charlemagne was broken up, but into separate states, which arose as so many barriers at all points where there was still danger. Up to the time of Charlemagne, the frontiers of Germany, Spain, and Italy were in continual fluctuation; no constituted public force had attained a permanent shape; he was compelled to be constantly transporting himself from one end to the other of his dominions, in order to oppose to the invaders the mobile and temporary force of his armies. After him, the scene is changed; real political barriers, states more or less organized, but real and durable, arose; the kingdoms of Lorraine, of Germany, Italy, the two Burgundies, Navarre, date from that time; and in spite of the vicissitudes of their destiny, they subsist, and suffice to oppose effectual resistance to the invading movement. Accordingly, that movement ceases, or continues only in the form of maritime expeditions, destructive to the points which they reach, but which cannot be made with great masses of men, nor produce great results.

Although, therefore, the vast domination of Charlemagne disappeared with him, it is not true that he founded nothing; he founded all the states which sprung from the dismemberment of his empire. His conquests entered into new combinations, but his wars attained their end: the foundation of the work subsisted, although its form was changed. It is thus that the action of great men is in general exercised. Charlemagne, as an administrator and legislator, appears to us under the same aspect.

His government is more difficult to sum up than his wars. Much has been said of the order which he introduced into his states, of the great system of administration which he attempted to found. I indeed believe he attempted it, but he was very far from succeeding in his attempt: despite the unity, despite the activity of his thought and of his power, the disorder around him was immense and invincible; he repressed it for a moment on one point, but the evil reigned wherever his terrible will did not come; and when it had passed, recommenced the moment it was at a distance. . . .

Now, I here reintroduce the question which I raised earlier concerning the wars of Charlemagne. Is it true, is it possible, that of this government, so active and vigorous, nothing remained—that all disappeared with Charlemagne—that he founded nothing for the internal consolidation of society?

What fell with Charlemagne, what rested upon him alone, and could not survive him, was the central government. After continuing some time under Louis le Debonnaire and Charles le Chauve, but with less and less energy and influence, the general assemblies, the *missi dominici,* the whole machinery of the central and sovereign administration, disappeared. Not so the local government, the dukes, counts, vicars, centeniers, beneficiaries, vassals, who held authority in their several neighbourhoods under the rule of Charlemagne. Before his time, the disorder had been as great in each locality as in the commonwealth generally; landed properties, magistracies were incessantly changing hands; no local positions or influences possessed any steadiness or permanence. During the forty-six years of his government, these influences had time to become rooted in the same soil, in the same families; they had acquired stability, the first condition of the progress which was destined to render them independent and hereditary, and make them the elements of the feudal regime. Nothing, certainly, less resembles feudalism than the sovereign unity which Charlemagne aspired to establish; yet he is the true founder of feudal society! It was he who, by arresting the external invasions, and repressing, to a certain extent, the internal disorders, gave to local situations, fortunes, influences, sufficient time to take real possession of the country. After him, his general government perished like his conquests; his unity of authority like his extended empire; but as the empire was broken into separate states, which acquired a vigorous and durable life, so the central sovereignty of Charlemagne resolved itself into a multitude of local sovereignties, to which a portion of the strength of his government had been imparted, and which had acquired under its shelter the conditions requisite for reality and durability; so that in this second point of view, in his civil as well as military capacity, if we look beyond first appearances, he accomplished and founded much.

I might show him to you accomplishing and leaving analogous results in the church; there also he arrested dissolution, until his time always increasing: there also he gave society time to rest, to acquire some consistency and to enter upon new paths. But time presses: I have yet at present to speak of the influence of Charlemagne in the intellectual order, and of the place occupied by his reign in the history of the human mind; scarcely shall I be able to point out the principal features.

It is more difficult here than anywhere else to sum up facts and present them in a table. The acts of Charlemagne in favour of moral civilization form no entirety, manifest no systematic form; they are isolated, scattered acts; at times the foundation of certain schools, at times measures taken for the improvement of ecclesiastical offices, and the progress of the knowledge which depends on them; also general recommendations for the instruction of priests and laymen; but most frequently an eager protection of distinguished men, and a particular care to surround himself with them. There is nothing systematic, nothing than can be estimated by the mere juxtaposition of figures and words. I wish, however, with a touch, and without entering into details, to place before you some facts which may give you an idea of that kind of action of Charlemagne, of which more is said than is known. It appears to me that a table of the celebrated men who were born and died under his reign—that is, of the celebrated men whom he employed, and those whom he made— would tend efficiently towards this end; this body of names and of works may be taken as a decided proof, and even as a correct estimate of the influence of Charlemagne over minds.

. . . .

At this point Guizot presented a "Table of the celebrated men born or who died under the reign of Charlemagne" starting with Alcuin and concluding with Duns Scotus, in which he included the major works of 23 figures of the ninth century. The list covered four pages in the original text.

Surely such a table is sufficient to prove that at this epoch, and under the star of Charlemagne, intellectual activity was great. Recal to your minds the times from whence we set out; call to mind from the sixth to the eighth century, we had great difficulty in finding any names, any works; that sermons and legends were almost the only monuments which we encountered. Here, on the contrary, you see reappear, and that almost at once, philosophical, historical, philological, and critical writings; you find yourself in the presence of study and science—that is to say, of pure and disinterested intellectual activity, of the real movement of mind. I shall soon discuss with you, in a more detailed manner, the men and the works I have just named, and you will see that they truly commence a new epoch, and merit the most serious attention.

Now, I ask, have we a right to say that Charlemagne has founded nothing, that nothing remains of his works? I have merely given you a glimpse, as in a transient panorama, of their principal results; and yet their permanence is thus shown therein as clearly as their grandeur. It is evident that, by his wars, by his government, and by his action upon minds, Charlemagne has left the most profound traces; that if many of the things he did perished with him, many others have survived him; that western Europe, in a word, left his hands entirely different from what it was when he received it.

What is the general, dominant character of this change, of the crisis over which Charlemagne presided?

Take in at one view, that history of the civilization in France under the Merovingian kings which we have just studied; it is the history of a constant, universal decline. In individual man as in society, in religious society as in civil society, everywhere we have seen anarchy and weakness extending itself more and more; we have seen everything become enervated and dissolved, both institutions and ideas, what remained of the Roman world and what the Germans had introduced. Up to the eighth century, nothing of what had formerly been could continue to exist; nothing which seemed to dawn could succeed in fixing itself.

Dating from Charlemagne, the face of things changes; decay is arrested, progress recommences. Yet for a long period the disorder will be enormous, the progress partial, but little visible, or often suspended. This matters not: we shall no more encounter those long ages of disorganization, of always increasing intellectual sterility: through a thousand sufferings, a thousand interruptions, we shall see power and life revive in man and in society. Charlemagne marks the limit at which the dissolution of the ancient Roman and barbarian world is consummated, and where really begins the formation of modern Europe, of the new world. It was under his reign, and as it were under his hand, that the shock took place by which European society, turning right round, left the paths of destruction to enter those of creation.

If you would know truly what perished with him, and what,

independently of the changes of form and appearance, is the portion of his works which did not survive him, if I mistake not, it is this:

In opening this course, the first fact which presented itself to your eyes, the first spectacle at which we were present, was that of the old Roman empire struggling with the barbarians. The latter triumphed; they destroyed the Empire. In combating it, they respected it; no sooner had they destroyed it, than they aspired to reproduce it. All the great barbaric chiefs, Ataulf, Theodoric, Euric, Clovis, showed themselves full of the desire of succeeding to the Roman emperors, of adapting their tribes to the frame of that society which they had conquered. None of them succeeded therein; none of them contrived to resuscitate the name and forms of the empire, even for a moment; they were overcome by that torrent of invasion, by that general course of dissolution which carried all things before it; barbarism, incessantly extended and renewed itself, but the Roman empire was still present to all imaginations; it was between barbarism and Roman civilization that, in all minds of any compass at all, the question lay.

It was still in this position when Charlemagne appeared; he also, he especially nursed the hope of resolving it, as all the great barbarians who went before him had wished to resolve it —that is to say, by reconstituting the empire. What Diocletian, Constantine, Julian, had attempted to maintain with the old wrecks of the Roman legions, that is, the struggle against the invasion, Charlemagne undertook to do with Franks, Goths, and Lombards: he occupied the same territory; he proposed to himself the same design. Without, and almost always on the same frontiers, he maintained the same struggle; within, he restored its name to the empire, he attempted to bring back the unity of its administration; he placed the imperial crown upon his head. Strange contrast! He dwelt in Germany; in war, in national assemblies, in the interior of his family, he acted as a German; his personal nature, his language, his manners, his external form, his way of living, were German; and not only were they German, but he did not desire to change them. "He always wore," says Einhard, "the habit of his fathers, the habit of the Franks. . . . Foreign costumes, however rich, he scorned, and suffered no one to be clothed with them. Twice only during the stay which he made at Rome, first at the request of pope Adrian, and then at the solicitation of Leo, the successor of that pontiff, he consented to wear the long tunic, the chalybs, and the Roman sandal." He was, in fact, completely German, with the exception of the ambition of his thought; it was towards the Roman empire, towards Roman civilization that it tended; that was what he desired to establish, with barbarians as his instruments.

This was, in him, a piece of egoism and illusion; and it was in this that he failed. The Roman empire, and its unity, were invincibly repugnant to the new distribution of the population, the new relations, the new moral condition of mankind; Roman civilization could only enter as a transformed element into the new world which was preparing. This idea, this aspiration of Charlemagne, was not a public idea, nor a public want; all that he did for its accomplishment perished with him. Yet even of this vain endeavor something remained. The name of the western empire, revived by him, and the rights which were thought to be attached to the title of emperor, resumed their place among the elements of history, and were for several centuries longer an object of ambition, an influencing principle of events. Even, therefore, in the purely egoistical and ephemeral portion of his operations, it cannot be said that the ideas of Charlemagne were absolutely sterile, nor totally devoid of duration.

. . . .

Lecture 30

We are come to the termination of this course. I would now undertake to review the whole, noticing the chief and predominant facts, which appear to me to result from it, and which characterize, during that long period, the history of our civilization.

I gave at the commencement a description of Gaul prior to the German invasion, at the end of the fourth and the beginning of the fifth century, under the Roman administration. We considered its social and intellectual state in civil and in religious society.

After I had thus made you acquainted with Roman Gaul, I took you across the Rhine. I directed your view towards Germany, prior to the invasion also, and in the infancy of its institutions and manners.

The Germans having invaded Gaul, we examined what were the consequences, whether immediate or probable, of this first contact of Roman with barbarous society. I drew your attention to their abrupt and violent collision.

From the sixth century to the middle of the eighth, we followed the progressive amalgamation of the two societies. In the civil order, we saw barbarous laws arise, and the Roman law perpetuated. I laboured to explain the character, generally misunderstood, in my opinion, of these first rudiments of modern legislation. We passed from thence to religious society; and considering it in its double element, priests and monks, the secular and regular clergy, we gave an account both of its relations with civil society, and of its own internal organization.

Such has been our progress, from the sixth to the eighth century, in the history of the social state; but we had also to consider the intellectual state of Frankish Gaul at the same period; we searched both in sacred and profane literature, and we endeavoured to ascertain their distinctive character and reciprocal influence.

We thus arrived at the great crisis which signalized the middle of the eighth century, the fall of the Merovingian kings and the accession of the Carolingians; I attempted to characterise this revolution, and to assign its real causes.

The Carolingian revolution being comprehended, the reign of Charlemagne especially occupied us; I considered its events, properly so called, its laws, its influence on men's minds. I desired particularly to distinguish that which he attempted, and that which he effectually accomplished, that which perished with him, and that which survived him.

After the death of Charlemagne, the rapid dissolution of his vast empire struck our attention; we endeavoured to take an account of it, and to make known to ourselves the progress as well as the causes of that phenomenon; we pursued it, on the one hand, in its events, on the other, in its laws; we inquired into the political and the legislative revolution, which, from the death of Charlemagne to the accession of Hugh Capet, led to the feudal system.

To this history of civil society, from the middle of the eighth to the end of the tenth century, succeeded the history of religious society at the same period, that is to say, the history of the Gallo-Frankish church, considered firstly in itself, that is, in its national existence; secondly, externally, in its relations with the government of the universal church, that is, the papacy.

Lastly, always remaining true to the essential idea of civilization, and always mindful to consider it under its double aspect, with respect to society and the human soul, the intellectual state of Frankish Gaul, from the eighth to the tenth century, was our concluding study. We saw ancient philosophy expire, and ecclesiastical theology arise: and we determined with some precision the profane and the sacred elements which have contributed to the modern development of the human mind.

Such is the vast career, the steps of which we have followed; such is the immense variety of objects which have passed under your view. Certainly; I have not arbitrarily or from mere fancy led you into this vast expanse, causing you continually to change the point of view and subject. The very nature of our study rigidly exacted it: the history of civilization can only be given at this expense.

This history is a new work, scarcely more than sketched. The idea of it has been first conceived in the eighteenth century, and it is in our own times, under our own eyes, that we see its true fulfilment begin. It is not, however, only in the present day that history is made a study of; not only facts, but their connexion and their causes, have been studied; philosophers and scholars have equally laboured in this field. But up to the present times, we may say, the study of history, both philosophical and scholastic, has been partial and limited; political, legislative, religious, and literary histories have been written; learned researches have been made, brilliant reflections have been presented on the destination and development of laws, manners, sciences, letters, arts, of all the works of human activity; but they have never been regarded together, at one view, in their intimate and fertile union. And wherever there has been an attempt to grasp at general results, or a desire to form a complete idea of the development of human nature, it is altogether on a partial foundation that the edifice has been raised. The *Discours sur l'Histoire Universelle,* and the *Esprit des Lois,* are glorious essays on the history of civilization; but who cannot see that Bossuet has almost exclusively confined his search to religious creeds, and Montesquieu to political institutions? These two geniuses have thus narrowed the horizon of their view. What are we to say concerning minds of an inferior order? It is evident that, scholastic or philosophical, history up to the present day has never really been general; it has never at one time followed man in all the careers wherein his activity exhibits itself. And yet the history of civilization is possible only under this condition; it is a summary of all histories; it requires them all for materials, for the fact which it relates is the summary of all other facts. An immense variety, without doubt; yet do not think that unity is destroyed thereby. There is unity in the life of a people, in the life of the human race, just as there is in that of an individual; but, as in fact all the circumstances of destiny and activity in an individual contribute to form his character, which is one and the same, so the unity and history of a people must have for its basis all the variety of its entire existence.

It is, then, wholly of necessity, and driven by the very nature of our subject, that we have gone over the political, ecclesiastical, legislative, philosophical, and literary history of Frankish Gaul, from the fifth to the tenth century: if we have arrived at any precise and positive results, we owe them to this method. You may have observed, especially, how much we have been enlightened by placing civil and religious society continually in juxtaposition, both of which are incomprehensible if we leave them separate. Let us now endeavour to understand clearly these results, which we have obtained, I think, with some certainty; let us endeavour to determine the point of departure of Gaulish civilization in the fifth century, and the point at which it had arrived at the end of the tenth.

You are aware that the essential, fundamental elements of modern civilization in general, and of French civilization in particular, reduce themselves to three: the Roman world, the Christian world, and the Germanic world; antiquity, Christianity, and barbarism. Let us see what transformation these three elements underwent between the fifth and tenth centuries, what they became in this last period, and what remained of them in the civilization of that period.

I commence with the Roman element. I wish to cast a slight glance at what the Roman world has furnished to France, under a social and an intellectual point of view; and we must discover what remained of it in the tenth century, in society and in mind.

Under the first point of view—that is to say, the influence of Roman on Gallo-Frankish society, from the fifth to the tenth century, the result of our inquiries is, that the Roman world, when it broke up, bequeathed to the future the wrecks of three great facts—first, central sole power, empire, and absolute royalty; second, imperial administration, government of provinces by the delegates of the central power; third, the municipal system, the primitive mode of existence of Rome and most of the countries which had successively formed the Roman empire.

What are the changes which these three facts underwent between the fifth and tenth centuries?

1. With respect to the central power, sole and sovereign, it perished, as you know, in the invasion; in vain some of the first barbarous kings tried to restore it, and to exercise it to their advantage; they were baffled in the attempt; imperial despotism was too complex an instrument for their rude hands. At the fall of the Merovingians, Charlemagne attempted to revive it, and to use it; the attempt had a momentary success; central power reappeared: but, after Charlemagne, as after the first invasion, it broke asunder, and was lost in the chaos. Nothing, surely, less resembled imperial power than the royalty of Hugh Capet. Some

remembrance of it, nevertheless, lay in the minds of men: Empire had left behind it profound traces. The names of emperor, imperial authority, sovereign majesty, had still a certain virtue, and recalled a certain type of government; these were now only words, yet words still powerful, and sufficient to produce deeds if the occasion offered. Such was the state in which, at about the end of the tenth century, this first legacy of the Roman world manifested itself.

2. The imperial administration underwent very nearly the same vicissitudes; the barbarous chiefs tried to use it, but with no better success. This mode of governing the several parts of a state was too complicated, too exact; it required the concurrence of too many agents, and intelligence of too developed a kind; the administrative machine of the empire was speedily deranged, if I may so speak, in the hands of its new masters. Charlemagne attempted to give it regularity and motion; it was a necessary consequence of the restoration of central power; and, by an analogous consequence, together with the central power of Charlemagne, perished also the provincial administration, which he had, as well as he could, reconstructed. After the complete dissolution of the new empire, however, when the feudal system had prevailed, and when the holders of fiefs had succeeded the ancient delegates of the sovereign, there remained, in the thoughts of the people and of the possessors of fiefs themselves, some recollection of their origin. That origin, I have been careful to point out to you, was of a double kind; the fiefs originated on the one hand in benefices, or lands conceded, whether by the sovereign or by other chiefs; on the other hand, in offices or appointments of dukes, counts, viscounts, centeniers, etc., that is, of officers, invested by the sovereign with local administration. This second origin was not, therefore, absolutely effaced from memory: it was vaguely remembered that these lords—now sovereigns, or nearly so—had formerly been delegates of a greater sovereign: that they had been the representatives of a general and superior power; and that instead of being then proprietors of the sovereignty on their own account, they were only magistrates or administrators in the name of another,

and that the portion of that sovereignty which they possessed might have been usurped from this sole and remote monarch, who was now lost sight of. This idea, which pervades the course of our history, and which has been the favourite theory of jurisconsults, and other writers upon public laws, is clearly a wreck of the ancient Roman administration—an echo which had survived the ruin of that vast and learned hierarchy. Such is all that we discern of it towards the end of the tenth century; but a potent germ of life lay buried under this remembrance.

3. The third fact bequeathed by the Roman to the modern world is the municipal system. You know what the state of towns was, at the end of the tenth century, into what depopulation, decay, and distress they had fallen. Nevertheless, so much as still remained of internal administration, especially in southern Gaul, was Roman in its origin; here was still some shadow of the curia, of consuls, duumvirs, and other ancient municipal magistrates. The Roman law presided over the acts of civil life, donations, contracts, etc. Municipal magistrates, deprived of their political importance, had become in a manner simple notaries who registered civil acts, and preserved records of them. A new municipal system of a different principle and character, the system of the communes of the middle age, was about to raise itself upon the ruins of the Roman municipality; but as yet it had scarcely begun to dawn; and, in general, all that we can discern as existing in the tenth century, of distinct administration in towns, is Roman. Let us now see what remained of Greco-Roman antiquity under an intellectual point of view, what the mind of the tenth century still retained of it. I cannot here enter into detail; I do not mean to search, in the theological tenets and popular opinions of that time, for those which were allied to Roman philosophy and opinions; I merely wish to characterize, in its most general features, the intellectual heritage which ancient society has bequeathed to us, and the condition of it at the end of the tenth century. An important fact, and far too little noticed, in my opinion, first strikes me; it is that the principle of liberty of thought, the principle of all philosophy, reason being its own point of departure and guide, is an idea essentially the daughter

of antiquity, an idea which modern society holds from Greece and Rome. We have received it evidently neither from Christianity nor from Germany; for it was included in neither of those elements of our civilization. It strongly prevailed on the contrary in Greco-Roman civilization: there is its true origin; there the most valuable legacy which antiquity has left to the modern world: the legacy which has never been absolutely set aside and without value; for you have seen the idea which is the mother of philosophy, namely, the right of reason to start from itself, animating the works and life of Duns Scotus, and the principle of liberty of thought still prevailing in the ninth century, in face of the principle of authority. A second intellectual legacy of Roman civilization to ours, is the body of beautiful works of antiquity. In spite of the general ignorance, in spite of the corruption of language, ancient literature has always been presented to the mind as a worthy object of study, of imitation, and of admiration, and as the type of the beautiful. The influence of this idea was very great, you are aware, from the fourteenth to the sixteenth century; it has never been lost completely, and in the eighth, ninth, and tenth centuries, we have encountered it at every step.

The philosophical and the classical spirit, the principle of liberty of thought and the model of the beautiful, are the gifts which the Roman has transmitted to the modern world, and which still survived in the intellectual order at the end of the tenth century.

I pass to the Christian element; I desire to ascertain what was its condition at this epoch, and what effects it had produced.

You have followed the changes of Christian society from the fifth to the tenth century; in its birth you have seen the origin and model of all the modes of organization, of all the systems which subsequently appeared; therein you have recognised the democratic, aristocratic, and monarchical principles; you have seen the lay community one time associated with the ecclesiastical community, and at another, excluded from all participation in power: all the combinations, in short, of religious social organization offered themselves to your view. During the period which we have considered, the aristocratic system prevailed;

episcopacy became soon the ruling and almost the sole power. At the end of the tenth century, the papacy raised itself above episcopacy, the monarchical overcame the aristocratic principle. Under a social point of view, therefore, the state of the church at that time reduced itself to two facts: the preponderance of the church in the state, and the preponderance of papacy in the church. Such are the results which at this epoch we may regard as established.

From an intellectual point of view, it is more difficult, and still more important, to render to ourselves an account of what the Christian element had at that time furnished to modern civilization. Let me here ascend a step higher, and compare for a moment what has passed in antiquity with that which passed in Christian society.

Spiritual and temporal order, human thought and human society, developed themselves amongst the ancients parallel rather than together, not without an intimate correspondence, but without exercising a prompt and direct influence one upon the other. I will explain myself: without speaking of the earlier times of philosophy, but taking it at the epoch of its highest glory, Plato, Aristotle, and most of the philosophers, whether of Grecian, or more latterly of Greco-Roman antiquity, had full liberty of thought, or nearly so. The State, public policy interfered but little with their labours to cramp them and give them a particular tendency. They, on their part, concerned themselves little about politics, nor cared much to influence immediately and decisively the society in which they lived: undoubtedly they exerted that indirect and remote influence which belongs to all great human thought cast into the midst of mankind; but the ancient philosophers made few pretensions to the action or direct influence of thought over exterior facts, of pure knowledge over society; they were not essentially reformers; they aspired to govern neither the private conduct of individuals, nor society in general. The ruling character, in one word, of intellectual development in antiquity, is liberty of thought and its practical disinterestedness; it is a development essentially rational and scientific. Upon the triumph of Christianity in the Roman world, the character of intellectual development changed: that which was philosophy became religion; philosophy was enfeebled more and more; religion usurped the understanding; the form of thought was essentially religious. It aspired from that time to much more power over human affairs; the end of thought, in religion, is essentially practical; it aspires to govern individuals, frequently even society. The spiritual order, it is true, continued to be separate from the temporal order; the government of nations was not directly and completely committed to the clergy; its lay society and ecclesiastic society developed themselves independently. Nevertheless, the spiritual penetrated much further into the temporal order than it had done in ancient times; and whereas liberty of thought, and its purely scientific activity, had been, in Greece and Rome, the ruling character of intellectual development; its practical activity and pretension to power, was the distinguishing trait of intellectual development amongst Christian nations.

From this there resulted another change, which was not of less importance. In proportion as human thought, under the religious form, aspired to more power over the conduct of mankind, and the fate of states, it lost its liberty. Instead of remaining open and free to competition, as amongst the ancients, intellectual society was organized and governed; instead of philosophical schools, there was a church. It was at the cost of its independence that thought purchased empire; it no longer developed itself in all directions, and according to its simple impulse; but it acted forcibly and immediately on mankind and on societies.

This fact is important; it has exercised a decisive influence on the history of modern Europe, so decisive, as still to subsist and to manifest itself around us in our own days. The religious form has ceased to hold exclusive dominion in human thought; scientific and rational development has recommenced; and yet what is come to pass? Have philosophers thought, have they wished to treat pure knowledge in the same manner as those of antiquity have done? No: human reason aspires in the present day to govern and reform societies after its own conceptions, to rule the exterior world according to general principles; that is to say, thought, again become philosophical, has preserved the pretensions it held under the religious form; with this immense difference, it is true, that it would unite the liberty of thought with its power, and that even whilst it tries to take possession of societies, to govern them, and place the power in the hands of intelligence, it does not wish intelligence to be organized nor subjected to forms and a legal yoke. It is in the alliance of intellectual liberty, as it shone in antiquity, with intellectual power, as it showed itself in Christian societies, that we find the great and original character of modern civilization; and it is without doubt, in the bosom of the revolution effected by Christianity in the relations of the spiritual and temporal orders of thought and of the exterior world, that this new revolution has taken its origin and its first point of support.

At the epoch to which we are now come, at the end of the tenth century, the double fact which characterizes the first revolution, I mean the abdication of the liberty of the human intellect, and the increase of its social power, was already consummated. From the tenth century, you observe spiritual society aspiring to the government of temporal society, that is, announcing that thought has a right to govern the world; and, at the same time, you observe thought subjected to the rules, the yoke of the church, and organized according to certain laws. These are the two most considerable results of the vicissitudes which intellectual order has suffered from the fifth to the tenth century, the two principal facts which the Christian element has thrown into modern civilization.

We come to the third primitive element of this civilization, the Germanic world or barbarism. Let us see what modern society had already received from it in the tenth century.

When we considered the condition of the Germans prior to the invasion, two facts especially, two forms of social organization, struck us:

1. The tribe formed of all the proprietary chiefs of family, governing itself by an assembly, where justice was rendered, and where public business was transacted—in one word, by the common deliberation of free men; a system very incomplete and

precarious, without doubt, in such a state of social relations and manners, but of which, however, glimpses may be caught of the principal rudiments.

2. Side by side with the tribe, we have met with the warlike band, a society where the individual lived in so free a manner, that he could adopt it or reject it, according to his taste, and where the social principle was not equality of free men, and common deliberation, but the patronage of a chief towards his companions, who served him, and lived at his expense, that is to say, aristocratic and military subordination; words which ill answer to the idea which must be formed of a band of barbarians, but which describe the system of social organization which was about to issue from it.

Such are the two principles, or rather the two germs of principles, which Germany has furnished in the earliest times, to modern society in its nascent state. The principle of common deliberation of free men no more existed in the Roman world, unless in the bosom of the municipal system; it was the Germans who restored it to the political order. The principle of aristocratic patronage, combined with a large portion of liberty, had become equally foreign to Roman society. Both the one and the other of these elements of our social organization are of German origin.

From the fifth to the tenth century they underwent great changes. At the end of this period, the assemblies, or government, by the voice of common deliberation, had disappeared; in fact, there remained scarcely any trace of the ancient *mâls*, fields of *Mars* and *Mai*, or Germanic courts. The remembrance, however, of national assemblies, the right of free men to join together, to deliberate and transact their business together, resided in the minds of men as a primitive tradition and a thing which might again come about. It was with the ancient German assemblies as with imperial sovereignty: neither the one nor the other any longer existed; government by the voice of free deliberation and absolute power had equally fallen, yet without absolutely perishing. They were germs buried under immense heaps of ruins, but which yet might one day reappear and be fruitful. Such was, in fact, what really happened.

With respect to the patronage of the chief towards his companions, the acquisition of large domains and the territorial life had much changed this relation of the ancient Germans. We can no more find, in any degree worth mentioning, the same liberty which used to reign in the wandering band. Some had received benefices, and were settled in them; others had continued to live around their chief in his house and at his table. The chief had become eminently powerful; there was introduced into this little society much more inequality and fixedness. Nevertheless, although the aristocratic principle and the inequality which accompanies it, and which even constitutes it, had assumed a great development, they had not destroyed all the ancient relation between the chief and his companions. The inequality did not draw servility after it; and the society which resulted therefrom, and with which we will occupy ourselves more in detail hereafter, the feudal society reposed, for those at least who composed part of it, that is, the proprietors of fiefs, upon the principles of right and liberty.

In the tenth century, and from the social point of view, the Germanic element then had furnished to modern civilization in its nascent state, on the one hand, the remembrance of national assemblies, and the right of free men to govern themselves in common; on the other hand, certain ideas, certain sentiments of right and liberty implanted in the bosom of an entirely aristocratic organization.

From the moral point of view, although eminent writers have strongly insisted upon what modern Europe owes to the Germans, their assertions seem to me vague and too general; they make no distinction of epoch or country; and I think that, in western Europe, especially in France, the energetic sentiment of individual independence is the most important, I would willingly say the only great moral legacy which ancient Germany has transmitted to us.

There was, in the tenth century, a national German literature, consisting of songs and popular traditions which hold a high place in the literary history of Germany, and which have exerted a great influence on its manners. But the part played by these traditions, and by all primitive German literature, in the intellectual development of France, has been very limited and fugitive; this is the reason why I have not entered upon it with you, though this literature is positively full of originality and interest.

Such was the state of the three great elements of modern civilization in the tenth century; such are the changes, social and moral, which Roman antiquity, Christianity, and barbarism have experienced on our soil.

From thence flow, if I mistake not, two general facts, two great results, which it is necessary to exhibit.

The work of M. de Savigny on the history of Roman law, after the fall of the Empire, has changed the face of the science; he has proved that the Roman law had not perished; that, notwithstanding great modifications, without doubt, it was transmitted from the fifth to the fifteenth century, and had always continued to form a considerable part of the legislation of the west.

If I am not mistaken, the facts which I have laid before your view, in this course, have generalized this result. It follows, I think, evidently, that not only in municipal institutions and civil laws, as M. de Savigny has proved, but in political order and philosophy, in literature and all departments, in a word, of social and intellectual life, Roman civilization was transmitted far beyond the date of the Empire; that we may everywhere discern a trace of it; that no abyss separates the Roman from the modern world; that the thread is nowhere broken; that we may recognise everywhere the transition of Roman society into our own; in a word, that the part played by ancients in modern civilization is greater and more continuous than is commonly thought. A second result equally arises out of our labours, and characterizes the period which is the object of them. During all this period, from the fifth to the tenth century, we have nowhere been able to pause; we have been unable to find, either in social or intellectual order, any system, any fact, which became fixed, which took a firm, general, and regular hold on society or mind. The general

346

fact with which we have been struck is a continual and universal fluctuation, a constant state of uncertainty and of transformation. It was, then, from the fifth to the tenth century, that the work of fermentation and amalgamation of the three elements of modern civilization, namely, the Roman element, the Christian element, and the German element, was in operation; and it was only at the end of the tenth century that the ferment ceased, and the amalgamation became nearly accomplished, and that the development of the new order and truly modern society commenced.

The history which we have just concluded, then, is the history of its very conception and creation. All things rise out of the chaos, modern society among the rest. That which we have now studied is the chaos, the cradle of France: what we shall have to study hereafter is France itself. Dating only from the end of the tenth century, the social being which bears that name, if I may thus speak, has been formed and exists; we might attend it in its proper and exterior development. This development will merit, for the first time, the name of French civilization. Until now, we have spoken of Gaulish-Roman, Frankish, Gallo-Roman, and Gallo-Frankish civilization; we have been obliged to combine foreign names in order to characterize, with any justice, a society without unity and certainty. When we again enter upon our labours, it will be to speak of French civilization; we shall date therefrom; the question will no longer concern Gauls, Franks, and Romans, but Frenchmen, ourselves.

PART II

SECOND SERIES

Lecture 1
In commencing the last course, I was obliged to determine its subject, and to explain the motives of my choice. At present I have not anything of the kind to do. The subject of our study is known; the route is traced. I endeavoured to place you in the presence of the origins of French civilization under the two first

races; I propose to follow it through all its vicissitudes, in its long and glorious development up to the eve of our own times. I now, therefore, again take up the subject where we left it, that is to say at the end of the tenth century, at the accession of the Capetians. As I told you in concluding the past course, it is there that French civilization commences. Hitherto you will recollect, we have spoken of Gaulish, Roman, Gallo-Roman, Frankish, Gallo-Frankish, civilization; we were obliged to make use of foreign names which did not belong to us, in order to express with any fulness, a society without unity, without fixedness, without entirety. Dating from the end of the tenth century, there is no longer anything of this kind; it is now with the French, with French civilization, that we have to occupy ourselves.

And yet it was at this very epoch that all national and political unity was disappearing from our land. All books say this, and all facts show it. It was the epoch when the feudal system, that is to say, the dismemberment of the people and of power, entirely prevailed. At the eleventh century, the soil which we call France was covered with petty nations and petty sovereigns, almost strangers one to the other, almost independent of each other. Even the very shadow of a central government, of a general nation, seemed to have disappeared.

How comes it that truly French civilization and history commences exactly at the moment when it was almost impossible to discover a France?

It is because, in the life of nations, the external visible unity, the unity of name and government, although important, is not the first, the most real, not that which truly constitutes a nation. There is a more profound, more powerful unity; that which results, not from the identity of government and destiny, but from the similarity of social elements, from the similarity of institutions, manners, ideas, sentiments, languages; the unity which resides in the men themselves whom the society unites together, and not in the forms of their junction; moral unity, in point of fact, far superior to political unity, and which alone can give it a solid foundation.

Well, it is at the end of the tenth century that the cradle of this at once unique and complex being, which has become the French nation, is placed. She required many centuries and many long efforts to extricate herself, and to emerge in her simplicity and grandeur. Still, at this epoch, her elements existed, and we begin to catch glimpses of the work of their development. In the times which we studied in the last course, from the fifth to the tenth century, under Charlemagne, for example, external political unity was often greater and stronger than at the epoch with which we are about to occupy ourselves. But if you go thoroughly into the matter, into the moral state of the men themselves, you find there is an utter absence of unity. The races are profoundly different and even hostile; the laws, traditions, manners, languages, likewise differ and struggle; situations, social relations have neither generality nor fixedness. At the end of the tenth and at the commencement of the eleventh century, there was no kind of political unity like that of Charlemagne, but races began to amalgamate; diversity of laws according to origin is no longer the principle of all legislation. Social situations have acquired some fixedness; likewise, feudal institutions, not the same but everywhere analogous, have prevailed, or nearly so, over all the land. In place of the radical, imperishable diversity of the Latin language and the Germanic languages, two languages begin to be formed, the Roman language of the south, and the Roman language of the north, doubtless different, but still of the same origin, of the same character, and destined one day to become amalgamated. Diversity also begins to be effaced from the soul of men, from their moral existence. The German is less addicted to his Germanic traditions and habits; he gradually detaches himself from the past to belong to his present situation. It is the same with the Roman; he thinks less of the ancient empire, of its fall, and of the sentiments which it gave rise to in him. Over conquerors and conquered, the new, actual facts, which are common to them, daily exercise more influence. In a word, political unity is almost null, real diversity still very great, and yet at bottom there is more of true unity than there has been for five centuries. We begin to catch glimpses of

349

the elements of a nation; and the proof is, that from this epoch the tendency of all these social elements to conjoin, to assimilate and form themselves into great masses, that is to say, the tendency towards national unity, and thence towards political unity, becomes the dominant characteristic, the great fact of the history of French civilization, the general and constant fact around which all our study will turn.

The development of this fact, the triumph of this tendency, has made the fortune of France. It is by this especially that she has outstripped the other nations of the continent in the career of civilization. Look at Spain, Italy, even Germany: what is it that they want? They have progressed far more slowly than France towards moral unity, towards the formation into a single people. Even there where moral unity has been formed, or nearly so, as in Italy and Germany, its transformation into political unity, the birth of a general government, has been slackened or almost entirely stopped. France, more happy, arrived more rapidly and more completely at that double unity, not the only principle, but the only pledge of the strength and grandeur of nations. It was at the end of the tenth century that it, so to speak, commenced its progress towards this important result. It is, therefore, from this epoch that French civilization really dates; it is there that we may begin to study it under its true name.

The feudal period, that is, the period when the feudal system was the dominant fact of our country, will be the subject of the present course.

It includes Hugh Capet and Philippe de Valois; that is, it embraces the eleventh, twelfth, and thirteenth centuries.

That these are the true limits, the career of the feudal system, it is easy I think to establish.

The peculiar general character of feudalism, as I have just repeated, and as every one knows, is the dismemberment of the people and of power into a multitude of petty nations, and petty sovereigns; the absence of any universal nation, of any central government. Let us see the limits in which this fact is contained. These limits will necessarily be those of the feudal period.

We may, if I do not deceive myself, recognise them especially by three symptoms.

First, to what enemies did feudalism succumb? Who opposed it in France? Two powers; royalty on the one hand, on the other, the commons. By royalty a central government was formed in France, by the commons was formed an universal nation, which grouped itself around the central government.

At the end of the tenth century, royalty and the commons were not visible, or at all events scarcely visible. At the commencement of the fourteenth century, royalty was the head of the state, the commons were the body of the nation. The two forces to which the feudal system was to succumb had then attained, not, indeed, their entire development, but a decided preponderance. By this symptom we may then say that there the feudal period, properly so called, stops, since the absence of any universal nation, and of all central power, is its essential characteristic.

Here is a second symptom which assigns the same limits to the feudal period.

From the tenth to the fourteenth century, wars, which were then the principal event of history, have, at least the greater part of them, the same characteristic. They are internal, civil wars, as it were in the bosom of feudalism itself. It is a suzerain who endeavours to acquire the territory of his vassals; vassals who dispute among themselves certain portions of the territory. Such appear to us, with the exception of the crusades, almost all the wars of Louis le Gros, of Philip Augustus, Saint Louis, and Philippe le Bel. It is from the very nature of the feudal society that their causes and effects arise.

With the fourteenth century the character of war changed. Then began the foreign wars; no longer a vassal against suzerain, or vassal against vassal, but nation against nation, government against government. On the accession of Philippe de Valois, the great wars between the French and the English broke out—the claims of the kings of England, not upon any particular fief, but upon the whole land, and upon the throne of France—and they continued up to Louis XI. They were no longer feudal, but national wars; a certain proof that the feudal period stopped at this limit, that another society had already commenced.

Lastly, if we address ourselves to a third kind of indication, if we interrogate the great events which we are accustomed, and with reason, to look upon as the result, as the expression of feudal society, we shall find that they are all included within the epoch of which we speak. The crusades, that great adventure of feudalism and its popular glory, finished, or nearly finished, with Saint Louis and the thirteenth century; we hear afterwards but a futile echo of them. Chivalry, that poetical daughter, that ideal, so to speak, of the feudal system, is equally inclosed in the same limits. In the fourteenth century it was on the decline, and a knight errant already appears a ridiculous personage. Romantic and chivalrous literature, the troubadours, the trouvères, in a word, all the institutions, all the facts which may be looked upon as the results, the companions of feudalism, alike belong to the eleventh, twelfth, and thirteenth centuries. That, therefore, is evidently the feudal period; and when I confine it to these limits, I do not adopt an arbitrary, purely conventional classification; it is the fact.

Now, how shall we study this epoch? What method will best make it known to us?

It will, I hope, be borne in mind, that I have regarded civilization as the result of two great facts; the development, on the one hand of society, on the other, of individual man. I have therefore always been careful to retrace external and internal civilization, the history of society and the history of man, of human relations and of human ideas, political history and intellectual history.

We shall follow the same method here, we shall examine the feudal period from this twofold point of view.

From the political point of view, in confining ourselves to the history of society, we shall find from the tenth to the fourteenth century, as from the fifth to the tenth, two societies closely bordering on each other, dovetailed, as it were, into one another, yet essentially distinct: the civil society and the religious society, the church and the state; we shall study them separately, as we have hitherto done.

Civil society is to be considered, first, in the facts which constitute it, and which show us what it has been; secondly, in the legislative and political movements which emanate from it, and upon which its character is imprinted.

The three great facts of the feudal period, the three facts whose nature and relations comprehend the history of civilization during these three centuries, are (1) the possessors of fiefs, the feudal association itself; (2) above and by the side of the feudal association, in intimate relation with it, and yet reposing upon other principles, and applying itself to create a distinct existence, royalty; (3) below and by the side of the feudal association, also in intimate relation with it, and yet also reposing upon other principles, and labouring to separate itself, the commons. The history of these three facts, and of their reciprocal action is, at this epoch, the history of civil society.

With regard to the written monuments that remain to us, there are four principal ones: two collections of laws which modern learning, wrongly I think, would call codes; and two works of jurisconsults. The legislative monuments are (1) the collection of the ordinances of the kings of France, and especially the *Etablissements* of Saint Louis; (2) his *assises* of the Frank kingdom of Jerusalem, drawn up by order of Godefry de Bouillon, which reproduce the image of the feudal society more completely and more faithfully than any other document.

The two works of jurisconsults are (1) the *Coutume de Beaucasis*, by Beaumanoir; (2) the *Traité de l'ancienne Jurisprudence des Français; ou Conseils à un Ami*, by Pierre de Fontaines.

I shall study with you these monuments of the feudal legislation as I have studied the barbarian laws and capitularies, by carefully analyzing them, and attempting to thoroughly comprehend their contents, and to exactly understand their nature.

From civil society we shall pass to religious society; we shall consider it, as we have already done, (1) in itself, in its peculiar and internal organization; (2) in its relations with civil society, with the state; (3) finally, in its relations with the external government of the universal church—that is, with the papacy.

The history of society, if I do not deceive myself, will thus be completed; we shall then enter into the history of the human mind. At this epoch it resides in two great facts, two distinct literatures: (1) a learned literature, written in Latin, addressed solely to the learned classes, lay or ecclesiastical, and which contains the theology and philosophy of the time; (2) a national, popular literature, entirely in the vulgar tongue, addressed to the whole community, particularly to idlers and to the lower classes. Whosoever neglects either of these two facts, whoever does not thoroughly understand these two literatures, who does not see them marching abreast, rarely close to each other, rarely acting upon one another, but both powerful and holding an important place, who does not see all this, will have but an incomplete and false idea of the intellectual history of this epoch, of the state and progress of mind.

Such, in its whole, is the plan of the present course.

Here, most assuredly, is a vast field opened to our study. There is here enough long to excite and nourish learned curiosity. But is so great an epoch of our history—is France in the rudest crisis of her development—in a word, the middle ages, are they with us a mere matter of learning, a mere object of curiosity? Have we not the most universal and pressing interest in thoroughly understanding it? Has the past no other value attached to it than for erudition? has it become totally foreign to the present, to our life?

Two facts, if I mistake not, two contemporary visible facts, prove that such is not the case.

The imagination at the present day is evidently gratified in carrying itself back towards this epoch. Its traditions, its manners, its adventures, its monuments, have an attraction for the public which cannot be mistaken. We may, upon this subject, interrogate letters and the arts; we may open the histories, romance, poems of our time; we may enter the furniture and curiosity shops; everywhere we shall see the middle ages cultivated, reproduced, occupying the thought, amusing the taste of that portion of the public which has time to spare for its intellectual wants and pleasures.

At the same time there is manifested, on the part of some enlightened and honourable men, sincere friends to the learning and progress of humanity, an increasing aversion towards this epoch and all which recals it. In their eyes, those who there seek inspirations, or merely poetical pleasure, carry literature back towards barbarism; in their eyes, those who, from a political point of view, and amidst an enormous mass of error and of evil, seek to find in it anything of good, those, whether they wish it or not, favour the system of despotism and privilege. These unrelenting enemies of the middle ages deplore the blindness of the public who can take any pleasure in going back, if only in imagination, amidst those barbarous ages, and seem to predict, if this despotism continues, the return of all the absurdities, of all the evils, which then weighed upon nations.

This clearly proves that the middle ages are quite other than a matter of learning to us; that they correspond to interests more real, more direct than those of historical erudition and criticism, to sentiments more general, more full of life than that of mere curiosity.

How can we be surprised at this? The twofold fact which I spoke of is exactly the result, and as it were a new form of the two essential characteristics of the middle ages, the two facts by which that epoch has held so great a place in the history of our civilization, and influenced posterior ages so powerfully.

On the one hand, it is impossible to overlook the fact that there is the cradle of modern societies and manners. Thence date (1) modern languages, and especially our own; (2) modern literatures, precisely in all that there is in them of the national, the original, of the foreign to all mere learning, to all imitation of other times, of other countries; (3) the greater portion of modern monuments, monuments in which, for many centuries, the people have assembled, and still continue to assemble, churches, palaces, town halls, works of art and public utility of every kind; (4) almost all historical families, families who have played a part and placed their name in the various phases of our destiny; (5) a large number of national events, important in themselves, and for a long time popular, the crusades, chivalry; in a word, almost everything which for centuries has filled and agitated the imagination of the French people.

This is evidently the heroic age of modern nations, among others, of France. What more natural than its poetical richness and poetical attraction?

By the side of this fact, however, we encounter another no less incontestable: the social state of the middle ages was constantly insupportable and odious, and especially so in France. Never did the cradle of a nation inspire it with such antipathy; the feudal system, its institutions and principles, never obtained that unhesitating adhesion, the result of habit, which nations have often given to the very worst systems of social organization. France constantly struggled to escape from them, to abolish them. Whosoever dealt them a blow, kings, jurisconsults, the church, was sanctioned and became popular; despotism itself, when it seemed a means of deliverance from them, was accepted as a benefit.

The eighteenth century and the French revolution have been for us the last phase, the definitive expression of this fact of our history. When they occurred, the social state of the middle ages had long been changed, enervated, dissolved. Yet it was against the consequences and recollections of the middle ages that, in the popular mind and intention, this great shock was especially felt. The society which then perished, was the society which the Germanic invasion had created in the west, and of which feudalism was the first and essential form. It was, in truth, no longer in existence: yet it was against it that the revolution was directed.

But precisely because of this fact, precisely because the eighteenth century and the revolution were the definitive explosion of the national antipathy to the social state of the middle ages, two things were inevitably destined to happen, and in fact did happen: In their violent efforts against the memory and remains of this epoch, the eighteenth century and the revolution would necessarily fail in impartiality towards it, and would not recognise the good which might be met with in it; and it would in like manner overlook its poetical character, its merit, and its attractions as the cradle of certain elements of the national life. The epochs in which the critical spirit dominates, that is to say, those which occupy themselves more especially with examining and demolishing, generally understand but little of the poetical times, those times when man complacently gives himself to the impulsion of his manners and the facts which surround him.

They understand more especially little of what there is of the true and poetical in the times against which they make war. Open the writings of the eighteenth century, those at least which really have the character of the epoch, and contributed to the great revolution then accomplished; you will see that the human mind there shows itself very little sensible of the poetical merit of any social state much differing from the type which they then conceived and followed, especially of the poetical merit of the rude and unrefined times, and, among those times, of the middle ages. The *Essai sur les mœurs et l'esprit des nations* is in this way the most faithful image of the general disposition of the age: look there for the history of the middle ages: you will see that Voltaire incessantly applied himself to the task of extracting all that is gross, absurd, odious, calamitous, in this epoch. He was right, thoroughly right in the definitive judgment which he gave of it, and in his efforts to abolish its remains. But that is all that he sees of it; he thinks only of judging and abolishing, in his historical writings, that is to say, in his works of polemical criticism; for Voltaire has done other things than criticism. Voltaire was also a poet, and when he gave himself up to his imagination, to his poetical instincts, he found impressions greatly differing from his judgment. He has spoken of the middle ages elsewhere than in the *Essai sur les mœurs et l'esprit des nations,* and how has he spoken of it?

> Oh! l'heureux temps que celui de ces fables,
> Des bons démons, des esprits familiers,
> Des farfadets, aux mortels secourables!
> On écoutait tous ces faits admirables
> Dans son chateâu, pres d'un large foyer.
> Le père et l'oncle, et la mère et la fille,
> Et les voisins, et toute la famille,
> Ouvraient l'oreille à monsieur l'aumônier,
> Qui leur faisait des contes de sorcier.
> On a banni les démons et les fées;
> Sous la raison les graces étouffées
> Livrent nos cœurs à l'insipidité;
> Le raisonner tristement s'accrédité;
> On court, hélas! après la vérité:
> Ah! croyez moi, l'erreur a son merite.

Voltaire is wrong to call the poetical side of these old times *erreur;* Poetry there doubtless associated herself with many errors; but in herself she was true, although of a truth very different from philosophical truth, and she answered to very legitimate needs of human nature. This incidental observation, however, is of but little importance; what is necessary to be remarked, is the singular contrast between Voltaire the poet, and Voltaire the critic. The poet acutely feels for the middle ages impressions to which the critic shows himself an entire stranger; the one deplores the loss of those impressions which the other applies himself to destroy: nothing, surely, better manifests that want of political impartiality and poetical sympathy in the eighteenth century, of which I just now spoke.

We are now in the reaction against the tendency of the age which preceded us. This fact is evidenced in the direction now taken, at least for the most part, by historical studies, by works of general literature following the public taste, and also in the indignation of the exclusive partisans of the eighteenth century. Is this indignation legitimate? Is the danger denounced from this reaction so great? Is there any danger at all?

From a literary point of view I shall not absolutely deny it. I would not say that there is not some exaggeration, something of mania in this return of the imagination towards the middle ages, and that good sense and good taste have not a little suffered from it. The reaction, followed with much talent, appears to me, upon the whole, a groping rather than a regeneration. In my opinion, it proceeds from very distinguished men, sometimes sincerely inspired, but who often deviate in seeking a good vein, rather than from people who have found one, and are working it with confidence. But in truth, in the actual state of society and mind, the evil cannot become very grave. Are not publicity and criticism always at hand in the literary world as well as in the political world, and always ready to render everywhere the same services, to warn, restrain, to combat, in fine to prevent us from falling under the exclusive domination of a coterie or system? They do not spare the new school; and the public, the genuine and general public, while receiving it with gentleness, does not seem disposed to become subjected by it. It judges it, and sometimes even rebukes it rather roughly. Nothing, therefore, seems to me to indicate that barbarism is about to resume sway over the national taste.

Besides, we must take life where life manifests itself; the wind, from whatever quarter it blows; talent, wherever it has pleased Heaven to bestow it. For we need above all things in the literary world talent and life. The worst that can happen to us here is immobility and sterility.

Is danger to political impartiality the character of the reaction which they deplore? This must be absolutely denied. Impartiality will never be a popular tendency, the error of the masses; they are governed by simple, exclusive ideas and passions: there is no fear of their ever judging too favourably of the middle ages and their social state. Present interests, national traditions in this respect preserve, if not all their potency, at least sufficient influence to prevent all excess. The impartiality which is spoken of will scarcely penetrate below the regions of science and of philosophical discussion.

And what is it in these regions themselves, and among the very men who most pique themselves on it? Does it impel them in any way towards the doctrines of the middle ages? To any approbation of their institutions—of their social state? Not in the least degree. The principles upon which modern societies rest, the progress and the requirements of reason and of human liberty, have certainly not firmer, more zealous defenders, than the partisans of historical impartiality; they are first in the breach, and more exposed than any others to the blows of their enemies. They have no esteem for the old forms, the fanatic and tyrannical classification of feudal France, the work of force, which ages and enormous labours have had such difficulty in reforming. What they claim is a full and free judgment of this past of the country. They do not believe that it was absolutely destitute of virtue, liberty, or reason, nor that we are entitled to condemn it for its errors and failings in a career in which, even in the present day, after such progress, so many victories, we are ourselves advancing so laboriously.

There is evidently therein no danger either for the liberty of the human mind, or for the good organization of society.

Might there not be, on the other hand, great advantages in this historical impartiality, this poetical sympathy for ancient France?

And first, is it nothing to have a source of emotions and pleasures opened to the imagination? All this long epoch, all this old history, in which one hitherto saw nothing but absurdity and barbarism, becomes for us rich in great memories, in noble adventures, in events and sentiments in which we feel a vivid interest. It is a domain restored to that need of emotion, of sympathy, which, thanks to God, nothing can stifle in our nature. The imagination plays an immense part in the life of men and of nations. In order to occupy it, to satisfy it, an actual energetic passion is necessary, like that which animated the eighteenth century and the revolution, a rich and varied spectacle. The present alone, the present without passion, the calm and regular present, does not suffice for the human soul; it feels narrow and poor in it; it desires more extension, more variety. Hence the importance and the charm of the past, of national traditions, of all that portion of the life of nations in which imagination wanders and freely enjoys itself, amidst a space far more vast than actual life. Nations may one moment, under the influence of a violent crisis, deny their past—even curse it; they cannot forget it, nor long or absolutely detach themselves from it. On a certain occasion, in one of the ephemeral parliaments held in England under Cromwell, in that which took the name of one of its members, a ridiculous personage, in the Barebone parliament, a fanatic arose, and demanded that in all the offices, in all public establishments, they should destroy the archives, the records, all the written monuments of old England. This was an excess of that fever which sometimes seizes nations, amidst the most useful, the most glorious regenerations; Cromwell, more sensible, had the proposition rejected. Is it to be supposed that it would long have had the assent of England, that it would truly have attained its end?

In my opinion, the school of the eighteenth century has more than once committed this mistake of not comprehending the whole of the part which imagination plays in the life of man and of society. It has attacked, cried down, on the one hand, everything ancient, on the other, all which assumed to be eternal, history and religion: that is, it has seemed to dispute, to wish to take from men the past and the future, in order to concentrate them in the present. The mistake explains itself, even excuses itself by the ardour of the struggle then afoot, and by the empire of the passion of the moment, which satisfied those requirements of emotion and of imagination, imperishable in human nature. But it is no less serious, and of serious consequence. It would be easy to show the proof and effects of this in a thousand details of our contemporaneous history.

It has, moreover, been made matter of complaint, and with reason, that our history was not national, that we were in want of associations, of popular traditions. To this fact some of the faults of our literature, and even of our character, have been imputed. Should it then be extended beyond these natural limits? Is it to be regretted that the past should again become something for us, that we should again take some interest in it?

From a political point of view, and in an entirely positive aim, this was a valuable advantage. The power of associations in fixing and fertilizing institutions is very great. Our institutions are beneficial and powerful; they rest upon truly national interests, upon ideas which have penetrated deeply into minds. Still they are young; they do not claim the authority of long experience, at all events not of a long national experience. It was in the name of reason, of philosophy, that they first appeared: they took birth in doctrines: a noble origin, but for some time subject to the uncertainties, the vicissitudes of the human mind. What more useful than to make them thus strike root in the past; to unite the principles and guarantees of our social order to principles half seen, to guarantees sought in the same path through ages? Facts are at present popular; facts have favour and credit. Well, let the institutions, the ideas which are dear to us, be strongly established in the bosom of facts, of the facts of all time; let the trace of them be everywhere found; let them everywhere reappear in our history. They will thence derive force, and we ourselves dignity; for a nation has higher esteem for itself, and has greater pride in itself, when it can thus, in a long series of ages, prolong its destiny and its sentiments.

Lastly, another advantage, an advantage of an entirely different nature, but no less considerable, must result from impartiality towards the middle ages, and from an attentive and familiar contemplation of that epoch.

That the social reform which is brought about in our times, under our eyes, is immense, no man of sense can deny. Never were human relations regulated with more justice, never has the result been a more general well-being.

Not only is social reform great, but I am convinced that a correspondent moral reform has also been accomplished; that, perhaps, at no epoch has there been, upon the whole, so much propriety in human life, so many men living regularly, that never has less public force been necessary to repress individual wills. Practical morality, I am convinced, has made almost as much progress as the well-being and the prosperity of the country.

But from another point of view we have, I think, much to gain, and we are justly reproachable. We have lived for fifty years under the influence of general ideas, more and more accredited and powerful, under the weight of formidable, almost indescribable events. Thence has resulted a certain weakness, a certain effeminacy in minds and in characters. Individual wills and convictions want energy and confidence in themselves. They think with a common opinion, they obey a general impulse, they give way to an external necessity. Whether to resist or to act, each has but little idea of his own strength, little confidence in his own thoughts. The individuality, in a word, the inward and personal energy of man, is weak and timid. Amidst the progress of general liberty, men seem to have lost the proud sentiment of their own liberty.

Such were not the middle ages; the social condition of those ages was deplorable; human morality very inferior, according to what is told us, to that of our times. But in men, individuality was strong, and the will, energetic.

There were then few general ideas which governed all minds, few events which, in all parts of the territory, in all situations, weighed upon characters. The individual displayed himself upon his own account, according to his own inclination, irregularly, and with confidence; the moral nature of man appeared here and there with all its ambition, all its energy. A spectacle not only dramatic and attractive, but instructive and useful; which offers us nothing to regret, nothing to imitate, but much to learn from, were it only by constantly recalling our attention to that wherein we are deficient, by showing us what a man may do when he knows how to believe and to will.

Such merits certainly will justify the care which we shall take in our study; and it will, I hope, be seen, that in being just, fully just, towards this great epoch, there is for us no danger and some benefit.

Lecture 5

In the opening pages of this lecture, Guizot proposes the methodology for his course, how he plans to study the whole of feudal society, including royalty and the towns. He will begin with the fief, "the primitive feudal molecule."

Such will be our progress in the study of civil society in France, during the feudal period. Let us immediately approach it, let us enter, and confine ourselves to the simple fief.

Let us first occupy ourselves with its possessor; let us study the situation and the life of the sovereign of this little state, the interior of the castle which contained him, and his people.

The single word *castle* evokes the idea of feudal society; it seems to rise up before us. Nothing can be more natural. These castles which once covered our soil, and the ruins of which are still scattered about, were constructed by feudalism; their very elevation was, so to speak, the declaration of its triumph. Nothing of the kind existed on the Gallo-Roman soil. Before the German invasion, the great proprietors lived either in cities, or in beautiful houses, agreeably situated near cities, or in rich plains upon the banks of rivers. In the country districts, properly so called, were dispersed the *villæ*, a species of farms, great buildings serving for the improvement of estates, and for the dwelling of the labourers or serfs who cultivated them.

Such was the distribution and habitation of the various classes, which the Germanic nations found in Gaul at the time of the invasion.

It must not be supposed that they disliked and were eager to change it; that they immediately sought the mountains, steep and savage places, in order to construct new and entirely different dwellings. They first established themselves in the habitations of the Gallo-Romans, whether in the cities, or in the *villæ*, amidst the country districts and the agricultural population, and rather in the latter dwellings, whose situation was more conformable to their national habits. Accordingly the *villæ*, of which constant mention is made under the first race, were the same, or almost the same, as they had been before the invasion; that is to say, they were the centre of improvement and habitation of great domains, buildings scattered throughout the country districts, where barbarians and Romans, conquerors and conquered, masters, free men, labourers, slaves, lived together.

Still a change soon became visible. The invasion continued; disorder and pillage were incessantly renewed; the inhabitants of the country districts, of ancient or new origin, had need to guard themselves, and incessantly keep on the defensive. We find the *villæ* gradually becoming surrounded by moats, ramparts of earth, with some appearances of fortifications. Hence arises a pretended etymology of the world *villa,* which we read in the *Glossary* of Du Cange thus:

Villa dicitur à vallis, quasi vallata, eo quod vallata sit solum vallatione vallorum, et non munitione murorum. Indè villanus.

The etymology is incorrect; the word *villa* is far anterior to the epoch when the inhabitants of this kind of dwelling had need to surround them with moats or ramparts; the word is commonly derived from *vehilla, vehere,* which probably means the place where the agricultural carts were made. But whatever may be its merit, the mere etymology of the word is not the less a remarkable fact; it proves that the *villæ* were not long before they were in a measure fortified.

There is another circumstance which prevents any doubt of this: in certain parts of France, in Normandy, Picardy, etc., the names of many castles terminate with *ville*, Frondeville, Aboville, Méréville, etc.; and many of these castles are not situated, as most feudal castles properly so called were, in steep, isolated places, but amidst rich plains, in valleys upon the site which the *villæ* doubtless formerly occupied: a sure sign that more than one Anglo-Roman *villa* in fortifying itself, and after many vicissitudes, ended by being metamorphosed into a castle.

As for the rest, even before the invasion was consummated, and in order to resist its disorders, to escape its dangers, the population of the country districts had begun, in many places, to seek refuge in the heights, in places difficult of access, and to surround them with fortifications. We read in the life of St. Nicet, bishop of Trèves, written by Fortunat, bishop of Poitiers:

> In going through these districts, Nicet, that apostolic man, that good pastor, constructed there for his flock a protecting fold: he surrounded the hill with thirty towers, which enclosed it on all sides, and thus raised an edifice where formerly was a forest.[5]

I might quote many analogous examples. Is not this evidently a first attempt of that choice of places, and of that kind of construction, which was adopted at a later period for feudal castles?

In the dreadful anarchy of the following centuries, the causes which had impelled the population to seek such places of refuge, and to surround them with fortifications, became more and more pressing; it was necessary for it to fly from places easy of access; to fortify its dwelling. And not only did men thus seek security, they also found in it a means of abandoning themselves without fear to depredation, and to secure to themselves its fruits. Among the conquerors, many still led a life of hunting and pillage; they were forced to have a fortress where they might shut themselves up after an expedition, repel the vengeance of their adversaries, resist the magistrates who attempted to maintain any

5. Venantius Honorius Fortunatus, *Carmen,* bk. 3, c. 12.

order in the country. Such was the aim which originally caused the construction of many of the feudal castles. It was more especially after the death of Charlemagne, under the reigns of Louis le Debonnaire and Charles le Chauve, that we find the country covered with these haunts; they even became so numerous and so formidable, that Charles le Chauve, despite his weakness, and for the sake of the public order, as well as of his own authority, thought it his duty to attempt to destroy them. We read in the capitularies drawn up at Pistes in 864:

> We will and expressly order that, whosoever in these times shall, without our consent, have constructed castles, fortifications, and embankments (*haias*), shall entirely destroy them between this and the latter end of August, seeing that the neighbours and inhabitants have suffered much uneasiness and many depredations from them; and if any one refuse to demolish these works, let the counts, in whose counties they have been constructed, themselves cause them to be demolished; and if any one resist them, let them immediately inform us. And if the counts neglect to obey us in this, let them know that, according to what is written in these capitularies, and in those of our predecessors, we shall order them to our presence, and we shall ourselves establish in their counties men who can and will cause our orders to be executed.[6]

The tone and precision of the injunctions addressed to all the royal officers, prove the importance which was attached to the matter; but Charles le Chauve was evidently not in a condition to accomplish such a work. We do not find that this capitulary had any effect, and his successors do not even claim its execution. Accordingly, the number of castles went on increasing under the last Carolingians with extraordinary rapidity. Still the struggle did not cease between those whose interest it was to prevent, and those who felt the need of raising buildings of this kind: we find it protracted to the eleventh, twelfth, and thirteenth centuries. And it was not merely between the king and the possessors of fiefs that it subsisted, it also broke out among the possessors of

6. *Capitularies of Charles le Chauve*, at Pistes in 864, in Etienne Baluze *Recueil des Capitulaires* [*Capitularia regum Francorum*] (Paris, 1780), vol. 2, col. 195.

fiefs themselves. It was not a mere question, in fact, of the maintenance of public order in the whole territory, nor of a duty or
interest of royalty. Every suzerain saw with displeasure his vassal
constructing a castle on his fief, for the vassal thus insured himself
a powerful means of independence and resistance. Local wars
then became more and more fierce, the castle served for aggression as well as for defence, and the powerful, who desired alone to
have them, like the weak who had none at all, greatly feared to see
them constructed around them. There was here, accordingly,
a subject for continual complaints and protest. About the year
1020, and on a similar occasion, Fulbert, bishop of Chartres, wrote
to King Robert a letter which I shall quote entire, because it
gives a clear and lively idea of the importance which such a
dispute must have had:

> To his lord Robert, his most gracious king, whom Fulbert,
> humble bishop of Chartres, prays may remain in the grace
> of the King of kings.

> We return thanks to your goodness for that you have lately
> sent us a messenger charged with rejoicing us by bringing news of
> your good health, and to instruct your majesty of the condition of
> our affairs, after having demanded from us an account thereof.
> We then wrote to you concerning the evils done to our church by
> viscount Geoffrey, of Chateaudun, who shows sufficiently, and
> even more than enough, that he has no respect for God or your
> excellence, for he rebuilt the castle of Galardon, formerly de-
> stroyed by you; and upon this occasion we may say, *See! the evil
> comes from the east* upon our church; and lo! again he dares to
> undertake the building of another castle at Illiers, in the midst of
> the domains of Saint Mary, concerning which we may well say,
> and also in good truth, *See! the evil comes from the west.* Now,
> therefore, forced to write to you by reason of these evils, we bring
> complaint to your mercy, and ask help and counsel of it; for in
> this calamity we have received neither aid nor consolation from
> your son Hugh. Accordingly, penetrated to the depths of our
> heart with a lively grief, we have already manifested it to such a
> degree, that, according to our order, our bells, accustomed to
> announce our joy and gladness, have ceased to sound, as the more
> to show our sadness; and divine service, which, up to the present
> time, and by the grace of God, we have been accustomed to
> celebrate with great rejoicing of heart and mouth, is no longer

celebrated, except in a lamentable manner, with a low voice, and almost in silence.

. . . .

Assuredly, the construction of the castles of Galardon and Illiers must have appeared a grave fact, for it to cause a bishop, in the mere hope of making its gravity felt, to silence the bells of his church, and have divine service almost suspended. The successors of Fulbert, in the bishopric of Chartres, took a different course; they fortified the episcopal house, and were in their turn obliged to demolish their fortifications. We read, in a charter granted to Yves, bishop of Chartres, by Stephen, count of Chartres and of Blois, who died in 1101, the following clause:

> If any future bishop cause to be constructed, in the said episcopal house, a tower or ramparts, let that tower and those ramparts alone be demolished, and let the house itself remain standing, with its dependencies.[7]

Doubtless, between Fulbert and Yves, some bishop of Chartres had added such works to his house, and Count Stephen wished to prevent their being renewed.

The lords who each held fiefs, often had quarrels among them, arising from the construction of castles, whether within the fief, or on the frontiers of neighbouring fiefs.

> In 1228, Guy, count of Forest and Nevers, and Thibaut, count of Champagne, were at war with one another, because of fortresses which they had respectively caused to be constructed upon the borders of their counties of Champagne and Nevers. This war having lasted for a long period, the two counts put it to the arbitration of the cardinal legate, who then gave his judgment as umpire, by which it was said that so long as Guy, count of Forest, should hold the county of Nevers, the fortresses which were on the confines of the county of Champagne, and on those of the county of Nevers, should subsist, and that they might even be fenced around with new works, provided, however, that it was only to the distance of the shot of a crossbow; but that the counts could not make new fortresses on the same borders, nor suffer others to make them.[8]

7. Edmond Martène, *Amplissima Collectio*, vol. 1, p. 621.
8. Nicolas Brussel, *Nouvel examen de l'Usage général des Fiefs*, vol. 1, p. 383.

And in 1160, under the reign of Louis le Jeune, a charter of his brother Robert, count of Dreux, is expressed in the following terms:

> I, Robert, count, brother of the king of France, make known to all present and to come, that there was a certain contest between Henry, count of Champagne and Brie, and myself, concerning a certain house which is called Savegny, and a part of which I fortified by a moat of two outlets. The affair has been arranged as follows, namely: that what is already fortified by a moat of two outlets, shall so remain, but that the remainder shall be fortified with a moat of one outlet only, and a fence without battlements. If I make war against the said count, or against any other, I shall immediately give him up the said house. I have guaranteed it to him on my faith and by hostages, and he has promised me that he will keep the said house, with the ponds and mills, in good faith and without ill design; and that he will immediately return it to me, the war being finished.[9]

It would be easy to multiply this example of the resistance, or more correctly speaking, various resistances, which, down to the middle of the thirteenth century, the construction of castles had to surmount.

It did surmount them, as it happens with everything which is the work of necessity. At this epoch, there was war everywhere; everywhere would necessarily be also the monuments of war, the means of making it and repelling it. Not only were strong castles constructed, but all things were made into fortifications, haunts, or defensive habitations. Towards the end of the eleventh century, we find, at Nîmes, an association called *Les Chevaliers des Arénes*. When the meaning of this is sought, we find that they were knights who had taken up their abode in the Roman amphitheatre, the Arénes still remaining in the present day. It was easy to fortify them: they were strong in themselves. These knights established themselves in them, and intrenched themselves therein when necessary, and this is not an isolated fact; most of the ancient circuses, the arena of Arles, as well as that of Nîmes, have been put to the same use, and occupied for some time as a castle. It was not necessary to be a knight, or even a layman, in order to act thus, and to live amidst fortifications. Monasteries

9. Ibid., p. 382, note b.

and churches also fortified themselves; they were surrounded by towers, ramparts, and moats; they were assiduously guarded, and long sieges were sustained by them. The bourgeois did like the nobles; towns were fortified. War so constantly menaced them, that, in many of them, a child was kept, at a fixed post and by way of sentinel, in the bell tower of the church, to observe what passed at a distance, and to announce the approach of an enemy. Moreover, the enemy was within the walls, in the neighbouring street, in the intermediate house; war might break out, in fact did break out, between one quarter and another, from door to door, and fortifications, like war, penetrated everywhere. Each street had its barriers, each house its tower, its loop-hole, its platform, in the fourteenth century.

> Rhodez was divided into two parts, surrounded with ramparts and towers. One was called the city, the other the commune; the inhabitants of the city and those of the commune made war with each other from time to time; and even when they were at peace, they shut the gates of their inclosure every night, and were more particular in setting the watch upon the walls which separated them, than upon those which protected the town on the side towards the country.[10]

And many other towns, among others Limoges, Auch, Perigueux, Angoulême, Meaux, were the same, or almost the same, as Rhodez.

Would you have a somewhat exact idea of what a castle was, not exactly at the epoch which now occupies us, but at a rather later epoch? I shall borrow its description from a very recent work, and which as yet is not even finished; a work which, in my opinion, is often deficient in a due sentiment for the ancient times, and in moral truth, but which, concerning the actual state of society in the fourteenth and fifteenth centuries, concerning the employment of time, manners, and domestic, industrial, agricultural life, etc., contains very complete information, collected with a great deal of learning, and well arranged. I speak of the *Histoire des Français des divers Etats pendant les cinq derniers Siècles*, by A. A. Monteil, the first four volumes of which are

10. A. A. Monteil, *Histoire des Français des divers états*, vol. 1, p. 196.

published. The author describes, in the following terms, the castle of Montbazon, near Tours, in the fourteenth century.

First, imagine to yourself a superb position, a steep mountain, bristling with rocks, furrowed with ravines and precipices; upon the declivity is the castle. The small houses which surround it set off its grandeur; the Indre seems to turn aside with respect; it forms a large semicircle at its feet.

This castle must be seen when, at sunrise, the outward galleries glimmer with the armour of the sentinels, and the towers are shown all brilliant with their large, new gratings. Those high buildings must be seen, which fill those who defend them with courage, and with fear those who should be tempted to attack them.

The door presents itself all covered with heads of boars or wolves, flanked with turrets, and crowned with a high guardhouse. Enter, there are three inclosures, three moats, three drawbridges to pass. You find yourself in a large, square court, where are cisterns, and on the right and left the stables, hen houses, pigeon houses, coach houses; the cellars, vaults, and prisons are below; above are the dwelling apartments; above these are the magazine, larders, or salting rooms and arsenals. All the roofs are bordered with machicolations, parapets, guard walks, and sentry boxes. In the middle of the court is the donjon, which contains the archives and the treasure. It is deeply moated all round, and can only be entered by a bridge, almost always raised. Although the walls, like those of the castle, are six feet thick, it is surrounded up to half its height with a chemise, or second wall, of large cut stones.

This castle has just been rebuilt. There is something light, fresh, laughing, about it, not possessed by the heavy, massive castles of the last century.[11]

This last phrase will cause some astonishment; one would scarcely expect to hear such a castle qualified with the names of *light, fresh, laughing;* and yet the author is right; and, compared with those of the eleventh and twelfth centuries, the castle of Montbazon really merited these titles. The former were entirely the reverse—heavy, massive, and gloomy; there were not so many courts in them, not so much interior space, nor so judicious a distribution of it. All idea of art or convenience was foreign to

11. Ibid., vol. 1, p. 101.

their construction; they had no monumental character, no idea of the agreeable; defence, safety, was the only thought manifested in them. Men selected the steepest and most savage places; and there, according to the accidents of the ground, the edifice was raised, destined solely to repel attacks effectually, and to shut up the inhabitants. But buildings so conceived were put up by every one, bourgeois as well as lords, ecclesiastics as well as laymen; the territory was covered with them, and they all had the same character, that of dens, or asylums.

Now that we know what was the actual state of feudal habitations at their origin, what passed within? What life was led there by the possessor? What influence must have been exercised over him and his people by such a dwelling, and the material circumstances which arose from it? How and in what direction developed the petty society contained by the castle, and what was the constitutive element of feudal society?

The first feature of its situation was isolation. At no epoch, perhaps, in the history of any society, do we meet with isolation so complete. Take the patriarchal system, the nations which were formed in the plains of western Asia; take the nomadic nations, the tribes of shepherds; take those German tribes I described in one of the last lectures; be present at the birth of the Greek or Roman society; transport yourself to the midst of those villages which afterwards became Athens; to the seven hills whose population formed Rome: everywhere you will find men in infinitely closer connexion, far more disposed to act upon one another, that is to say, to become civilized, for civilization is the result of the reciprocal and continual action of individuals. The primitive social molecule was never elsewhere so isolated, so separated from other like molecules; the distance was never so great between the essential and simple elements of society.

With this first feature, with the isolation of the castle and its inhabitants was combined a singular indolence. The possessor of the castle had nothing to do; no duties, no regular occupation. Among other nations, at their origin, even in the superior classes, men were occupied, sometimes with public affairs, sometimes with frequent and various kinds of relations with neighbouring families. We never find them at a loss how to fill up their time, to satisfy their activity: here they cultivated and improved large estates; there they managed great flocks; elsewhere they hunted for a livelihood; in a word, they had a compulsory activity. Within the castle, the proprietor had nothing to do; it was not he who improved his fields; he did not hunt for his support; he had no political activity, no industrial activity of any kind; never has there been seen such leisure in such isolation.

Men cannot remain in a situation of this kind; they would die of impatience and ennui. The proprietor of the castle thought only of getting out of it. Shut up there when it was absolutely necessary to his safety and independence, he left it as often as he was able, to seek abroad what he was in want of, society, activity. The life of the possessors of fiefs was passed upon the high roads, in adventures. That long series of incursions, pillages, wars, which characterises the middle ages, was in a great measure, the effect of the nature of the feudal habitation, and of the material situation amidst which its masters were placed. They everywhere sought the social movement which they could not find within their own castles.

Horrible pictures of the life which the possessors of fiefs led at this epoch, have been seen in many works. These pictures have often been traced with a hostile hand, in a partial design. Upon the whole, however, I do not think them exaggerated. Historical events on the one hand, and contemporaneous monuments on the other, prove that such was in fact, for a very long period, the feudal life, the life of the seigneurs.

Among the contemporaneous monuments, I shall refer you to three only, in my opinion the most striking, and which give the most exact idea of the state of society at this epoch: first, the *Histoire de Louis le Gros,* by Suger; secondly, the *Vie de Guibert de Nogent,* by himself, a book less known, but curious, and to which I shall immediately return; thirdly, *l'Histoire Ecclésiastique et civile de Normandie,* by Orderic Vital. You will there see to what an extent the life of possessors of fiefs was passed away from home, entirely employed in depredations, incursions, disorders of every description.

Consult events instead of monuments. That which has astonished all historians, the crusades, first presents itself to the mind. Can it be supposed that the crusades would be possible among a people who had not been accustomed, brought up from childhood to this wandering adventurous life? In the twelfth century, the crusades were not nearly so singular as they appear to be to us. The life of the possessors of fiefs, with the exception of the pious motive, was an incursion, a continual crusade in their own country. They here went farther and from other causes; that is the great difference. For the rest, they did not leave their habits; they did not essentially change their mode of life. Could one conceive in the present day a nation of proprietors, who should suddenly displace itself, abandon their estates, or their families, to go, without any absolute necessity, and seek elsewhere such adventures? Nothing of the kind would have been possible, if the daily life of the possessors of fiefs had not been, so to speak, a foretaste of the crusades, if they had not found themselves all prepared for such expeditions.

Thus, whether you consult monuments or events, it will be seen that the need to seek activity and amusement abroad prevailed in the feudal society at this epoch, and that it had a large share, among other causes, in the material circumstances amidst which the possessors of fiefs lived.

Two characteristic traits manifest themselves in feudalism. The one is the savage and fantastical energy of the development of individual characters: not only are they brutal, ferocious, cruel, but they are so in a singular, strange fashion, such as we might look for in an individual who lives alone, abandoned to himself, to the originality of his nature, and to the caprices of his imagination. The second trait, equally striking, in feudal society, is the stubbornness of manners, their long opposition to change, to progress. Into no other society have new ideas, or manners, had so much trouble to penetrate. Civilization was more slow and difficult in modern Europe than anywhere else; it was not till after the tenth century that it actually conquered and settled in the territory. Nowhere was, during so long a period, so little progress with so much movement.

How can we but recognise, in these two facts, the influence of the material circumstances under the empire of which the constitutive element of feudal society lived and was developed? Who does not see therein the effect of the situation of the possessor of the fief, isolated within his castle, surrounded by an inferior and a despised population, obliged to seek afar off, and by violent means, the society and activity which he had not about him? The ramparts and moats of the castles formed obstacles to ideas as to enemies, and civilization had as much trouble as war to penetrate and invade them.

But at the same time that the castles opposed so strong a barrier to civilization, at the same time that it had such difficulty in penetrating therein, they were in some respects a principle of civilization; they protected the development of sentiments and manners which have played a powerful and beneficial part in modern society. There is no one but knows that the domestic life, the spirit of family, and particularly the condition of women, were developed in modern Europe, much more completely, more happily, than elsewhere. Among the causes which contributed to this development, must be reckoned as one of the principal, the life of the castle, the situation of the possessor of the fief in his domains. Never, in any other form of society, has the family reduced to its most simple expression, the husband, the wife, and the children, been found so bound, so pressed together, separated from all other powerful and rival relation. In the various states of society which I have just enumerated, the chief of the family, without quitting home, had numerous occupations, diversions, which drew him from the interior of his dwelling, which at least prevented that from being the centre of his life. The contrary was the case in feudal society. So long as he remained in his castle, the possessor of the fief lived there with his wife and children, almost his only equals, his only intimate and permanent company. Doubtless, he often left it, and abroad led the brutal and adventurous life which I have just described; but he was obliged to return to it. It was there that he shut himself up in times of danger. Now whenever a man is placed in any particular position, the part of his moral nature which corresponds to that position is forcibly developed in him. If he be obliged to live habitually in the bosom of his family, with his wife and children, the ideas, the sentiments in harmony with this fact cannot fail to have great influence. Thus it happened in feudalism.

Moreover, when the possessor of the fief left his castle to seek war and adventures, his wife remained in it, and in a situation wholly different from that in which women had hitherto almost always been placed. She remained mistress, chatelaine, representing her husband, charged in his absence with the defence and honour of the fief. This elevated and almost sovereign position, in the very bosom of domestic life, often gave to the women of the feudal period a dignity, a courage, virtues, a distinction, which they have displayed nowhere else, and it has doubtless powerfully contributed to their moral development and to the general improvement of their condition.

This is not all. The importance of children, of the eldest son more especially, was much greater in the feudal mansion than anywhere else. There developed not only natural affection, and the desire to transmit his property to his children, but also the desire to transmit to them that power, that superior position, that sovereignty, inherent in the domain. The eldest son of the lord was, in the eyes of his father and all his people, a prince, an heir presumptive, the depositary of the glory of a dynasty. So that the weaknesses as well as the good feelings of human nature, domestic pride as well as affection, combined to give the spirit of family more energy and power.

Add to this the influence of Christian ideas, which I here merely point out in passing, and you will comprehend how this life of the castle, this solitary, gloomy, hard situation, was favourable to the development of domestic life, and to that elevation of the condition of women which holds so great a place in the history of our civilization.

This great and beneficial revolution was accomplished between the ninth and twelfth centuries. We cannot follow the trace of it step by step; we can but very imperfectly mark the particular facts which have served it as steps, for we are deficient in documents. But that at the eleventh century it was almost consummated, that the position of women was changed, that the spirit of family, the domestic life, the ideas and sentiments connected with it, acquired a development, an empire, till then unknown, is a general fact which it is impossible to overlook. Many of you will still have before you the spirit of the monuments of the eleventh century, which I placed before you in the last course; compare them with the three pages I shall here quote from the *Vie de Guibert de Nogent,* of which I just now spoke. They have no historical importance, and no other merit than that of showing to what dignity, to what refined and delicate sentiments, women and domestic manners were elevated from the ninth to the eleventh century; but, under this point of view, they appear to me conclusive, and of a genuine interest.

Guibert de Nogent gives an account in this work, both of the public events at which he was present, and of the personal events which passed within his own family. He was born in 1053, in a castle of Beauvaisis. Let us see how he speaks of his mother, and of his relations with her. Call to mind the narrative, or rather the language (for narrative is entirely wanting,) of writers contemporaneous with Charlemagne, Louis le Debonnaire, and Charles le Chauve, on a similar matter, and say if this is the same state of relations and of souls. . . .

> The eighth month of my birth had scarcely elapsed, when my father in the flesh died; . . . although my mother was still fair and of fresh age, she resolved to remain a widow, and how great was the firmness which she used to accomplish this vow! How great were the examples of modesty which she gave! . . . Living in great fear of the Lord, and with an equal love for her neighbours, especially those who were poor, she managed us prudently, us and our property. . . . Her mouth was so accustomed to continually repeat the name of her dead husband, that it seemed as if her soul had never any other thought; for, whether in praying or distributing alms, even in the most ordinary acts of life, she continually pronounced the name of that man, which showed that her mind was always preoccupied with him. In fact, when the heart is absorbed in a feeling of love, the tongue forms itself in a manner to speak, as it were unconsciously, of him who is its object.[12]

12. *Vie de Guibert de Nogent,* bk. 1, chap. 4, p. 355; chap. 12, p. 385; chap. 13, pp. 396, 397, in Guizot, *Collection des Mémoires relatifs à l'Histoire de France,* vol 9.

My mother brought me up with the most tender care . . . Scarcely had I learned the first elements of letters, when, eager to have me instructed, she confided me to a master of grammar. . . . There was shortly before this epoch, and even at this time, so great a scarcity of masters of grammar, that, so to speak, scarce one was to be seen in the country, and hardly could they be found in the great towns. . . . He to whom my mother resolved to confide me had learned grammar in a rather advanced age, and was so much the less familiar with this science, as he had devoted himself to it at a later period; but what he wanted in knowledge, he made up for in virtue. . . . From the time that I was placed under his care, he formed in me such a purity, he so thoroughly eradicated from me all the vices which generally accompany youth, that he preserved me from the most frequent dangers. He allowed me to go nowhere except in his company, to sleep nowhere but in my mother's house, to receive a present from no one without her permission. He required me to do everything with moderation, precision, attention, and exertion. . . . While most children of my age ran here and there, according to their pleasure, and were allowed from time to time the enjoyment of the liberty which belongs to them, I, held in continual restraint, muffled up like a clerk, looked upon the bands of players as if I had been a being above them.

Every one, seeing how my master excited me to work, hoped at first that such great application would sharpen my wits; but this hope soon diminished, for my master, altogether unskilful at reciting verses, or composing them according to rule, almost every day loaded me with a shower of cuffs and blows, to force me to know what he himself was unable to teach me. . . . Still he showed me so much friendship; he occupied himself concerning me with so much solicitude, he watched so assiduously over my safety, that, far from experiencing the fear generally felt at that age, I forgot all his severity, and obeyed with an inexpressible feeling of love. . . . One day, when I had been struck, having neglected my work for some hours in the evening, I went and sat myself at my mother's knee, severely bruised, and certainly more so than I had deserved. My mother having, according to her custom, asked if I had been beaten that day, I, in order to avoid accusing my master, assured her that I had not. But she pulling aside, whether I would or no, the garment they call a shirt, saw my little arms all black, and the skin of my shoulders all raised up and swollen by the blow of the rod which I had received. At this sight, complaining that they treated me with too much cruelty at so tender an age, all troubled and beside herself, her eyes full of tears, she cried "I will no longer have thee become a priest, nor in order to learn letters, that thou thus endure such treatment." But I, at these words, regarding her with all the rage of which I was capable, said to her: "I would rather die than cease learning letters, and wishing to be a priest."[13]

Who can read this account without being struck with the prodigious development which, in two centuries, had been taken by the domestic sentiments, the importance attached to children, to their education, to all the ties of family? You might search through all the writers of the preceding centuries, and never find anything resembling it. We cannot, I repeat, give an exact account of the manner in which this revolution was accomplished; we do not follow it in its degrees, but it is incontestable.

I must close this lecture. I have given you a glimpse of the influence which the internal life of the feudal castles exercised over the domestic manners, and to the advantage of the sentiments which arose from it. You will immediately see this life take a great extension; new elements will become joined to it, and will contribute to the progress of civilization. It was in the castles that chivalry took birth and grew. We shall occupy ourselves with it in our next lecture.

Lecture 6

Isolation and idleness were, as you have seen, the most prominent features of the situation of the possessor of the fief in his castle, the natural effect of the material circumstances in which he was placed. Hence, as you have also seen, arose two results apparently contradictory, and which yet wonderfully accorded. On the one hand, the need, the passion for that life of incursions, war, pillage, adventures, which characterises the feudal society; on the other, the power of domestic life, the progress of the position of women, of the spirit of family, and of all the sentiments connected with it. Without premeditation, by the mere effect of their situation, and of the manners which it gave rise to, the possessors

13. Ibid., bk. 1, chap. 4, pp. 355, 356; chap. 5, p. 358; chap. 6, pp. 363, 364.

of fiefs sought at once afar off and within their dwelling, in the most tempestuous, the most unforeseen chances, in the nearest and most habitual interests, wherewith to fill up their life and to occupy their soul, a twofold satisfying of that need for society and activity, one of the most powerful instincts of our nature.

Neither one nor the other of these means sufficed. Those wars, those adventures, which in the present day, at a distance of seven or eight centuries, appear to us so multiplied, so continual, were probably, in the eyes of the men of the eleventh century, rare, soon terminated, mere transitory incidents. The days of the year seem very numerous and long to him who has nothing to do, no necessary, regular, or permanent occupation. The family, in its proper and natural limits, reduced to the wife and children, did not suffice to fill them up. Men with manners so rude, with a mind so little developed, soon exhausted the resources which they found in them. To fertilize, so to speak, the sensible nature of man, and make it give rise to a thousand means of occupation and interest, is the result of a very advanced civilization. This moral abundance is unknown in rising societies; its sentiments are strong, but abrupt, and brief, as it were; the influence which they exercise over life is greater than the place which they hold in it. Domestic relations, as well as external adventures, assuredly left a great void to fill up in the time and soul of the possessors of fiefs of the eleventh century.

Men must have sought, in fact did seek, to fill it up, to animate, to people the castle, to draw thither the social movement which it wanted; and they found the means.

You will recollect the life which, before the invasion, the German warriors led around their chief, that life of banquets, of games, of festivals, and which was always passed in common.

"Feasts," says Tacitus, "banquets ill prepared but abundant, are given them instead of pay . . . no one is ashamed to pass the day or night drinking. . . . They most frequently treat at the banquets, of enemies to be reconciled, alliances to be formed, chiefs to be chosen, of peace and of war."[14]

14. Tacitus, *De Moribus Germanorum*, c. 14, 22.

After the invasion and the territorial establishment, this con-glomeration of warriors, this life in common (as I have already had occasion to observe), did not immediately cease; many com-panions still continued to live around their chief, upon his domains, and in his house. Moreover, we find the chiefs, the prin-cipal of them at least, kings or others, forming a court, a palace, upon the model of the palace of the Roman emperors. The multitude and titles of officers, and servants of all kinds, who all at once make their appearance in the house of the great barbarians, are inexplicable to those who do not know the organi-zation of the imperial palace. Referendary, seneschal, marshal, falconers, butlers, cup-bearers, chamberlains, porters, harbin-gers, etc., such are the offices which are found from the sixth century, not only in the establishments of the Frank, Burgundian, and Visigoth kings, but among their more considerable ben-eficiaries, of which the greater part are borrowed from the *notitia dignitatum*, the imperial almanac of the time.

Soon, you have seen, the taste for and habit of territorial prop-erty gained more influence; the greater part of the companions left the chief; some went to live in benefices which they held of him; others fell into a subaltern condition, into that of coloni. This revolution was operated more especially in the course of the seventh and eighth centuries. We then see the home of the chief broken up, or at least very much contracted; only a few companions remained near his person. He was not entirely alone, or absolutely reduced to his family, properly so called; but he was no longer surrounded by a band of warriors as before the in-vasion, nor at the head of a little imperial palace, as in the cen-tury which followed it.

When we arrive at the end of the tenth century, or rather at the middle of the eleventh, at the epoch when feudalism attains its complete development, we find, around the great possessors of fiefs, numerous officers, a considerable train, a little court. We find there not only most of the offices which I have just named, and which they had borrowed from the empire, not only the count of the palace, the seneschal, the marshal, the cup-bearers, falconers, etc., but new officers and names, pages, varlets, grooms, and squires of all kinds: squire of the body, squire of the chamber, squire of the stable, squire of the pantry, carving squire, etc., and most of these charges are evidently filled by free men; indeed by men, if not equal to the lord with whom they live, at least in the same state, the same condition with him. When La Fontaine said:

> Tout petit prince a des ambassadeurs,
> Tout marquis veut avoir des pages,

he ridiculed a foolish pretension, an absurdity of his time. This pretension, not ridiculous then, was in the eleventh and twelfth centuries a simple general fact, and it was not necessary to be a prince in order to have ambassadors, or a marquis to have pages; every lord, every possessor of a fief, of *reasonable* greatness, as La Fontaine would have said, had many around him.

How was this fact brought about? How was this numerous and regularly constituted train formed in the interior of the castle, around the suzerain?

To this, I think, two principal causes contributed: (1) the creation and perpetuation of a certain number of interior domestic offices, given in fief, as well as estates; (2) the custom soon adopted by the vassals, of sending their sons to the suzerain, to be brought up with his sons in his house.

The principal, in fact, of the offices which I have just named, those among others of the constable, marshal, seneschal, chamberlain, butler, etc., were at an early period given in fief, like lands. The benefices in lands, as has been seen, had the inconvenience of dispersing the companions, of separating them from the chief. Offices given in fief, on the contrary, retained them, at all events very frequently, about him, and so far better secured to him their services and fidelity. Thus, from the time that this invention of the feudal mind appeared, we see it spreading with great rapidity; all kinds of offices were given in fief, and the proprietors, ecclesiastics as well as laymen, thus surrounded themselves with a numerous train.

. . . .

Thus was the interior of the castle peopled and animated, thus was the circle of feudal domestic life enlarged. All these officers, all these young sons of vassals, formed part of the household, acquitted themselves of services of all kinds; and the social movement, the intercourse between equals, returned to these habitations so isolated and of so austere an appearance.

At the same time, and also in the interior of the chateau, was developed another fact of equally ancient origin, and which, in order to arrive at that which it was destined to become in feudal society, had many transformations to undergo.

Before the invasion, beyond the Rhine and the Danube, when the young Germans arrived at the age of men, they solemnly received, in the assembly of the tribe, the rank and arms of warriors.

"It is the custom," says Tacitus, "that none of them should take arms until the tribe have judged him capable of them. Then, in the assembly itself, one of the chiefs, either the father, or a relation, invests the young man with the shield and lance, equivalent to our assumption of the toga, and with them the first honour of youth. Before this they appear only a part of the house; afterward they become members of the republic."[15]

The declaration that a man was entering the class of warriors, was therefore among the Germans a national act, a public ceremony.

We see this fact perpetuated, after the invasion, upon the Gallo-Roman territory. Without citing a great number of obscure examples: in 791, at Ratisbon, Charlemagne solemnly girt the sword (that is the expression of the old chroniclers) about his son Louis le Debonnaire. In 838, Louis le Debonnaire conferred the same honour, with the same solemnity, upon his son Charles le Chauve. The old German custom still subsists, only some religious ceremonies are now joined to it. "In the name of the Father, the Son, and the Holy Ghost," the young warrior receives a kind of consecration.

In the eleventh century, in the feudal castle, when the son of the lord arrives at the age of manhood, the same ceremony is performed: they gird on the sword, they declare him admitted to the rank of warrior.

15. Tacitus, c. 13.

And it was not upon his own son alone, but also upon the young vassals brought up within his house, that the lord conferred this dignity; they deemed it an honour to receive it from the hands of their suzerain, amidst their companions; the court of the castle replaced the assembly of the tribe; the ceremonies were changed; essentially the facts were the same.

Chivalry practically consists in the admission to the rank and honours of warriors, in the solemn delivering of the arms and titles of the warlike life. It was by this that it commenced; we see at first only a simple and uninterrupted prolongation of the ancient Germanic manners.

It is at the same time a natural consequence of feudal relations. We read in the *Histoire de la pairie de France et du parlement de Paris,* by Le Laboureur, a work not without ingenious and solid views:

> The ceremonies of chivalry are a species of investiture, and represent a manner of homage; for the proposed knight appears without cloak, without sword, without spurs: he is invested with them, after the accolade. As the vassal, after the consummation of the act of his homage, he resumes his cloak, which is the mark of chivalry or vassalage; the girdle, which is the ancient military baldric; the spurs, and finally a sword, which is a token of the service he owes to his seigneur; and the analogy holds in reference to the kiss, which forms part of each ceremony. We may add farther, that it was upon the same theory that their subjects were obliged to pay a tax to their lord for the knighthood of their eldest sons, as the first acknowledgment of their future seigneury.[16]

There is a little exaggeration in this language. We cannot consider the admission of the young man to the title of knight as a *manner of hommage;* for it was not the actual vassal, but his son, who was received as a knight by the suzerain. There is, therefore, no true investiture in it. Still the suzerain, in arming the young man knight, accepted him, in a manner, for his man, and declared that he should one day be his vassal. This was like an investiture given in advance, a reciprocal and anticipated engagement, on the part of the suzerain to receive, on the part of the young man to do, at some future day, the feudal homage.

16. Le Laboureur, *Histoire de la pairie de France* (London, 1740), p. 278.

You are aware that people have formed an entirely different idea of chivalry and its origin. It has been represented as a great institution invented in the eleventh century, and with a moral design, with a design of struggling against the deplorable state of society, of protecting the weak against the strong of devoting a certain class of men to the defence of the weak, to the redress of injustice; and this idea has been so general, so powerful, that we even find it in the *Histoire des Français* of M. de Sismondi, generally so clear sighted, so far removed from the routine of his predecessors. The following are the terms in which he states the origin of chivalry:

"Chivalry broke forth," he says, "in all its splendour at the time of the first crusade, that is to say, during the reign of Philip I. . . . The consecration of the arms of the nobility, become the only public force for the defence of the oppressed, seems to have been the fundamental idea of chivalry. At an epoch when religious zeal became reanimated, when valour still seemed the most worthy of all offerings that men could present to the Divinity, it is not surprising that they should have invented a military ordination, after the example of the sacerdotal ordination, and that chivalry should have appeared a second priesthood, destined in a more active manner to the Divine service.[17]

Of a surety, if the picture which I have just traced of the origin of chivalry be true; if the form which I have, so to speak, made rise up before your eyes, be legitimate, the idea which most historians have conceived, and which M. de Sismondi thus sums up, is fallacious. Chivalry, at the eleventh century, was by no means an innovation, an institution brought about by special necessity, and constructed with the design of obviating that necessity. It was formed much more simply, much more naturally, much more obscurely; it was the progressive development of ancient facts, the spontaneous consequence of Germanic manners and feudal relations; it took rise in the interior of castles, without any other intention than of declaring: first, the admission of the young man to the rank and life of warriors; secondly, the tie which united him to his suzerain, to the lord who armed him knight.

17. Sismondi, *Histoire des Français,* vol. 4, pp. 199–201.

An incontestable proof, the history of the very word which designated the knight, of the word *miles,* fully confirms this idea. What follows is that history, and it results from the various senses through which the word passed from the fourth to the fourteenth century, and which Du Cange has verified. Towards the end of the Roman empire, *militare* signified simply *to serve,* to acquit oneself of some service towards a superior, not merely of a military service, but also of a civil service, an office, a function. In this sense we find it said, "Such a one serves (*militat*) in the office of the count, of the governor of the province": *militia clericatûs,* ecclesiastical militia, etc. Doubtless the service originally designated by the word *miles* was the military service; but the word had been successively applied to all kinds of service.

After the invasion, we frequently find it employed in speaking of the palace of barbaric kings, and of the offices filled around them by their companions. Soon afterwards, by a natural reaction, for it is the expression of the social state, the word *miles* resumed its almost exclusively warlike character, and designates the companion, the faithful of a superior. It then becomes synonymous with *vassus, vassalus,* and indicates that one man holds a benefice from another, and is attached to him upon that consideration.

These princes are very noble, and the *knights* (milites) of my lord—Gerbert and his *knight* (miles) Arser. We order that no *knight* (miles) of a bishop, of an abbot, of a marquis, etc., lose his benefice without certain and proved fault. The pope excommunicated Philip, king of the Gauls, because, having repudiated his own wife, he had taken in marriage the wife of his knight (militis suî). The lord Guillaume Hunald, on his knees, and his hands clasped in those of the said count, received from him the aforesaid land, and acknowledged himself his *knight.*[18]

I might multiply these examples: they evidently prove that, from the ninth to the twelfth century, and even later, the word *miles* meant, not the knight, such as he is generally conceived,

18. *Recognovit se esse militem dom. comitis.* See the *Glossary* of Du Cange, at the word *Miles.*

and has just been described by M. de Sismondi but simply the companion, the vassal of a suzerain.

Here is clearly stamped the origin of chivalry. But in proportion as it was developed, when once the feudal society had acquired some fixity, some confidence in itself, the customs, feelings, facts of all kinds, which accompanied the admission of the young men to the rank of vassal warriors, fell under the empire of influences which were not long in imprinting upon them a new turn, another character. Religion and imagination, the church and poetry, took possession of chivalry, and made it a powerful means of attaining the ends which they pursued, of fulfilling the moral needs which it was their mission to satisfy. You have already seen, in the ninth century, some religious ceremonies associated in this matter with German forms. I am about to describe to you the reception of a knight, such as it took place in the twelfth century: you will see what progress the alliance had made, and with what empire the church had penetrated into all the details of this great act of feudal life.

The young man, the squire, who aspired to the title of knight, was first divested of his clothes, and put into the bath, a symbol of purification. Upon coming out of the bath, they clothed him in a white tunic, a symbol of purity in a red robe, a symbol of the blood which he was bound to shed in the service of the faith; in a sagum, or close black coat, a symbol of the death which awaited him as well as all men.

Thus purified and clothed, the recipient observed a rigorous fast for twenty-four hours; then, in the evening, he entered the church, and there passed the night in prayers, sometimes alone, sometimes with a priest and godfathers, who prayed with him.

The following day, his first act was confession; after the confession, the priest administered the communion to him; after the communion, he was present at the mass of the Holy Ghost, and generally at a sermon upon the duties of knights, and the new life which he was about to enter. The sermon finished, the recipient advanced towards the altar, the sword of the knight suspended from his neck; the priest detached it, blessed it, and again put it on his neck. The recipient then went and kneeled before the lord, who was to arm him knight. "With what design," asked the lord, "do you desire to enter into the order? If it is in order to become rich, to repose yourself, and be honoured without doing honour to chivalry, you are unworthy of it, and you would be to the order of chivalry which receives you, what the simoniacal priest is to the prelacy." And, upon the answer of the young man, who promised to acquit himself well of the duties of a knight, the lord granted his request.

Then there approached knights, and sometimes ladies, to clothe the recipient with all his new equipments; they put on him (1) the spurs; (2) the hauberk, or coat of mail; (3) the cuirass; (4) the vambrances and gauntlets; lastly, they girded on his sword.

He was then what they called *adoubé*—that is to say, adopted, according to Du Cange. The lord arose, went to him, and gave him the *accolade* or *accolée*, or *colée*, three blows with the flat of his sword on his shoulder, or nape of the neck, and sometimes a blow with the palm of the hand on his cheek, saying, "In the name of God, of Saint Michael, and Saint George, I dub[19] thee knight;" and he sometimes added, "Be brave, adventurous, and loyal."

The young man thus armed knight, they brought him his helmet and horse, upon which he sprang generally without the help of the stirrups, and caracolled about, brandishing his lance, and making his sword glitter. He finally left the church, and went to caracol around the square at the foot of the castle, before the people, ever eager to take its part in the spectacle.

Who does not recognise ecclesiastical influence in all these details? Who does not see in them a constant anxiety to associate religion with all the phases of an event so solemn in the life of warriors? The most august part of Christianity, its sacraments, take place in it; many of the ceremonies are assimilated, as much as possible, to the administration of the sacraments.

Such is the share which the clergy took in the external, material portion, so to speak, of the reception of knights, in the

19. *Adoubis,* Adopt.

forms of the spectacle. Let us enter into the heart of chivalry, into its moral character, into the ideas, the sentiments with which they endeavoured to penetrate the knight; here again religious influence will be visible.

Look at the series of oaths which the knights had to take. The twenty-six articles which I am about to quote do not form a single act, drawn up at one time and altogether: it is a collection of the various oaths exacted from the knights at different epochs, and in a manner more or less complete, from the eleventh to the fourteenth century. You will easily see that many of these oaths belong to widely different times and states of society; but they do not the less indicate the moral character which it was endeavoured to impress upon chivalry.

The recipients swore:

To fear, revere, and serve God religiously, to fight for the faith with all their strength, and to die a thousand deaths rather than ever renounce Christianity;

To serve their sovereign prince faithfully, and to fight for him and their country most valorously;

To maintain the just right of the weak, such as of widows, orphans, and maidens in a good quarrel, to expose themselves for them according as necessity required, provided that it was not against their own honour, or against their king or natural prince.

. . . . .

That they would fight for the good and profit of the state;

. . . . .

That they would never fight more than one against one, and that they would avoid all fraud and deceit;

. . . . .

That in a tournay, or other combat *à plaisance*, they would never make use of the point of their sword;

. . . . .

That they would never take wages or pension from a foreign prince.

. . . . .

That they would never do violence to ladies or maidens, although they had gained them by arms, without their will and consent.

. . . . .

That they would be faithful observers of their word and pledged faith, and that being taken prisoners in fair war, they would pay exactly the promised ransom, or return to prison at the day and time agreed upon, according to their promise, on pain of being declared infamous and perjured.

. . . . .

That above all things, they would be faithful, courteous, humble, and would never fail in their word, for any ill or loss that might thence happen to them.[20]

Of a surety, there is in this series of oaths, in the obligations imposed upon knights, a moral development very foreign to the lay society of this epoch. Moral notions so elevated, often so delicate, so scrupulous, above all so humane, and always impressed with the religious character, evidently emanated from the clergy. The clergy alone, at that time, thought thus of the duties and relations of men. Its influence was constantly employed in directing the ideas and customs which chivalry had given rise to, towards the accomplishment of these duties, towards the amelioration of these relations. It was not, as has been said, instituted for the protection of the weak, the re-establishment of justice, the reform of manners; it arose, I repeat, simply, undesignedly, as a natural consequence of the Germanic traditions and the feudal relations. But the clergy immediately took hold of it, and made it a means of labouring at the establishment of peace in society, of a more extended, more rigorous morality in individual conduct, that is to say, to the advancement of the general work which they pursued.

The canons of the councils from the eleventh to the fourteenth centuries, if time would allow of the investigation, would also show you the clergy playing the same part in the history of chivalry, applied to bring about the same result.

In proportion as it succeeded, in proportion as chivalry appears more and more under a character at once warlike, religious, and moral, at once conformable and superior to existing manners, it more and more invaded and exalted the imagination of men; and as it was intimately connected with their belief, it soon became the ideal of their thoughts, the source of their most noble

20. Vulson de la Colombière, *Le vrai Théâtre d'honneur et de Chevalerie,* folio, vol. 1, p. 22.

pleasures. Poetry, as well as religion, took possession of it. From
the eleventh century, chivalry, its ceremonies, duties, adventures,
were the mine whence the poets drew, in order to charm the
people, at once to satisfy and to excite that movement of imagination, that want of more varied, more striking events, of more
elevated and purer emotions, than real life could furnish. For,
in the youth of societies, poetry is not only a pleasure, a national
pastime, it is also a progress; it elevates and develops the moral
nature of men, at the same time that it amuses and excites them.
I have just enumerated the oaths which the knights took before
the priests. The following is an old ballad which will show that
the poets imposed the same duties, the same virtues, upon them,
and that the influence of poetry tended towards the same end as
that of religion. It is taken from the manuscript poems of Eustace
Deschamps, and is quoted by M. de Sainte-Palaye.

> You who would enter the order of chivalry, befits you to lead a
> new life; devoutly to watch and pray; to fly sin or pride and all
> villainy; you must defend the church, and take under your charge
> the widow and the orphan; you must be valiant and defend the
> weak; upright, loyal, taking nothing of other men's; by this rule
> must the knight govern himself.
> Let your heart be humble; ever labour and pursue deeds of
> chivalry; be your warfare loyal; travel far and near; seek tournay,
> and joust for your mistress' honour; a true knight must in all things
> pursue honour, so that no blame may befal him, nor cowardice be
> found in his life; let him ever esteem himself least of all; by this
> rule must the knight govern himself.
> He must love his seigneur truly and fully, and above all things
> guard his seigneurie; he must be liberal and a true lover of justice;
> he must seek the company of upright men; hear their sayings, and
> profit by them; he must study the prowesses of valiant warriors,
> that he himself may achieve great deeds, after the example of
> King Alexander; by this rule must the knight govern himself.[21]

Many have said that all this was pure poetry, a beautiful
chimera, having no relation with reality. And, in fact, when we
look at the state of manners in these three centuries, at the daily

21. The original French version from *Poésies Manuscripts d'Eustache
Deschamps* (as quoted in Sainte-Palaye's *Mémoires sur la Chevalerie*, vol.
1) has been deleted.—EDITOR.

incidents which filled the life of men, the contrast with the duties and life of knights is repulsive. The epoch which occupies us is, without doubt, one of the most brutal, one of the rudest in our history; one of those in which we meet with the greatest amount of crime and violence; when the public peace was the most constantly troubled; when the greatest disorder pervaded manners. To him who merely takes into consideration the positive and practical state of society, all this poetry, all this morality of chivalry appears like a mere falsehood. And still we cannot deny but that chivalric morality, poetry existed side by side with these disorders, this barbarism, this deplorable social state. The monuments are there to prove it; the contrast is offensive, but real.

It is precisely this contrast which forms the great characteristic of the middle ages. Carry back your thoughts towards other societies, towards Greek or Roman society, for example, towards the first youth of Greek society, towards its heroic age, of which the poems which bear the name of Homer are a faithful mirror. There is nothing there resembling that contradiction which strikes us in the middle ages. The practice and theory of manners are nearly conformable. We do not find that men have ideas far more pure, more elevated, more generous than their daily actions. The heroes of Homer do not seem to have an idea of their brutality, their ferocity, their egoism, their avidity; their moral knowledge is no better than their conduct; their principles do not rise above their acts. It is the same with almost all other societies in their strong and turbulent youth. In our Europe, on the contrary, in those middle ages which we are studying, facts are habitually detestable; crimes, disorders of all kinds abound; and still men have in their minds, in their imaginations, pure elevated instincts and desires; their notions of virtue are far more developed, their ideas of justice incomparably better than what is practised around them, than what they often practise themselves. A certain moral idea hovers over this rude tempestuous society, and attracts the regard, obtains the respect of men whose life scarcely ever reflects its image. Christianity must, doubtless, be ranked among the number of the principal causes of this fact: its precise characteristic is to inspire men with a great moral ambition, to hold constantly before their eyes a type infinitely superior to human reality, and to excite them to reproduce it. But whatever the cause, the fact is indubitable. We everywhere encounter it in the middle ages, in the popular poems as in the exhortations of priests. Everywhere the moral thought of men aspires far above their life. We should be careful not to suppose that because it does not immediately govern actions, because practice incessantly and strangely gives the lie to theory, the influence of the theory was, therefore, null and worthless. It is much for men to exercise a judgment upon human actions; sooner or later this becomes efficacious. "I prefer a bad action to a bad example," says Rousseau somewhere, and he was right; a bad action may remain isolated; a bad principle is always fertile; for, after all, it is the mind which governs, and man acts according to his thought much more frequently than he himself supposes. Now, in the middle ages, principles were infinitely better than actions. Never, perhaps, for instance, have the relations between men and women been more licentious, and yet never has propriety of manners been more strongly inculcated, and described with more esteem and charm. And it was not the poets only who celebrated it, it was not a mere matter of praises and of songs; we recognise by numerous testimonies that the public thought as the poet spoke, and judged in the same way of this kind of action. . . .

It is true, I cannot guarantee the authenticity of all these details; the romantic is always mixed with the real in documents of this epoch; but what here concerns us is, the state of moral ideas: now, they appear beautiful and pure amidst the licentiousness and grossness of actions.

That is the great characteristic of chivalry; it is for this reason that it holds a great place in the history of our civilization. If we consider it not under a moral point of view, but under a social point of view, not as an idea, but as an institution, there is little in it: not but that it made a great deal of noise, and led to many events, but it was not a true, special institution. Lords, possessors of fiefs, alone were knights, alone had the right to become such. It was somewhat different in the south of France; there the citizens also were often knights, and chivalry was not purely feudal. Even in the north we meet with exceptions; but they are exceptions against which chivalry protested, and which even occasioned prosecutions, legal interdictions. The knights did not form a separate class, which had distinct functions and duties in society; chivalry was a feudal dignity, a character which most of the possessors of fiefs received at a certain age and under certain conditions. It played a great part, greater and more enduring, in my opinion, than it has been represented as having done, in the moral development of France; in social development it held but a small place, and possessed but little consistency.

. . . .

7

Character and Influence of Washington

Two difficult and important duties are assigned to man, and may constitute his true glory; to support misfortune and resign himself to it with firmness; to believe in goodness and trust himself to it with unbroken confidence.

There is a spectacle not less noble or less improving, than that of a virtuous man struggling with adversity; it is that of a virtuous man at the head of a good cause, and giving assurance of its triumph.

If there were ever a just cause, and one which deserved success, it was that of the English colonies in their struggle to become the United States of America. In their case, open insurrection had been preceded by resistance. This resistance was founded upon historical right and upon facts, upon natural right and upon opinions.

It is the honorable distinction of England to have given to her colonies, in their infancy, the seminal principle of their liberty. Almost all of them, either at the time of their being planted or shortly after, received charters which conferred upon the colonists the rights of the mother country. And these charters were not

Excerpts from "Character and Influence of Washington," Guizot's introduction to Jarred Sparks's *Life of Washington* (London: John Murray, 1840). The introduction—written by Guizot for the French edition—was translated into English by Henry Reeve.

a mere deceptive form, a dead letter, for they either established or recognised those powerful institutions, which impelled the colonists to defend their liberties and to control power by dividing it; such as the levying of taxes by vote, the election of the principal public bodies, trial by jury, and the right to meet and deliberate upon affairs of general interest.

Thus the history of these colonies is nothing else than the practical and sedulous developement of the spirit of liberty, expanding under the protecting influence of the laws and traditions of the country. Such, indeed, was the history of England itself.

A still more striking resemblance is presented in the fact, that the colonies of America, at least the greater part of them and the most considerable among them, either were founded, or received their principal increase, precisely at the period when England was preparing to sustain, or was already sustaining, those bold conflicts against the claims of absolute power, which were to confer upon her the honorable distinction of giving the world the first example of a great nation, free and well governed.

From 1578 to 1704, under Elizabeth, James the First, Charles the First, the Long Parliament, Cromwell, Charles the Second, James the Second, William the Third, and Queen Anne, the charters of Virginia, of Massachusetts, of Maryland, of Carolina, and of New York, were, one after another, recognised, contested, restrained, enlarged, lost, regained; incessantly exposed to those struggles and those vicissitudes, which are the condition, indeed the very essence, of liberty; for it is victory, and not peace, that free communities can lay claim to.

At the same time with their legal rights, the colonists had also religious faith. It was not only as Englishmen, but as Christians, that they wished to be free; and their faith was more dear to them than their charters. Indeed, these charters were, in their eyes, nothing more than a manifestation and an image, however imperfect, of the great law of God, the Gospel. Their rights would not have been lost, even had they been deprived of their charters. In their enthusiastic state of mind, supported by divine favor, they would have traced these rights to a source superior and inaccessible to all human power; for they cherished sentiments more elevated than even the institutions themselves, over which they were so sensitively watchful.

It is well known, that, in the eighteenth century, the human understanding, impelled by the accumulation of wealth, the growth of population, and the increase of every form of social power, as well as by its own impetuous and self-derived activity, attempted the conquest of the world. Political science, in all its forms, woke into new and vigorous life; as did, to a still greater degree, the spirit of philosophy, proud, unsatisfied, eager to penetrate and to regulate all things. English America shared in this great movement, but serenely and dispassionately; obeying its inherent tendency rather than rushing into new and untried paths. Philosophical opinions were there combined with religious belief, the triumphs of reason with the heritage of faith, and the rights of man with those of the Christian.

A noble spectacle is presented to us, when we see the union of historical and rational right, of traditions and opinions. A nation, in such a case, gains in prudence as well as in energy. When time-honored and esteemed truths control man without enslaving him, restrain at the same time that they support him, he can move onward and upward, without danger of being carried away by the impetuous flight of his own spirit; soon to be either dashed in pieces against unknown obstacles, or to sink gradually into a sluggish and paralyzing inactivity. And when, by a further union, still more beautiful and more salutary, religious belief is indissolubly linked, in the very mind of man, to the general progress of opinions, and liberty of reason to the firm convictions of faith—it is then that a people may trust themselves to the boldest institutions. For religious belief promotes, to an incalculable extent, the wise management of human affairs. In order to discharge properly the duty assigned to him in this life, man must contemplate it from a higher point of view; if his mind be merely on the same level with the task he is performing, he will soon fall below it, and become incapable of accomplishing it in a worthy manner.

Such was the fortunate condition, both of man and of society, in the English colonies, when, in a spirit of haughty aggression,

England undertook to control their fortunes and their destiny, without their own consent. This aggression was not unprecedented, nor altogether arbitrary; it also rested upon historical foundations, and might claim to be supported by some right.

It is the great problem of political science, to bring the various powers of society into harmony, by assigning to each its sphere and its degree of activity; a harmony never assured, and always liable to be disturbed, but which, nevertheless, can be produced, even from the elements of the struggle itself, to that degree which the public safety imperatively demands. It is not the privilege of states in their infancy to accomplish this result. Not that any essential power is in them absolutely disregarded and annihilated; on the contrary, all powers are found in full activity; but they manifest themselves in a confused manner, each one in its own behalf, without necessary connexion or any just proportion, and in a way to bring on, not the struggle which leads to harmony, but the disorder which renders war inevitable.

In the infancy of the English colonies, three different powers are found, side by side with their liberties, and consecrated by the same charters—the crown, the proprietary founders, whether companies or individuals, and the mother country. The crown, by virtue of the monarchical principle, and with its traditions, derived from the Church and the Empire. The proprietary founders, to whom the territory had been granted, by virtue of the feudal principle, which attaches a considerable portion of sovereignty to the proprietorship of the soil. The mother country, by virtue of the colonial principle, which, at all periods and among all nations, by a natural connexion between facts and opinions, has given to the mother country a great influence over the population proceeding from its bosom.

. . . .

However, to say nothing of eloquence, Washington had not those brilliant and extraordinary qualities, which strike the imagination of men at the first glance. He did not belong to the class of men of vivid genius, who pant for an opportunity of display, are impelled by great thoughts or great passions, and diffuse around them the wealth of their own natures, before any outward occasion or necessity calls for its employment. Free from all internal restlessness and the promptings and pride of ambition, Washington did not seek opportunities to distinguish himself, and never aspired to the admiration of the world. This spirit so resolute, this heart so lofty, was profoundly calm and modest. Capable of rising to a level with the highest destiny, he might have lived in ignorance of his real power without suffering from it, and have found, in the cultivation of his estates, a satisfactory employment for those energetic faculties, which were to be proved equal to the task of commanding armies and founding a government.

But, when the opportunity presented itself, when the exigence occurred, without effort on his part, without any surprise on the part of others, indeed rather, as we have just seen, in conformity with their expectations, the prudent planter stood forth a great man. He had, in a remarkable degree, those two qualities which, in active life, make men capable of great things. He could confide strongly in his own views, and act resolutely in conformity with them, without fearing to assume the responsibility.

It is always a weakness of conviction, that leads to weakness of conduct; for man derives his motives from his own thoughts, more than from any other source. From the moment that the quarrel began, Washington was convinced, that the cause of his country was just, and that success must necessarily follow so just a cause, in a country already so powerful. Nine years were to be spent in war to obtain independence, and ten years in political discussion to form a system of government. Obstacles, reverses, enmities, treachery, mistakes, public indifference, personal antipathies, all these incumbered the progress of Washington, during this long period. But his faith and hope were never shaken for a moment. . . .

To this strong and independent understanding, he joined a great courage, always ready to act upon conviction, and fearless of consequences. "What I admire in Christopher Columbus," said Turgot, "is, not his having discovered the new world, but his having gone to search for it on the faith of an opinion." Whether the occasion was of great or little moment, whether the consequences were near at hand or remote, Washington, when once convinced, never hesitated to move onward upon the faith of his conviction. One would have inferred, from his firm and quiet resolution, that it was natural to him to act with decision, and assume responsibility—a certain sign of a genius born to command; an admirable power, when united to a conscientious disinterestedness.

On the list of great men, if there be some who have shone with a more dazzling lustre, there are none who have been exposed to a more complete test, in war and in civil government; resisting the king, in the cause of liberty, and the people, in the cause of legitimate authority; commencing a revolution and ending it. From the first moment, his task was clearly manifest in all its extent and all its difficulty. To carry on the war, he had not merely to create an army. To this work, always so difficult, the creating power itself was wanting. The United States had neither a government nor an army. Congress, a mere phantom, whose unity was only in name, had neither authority, nor power, nor courage, and did nothing. Washington was obliged, from his camp, not only to make constant solicitations, but to suggest measures for adoption, to point out to Congress what course they should pursue, if they would prevent both themselves and the army from becoming an idle name. His letters were read while they were in session, and supplied the subject of their debates; debates, characterized by inexperience, timidity, and distrust. They rested satisfied with appearances and promises. They sent messages to the local governments. They expressed apprehensions of military power. Washington replied respectfully, obeyed, and then insisted; demonstrated the deceptiveness of appearances, and the necessity of a real force to give him the substance of the power, of which he had the name, and to insure to the army the success which they expected of it. Brave and intelligent men, devoted to the cause, were not wanting in this assembly, so little experienced in the art of government. Some of them went to the camp, examined for themselves, had interviews with Washington, and brought with them, on their return, the weight of their own observations and of his advice. The assembly gradually grew wiser and bolder, and gained confidence in themselves and in their general. They adopted the measures, and conferred upon him the powers, which were necessary. He then entered into correspondence and negotiations with local governments, legislatures, committees, magistrates, and private citizens; placing facts before their eyes; appealing to their good sense and their patriotism; availing himself, for the public service, of his personal friendships; dealing prudently with democratic scruples and the sensitiveness of vanity; maintaining his own dignity; speaking as became his high station, but without giving offence, and with persuasive moderation; though wisely heedful of human weakness, being endowed with the power, to an extraordinary degree, of influencing men by honorable sentiments and by truth.

.   .   .   .

No man can separate himself from the place in which he has once held a distinguished position. "Retired as I am from the world," he writes in 1786, "I frankly acknowledge I cannot feel myself an unconcerned spectator." The spectacle deeply affected and disturbed him. The Confederation was falling to pieces. Congress, its sole bond of union, was without power, not even daring to make use of the little that was intrusted to it. The moral weakness of men was added to the political weakness of institutions. The States were falling a prey to their hostilities, to their mutual distrust, to their narrow and selfish views. The treaties, which had sanctioned the national independence, were executed only in an imperfect and a precarious manner. The debts contracted, both in the old and new world, were unpaid. The taxes destined to liquidate them never found their way into the public treasury. Agriculture was languishing; commerce was declining; anarchy was extending. In all parts of the country itself, whether enlightened or ignorant, whether the blame was laid on the government, or the want of government, the discontent was general. In Europe, the reputation of the United States was rapidly sinking. It was asked if there would ever be any United States. England encouraged this doubt, looking forward to the hour when she might profit by it.

The sorrow of Washington was extreme, and he was agitated and humbled as if he had been still responsible for the course of events. "What, gracious God!" he wrote, on learning of the troubles in Massachusetts, "is man, that there should be such inconsistency and perfidiousness in his conduct? It was but the other day, that we were shedding our blood to obtain the constitutions under which we now live; constitutions of our own choice and making; and now we are unsheathing the sword to overturn them. The thing is so unaccountable, that I hardly know how to realize it, or to persuade myself, that I am not under the illusion of a dream." . . . "We have probably had too good an opinion of human nature in forming our confederation. Experience has taught us, that men will not adopt and carry into execution measures the best calculated for their own good, without the intervention of a coercive power." . . . "From the high ground we stood upon, to be so fallen, so lost, is really mortifying." . . . "In regretting, which I have often done with the keenest sorrow, the death of our much lamented friend, General Greene, I have accompanied it of late with a query, whether he would have preferred such an exit to the scenes which, it is more than probable, many, of his compatriots may live to bemoan."

Nevertheless, the course of events, and the progress of general good sense, were also mingling hope with this patriotic sorrow— a hope full of anxiety and uneasiness, the only one which the imperfection of human things permits elevated minds to form, but which is sufficient to keep up their courage. Throughout the whole Confederation, the evil was felt and a glimpse was caught of the remedy. The jealousies of the States, local interests, ancient habits, democratic prejudices, were all strongly opposed to the sacrifices which were requisite in order to form a government in which the central power should be stronger and more prominent. Still, the spirit of order and union; the love of America as their country; regret at seeing it decline in the esteem of mankind; the disgust created by the petty, interminable, and profitless disturbances of anarchy; the obvious nature of its evils, the perception of its dangers; all the just opinions and noble sentiments which filled the mind of Washington, were gradually extending themselves, gathering additional strength, and preparing the way for a happier future. . . .

Two powers act in concurrence to develop and maintain the life of a people; its civil constitution and its political organization, the general influences of society and the authorities of the State; the latter were wanting to the infant American commonwealth, still more than the former. In this society, so disturbed, so slightly connected, the old government had disappeared, and the new had not yet been formed. I have spoken of the insignificance of Congress, the only bond of union between the States, the only central power; a power without rights and without strength; signing treaties, nominating ambassadors, proclaiming that the public good required certain laws, certain taxes, and a certain army; but not having itself the power of making laws, or judges or officers to administer them; without taxes, with which to pay its ambassadors, officers, and judges, or troops to enforce the payment of taxes and cause its laws, judges, and officers to be respected. The political state was still more weak and more wavering than the social state.

The Constitution was formed to remedy this evil, to give to the Union a government. It accomplished two great results. The central government became a real one, and was placed in its proper position. The Constitution freed it from the control of the States, gave it a direct action upon the citizens without the intervention of the local authorities, and supplied it with the instruments necessary to give effect to its will; with taxes, judges, officers, and soldiers. In its own interior organization, the central government was well conceived and well balanced; the duties and relations of the several powers were regulated with great good sense, and a clear understanding of the conditions upon which order and political vitality were to be had; at least for a republican form and the society for which it was intended.

In comparing the Constitution of the United States with the anarchy from which it sprang, we cannot too much admire the wisdom of its framers and of the generation which selected and sustained them. But the Constitution, though adopted and promulgated, was as yet a mere name. It supplied remedies against

403

the evil, but the evil was still there. The great powers, which it had brought into existence, were confronted with the events which had preceded it and rendered it so necessary, and with the parties which were formed by these events, and were striving to mould society and the Constitution itself according to their own views.

At the first glance, the names of these parties excite surprise. Federal and democratic; between these two qualities, these two tendencies, there is no real and essential difference. In Holland in the seventeenth century, in Switzerland even in our time, it was the democratic party which aimed at strengthening the federal union, the central government; it was the aristocratic party which placed itself at the head of the local governments, and defended their sovereignty. The Dutch people supported William of Nassau and the Stadtholdership against John de Witt and the leading citizens of the towns. The patricians of Schweitz and Uri are the most obstinate enemies of the federal diet and its power.

In the course of their struggle, the American parties often received different designations. The democratic party arrogated to itself the title of *republican,* and bestowed on the other that of *monarchists* and *monocrats.* The federalists called their opponents *anti-unionists.* They mutually accused each other of tending, the one to monarchy, and the other to separation; of wishing to destroy, the one the republic, and the other the union.

This was either a bigoted prejudice or a party trick. Both parties were sincerely friendly to a republican form of government and the union of the States. The names, which they gave one another for the sake of mutual disparagement, were still more false than their original denominations were imperfect and improperly opposed to each other.

Practically, and so far as the immediate affairs of the country were concerned, they differed less, than they either said or thought, in their mutual hatred. But, in reality, there was a permanent and essential difference between them in their principles and their tendencies. The federal party was, at the same time, aristocratic, favorable to the preponderance of the higher

404

classes, as well as to the power of the central government. The democratic party was, also, the local party; desiring at once the rule of the majority, and the almost entire independence of the State governments. Thus there were points of difference between them respecting both social order and political order; the constitution of society itself, as well as of its government. Thus those paramount and eternal questions, which have agitated and will continue to agitate the world, and which are linked to the far higher problem of man's nature and destiny, were all involved in the American parties, and were all concealed under their names.

It was in the midst of this society, so agitated and disturbed, that Washington, without ambition, without any false show, from a sense of duty rather than inclination, and rather trusting in truth than confident of success, undertook actually to found the government which a new-born constitution had just decreed. He rose to his high office, invested with an immense influence, which was acknowledged and received even by his enemies. But he himself has made the profound remark, that "influence is not government."

. . . .

The democratic party, not the turbulent and coarse democracy of antiquity or of the middle ages, but the great modern democracy, never had a more faithful or more distinguished representative than Jefferson. A warm friend of humanity, liberty, and science; trusting in their goodness as well as their rights; deeply touched by the injustice with which the mass of mankind have been treated, and the sufferings they endure, and incessantly engaged, with an admirable disinterestedness, in remedying them or preventing their recurrence; accepting power as a dangerous necessity, almost as one evil opposed to another, and exerting himself not merely to restrain, but to lower it; distrusting all display, all personal splendor, as a tendency to usurpation; of a temper open, kind, indulgent, though ready to take up prejudices against, and feel irritated with, the enemies of his party; of a mind bold, active, ingenious, inquiring, with more penetration than forecast, but with too much good sense to push things to the extreme, and capable of employing, against a pressing danger or evil, a prudence and firmness, which would perhaps have prevented it, had they been adopted earlier or more generally.

It was not an easy task to unite these two men, and make them act in concert in the same cabinet. The critical state of affairs at the first adoption of the Constitution, and the impartial preponderance of Washington alone could accomplish it. He applied himself to it with consummate perseverance and wisdom. At heart, he felt a decided preference for Hamilton and his views. "By some," said he, "he is considered an ambitious man, and therefore a dangerous one. That he is ambitious, I shall readily grant; but it is of that laudable kind, which prompts a man to excel in whatever he takes in hand. He is enterprising, quick in his perceptions, and his judgment intuitively great." But it was only in 1798, in the freedom of his retirement, that Washington spoke so explicitly. While in office, and between his two secretaries, he maintained towards them a strict reserve, and testified the same confidence in them both. He believed both of them to be sincere and able; both of them necessary to the country and to himself. Jefferson was to him, not only a connecting tie, a means of influence, with the popular party, which was not slow in becoming the opposition; but he made use of him in the internal administration of his government, as a counterpoise to the tendencies, and especially to the language, sometimes extravagant and inconsiderate, of Hamilton and his friends. He had interviews and consultations with each of them separately, upon the subjects which they were to discuss together, in order to remove or to lessen beforehand their differences of opinion. He knew how to turn the merit and the popularity of each with his own party, to the general good of the government, even to their own mutual advantage. He skilfully availed himself of every opportunity to employ them in a common responsibility. And when a disagreement too wide, and passions too impetuous, seemed to threaten an immediate rupture, he interposed, used exhortation and intreaty, and, by his personal influence, by a frank and touching appeal to the patriotism and right-mindedness of the two rivals, he at least postponed the breaking forth of the evil which he could not eradicate.

. . . .

There are some events which Providence does not permit those who live at the time of their occurrence to understand; so vast, so complicated, that they far surpass the comprehension of man, and, even when they are exploding, still remain for a long time darkly hidden in the depths, from which proceed those shocks, that ultimately decide the destinies of the world.

Such was the French revolution. Who has measured it? Whose judgment and forecast have not been a thousand times deceived by it, whether friends or foes, admirers or detractors? When the spirit of society and the spirit of man are shaken and convulsed to such a degree, results are produced which no imagination had conceived, no forethought could grasp.

That which experience has taught us, Washington caught sight of from the first day. At the time when the French Revolution had hardly begun, he was already suspending his judgment, and taking his position aloof from all parties and all spectators; free from the presumption of their predictions, from the blindness of their hostility or their hope. "The whole business is so extraordinary in its commencement, so wonderful in its progress, and may be so stupendous in its consequences, that I am almost lost in the contemplation. . . . Nobody is more anxious for the happy issue of that business, than I am; as no one can wish more sincerely for the prosperity of the French nation, than I do." "If it ends as our last accounts, to the first of August [1789], predict, that nation will be the most powerful and happy in Europe; but I fear, though it has gone triumphantly through the first paroxysm, it is not the last it has to encounter before matters are finally settled. . . . The mortification of the king, the intrigues of the queen, and the discontent of the princes and noblesse, will foment divisions, if possible, in the National Assembly; . . . the licentiousness of the people on one hand, and sanguinary punishments on the other, will alarm the best disposed friends to the measure. . . . To forbear running from one extreme to another is no easy matter; and, should this be the case, rocks and shelves, not visible at present, may wreck the vessel, and give a higher-toned despotism than the one which existed before." "It is a boundless ocean, whence no land is to be seen."

From that time, he maintained towards the nations and events of Europe an extreme reserve; faithful to the principles which had founded the independence and the liberties of America, animated by a grateful goodwill towards France, and seizing with earnestness upon every occasion to manifest it, but silent and self-restrained, as if under the presentiment of some grave responsibility of which he should be obliged to sustain the weight, and not wishing to pledge beforehand either his personal opinion or the policy of his country.

When the trying moment arrived, when the declaration of war between France and England caused the great revolutionary struggle to break out in Europe, the resolution of Washington was decided and prompt. He immediately made proclamation of the neutrality of the United States. . . .

No head of a state was ever more reserved than Washington in the exercise of power; more cautious in making engagements and taking new steps. But, also, no one ever maintained more firmly his declarations, his purposes, and his rights. He was President of the United States of America. He had, in their name, and by virtue of their constitution, proclaimed their neutrality. The neutrality was to be real and respected as well as his power. At five successive meetings, he laid before his cabinet the whole correspondence, and all the documents, relating to this singular contest; and the cabinet decided unanimously, that the recall of M. Genêt should be immediately demanded of the French government.

Genêt was recalled. In the opinion of America, as well as in his demand upon France, Washington gained a triumph. The federalists indignantly rallied around him. The pretensions and extravagant conduct of Genêt had alienated many persons of the democratic party. Jefferson had not hesitated to support the President against him. A favorable reaction took place, and the contest seemed at an end.

But in government, as well as in war, there are victories which cost dear, and leave the danger still existing. The revolutionary fever, once more kindled in the United States, did not depart with a recalled minister. Instead of that harmony of feeling, that calm after the storm of passions; instead of that course of prosperity and general moderation, upon which the American republic was lately congratulating itself, two parties were there in a hostile attitude, more widely separated, more violently irritated, than ever. The opposition no longer confined its attacks to the administration alone, to the financial measures of government, and to this or that doubtful application of legal powers. It had, concealed within itself, in the democratic associations, in the periodical press, and among the foreigners who swarmed throughout the country, a true revolutionary faction, eager to overturn society and its government, in order to reconstruct them upon other foundations. "There exists in the United States," writes Washington to Lafayette, "a party formed by a combination of causes, which oppose the government in all its measures, and are determined, as all their conduct evinces, by clogging its wheels, indirectly to change the nature of it, and to subvert the Constitution. To effect this, no means which have a tendency to accomplish their purposes are left unessayed. The friends of government, who are anxious to maintain its neutrality, and to preserve the country in peace, and adopt measures to secure these objects, are charged by them as being monarchists, aristocrats, and infractions of the Constitution, which, according to their interpretation of it, would be a mere cipher. They arrogated to themselves the sole merit of being the friends of France, when in fact they had no more regard for that nation than for the Grand Turk, further than their own views were promoted by it; denouncing those who differed in opinion (whose principles are purely American, and whose sole view was to observe a strict neutrality) as acting under British influence, and being directed by her counsels, or as being her pensioners." . . . "If the conduct of these men is viewed with indifference; if there are activity and misrepresentation on one side, and supineness on the other, their numbers accumulated by intriguing and discontented foreigners under proscription, who were at war with their own governments, and the greater part of them with *all* governments, they will increase, and nothing short of Omniscience can foretell the consequences."

. . . .

Washington did well to withdraw from public business. He had entered upon it at one of those moments, at once difficult and favorable, when nations, surrounded by perils, summon all their virtue and all their wisdom to surmount them. He was admirably suited to this position. He held the sentiments and opinions of his age without slavishness or fanaticism. The past, its institutions, its interests, its manners, inspired him with neither hatred nor regret. His thoughts and his ambition did not impatiently reach forward into the future. The society, in the midst of which he lived, suited his tastes and his judgment. He had confidence in its principles and its destiny; but a confidence enlightened and qualified by an accurate instinctive perception of the external principles of social order. He served it with heartiness and independence, with that combination of faith and fear which is wisdom in the affairs of the world, as well as before God. On this account, especially, he was qualified to govern it; for democracy requires two things for its tranquillity and its success; it must feel itself to be trusted and yet restrained, and must believe alike in the genuine devotedness and the moral superiority of its leaders. On these conditions alone can it govern itself while in a process of development, and hope to take a place among the durable and glorious forms of human society. It is the honor of the American people to have, at this period, understood and accepted these conditions. It is the glory of Washington to have been their interpreter and instrument.

He did the two greatest things which, in politics, man can have the privilege of attempting. He maintained, by peace, that independence of his country, which he had acquired by war. He founded a free government, in the name of the principles of order, and by reestablishing their sway.

When he retired from public life, both tasks were accomplished, and he could enjoy the result. For, in such high enterprises, the labor which they have cost matters but little. The sweat of any toil is dried at once on the brow where God places such laurels.

He retired voluntarily, and a conqueror. To the very last, his policy had prevailed. If he had wished, he could still have kept the direction of it. His successor was one of his most attached friends, one whom he had himself designated.

Still the epoch was a critical one. He had governed successfully for eight years, a long period in a democratic state, and that in its infancy. For some time, a policy opposed to his own had been gaining ground. American society seemed disposed to make a trial of new paths, more in conformity, perhaps, with its bias. Perhaps the hour had come for Washington to quit the arena. His successor was there overcome. Mr. Adams was succeeded by Mr. Jefferson, the leader of the opposition. Since that time, the democratic party has governed the United States.

Is this a good or an evil? Could it be otherwise? Had the government continued in the hands of the federal party, would it have done better? Was this possible? What have been the consequences, to the United States, of the triumph of the democratic party? Have they been carried out to the end, or have they only begun? What changes have the society and constitution of America undergone, what have they yet to undergo, under their influence?

These are great questions; difficult, if I mistake not, for natives to solve, and certainly impossible for a foreigner.

However it may be, one thing is certain; that which Washington did—the founding of a free government, by order and peace, at the close of the Revolution—no other policy than his could have accomplished. He has had this true glory; of triumphing, so long as he governed; and of rendering the triumph of his adversaries possible, after him, without disturbance to the state.

More than once, perhaps, this result presented itself to his mind, without disturbing his composure. "With me, a predominant motive has been to endeavour to gain time to our country to settle and mature its yet recent institutions; and to progress without interruption to that degree of strength and consistency, which is necessary to give it, humanly speaking, the command of its own fortunes."

The people of the United States are virtually the arbiters of their own fortunes. Washington had aimed at that high object. He reached his mark.

Who has succeeded like him? Who has seen his own success so near and so soon? Who has enjoyed, to such a degree and to the last, the confidence and gratitude of his country?

Still, at the close of his life, in the delightful and honorable retirement at Mount Vernon, which he had so longed for, this great man, serene as he was, was inwardly conscious of a slight feeling of lassitude and melancholy; a feeling very natural at the close of a long life employed in the affairs of men. Power is an oppressive burden; and mankind is hard to serve, when one is struggling virtuously against their passions and their errors. Even success does not efface the sad impressions which the contest has given birth to; and the exhaustion, which succeeds the struggle, is still felt in the quiet of repose.

The disposition of the most eminent men, and of the best among the most eminent, to keep aloof from public affairs, in a free democratic society, is a serious fact. Washington, Jefferson, Madison, all ardently sighed for retirement. It would seem as if, in this form of society, the task of government were too severe for men who are capable of comprehending its extent, and desirous of discharging the trust in a proper manner.

Still, to such men alone this task is suited, and ought to be intrusted. Government will be, always and everywhere, the greatest exercise of the faculties of man, and consequently that which requires minds of the highest order. It is for the honor, as well as for the interest, of society, that such minds should be drawn into the administration of its affairs, and retained there; for no institutions, no securities, can supply their place.

And, on the other hand, in men who are worthy of this destiny, all weariness, all sadness of spirit, however it might be permitted in others, is a weakness. Their vocation is labor. Their reward is, indeed, the success of their efforts, but still only in labor. Very often they die, bent under the burden, before the day of recompense arrives. Washington lived to receive it. He deserved and enjoyed both success and repose. Of all great men, he was the most virtuous and the most fortunate. In this world, God has no higher favors to bestow.

8

Memoir of Madame de Rumford

FIVE years ago, in a good and pleasant house, no longer in existence, and in the middle of a beautiful garden, now replaced by a street, a select and varied society was in the habit of assembling two or three times a week. In this circle were included members of the fashionable world, philosophers, scholars, foreigners, and natives; men of the old times and men of today; old and young people; members of the government, and the opposition. Amongst those who were thus associated, many met in no other place; or if they did meet occasionally, it was with mutual coldness and forced toleration. But there, all evinced towards one another extreme politeness and almost cordiality. Not that any one was attracted by a special interest or object which compelled dissimulation or reserve. It was not a house of political or literary patronage, where people went to push their fortunes or prepare success. A taste for good company, a desire of participation in the daily incidents of social life which form the amusement of the idle world and the relaxation of the busy— in these consisted the only incentive and charm that collected at the residence of Madame de Rumford such crowded and eager assemblies, and amongst them so many distinguished men of different classes and opinions.

From *Memoirs to Illustrate the History of My Time,* vol. 2, translated by J. W. Cole (London: Richard Bentley, 1858) from *Mémoires pour Servir à l'Histoire de mon Temps.*

Fontenelle, Montesquieu, Voltaire, Turgot, or D'Alembert, if they could return amongst us, would be greatly surprised at seeing such a house and its habits looked upon as either strange or rare. It was the general spirit and customary life of their day— a period of noble and liberal sociability which brought into play many important questions and matters, extracting only the gentler elements, the action of thought and hope, leaving to its heirs the burden of trial and practical experience.

When this inheritance became available, and the present generation entered on the stage of the world, the eighteenth century, so recently closed, was already at a great distance. An immense abyss, the Revolution, separated us from it, engulfing an entire past of several ages, the eighteenth included. Not one survived of the distinguished characters who had formed the power and glory of that great epoch. The salons of Paris, at once the theatre and implement of their success, that brilliant society, so passionately devoted to pleasures of the mind, had disappeared at the same time. Instead of courting mutual association and acquaintance as formerly, with one concurrent feeling, the nobility, the clergy, the bar, men of business, and men of letters, all classes belonging to the old system—or rather their ruins, for ruin alone remained of everything—separated from and almost shunned each other, concentrating themselves within the habits and interests of their individual position. The dispersion and isolation of coteries succeeded to the impulses of associated ideas. Emigrés, members of the Constituent Assembly and National Convention, Imperial functionaries, and men of letters, divided themselves into small circles, each living and thinking apart from the rest, with mutual indifference or malevolence.

The eighteenth century had also its own exclusive circle. A distinct coterie like the rest, but the sole inheritor of the ruling character of the time, the only faithful relic of the manners and tastes of that philosophical association which had itself perished in the ruin of the more extended society it had subverted.

A woman of seventy-nine years of age, two academicians— one eighty-two and the other seventy-six—formed in 1809 the sole remaining central points of the community, which in 1769 so many, and such powerful, leaders of public opinion had assembled and retained around them. The drawing rooms of Madame d'Houdetot, of M. Suard, and of the Abbé Morellet, were almost the only asylums in which the spirit of the old century still reflected itself faithfully and at perfect ease. Not that the memory of that age was disparaged elsewhere, or that many did not still claim to belong to it. How could the new men, the children of the Revolution and the Empire, repudiate the eighteenth century? But how little did they resemble it! Politics absorbed their faculties—practical, substantial politics. All their thoughts and energies were incessantly occupied with the affairs of their master or with their own. They had no leisure, no meditation; their lives consisted of movement and làbour, varied by labour and movement. The eighteenth century also took an interest in politics, but from taste and not through necessity. Politics considerably occupied their minds, but never engrossed their lives. They reflected, argued, and projected much, but indulged in little action. At no period have political questions engaged such general and expanded intellectual preoccupation; and perhaps no period was ever less familiar with the spirit of policy properly so designated; a single spirit, prompt, judicious, resolved, light in thought but serious in action, which sees nothing but facts and is anxious for results alone.

Apart from this opposition between science and practice, what an immense abyss exists between the policy of the last thirty years and that which was attempted half a century earlier! What had become of the doctrines, the hopes by which a whole nation —nay, even all nations—had been excited and charmed? How did the men of business of the nineteenth century fulfil the promise of the philosophers of the eighteenth? Some boldly, and others with timidity and embarrassment, deserted the ideas and institutions the very perspective of which had made their fortunes. Despotism, a learned and reasoning despotism, aspiring to erect itself into a system, beheld in its service the children of the most profound theories of liberty. Many persons of honourable feeling, attached in their hearts to their ancient faith, protested from time to time, but without effect, against the insults and attacks by which they were surrounded. The greater number, by defending Voltaire against Geoffroi, and the unbelievers against the devout, looked upon themselves as quits with philosophy and liberty. But what would the philosophers have said, or even Voltaire himself, in spite of his contempt for metaphysics and his complaisance for power, if they had been present at a dinner given by the Archchancellor, or at a sitting of the Imperial State Council? Can it be believed that the eighteenth century would have recognized itself in that society, or have accepted its successors as true representatives?

There was no greater resemblance between them either in manners, turn of mind, tone of thought, habits, and external forms. Men of the world as well as scholars, the philosophers of the eighteenth century had passed their lives in the most delightful and brilliant circles of that very society they attacked with bitterness. They had hailed and celebrated it, they had participated in all the enjoyments of its elegant and agreeable existence; they had indulged in all its tastes, habits, and refinements, in all the susceptibilities of a civilization at once decrepit and regenerated, aristocratic and literary; they belonged to that old system demolished by their very hands. But the philosophers of the second generation, the true offspring of the Revolution and the Empire, had no connection with that class, and had only known to destroy it. Between them and the select society of the eighteenth century, there existed no common tie. In place of the drawing rooms of Madame Geoffrin, Mademoiselle de Lespinasse, Madame Trudaine, the Maréchale de Beauveau, and Madame Necker, they had lived in public assemblies, clubs, and camps. With them, events of terrible significance had replaced the pleasures of society and the successes of the Academy. Far indeed from being fashioned for the enjoyment of social intercourse in an easy, idle life, everything connected with them bore the impress of the active and overwhelming times through which they had passed. Their manners were neither elegant nor gentle. They conversed and entertained abruptly and rudely, as if always in a hurry, and without leisure to attend to the conventionalities of life. If corrupt, they subsided into gross and cynical selfishness; if honest, their outward demeanour, without reference to their virtues, wanted the finish and harmony that seem exclusively peculiar to the habitual and tranquil enjoyment of a situation or a sentiment. They had little taste for conversation, reading, interchange of visits, and all those pursuits without definite end—those semi-superfluous relaxations in which but recently so many persons had found occupation, half serious and half frivolous, for their minds and time. . . .

Amongst these men of the new system, a few philosophers and writers alone, chiefly without office and suspected by the Imperial government, felt the necessity and sought occasional opportunities of assembling together, to converse, to inquire, and to enjoy in common the pleasures of intellectual recreation. They formed a liberal society, professing intense admiration of the eighteenth century, and flattering themselves that in them it was continued. But chiefly springing from the Revolution, they bore the stamp of that period, much more deeply impressed than that of its predecessor. Although men of totally different ideas and origin were mixed up with them, taken altogether the revolutionary spirit predominated in that circle, with its merits and defects, more independent than elevated, and more severe than independent; friendly to humanity and its advancement, but mistrustful, envious, and unsociable towards all who shrank from its yoke; uniting to the prejudices of a coterie the antipathies of a faction. The circle, moreover, was extremely concentrated within itself. There was little mixture of different classes and habits; little familiarity with men of the world, properly so named; nothing that recalled the composition and action of the old philosophic society. All the little crotchets of literary professionals, exhibited themselves there without restraint; not to speak of a certain indefinable discrepancy of manners, alternately familiar and laboured, equally destitute of reserve and freedom. Either I am much deceived, or in the assemblies of the *Philosophic Decade,* and notwithstanding a community of many ideas, the masters of the eighteenth century I have just named—Montesquieu, Voltaire, Buffon, Turgot, D'Alembert, and even Diderot and Rousseau, the least worldly of their time—would have sometimes felt themselves strangers out of place.

In very different salons, in the suburb of Saint-Germain, and in the midst of the remains of the aristocracy, almost recovered from their overthrow, they would not at first have felt the same surprise. They would have recognized there the manners, style, and all the forms and social appearances of their own age. Perhaps also they might have been gratified by finding some traditions of the old system, and the tie of common reminiscences so powerful even amongst the most opposite dispositions. But on the other hand, how many weighty objections would have driven them away! What a decided opposition of sentiments and ideas! In vain would they have sought some traces of the openness of mind, the liberality of heart, the taste for intellectual pleasures and progress, which fifty years before so remarkably distinguished a leading portion of the French nobility, and had so powerfully contributed to the movement of the century. Instead of these, they would have found a return of inordinate pretensions, and aristocratic pedantry; a bitter repentance for having ever temporarily abandoned it; a puerile anxiety to return its yoke, to reassume the livery of old customs and maxims; an arrogant antipathy to progressive knowledge, the culture of the mind, the philosophes, and all that resembled them.

In some corners, nevertheless, of this camp of the old regime, opposition to the Imperial government, the influence of M. de Châteaubriand, the single fact of independence towards a despot, and of enthusiasm for a celebrated writer, restored an impulse of moral and political generosity, operating as a sympathetic link between the survivors of the aristocracy and the relics of the philosophy of the last century. Undoubtedly Montesquieu and Voltaire would have been more at their ease in the drawing room of Madame de Duras, than in that of the Archchancellor; and M. Suard conversed with M. de Châteaubriand under less restraint than he would have felt with Chénier. But this restricted coterie, more liberal and animated, was then nearly lost in the great aristocratic coterie. Religious convictions divided its members from the philosophes, with whose political ideas they were disposed to concur; and in spite of certain points of contact, and a frequent similarity of sentiments, wishes, tastes, and manners, they appeared, after all, more as opponents than allies, giving themselves up to the movement of reaction, whose target was the eighteenth century.

Another coterie, still more confined, it is true, was even closer to that epoch, and almost seems to have reproduced its image. In this were collected the remains of that portion of the left-hand side of the Constituent Assembly, which in 1789 had declared for constitutional monarchy, neither more nor less; and in which were seated MM. de Clermont-Tonnerre, de la Rochefoucauld, de Broglie, Mounier, Malouet, etc.; a pure and patriotic party, whose ideas had commenced and conducted our revolution, but were unequal to its full accomplishment. Amongst these lovers of sense and probity, the greater part of those who remained faithful to their cause and principles, either keeping aloof from the Imperial government, or serving it with restraint and dignity, formed themselves, at the houses of Madame de Tessé, the Princess d'Hénin, and others, into a small select society, elegant in manners, liberal in opinions, void of all aristocratic folly or revolutionary bitterness; bound by habit to the old system, by sentiment to the new condition and necessities of the country.

It seems that the philosophical relics of the eighteenth century also found here their point of union; and that the few surviving members blended in with this coterie, where they often visited and encountered friends. But a real difference prevented a perfect amalgamation and complete revival of the bygone age. Politics had been the principal, almost the only topic of the Constituents; the link and predominant feature of their association. Issuing from the philosophy and literature of their time, they were neither literary nor philosophical. They paid respect to letters and doctrines, but in a secondary sense, as people who do not make it either their business or their pleasure. Now, the true school of the eighteenth century, that which constituted its centre and impulse, was essentially philosophic and literary. It took an interest in politics, but merely as one of its subjects of reflection, as an application of ideas, proceeding from more remote sources, and leading to very different results. In our days, purely devoted to politics as we are, we look upon that study as man's most attractive and important occupation; and it is almost solely because the eighteenth century originated constitutions and called nations back to liberty, that it appears illustrious in our eyes. Narrow-minded presumption! A field infinitely more vast and diversified than worldly society expands itself before the human faculties, and during its days of power and splendour, is far from feeling satisfied, or exhausting itself in the study of man's relations with his kind. Indisputably political in its desires and results, the eighteenth century embraced a wider scope, and enjoyed in its ideas, and in their truth and manifestation, a pleasure totally independent of the use to which they might be applied by publicists or legislators. Herein lies the true character of the spirit of philosophy, essentially different from the spirit of politics, which only attaches itself to ideas as they bear on social facts, and for the purpose of exclusive application. Certain minute fractions and sections of the eighteenth century, the economists for example, devoted themselves especially to politics; but the age in general, the society of the age in its extended sense, aspired above all other considerations to intellectual conquests and enjoyments of every class, under every signification, and at any price. The imagination of Voltaire, of Rousseau, or of Diderot, would have found itself in prison, if it had been restricted to forms of government and the political destiny of nations.

The last contemporaries of these great men, the survivors of the philosophic school, M. Suard and the Abbé Morellet were assuredly not gifted with such active and expansive ideas. M. Suard had no ardent desire to acquire or impart knowledge. Although literature alone had opened to him the doors of the world, he was more a man of fashion than a man of letters. In disposition, difficult, idle, inclined to aristocratic refinement and disdain, as long as he could lead an honourable life, mixed up with tender interests and agreeable relations, he cared little to display his talents or to win a name. Since work was no longer a necessity for him, he left or resumed it as a pastime; reading and composing at leisure, without definite object, for his gratification alone, with a sort of intellectual epicurism, but divested at the same time of either vanity or indifference. The studies of the Abbé Morellet had been more profound and persevering, but extremely confined. He had almost entirely devoted himself to political economy and a few applications of what he had learned at the Sorbonne. It might be supposed that both he and M. Suard would have been fully satisfied with the society of the Constituents, the traditions of their time, their elegant manners, their esteem for letters, and their political principles. But this was not the case. After the example of their masters, they both felt intellectual necessities extremely varied in character. They took a more disinterested interest, if I may use the expression, in the ideas and movements of the human mind; more exempt from any particular bias or close application. Separated, as we have seen, from all the coteries I have previously enumerated, they only extended half-sympathy to those which came the nearest to their own views and memories. They required that these coteries should present a more faithful and complete reflection of their times, and the society in which they had been formed.

Such was, in effect, their own. A circle composed of some old associates of the same origin and taste, M. de Boufflers, M. Dupont de Nemours, M. Gallois, etc.; of some academicians whose candidacy M. Suard had supported; of some rising young men whose talent he encouraged with exalted benevolence; of some members of the Senate, or other public bodies, who made profession of independence; and a few foreigners, who would never forgive themselves if they quitted Paris without knowing the last contemporaries of Voltaire and his age. They met on Thursdays at the house of the Abbé Morellet, and on Tuesdays and Saturdays at that of M. Suard. Sometimes more frequently on a select occasion. On the Wednesdays, Madame d'Houdetot gave a dinner to a certain number of guests, who received a general invitation, and could go when they pleased. They generally amounted to eight or ten, and sometimes more. There was no attempt at display or extraordinary fare. The dinner was nothing more than an excuse for meeting together. When it had concluded, Madame d'Houdetot, seated in her large arm chair by the corner of the fireplace, with her back bent, her head inclining towards her chest, speaking little in a low tone, and moving with difficulty, joined to a certain extent in conversation, without suggesting the topic; not obtruding herself as mistress of the house, but kind, considerate, and easy, taking a lively and curious interest in all that was said, in literary discussion, in anecdotes of society or of the theatres, in the slightest incident and the most trifling witticism: a striking and original mixture of age and youth, of tranquillity and excitement.

At M. Suard's there was less ease and freedom. Discussions *aside*, between immediate neighbours, seldom took place. The conversation was almost always general and sustained. Such was the rule of the house, and every one observed it. This led to a certain degree of coldness and restraint, particularly at the commencement of the evening; but as a compensation, full and unrestrained liberty was permitted in a more important matter. M. Suard never dreaded or forbade any particular subject. All were open to discussion at his house; never was perfect freedom of thought and language more openly permitted and called for by the master of a house. Those who have not witnessed the extent to which this indulgence was carried, can form no adequate idea on the subject; and many who have, forget how timid, at that time, were people's minds, how reserved their familiar intercourse, and to what an extent, when the slightest approach to politics manifested itself, controversy became frigid and language official. A censor of the day pointed out to one of his friends a certain passage in a play he had been ordered to examine. "You see no allusions there," he said; "the public will see none; nevertheless there are some, and I shall take good care to expunge them." From 1809 to 1814, this censor presented a general type. Every one conducted himself as if allusions existed where none would discern them, and on all political or exclusively philosophical subjects, conversation inclining to serious received a deathblow. M. Suard never allowed this mortal stroke to penetrate into his drawing room. No man was ever more free from political intentions or plots, more moderate in his opinions and desires. He had neither taste nor talent for active business; but liberty of thought and speech comprised his honour and his life. He would have felt degraded in his own eyes had he denounced either, and he maintained both for the general advantage of his guests. In other respects, the conversation at his parties was neither deficient in extent nor variety. The field was not closed against any special propensity or habit. Philosophy, literature, history, art, antiquity, modern times, foreign countries— all subjects were received with indulgence and attention. Young and new ideas, even though little in accord with the traditions of the eighteenth century, were not contemptuously rejected. Though unpalatable, they were pardoned in behalf of the intellectual exercise excited by their novelty. Movement was felt to be preeminently essential. In ideas and actual knowledge, the members of that circle were living off depleted land. The same persons, reflections, and anecdotes, were incessantly recurring. Activity, far from being real, had neither progress nor result; but they felt that sincerity and disinterestedness of the mind which form, perhaps, the principal charm of thought and conversation. They met and conversed without necessary or compulsive object, influenced by the sole attraction of intellectual intercourse. This certainly could not be considered the serious mission of devoted friends to truth and science; but it was still less the narrow egotism or mean employment of mere utilitarians, who never speak or act without a special purpose and with a definite end in view. It is true, they neither sought nor set forward ideas for their intrinsic values alone; they required and demanded social gratification, but nothing more.

Such was the peculiar feature that thirty years ago distinguished this particular coterie from all others, and gave it the truest, and indeed the only, resemblance to the society which half a century earlier had animated Paris, and Europe in the name of Paris. But it was a cold and colourless copy. Fifty years before, the circle of philosophers was not exclusively contracted round two old men. It was to be found everywhere: amongst courtiers, churchmen, lawyers and financiers. Haughty in one quarter,

424

complaisant in another; sometimes teaching, and at others amusing its followers; but at all times fresh, active, and confiding; recruiting and warring in all quarters; penetrating and attracting all classes, tastes, and pursuits. This great movement was not confined to Paris. It branched out from that centre into general expansion, and returned with augmented force. Grimm addressed his correspondence to the Empress of Russia, the Queen of Sweden, and the King of Poland; to eight or ten sovereign princes—all greedy for the smallest facts and reports emanating from the great workshop of intellectual labour and enjoyment. But it was not absolutely necessary to be a ruling potentate to maintain a correspondent in Paris. In Germany, in Italy, and in England, private individuals, rich and curious, were anxious to have their own, through whom, from month to month and week to week, they received information, whether correct or erroneous, of all that was said, done, or thought in Paris. D'Alembert, Diderot, and Grimm himself were applied to, to recommend correspondents of inferior pretension; and many young men, without fortune or name, on their entry into literary life, found through that source a means of existence, as they now do in the public journals.

An extensive society such as this, was certainly very different from the small, weak, and isolated philosophic circle of 1809, and furnished an idea of intellectual intercourse far beyond that supplied by the drawing room of M. Suard. Nevertheless the foundation, if not the celebrity, the direction, if not the movement, were exactly similar. There was the same taste for the pleasures and improvement of the mind, equally removed from pure meditation or selfish appliance. The same mixture of seriousness and levity; the same yearning after new action, without any ardent desire to innovate on the social situations of life; the same propensity to entertain political questions and interests, with the same preponderance of the literary and philosophic spirit, over the spirit of practical policy. The great picture had ceased to exist, but the surviving sketch was faithful and pure.

Madame de Rumford had been educated in the midst of the world, of which the various coteries I have just enumerated formed the last remains. Her father, M. Paulze, at first receiver-general, and afterwards the farmer-general of finance, a man highly accomplished in the science and skilful in the practice of his profession, married the niece of the celebrated comptroller-general, the Abbé Terrai, who held the knowledge and experience of his nephew in high estimation. The latter frequently supplied his uncle with sound advice on the administration of the finances, which was well taken and understood, for the Abbé Terrai was a man of quick perception, but with little following; as could not fail to happen in the case of a minister who wished to live in harmony with the entire court, and who was supplied by the country with means insufficient to satisfy at the same time the exigences of the State and the caprices of all the world. A long correspondence between the Abbé Terrai and M. Paulze has been preserved, or at least a considerable portion of it, in the family of the farmer-general, and contains some extremely curious details on the financial measures of that period.

Three great administrative epochs may be reckoned in French history. The first was created under Louis XIV, in the seventeenth century. The second, in the eighteenth, from 1750 to 1789, entered into the paths of scientific progress and universal civilization. It was in our days, and originally through the impulse of the Constituent Assembly, that administration received its systematic form, and assumed its destined place in society as well as in government, and, unless I deceive myself, will continue to increase in alliance with free institutions.

The second of these epochs conferred on France, in my opinion, benefits little known and appreciated. The first place must be accorded to the great problems of moral order. I am neither astonished at, nor do I complain of this preference. These questions, proposed at that time with so much brilliancy and effect, eclipsed all others. Administration was forgotten and lost in politics. Its labours and projects were unimportant, in the midst of the destruction, according to some, and the regeneration, in the opinion of others, of general society. But a great fact dates from that time—the creation of sciences which soar above administration and reveal to it the laws of the facts it is called on to regulate. No one has yet had a glimpse of, and may not perhaps be able to discover hereafter, the entire part which these branches of knowledge are destined to act in the world. An immense part, although it cannot and ought not to stand in the foremost rank. The principal honour belongs to the eighteenth century, and constitutes its most original work.

The theoretical portion of this work had nothing to complain of on the score of success. It created a great sensation at its birth. The various schools of economy, their systems and debates, have always powerfully attracted public attention. But the practical part of French administration during the second half of the eighteenth century—the general spirit by which it was governed; its respect for science and human nature; its efforts to secure, on the one hand, the empire of principles over facts, and, on the other, to direct facts and principles to the general advantage of society; the positive results of these efforts; the numberless and inestimable improvements accomplished, commenced, prepared, or meditated at that time in every department of public service; the labours in a word, and the merits of the administrators of every class and rank who then held in their hands the affairs of the country—all these achievements have been much obliterated by the storms and triumphs of politics, and have thus been deprived of their just proportion of gratitude and fame.

The house of M. Paulze was one of the centres of these useful studies and salutary reforms. It was there that Turgot, Malesherbes, Trudaine, Condorcet, and Dupont de Nemours, met in familiar intercourse; and there, in conversation at once serious and unstudied, without learned preparation, and with no object but truth, questions were proposed, facts related, and opinions discussed. M. Paulze did not only contribute his personal knowledge. He had established in the contractor-generalship a particular office, the duties of which were to collect statistics on the taxation and commerce of France, the exports and imports of the harbours, and all other points connected with the national resources. To promote the same object, he kept up a diligent correspondence with many foreign merchants and bankers. These documents were freely communicated to the enlightened men who frequented his house. The Abbé Raynal, amongst others, a particular friend of M. Paulze, collected from them the greater part of the facts and details he has accumulated in his *Philosophic History of the Indies*, and which are the only portions of his work that still retain their importance.

This society and these conversations contained nothing that could apply to the education of Mademoiselle Paulze, or even indirectly influence the formation of her character. But by living and gradually expanding in such an atmosphere, she obtained two acquirements, comprising the most salutary instruction that infancy can imbibe and bequeath for the regulation of future life—regard for serious studies and respect for personal merit.

She had scarcely completed her thirteenth year when the Abbé Terrai wished to contract a marriage for her at the court. Her father, little disposed to second this fancy, preferred one of his colleagues in the farmer-generalship, M. Lavoisier; and the Abbé Terrai submitted with a good grace. The marriage was celebrated in the chapel of the farmer-general's hôtel, on the 16th of December, 1771.

On quitting the house of her father for that of her husband, Madame Lavoisier changed the horizon without alteration of habits. To the action of economic science succeeded the science of physics, and the society of profound scholars to that of practical legislators. Professors of one particular pursuit conceive sometimes a marked contempt for the interest which men of the world may appear to take in their labours; and if the question were solely comprised in a judgment of their scientific merit, the feeling would be founded on reason. But the regard and taste of the public for science, with the frequent and animated manifestation of this sentiment, are highly important to science itself, and play an important part in general history. The periods when this sympathy, though a little tinged by ostentation and frivolity, have been strongly displayed, have ever been times of scientific advance; and to take things in a comprehensive sense, natural history and chemistry have profited as much by the social habits of M. de Buffon and M. Lavoisier as by their learned discoveries.

Whether from affection for her husband, or through a natural tendency, Madame Lavoisier associated herself in his labours as a companion or disciple. Those even who only became acquainted with her long after the season of youth had passed, were able to discover under a cold and somewhat repelling manner, almost entirely occupied with her love of society, that she was a person capable of being strongly moved by any particular sentiment or idea, and of giving herself up to it with enthusiasm. She lived in the laboratory of M. Lavoisier, took part in his experiments, copied notes under his dictation, and supplied him with translations and drawings. She learned to engrave, that he might be sure of a scrupulous assistant. The plates to the *Treatise on Chemistry* were really executed by her hands. She published, at her husband's desire, the translation of a work by the English chemist, Kirwan, *On the Strength of Acids and the Proportion of the Substances that compose Neutral Salts;* and she had acquired such a complete mastery of the science they cultivated together, that when, in 1805, eleven years after M. Lavoisier's death, she was desirous of collecting and publishing his scientific memoirs, she undertook and completed the work alone, with the addition of a preface simply written and totally divested of pedantic assumption.

A domestic interior thus regulated by reciprocal affection and pursuits, an ample fortune, much general esteem, an excellent house in the Arsenal, frequented by men of the most distinguished reputation, all the enjoyments of the mind, of riches, and of youth—here were indeed combined the ingredients of a happy and brilliant existence. This enviable life was suddenly assaulted and crushed, in common with all that surrounded it, by the thunder of the Revolution. In 1794, Madame Lavoisier saw her father and her husband ascend the scaffold on the same day, and only escaped herself, after a short imprisonment, by retiring, with exemplary patience, into the most complete and silent obscurity.

From the first outbreak of the Revolution, M. Lavoisier, although favourably disposed to reforms in the State, had contemplated the future with alarm. He was a man of just and even mind, modest and gentle in character, who pursued with disinterested ardour, and in the bosom of a happy domestic life, his noble and useful studies, which were too much interrupted by political storms to excite any favourable hopes for their tranquil continuance. In June, 1792, the King offered him the ministry of Public Taxes. M. Lavoisier declined the office in the following letter, replete with elevation of mind, simplicity, and rectitude:

Sire,

It is neither from pusillanimous fear, foreign to my character, nor from indifference to the public interest, nor, let me candidly own, from my conviction of personal inability, that I am constrained to decline the token of confidence with which your Majesty desires to honour me, by the offer of the ministry of Public Taxes. A witness, since I have belonged to the national treasury, of the patriotic sentiments of your Majesty, and of your tender solicitude for the happiness of your people, of your inflexible sincerity of principles and inalterable probity, I feel more acutely than I can express how much I renounce in losing the opportunity of becoming the organ of communicating these noble sentiments from your Majesty to the French nation.

But, Sire, it is the duty of an honest man and good citizen not to accept an important post, unless in the hope of fulfilling all its obligations in their fullest extent.

I am neither a Jacobin nor a Feuillant. I belong to no society or club. Accustomed to weigh everything by the measure of my reason and conscience, I have never allowed my opinions to be biassed by any particular party. I have sworn, in the sincerity of my heart, fidelity to the Constitution you have accepted, to the powers established by the people, and to you, Sire, who are the constitutional King of the French nation; to you, whose virtues and difficulties are not sufficiently appreciated. Convinced as I am that the legislative body has exceeded the limits traced out for it by the Constitution, what could a constitutional minister effect? Incapable of compromising his principles and conscience, he would appeal in vain to the authority of the law to which all Frenchmen are bound by the most imposing of oaths. The resistance he might recommend, through the means afforded to your Majesty by the Constitution, would be set forward against him as a crime. He would perish the victim of duty, and the very inflexibility of his character would become the source of new misfortunes.

Sire, permit me still to consecrate my vigour and my life to the service of the State in less elevated posts, but where I can discharge functions perhaps more useful, and more enduring. Devoted to public instruction, I shall endeavour to enlighten the people on their duties. A soldier-citizen, I shall carry arms in the defence of my country and the law, and for the protection of the irremovable representative of the French nation.

I am, with profound respect, Sire,
Your Majesty's most faithful and obedient subject,
Etc. etc. etc.

The illustrious scholar assumed too much when he asked permission to employ his life in an effort to "enlighten the people." He was sent to the scaffold in the name of the ignorant and oppressed nation!

He left his whole fortune to his widow, and she partly owed the preservation of it to the able attachment of a faithful servant, towards whom she evinced, to her last moments, the most devoted gratitude.

In 1798, when a cruel and shameful proscription, directed against herself, implicated several of her friends, and amongst the number one of the most intimate, M. de Marbois—a letter of credit from Madame Lavoisier upon her banker in London, reached them in the deserts of Sinamary.

When these proscriptions ceased, when order and justice once more returned to tranquillize and restore social intercourse, Madame Lavoisier resumed her position in the world, surrounded by an entire generation of distinguished scholars, the friends, disciples, and successors of Lavoisier. Lagrange, Laplace, Berthollet, Cuvier, Prony, Humboldt, and Arago, were delighted, while paying honour to his widow, to find in her house, in return for the reputation they brought to it, the enjoyments of elegant hospitality. M. de Rumford came with the rest. He was then in the service of the King of Bavaria, and extremely popular as a man of scientific acquirement. His mind was elevated, his conversation overflowing with interest, and his manners gentle and kind. He pleased Madame Lavoisier, by adapting himself to her habits, her tastes, and, we might almost say, to her reminiscences. She expected to find once more, in some degree, her former happiness. She married him on the 22nd of

October, 1805, delighted at offering to so distinguished a person a handsome fortune and an agreeable home.

Their characters assimilated badly. Youth, alone in the midst of affectionate enjoyment, can reconcile itself to the loss of independence. Delicate questions sprang up between them; reciprocal misunderstandings began to awaken. Madame de Rumford in this second marriage had formally stipulated in the contract that she should be called *Madame Lavoisier de Rumford.* M. de Rumford, who had consented to this, became dissatisfied with it. She insisted on the point. "I looked upon it as a duty, a tenet of religion," she wrote to a friend, in 1808, "not to give up the name of Lavoisier. . . . Trusting to the promise of M. de Rumford, I should not have had the stipulation entered as an article in my civil engagements with him, if I had not desired to place on record a public evidence of my respect for M. Lavoisier, and of the generosity of M. de Rumford. It is incumbent on me to persevere in a determination which has ever been one of the conditions of our marriage; and in my heart I have a profound conviction that M. de Rumford will not condemn me for this, and that after having taken time to reflect, he will allow me to continue in the fulfilment of a duty which I look upon as sacred."

Here was again a hope deceived. After some domestic differences, which M. de Rumford with a little tact might have rendered less notorious, a separation became necessary, and was amicably arranged on the 30th of June, 1809.

After that time, and during twenty-seven years, no event, or we may even say, no incident, disturbed Madame de Rumford in her delightful mode of existence. She gave herself up entirely to her friends and to the society, alternately extended and restricted, which she received at her own house with a singular mixture of rudeness and civility, ever evincing great knowledge of the world and excellent qualities, even in her eccentricities of language and whims of authority. Every Monday she gave a dinner, to which not more than ten or twelve persons were usually invited. On that day, the most distinguished Frenchmen or foreigners, frequenters of the house or incidental guests, assembled at her residence in a sort of extemporaneous intimacy, quickly established between minds so highly cultivated, through the pleasure of serious or witty conversation, ever varied and refined, which Madame de Rumford herself enjoyed rather than joined in. On Tuesday, she received all who presented themselves. On Friday there were large parties, composed of very different persons, but all belonging to the best company of their kind, and unanimously attracted by the excellent music, in which was combined the most celebrated artists and the most accomplished amateurs.

Under the Empire, besides its general charm, the house of Madame de Rumford had a special recommendation. Thought and speech were not there looked upon as official. A certain freedom of spirit and language predominated, without political hostility or reserve; liberty of mind, the habit of thinking and conversing at ease, without caring for the comments or interpretation of authority—a valuable privilege at that time, more so than can be estimated at present. We must have breathed under a pneumatic machine to feel the complete enjoyment of free respiration.

When the Restoration came round, in the midst of party movements and parliamentary debates, it was no longer liberty that was wanting to men of taste and intelligence. Another evil weighed heavily upon them—the evil of party spirit, animosities, and prejudices—a loathsome and pernicious infliction which shuts up every horizon, spreads over everything a false light, contracts the understanding, sours the heart, deprives the most enlightened minds of that expansion of ideas and generosity of sentiments which sat so gracefully upon them, and robs their lives of as much enjoyment as it diminishes the riches of their nature and the charms of their disposition. This scourge of society in free countries penetrated very sparingly into the house of Madame de Rumford. As freedom formerly, so did equity now, find an asylum there. Not only did men of the most opposite principles meet there in constant intercourse, but urbanity reigned amongst them. It seemed, as if by tacit convention, that all disagreements, antipathies, and variances were left at the door of that drawing room, and that avoiding by mutual concert all subjects likely to bring them into collision, their minds remained as unfettered, and their hearts as tolerant, as if they had never enlisted under the yoke of partisanship.

Thus, at the residence of Madame de Rumford, and through her controlling desire, the social spirit of the age and world in which she had been brought up, was faithfully perpetuated. I know not whether our descendants will ever see again a similar society, such exalted and graceful demeanour, such action of thought and facility of intercourse, a taste so animated for the progress of civilization and for the exercise of mental powers unmingled with those bitter passions, those inelegant and harsh manners, which often accompany and render painful or impracticable the most desirable intimacies. What was wanting to the eighteenth century—what it possessed of superficiality in ideas and feebleness of principle, of folly in assumption and vain pretence in creative power—experience has signally developed, and taught us to our cost. We know and feel evil which that memorable epoch has bequeathed to us. It has preached doubt, selfishness, and materialism. It has touched with an impure hand, and withered for a time, the noblest and most beautiful elements of human nature. But if the eighteenth century had done no more—if this had been its chief characteristic—can it be believed that it would have led to such important consequences, and have shaken, as it has, the social frame of the world? It was, in fact, far superior to its cynical scepticisms. Why do I say superior? It was directly opposed to them, and continually giving them the lie. In spite of the weakness of its morals, the frivolity of its manners, the barrenness of some of its doctrines, and its critical and destroying tendency, it was still a sincere and impulsive age, an age of faith and disinterestedness. It had faith in truth, for it claimed for truth the right of governing the world. It had faith in humanity, for it acknowledged its faculty of self-improvement, and wished to see it exercised without fetters. It bewildered and abused itself in this double confidence, and attempted things beyond its strength and mission. It judged erroneously of the moral state of man, and the conditions of social life. Its ideas, as well as its acts, were infected by the contamination of its vices. But this being admitted, the original and predominating thought of the eighteenth century, the belief that man, truth, and society, were made for each other, mutually worthy of the union to which they are called—that just and wholesome creed rises beyond all other points of its history. It took the lead in proclaiming this faith, and laboured for its establishment. Hence the power and popularity it has acquired throughout the world.

From that source also, to descend from great considerations to small ones, from the destiny of man to the character of a drawing room—from that source were derived the attractions of the age, and the charm it imparted to social life. Never before had all the various classes which form the select portion of a great people, however different their former history and present position, been seen to forget so entirely their antecedents and personalities, to mingle and associate in the interchange of the most delightful habits, and, solely occupied with their own pleasure, to enjoy and hope together during half a century, one destined to conclude with the most terrible dissensions among them.

This is the rare and delightful fact of which I witnessed the gradual extinction in the surviving drawing rooms of the eighteenth century. Madame de Rumford's was closed the last of all.

It closed naturally, without check or alteration, ever consistent and like itself. Men have their inherent points of character, and maintain them to the end; the selected breach in which they prefer to die. Marshal Villars envied the Duke of Berwick the cannon shot that killed him. Every orator in the British Parliament looked with a jealous eye on Lord Chatham, as he fell back exhausted in the arms of those who stood near him, in the midst of a sublime effusion of eloquence. The President Molé would have rejoiced to have died in his place, while vindicating the State against faction. Vespasian said, "An Emperor should die standing." Madame de Rumford had passed her life in the world, in seeking for herself and in offering to others the pleasures of social intercourse. Not that the world entirely absorbed her cares, or that when occasion required she was not ever ready with serious and valuable counsel for her friends, and with liberal benefactions to relieve the unfortunate. But the world and society were her leading objects; she lived in her drawing room. It may almost be said that she died there, on the 10th of February, 1836; having been surrounded, the evening before, by those in whose presence she most delighted, and who will never forget either the attractions of her house or the steadiness of her friendship.

Index

Index